My love STORY!!

Story KAZUNE KAWAHARA

Art ARUKO

10

MY love STORY!!

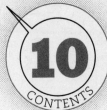

10

CONTENTS

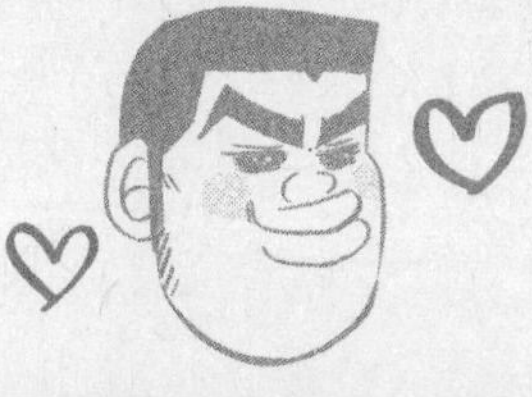

STORY Thus Far...

Takeo Goda, a first-year high school student, is a hot-blooded guy who is 6'6" tall and weighs 265 pounds. Boys look up to him, but the girls he falls in love with all end up liking his handsome best friend, Makoto Sunakawa! But that all changes when Takeo saves Rinko Yamato from a groper on the train, and she becomes his girlfriend.

During summer break of their second year of high school, Yamato starts working at a cake shop. Takeo watches over her from the shadows. However, a handsome pastry chef by the name of Ichinose takes a liking to Yamato and starts calling her by her first name, Rinko! Naturally, Takeo is disturbed by the appearance of this rival. Furthermore, Ichinose even tells Takeo to break up with Yamato! Ichinose says that he will confess his love to Yamato if he wins a pastry competition that he is participating in. Takeo wishes him luck since he knows how hard Ichinose devotes himself to being a pastry chef. On the day of the contest, Takeo can't help feeling worried...

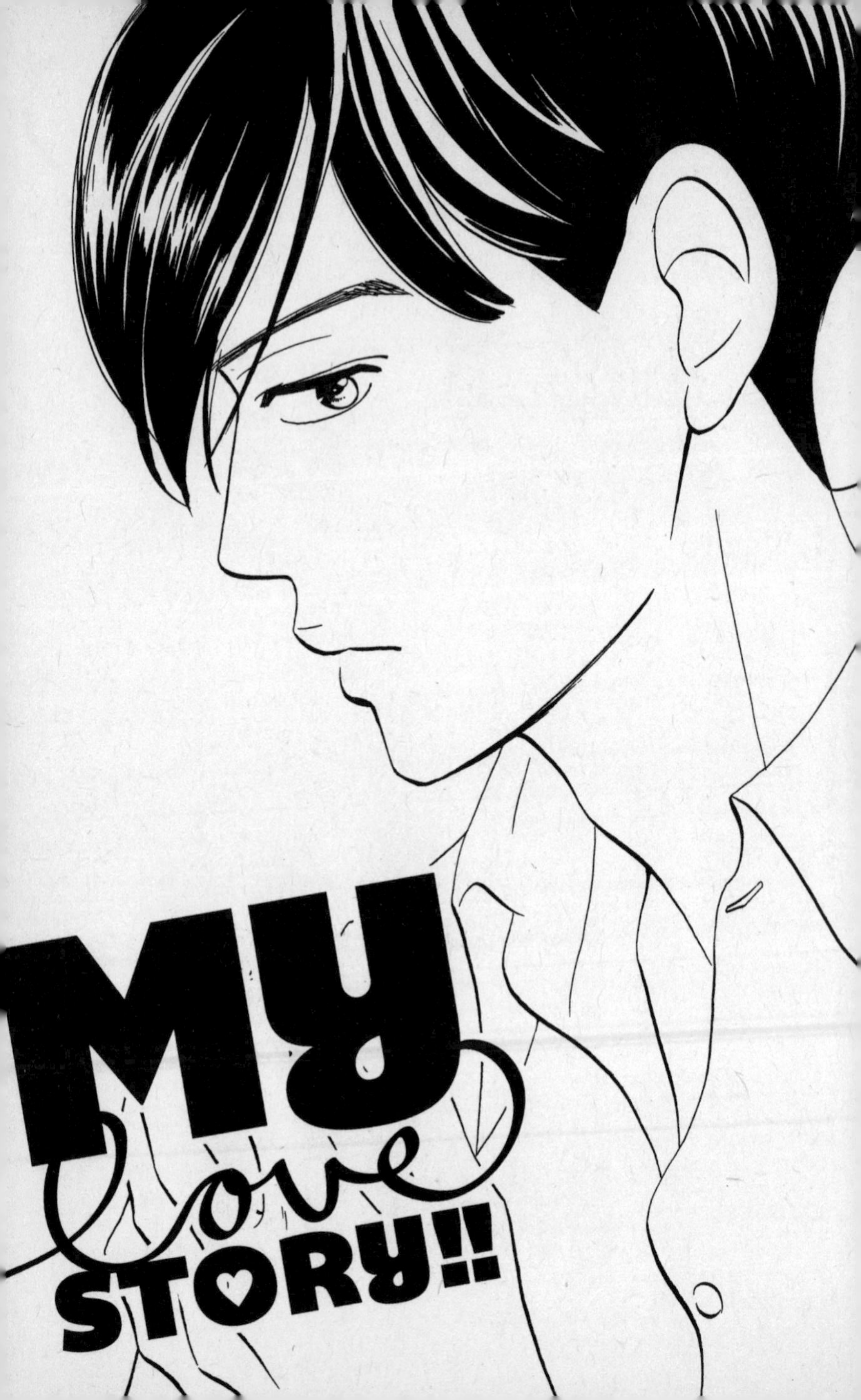
MY
Love
STORY!!

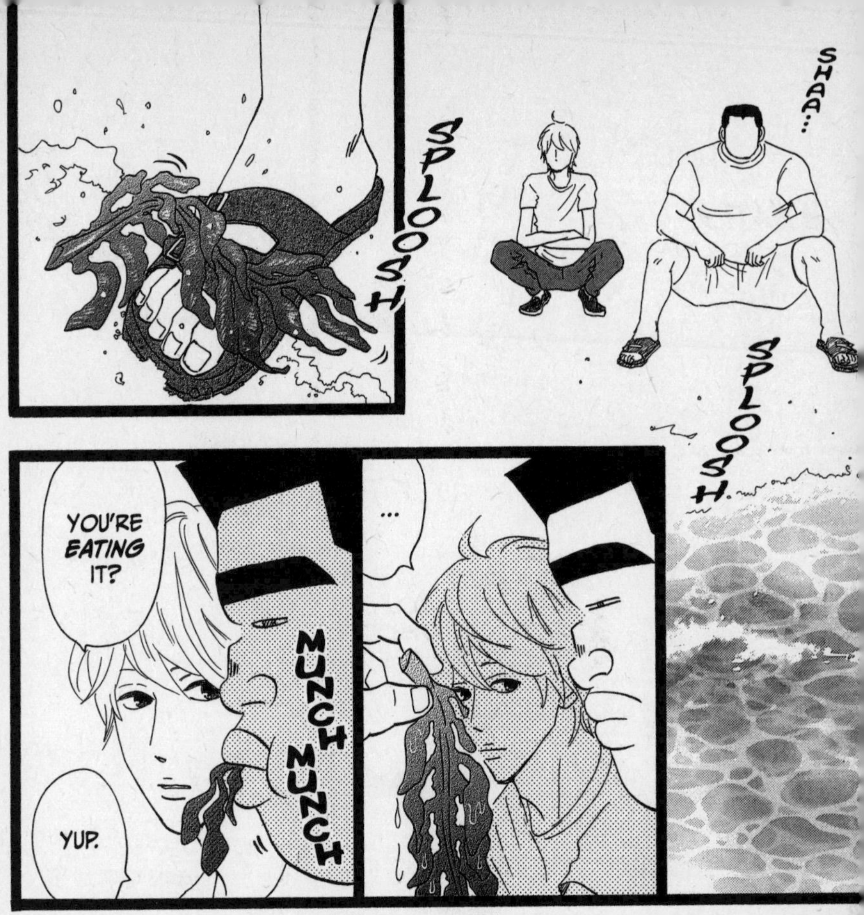
SHAA...
SPLOOSH
SPLOOSH
...
YOU'RE EATING IT?
MUNCH MUNCH
YUP.

MY love STORY!!

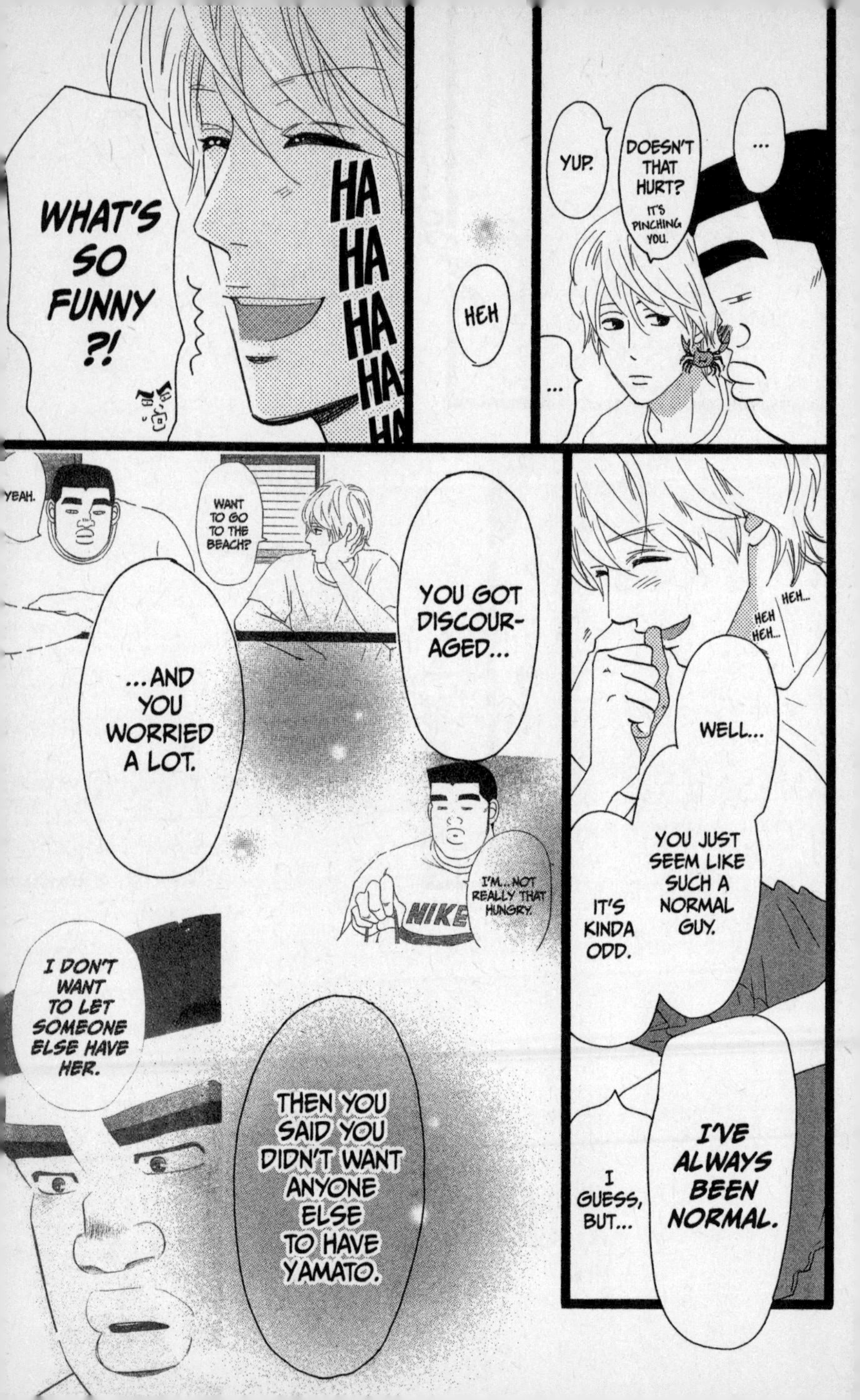
...
DOESN'T THAT HURT?
IT'S PINCHING YOU.
YUP.
HEH
...
HA HA HA HA HA
WHAT'S SO FUNNY?!
HEH HEH HEH...
WELL...
YOU JUST SEEM LIKE SUCH A NORMAL GUY.
IT'S KINDA ODD.
I'VE ALWAYS BEEN NORMAL.
I GUESS, BUT...
YOU GOT DISCOURAGED...
WANT TO GO TO THE BEACH?
YEAH.
...AND YOU WORRIED A LOT.
I'M...NOT REALLY THAT HUNGRY.
THEN YOU SAID YOU DIDN'T WANT ANYONE ELSE TO HAVE YAMATO.
I DON'T WANT TO LET SOMEONE ELSE HAVE HER.

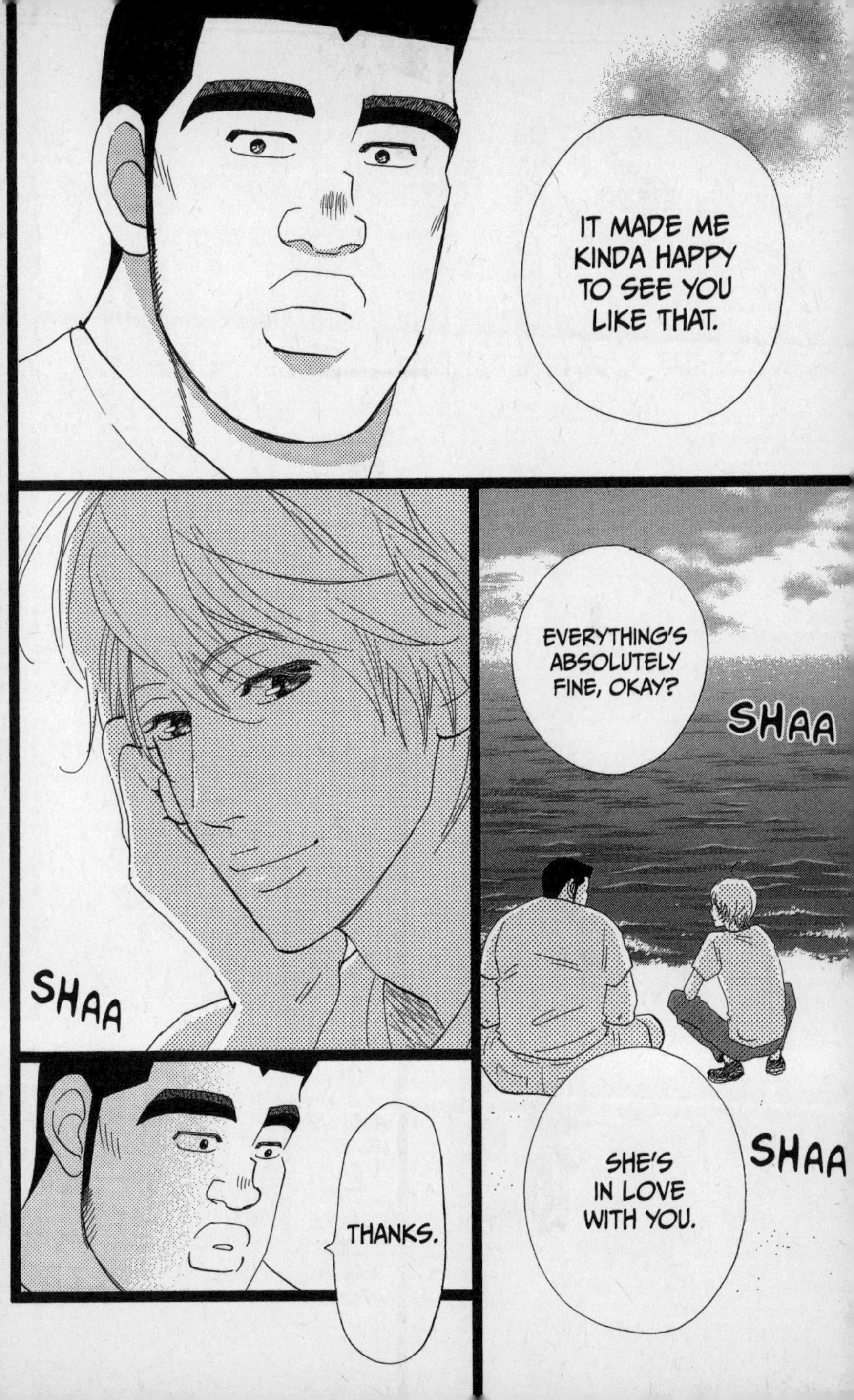
IT MADE ME KINDA HAPPY TO SEE YOU LIKE THAT.
EVERYTHING'S ABSOLUTELY FINE, OKAY?
SHAA
SHAA
SHE'S IN LOVE WITH YOU.
SHAA
THANKS.

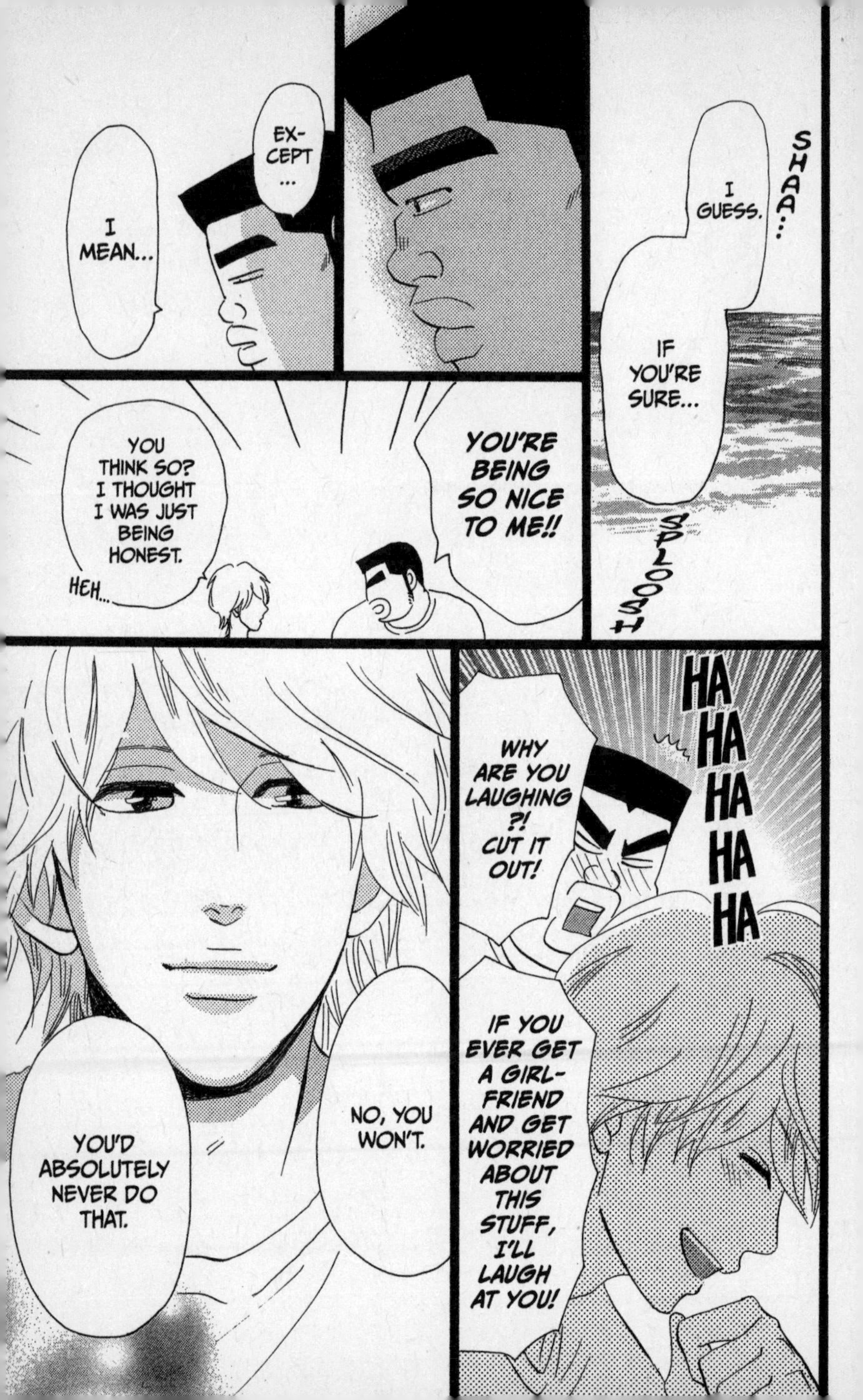
SHAAA...
I GUESS.
IF YOU'RE SURE...
SPLOOSH
EX-CEPT...
I MEAN...
YOU'RE BEING SO NICE TO ME!!
YOU THINK SO? I THOUGHT I WAS JUST BEING HONEST.
HEH...
HA HA HA HA HA
WHY ARE YOU LAUGHING?! CUT IT OUT!
IF YOU EVER GET A GIRL-FRIEND AND GET WORRIED ABOUT THIS STUFF, I'LL LAUGH AT YOU!
NO, YOU WON'T.
YOU'D ABSOLUTELY NEVER DO THAT.

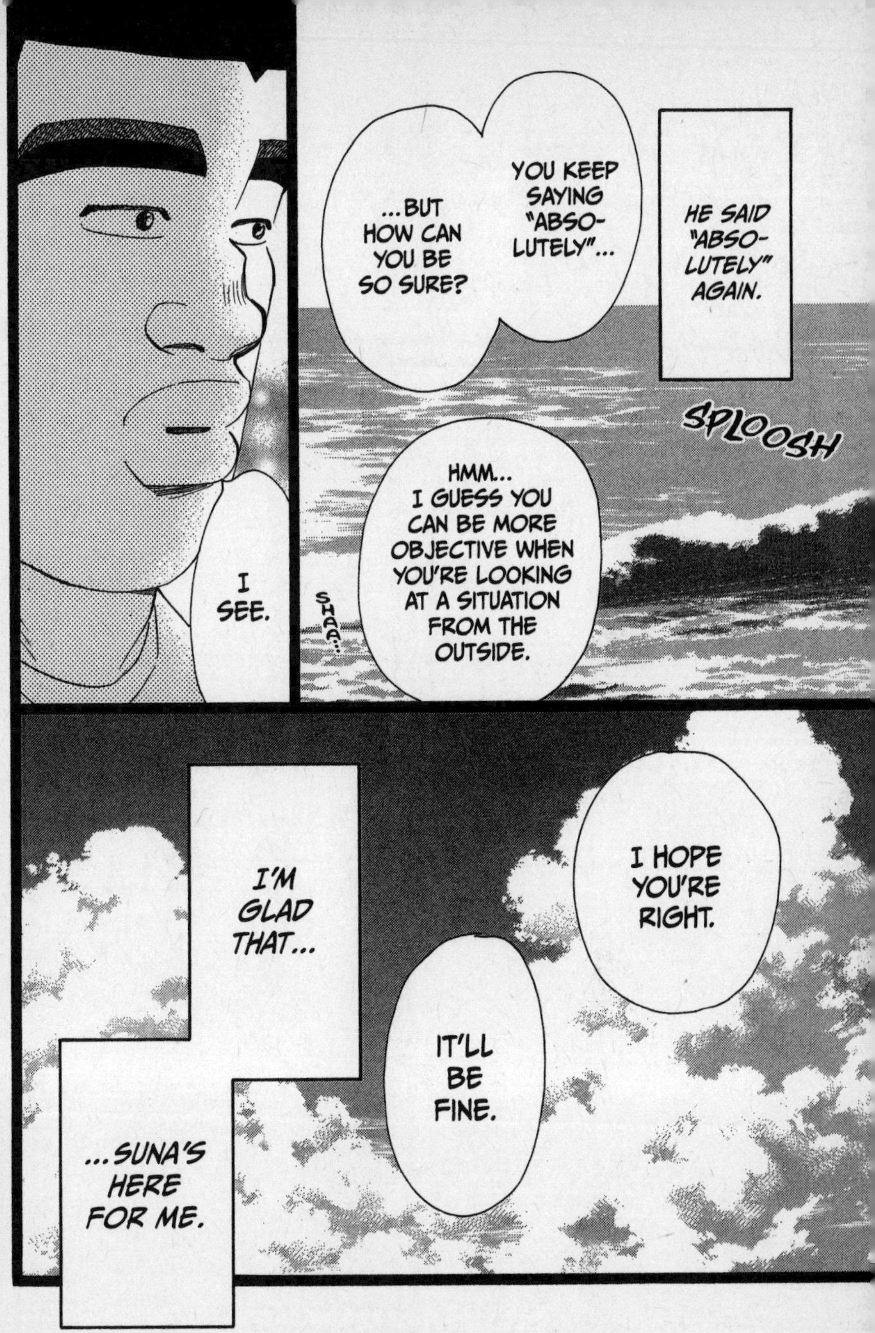
HE SAID "ABSO-LUTELY" AGAIN.
YOU KEEP SAYING "ABSO-LUTELY"...
...BUT HOW CAN YOU BE SO SURE?
SPLOOSH
HMM... I GUESS YOU CAN BE MORE OBJECTIVE WHEN YOU'RE LOOKING AT A SITUATION FROM THE OUTSIDE.
SHAA...
I SEE.
I HOPE YOU'RE RIGHT.
IT'LL BE FINE.
I'M GLAD THAT...
...SUNA'S HERE FOR ME.

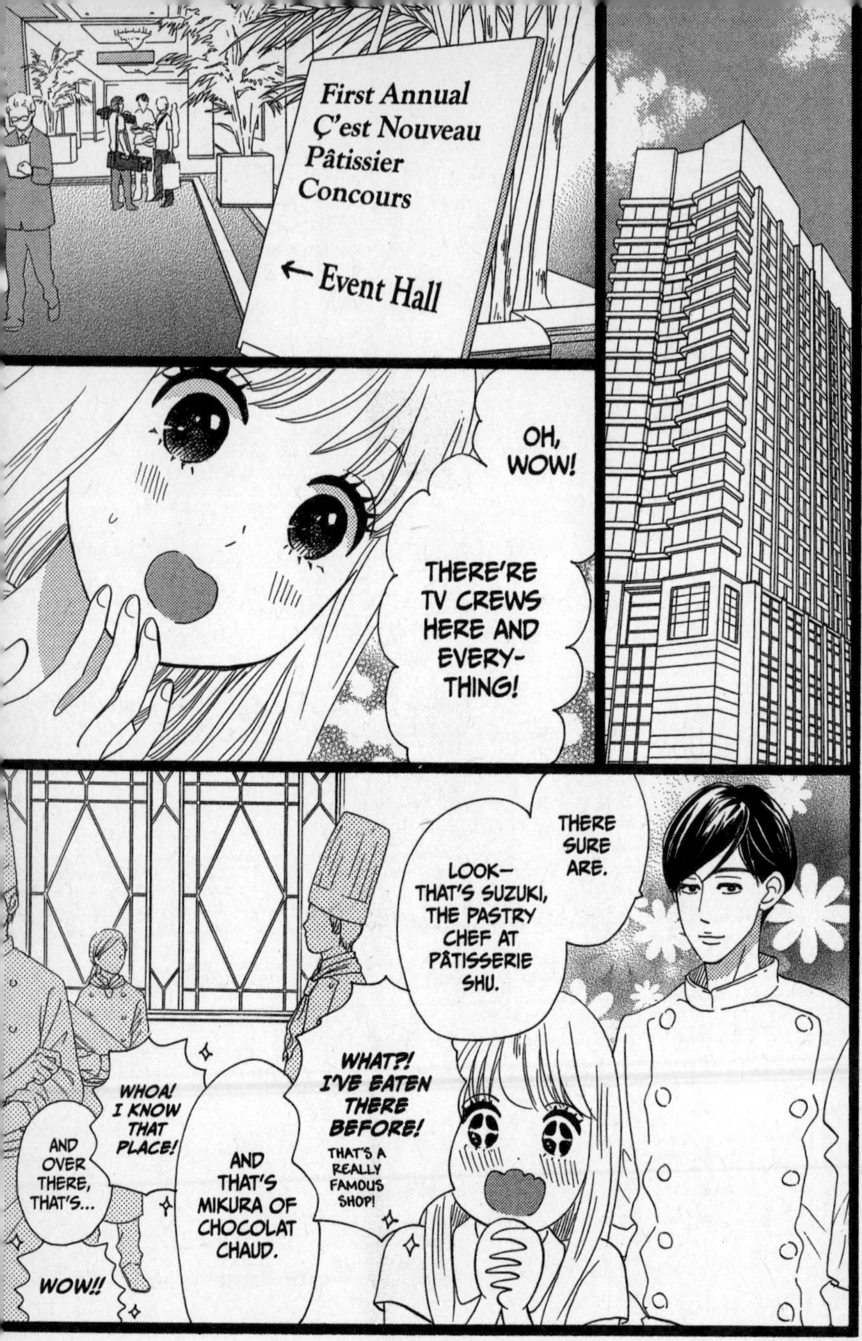
First Annual Ç'est Nouveau Pâtissier Concours
← Event Hall
OH, WOW!
THERE'RE TV CREWS HERE AND EVERY-THING!
THERE SURE ARE.
LOOK—THAT'S SUZUKI, THE PASTRY CHEF AT PÂTISSERIE SHU.
WHAT?! I'VE EATEN THERE BEFORE!
THAT'S A REALLY FAMOUS SHOP!
WHOA! I KNOW THAT PLACE!
AND THAT'S MIKURA OF CHOCOLAT CHAUD.
AND OVER THERE, THAT'S...
WOW!!

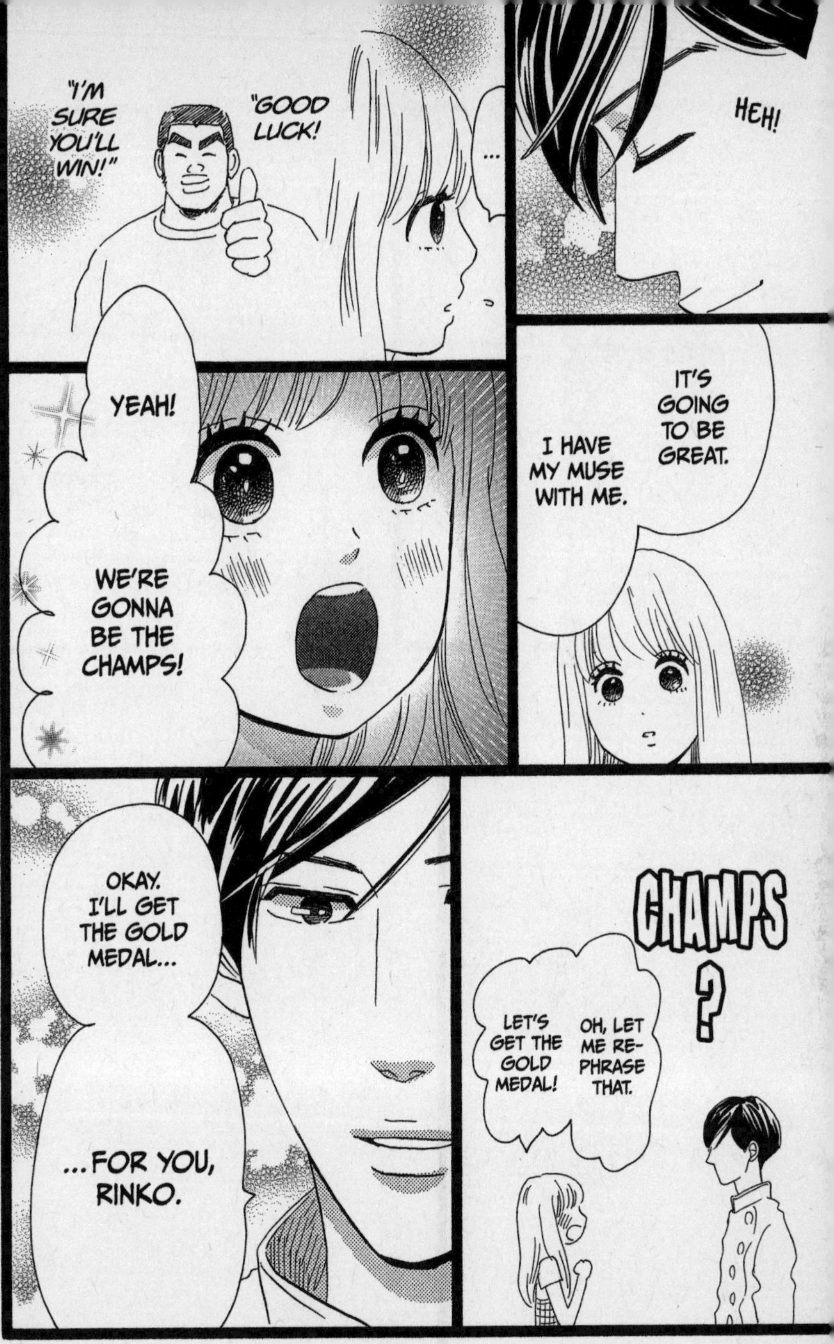
HEH!
...
"GOOD LUCK!
"I'M SURE YOU'LL WIN!"
IT'S GOING TO BE GREAT.
I HAVE MY MUSE WITH ME.
YEAH!
WE'RE GONNA BE THE CHAMPS!
CHAMPS?
OH, LET ME RE-PHRASE THAT.
LET'S GET THE GOLD MEDAL!
OKAY. I'LL GET THE GOLD MEDAL...
...FOR YOU, RINKO.

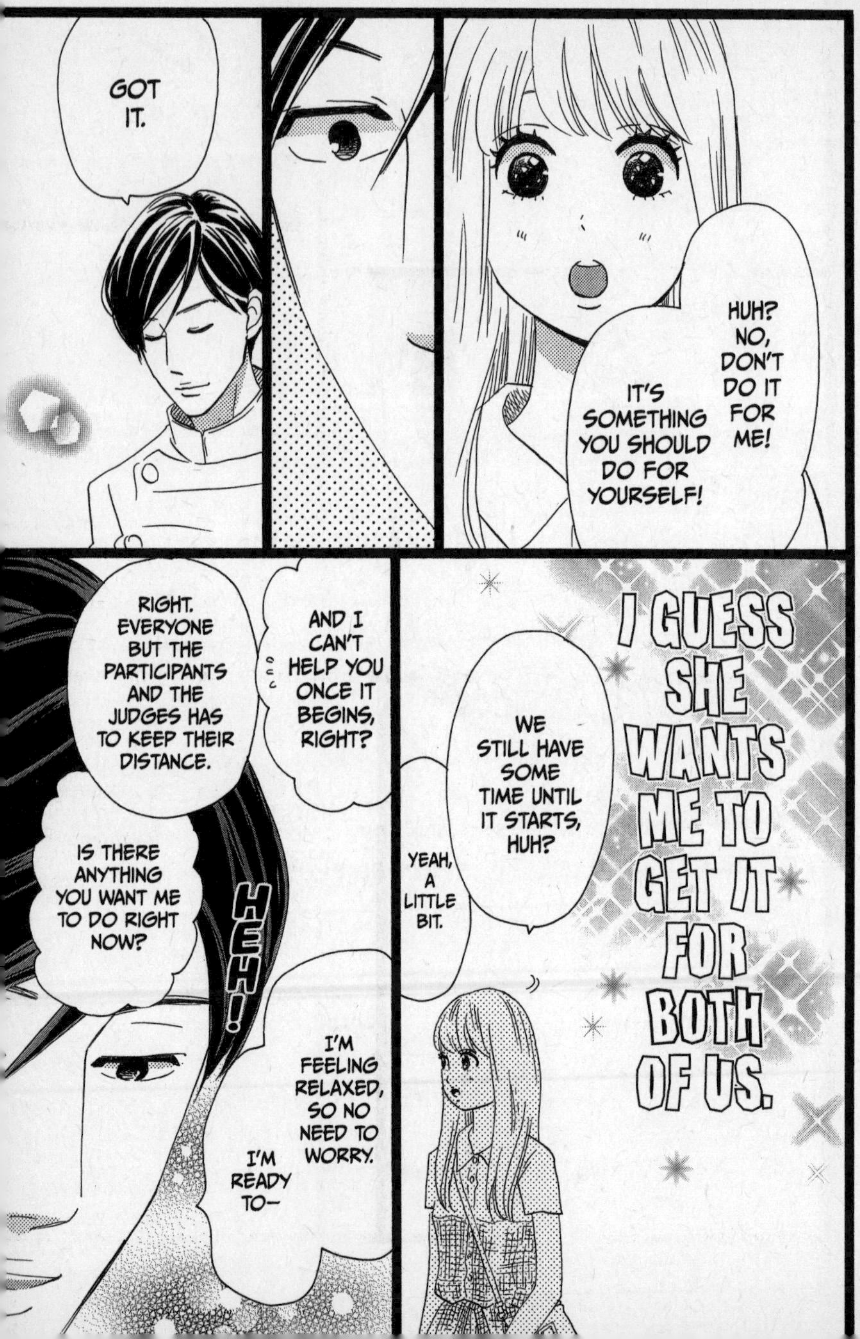
HUH? NO, DON'T DO IT FOR ME!
IT'S SOMETHING YOU SHOULD DO FOR YOURSELF!
GOT IT.
I GUESS SHE WANTS ME TO GET IT FOR BOTH OF US.
WE STILL HAVE SOME TIME UNTIL IT STARTS, HUH?
YEAH, A LITTLE BIT.
AND I CAN'T HELP YOU ONCE IT BEGINS, RIGHT?
RIGHT. EVERYONE BUT THE PARTICIPANTS AND THE JUDGES HAS TO KEEP THEIR DISTANCE.
IS THERE ANYTHING YOU WANT ME TO DO RIGHT NOW?
HEH!
I'M FEELING RELAXED, SO NO NEED TO WORRY.
I'M READY TO—

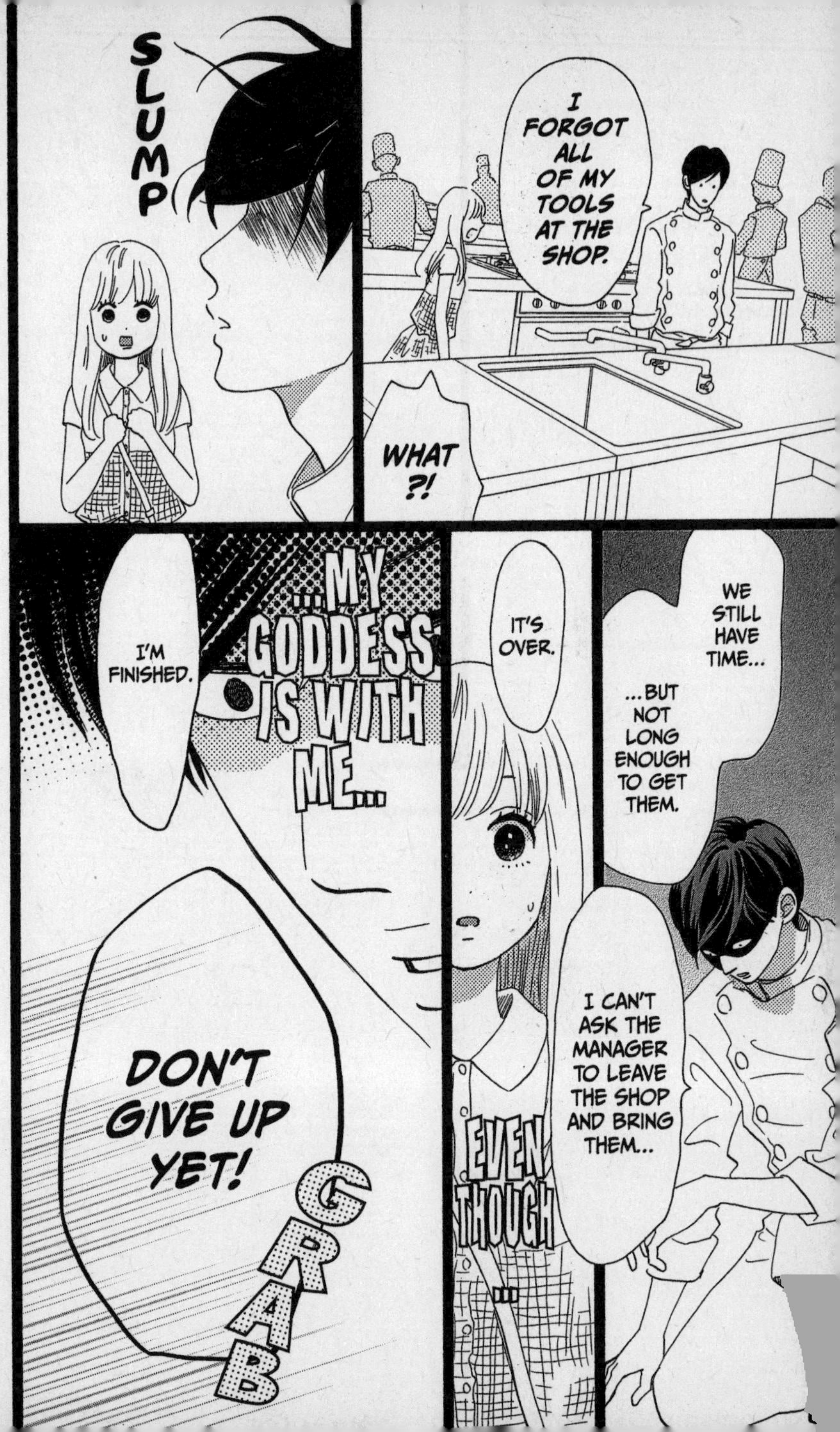

I FORGOT ALL OF MY TOOLS AT THE SHOP.
WHAT?!
SLUMP
WE STILL HAVE TIME...
...BUT NOT LONG ENOUGH TO GET THEM.
I CAN'T ASK THE MANAGER TO LEAVE THE SHOP AND BRING THEM...
IT'S OVER.
EVEN THOUGH...
I'M FINISHED.
...MY GODDESS IS WITH ME...
DON'T GIVE UP YET!
GRAB

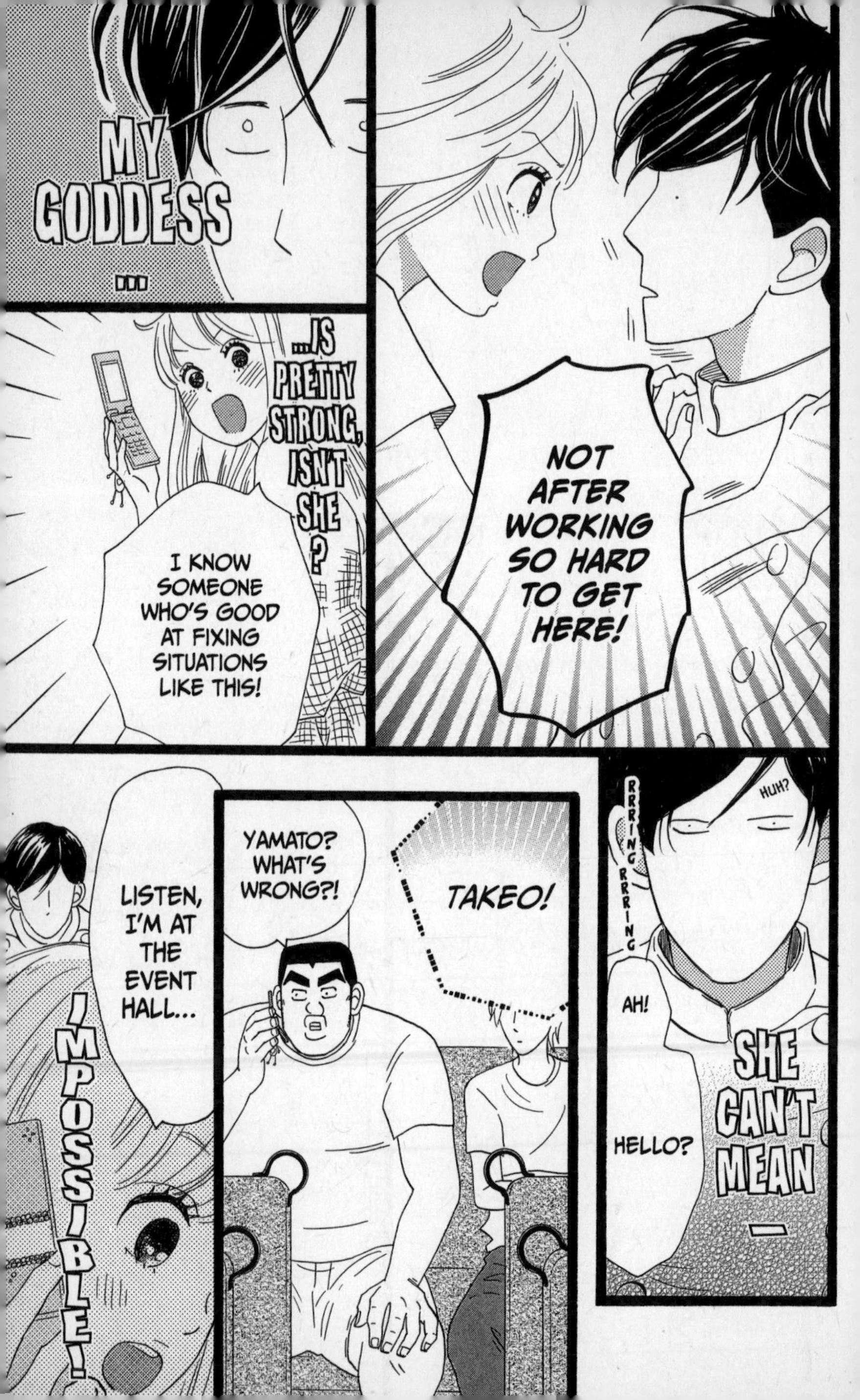
NOT AFTER WORKING SO HARD TO GET HERE!
MY GODDESS ...
...IS PRETTY STRONG, ISN'T SHE?
I KNOW SOMEONE WHO'S GOOD AT FIXING SITUATIONS LIKE THIS!
HUH?
RRRING RRRING
AH!
HELLO?
SHE CAN'T MEAN —
TAKEO!
YAMATO? WHAT'S WRONG?!
LISTEN, I'M AT THE EVENT HALL...
IMPOSSIBLE!

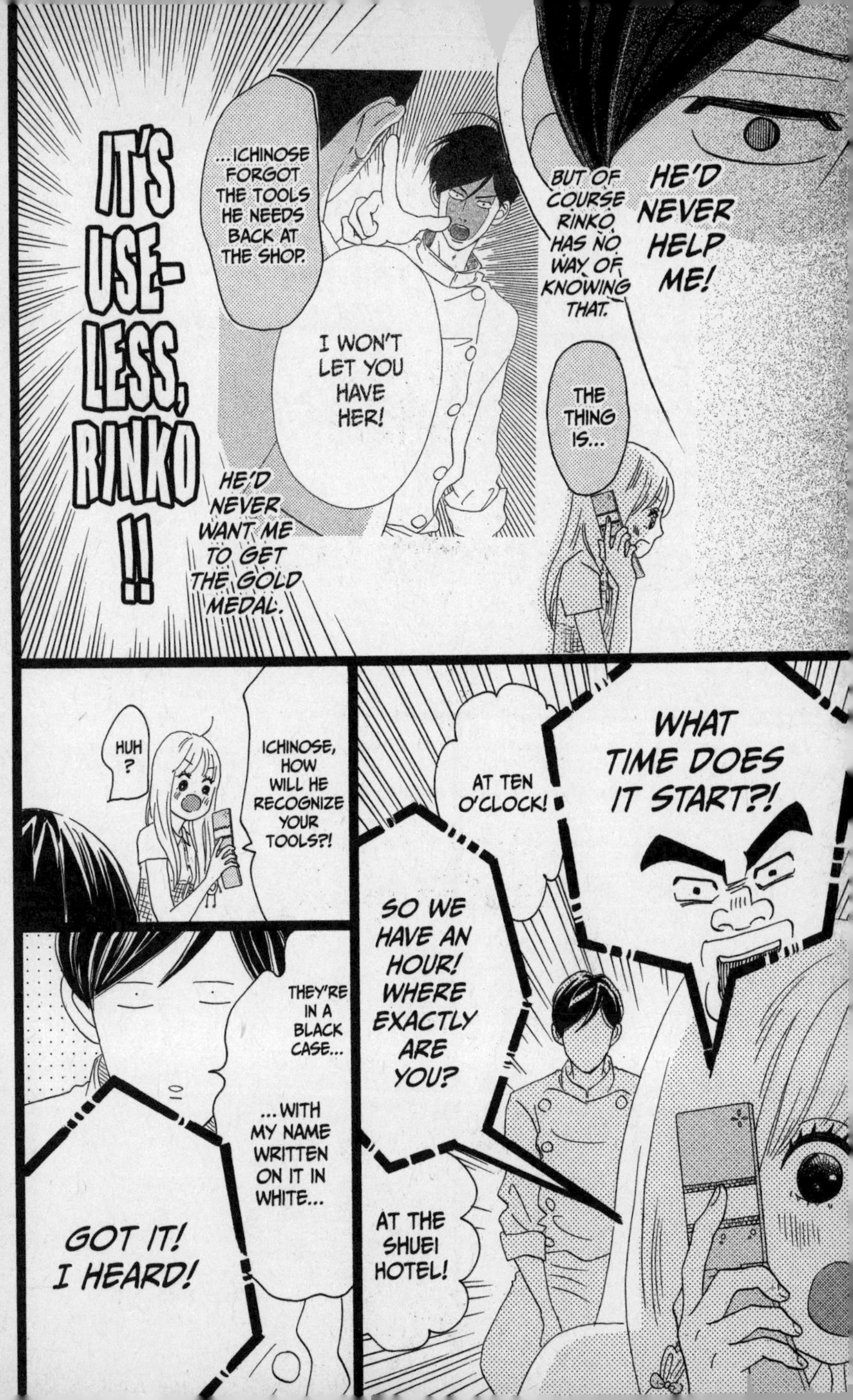
HE'D NEVER HELP ME!
BUT OF COURSE RINKO HAS NO WAY OF KNOWING THAT.
THE THING IS...
...ICHINOSE FORGOT THE TOOLS HE NEEDS BACK AT THE SHOP.
I WON'T LET YOU HAVE HER!
HE'D NEVER WANT ME TO GET THE GOLD MEDAL.
IT'S USE-LESS, RINKO!!
WHAT TIME DOES IT START?!
AT TEN O'CLOCK!
SO WE HAVE AN HOUR! WHERE EXACTLY ARE YOU?
AT THE SHUEI HOTEL!
ICHINOSE, HOW WILL HE RECOGNIZE YOUR TOOLS?!
HUH?
THEY'RE IN A BLACK CASE...
...WITH MY NAME WRITTEN ON IT IN WHITE...
GOT IT! I HEARD!

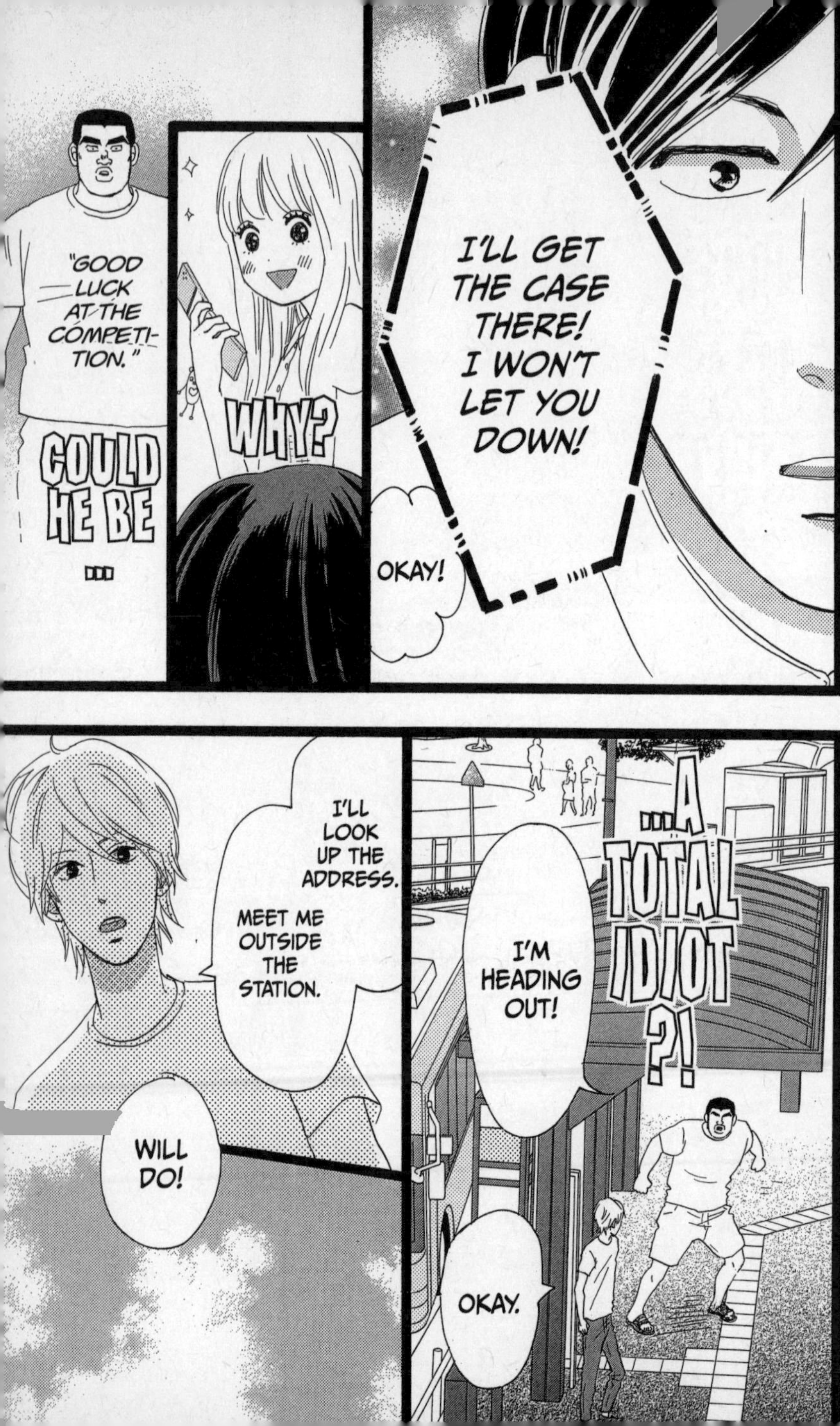

I'LL GET THE CASE THERE! I WON'T LET YOU DOWN!
OKAY!
WHY?
"GOOD LUCK AT THE COMPETI-TION."
COULD HE BE
...
...A TOTAL IDIOT ?!
I'M HEADING OUT!
OKAY.
I'LL LOOK UP THE ADDRESS.
MEET ME OUTSIDE THE STATION.
WILL DO!

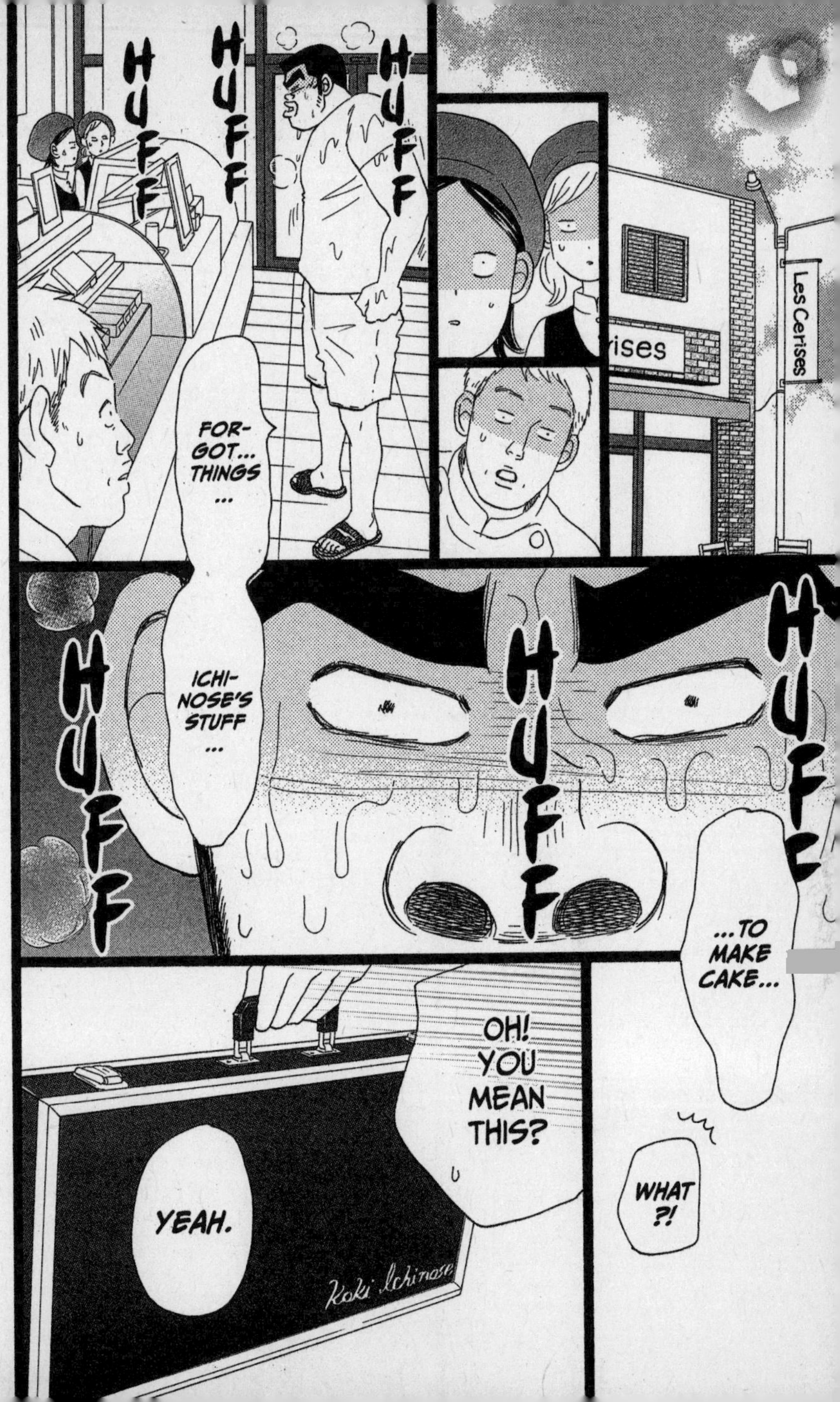
Les Cerises
rises
HUFF
HUFF
HUFF
FOR-GOT... THINGS ...
HUFF
HUFF
HUFF
ICHI-NOSE'S STUFF ...
...TO MAKE CAKE...
WHAT ?!
OH! YOU MEAN THIS?
YEAH.
Koki Ichinose

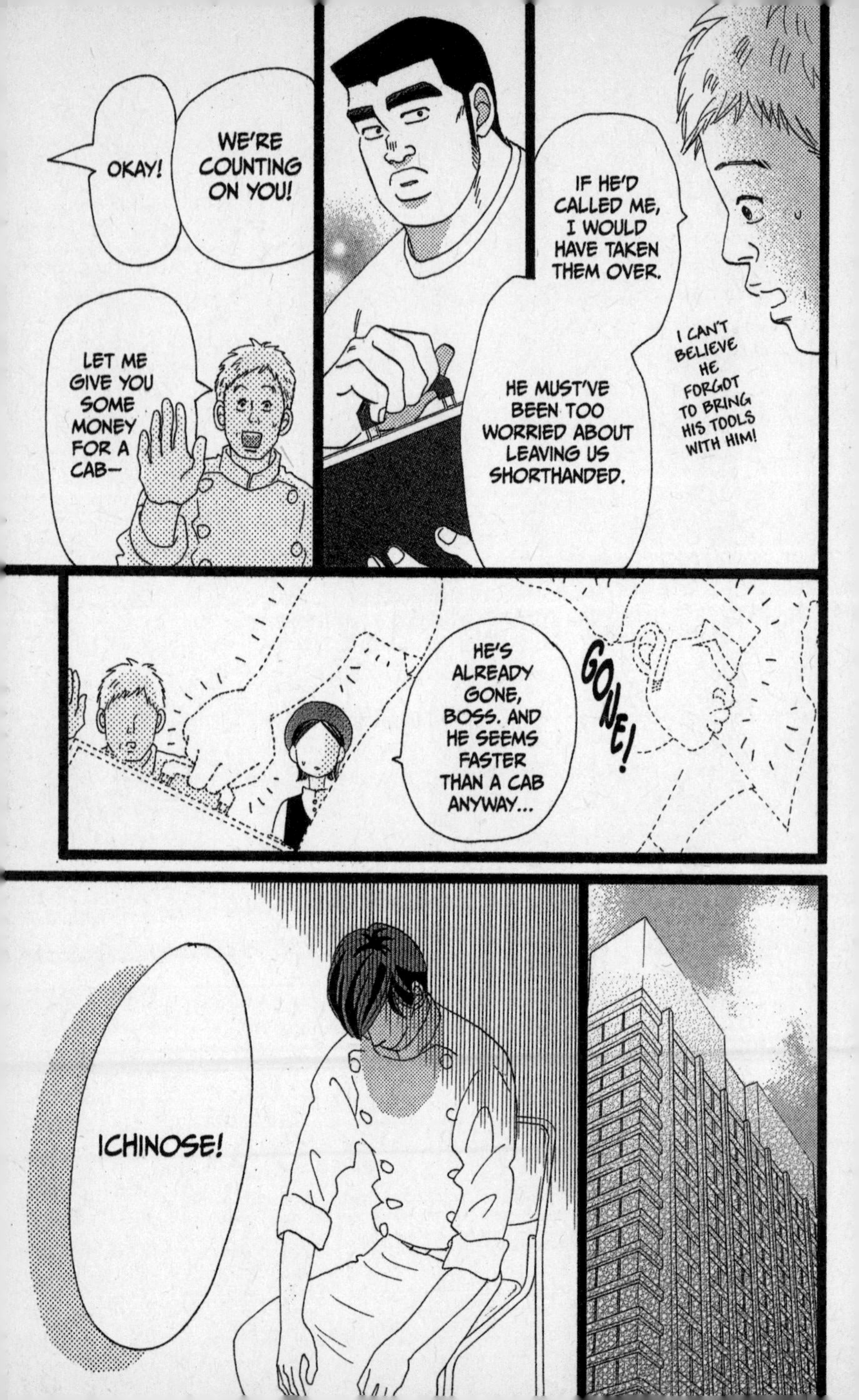
IF HE'D CALLED ME, I WOULD HAVE TAKEN THEM OVER.
I CAN'T BELIEVE HE FORGOT TO BRING HIS TOOLS WITH HIM!
HE MUST'VE BEEN TOO WORRIED ABOUT LEAVING US SHORTHANDED.
WE'RE COUNTING ON YOU!
OKAY!
LET ME GIVE YOU SOME MONEY FOR A CAB—
GONE!
HE'S ALREADY GONE, BOSS. AND HE SEEMS FASTER THAN A CAB ANYWAY...
ICHINOSE!

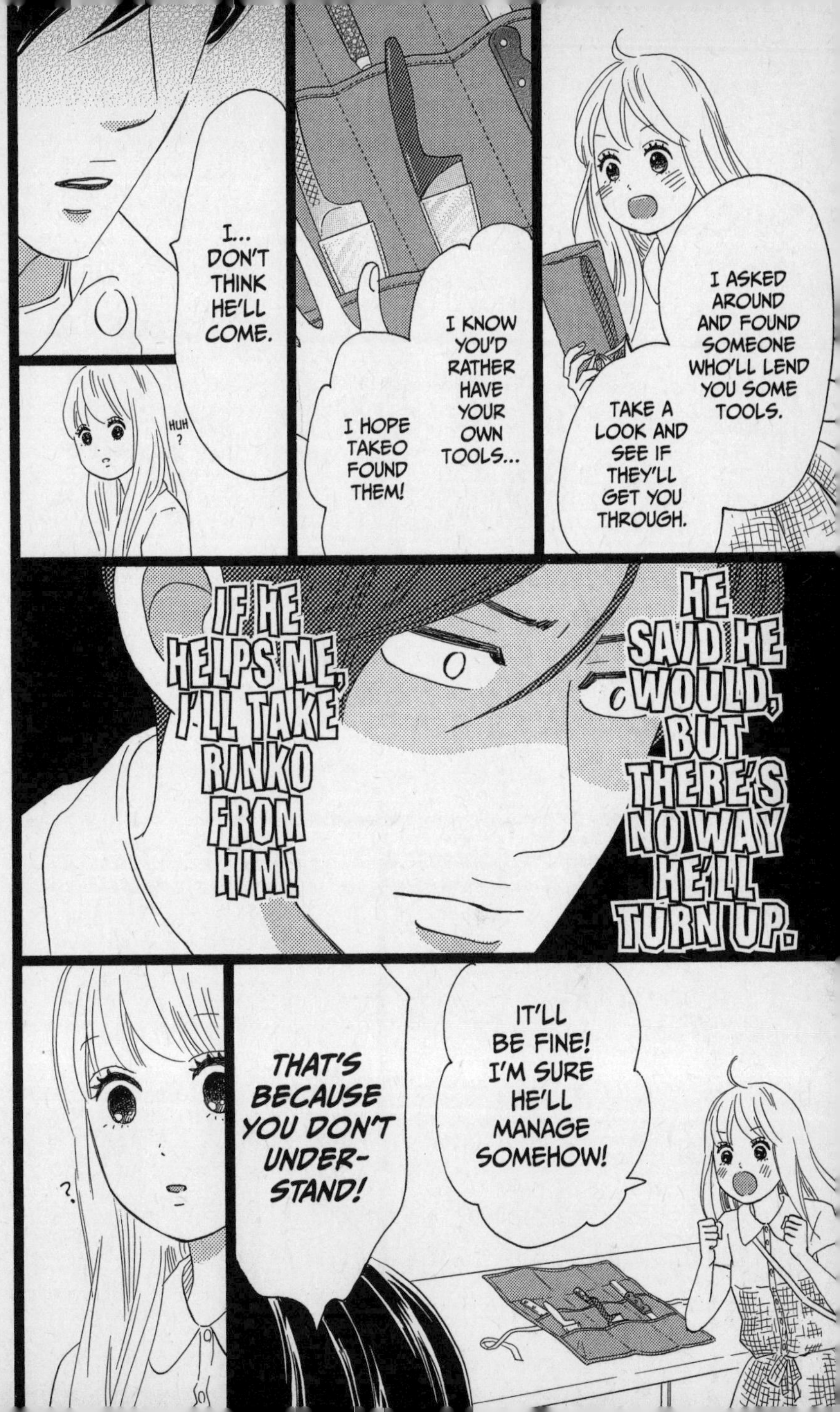
I ASKED AROUND AND FOUND SOMEONE WHO'LL LEND YOU SOME TOOLS.
TAKE A LOOK AND SEE IF THEY'LL GET YOU THROUGH.
I KNOW YOU'D RATHER HAVE YOUR OWN TOOLS...
I HOPE TAKEO FOUND THEM!
I... DON'T THINK HE'LL COME.
HUH ?
HE SAID HE WOULD, BUT THERE'S NO WAY HE'LL TURN UP.
IF HE HELPS ME, I'LL TAKE RINKO FROM HIM!
IT'LL BE FINE! I'M SURE HE'LL MANAGE SOMEHOW!
THAT'S BECAUSE YOU DON'T UNDER-STAND!
?

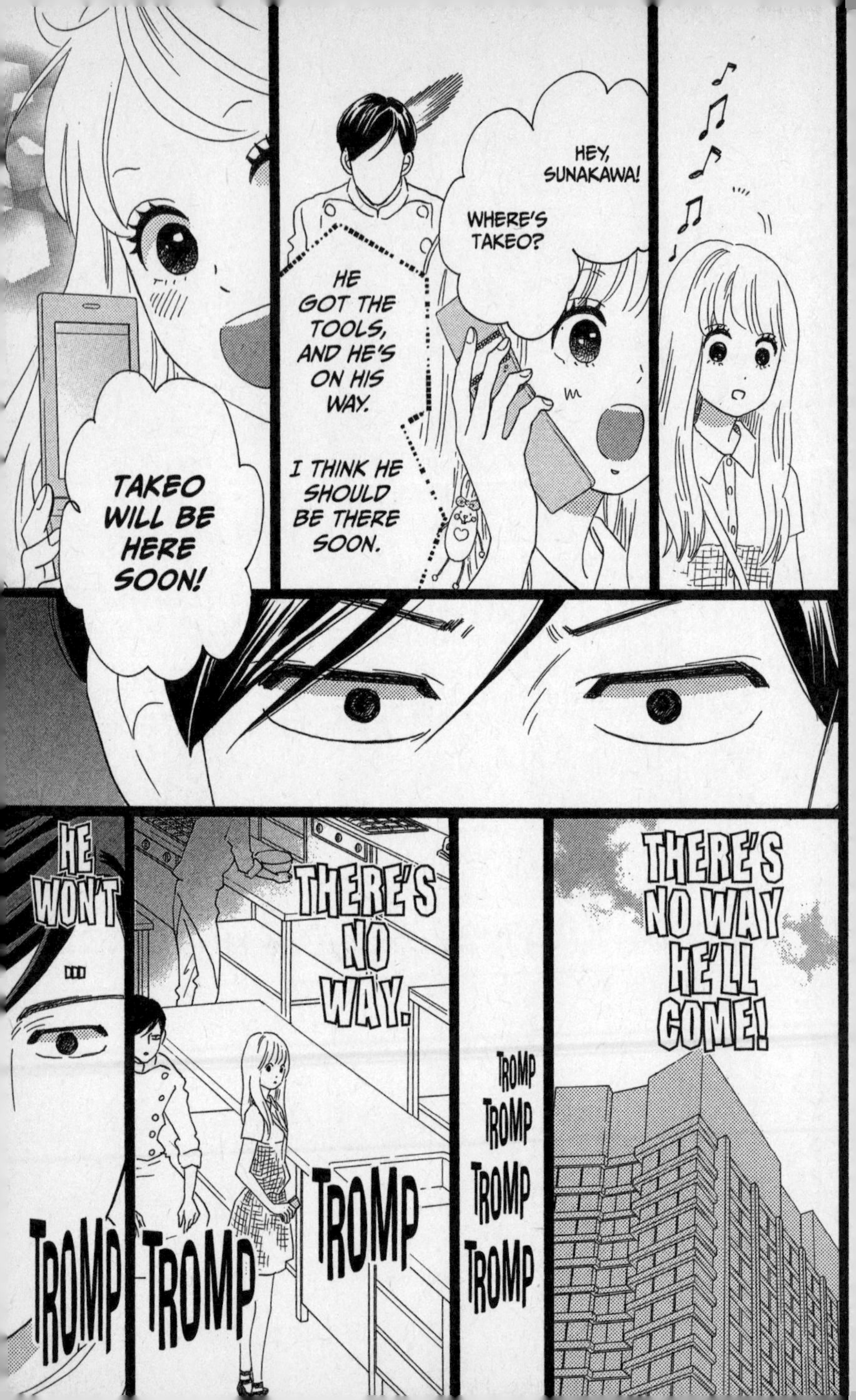
HEY, SUNAKAWA!
WHERE'S TAKEO?
HE GOT THE TOOLS, AND HE'S ON HIS WAY.
I THINK HE SHOULD BE THERE SOON.
TAKEO WILL BE HERE SOON!
THERE'S NO WAY HE'LL COME!
TROMP
TROMP
TROMP
TROMP
THERE'S NO WAY.
TROMP
TROMP
HE WON'T...
TROMP

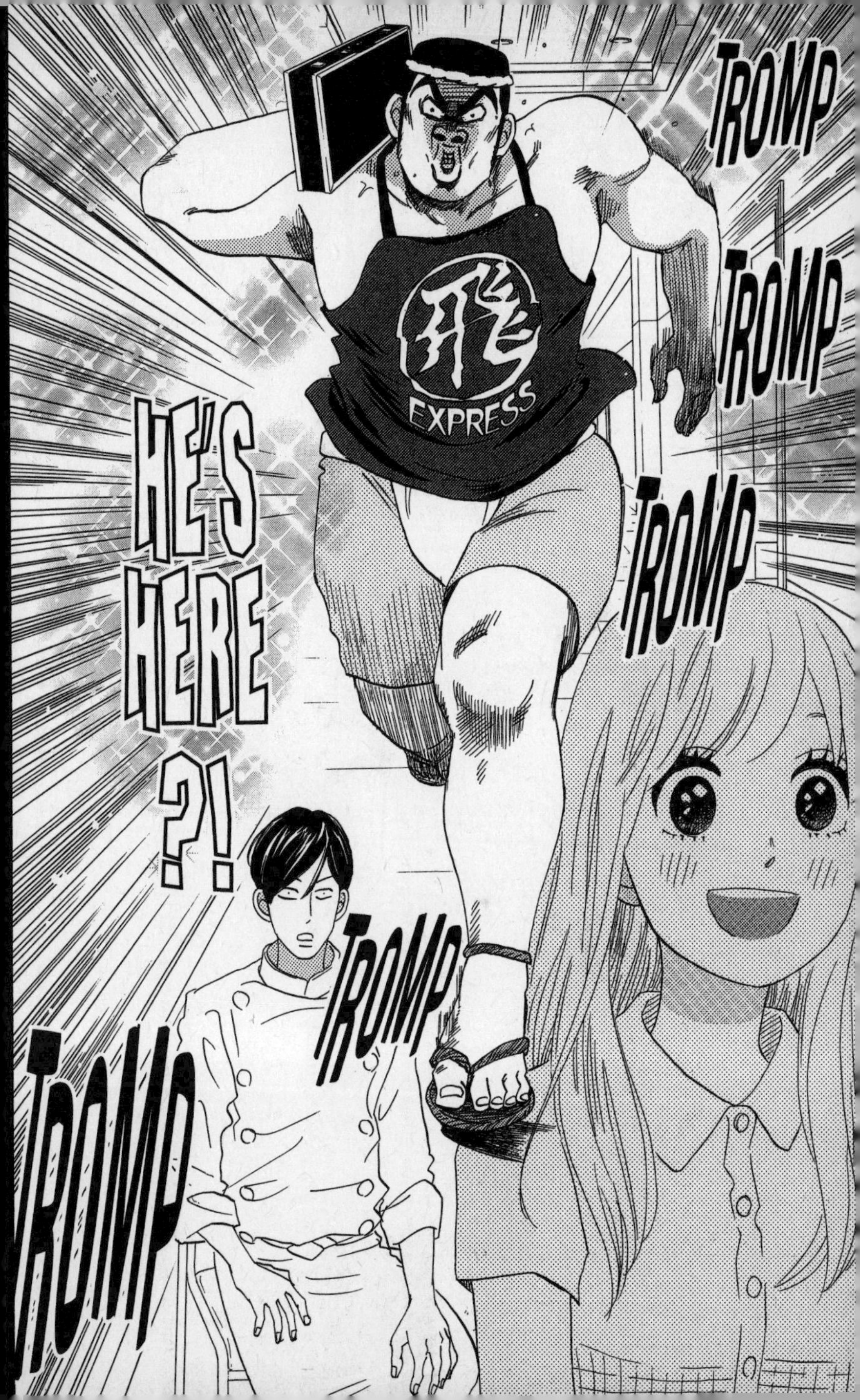
TROMP
TROMP
EXPRESS
TROMP
HE'S HERE ?!
TROMP
TROMP

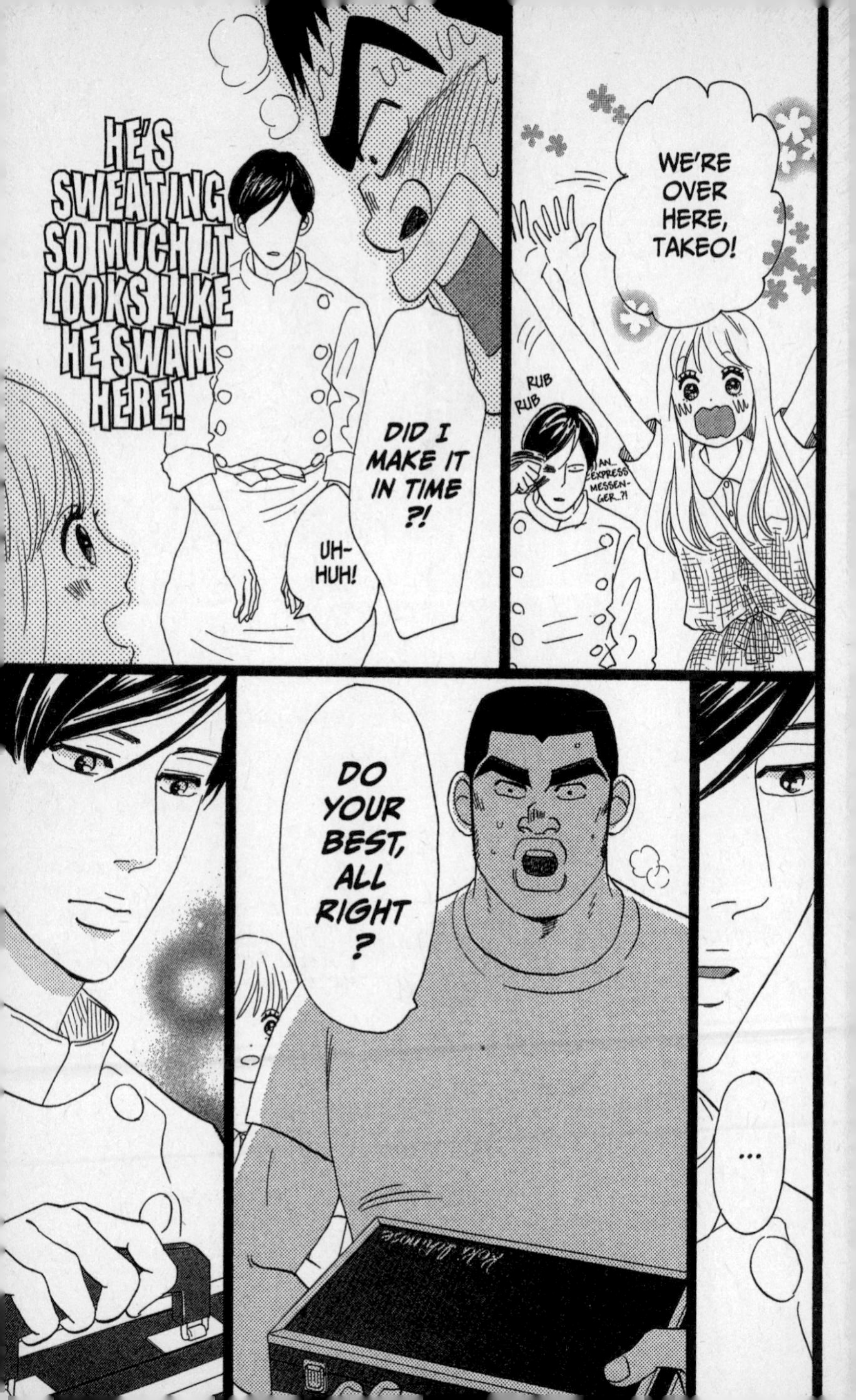
WE'RE OVER HERE, TAKEO!
RUB RUB
AN... EXPRESS MESSENGER...?!
DID I MAKE IT IN TIME ?!
UH-HUH!
HE'S SWEATING SO MUCH IT LOOKS LIKE HE SWAM HERE!
...
DO YOUR BEST, ALL RIGHT ?

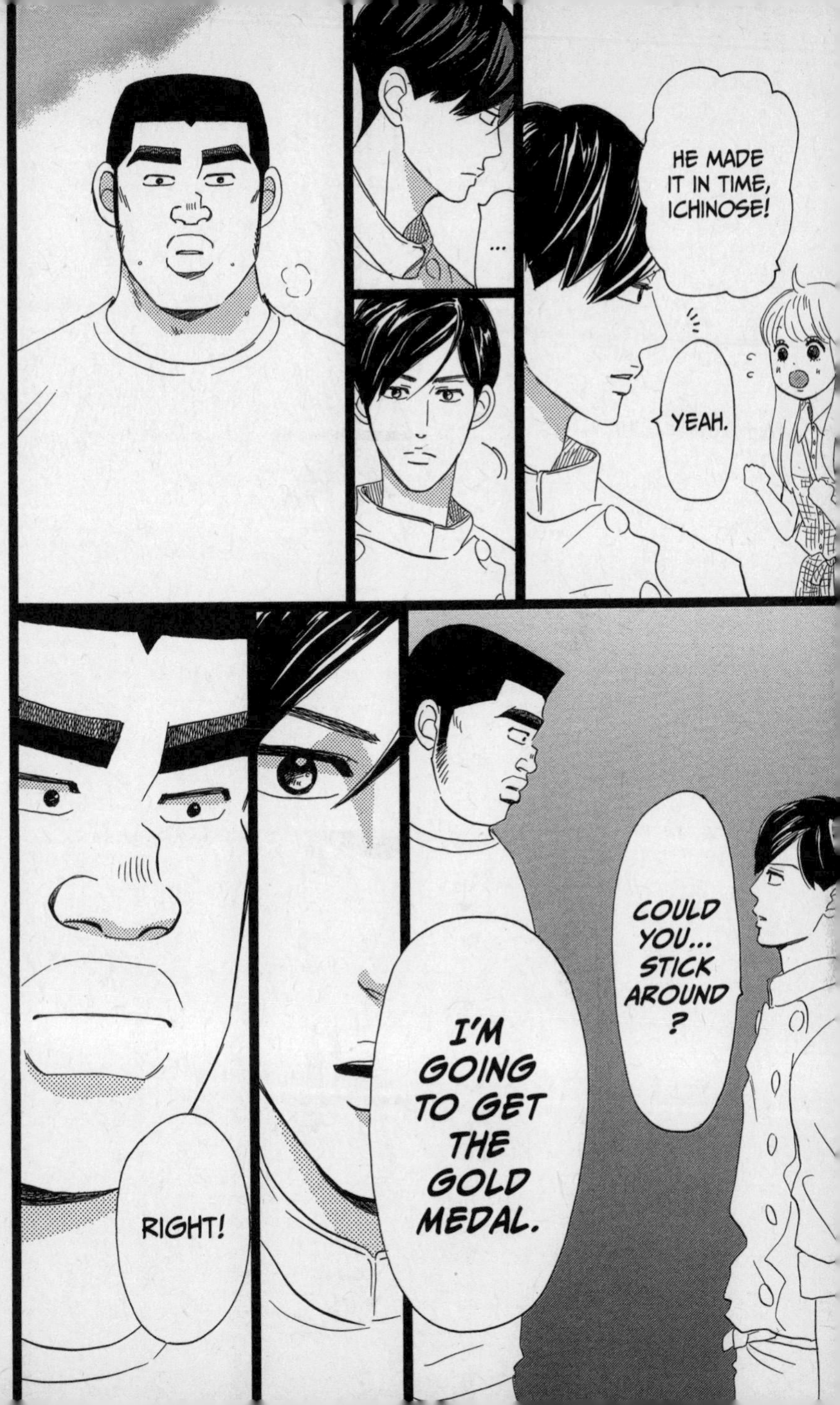
HE MADE IT IN TIME, ICHINOSE!
YEAH.
...
COULD YOU... STICK AROUND?
I'M GOING TO GET THE GOLD MEDAL.
RIGHT!

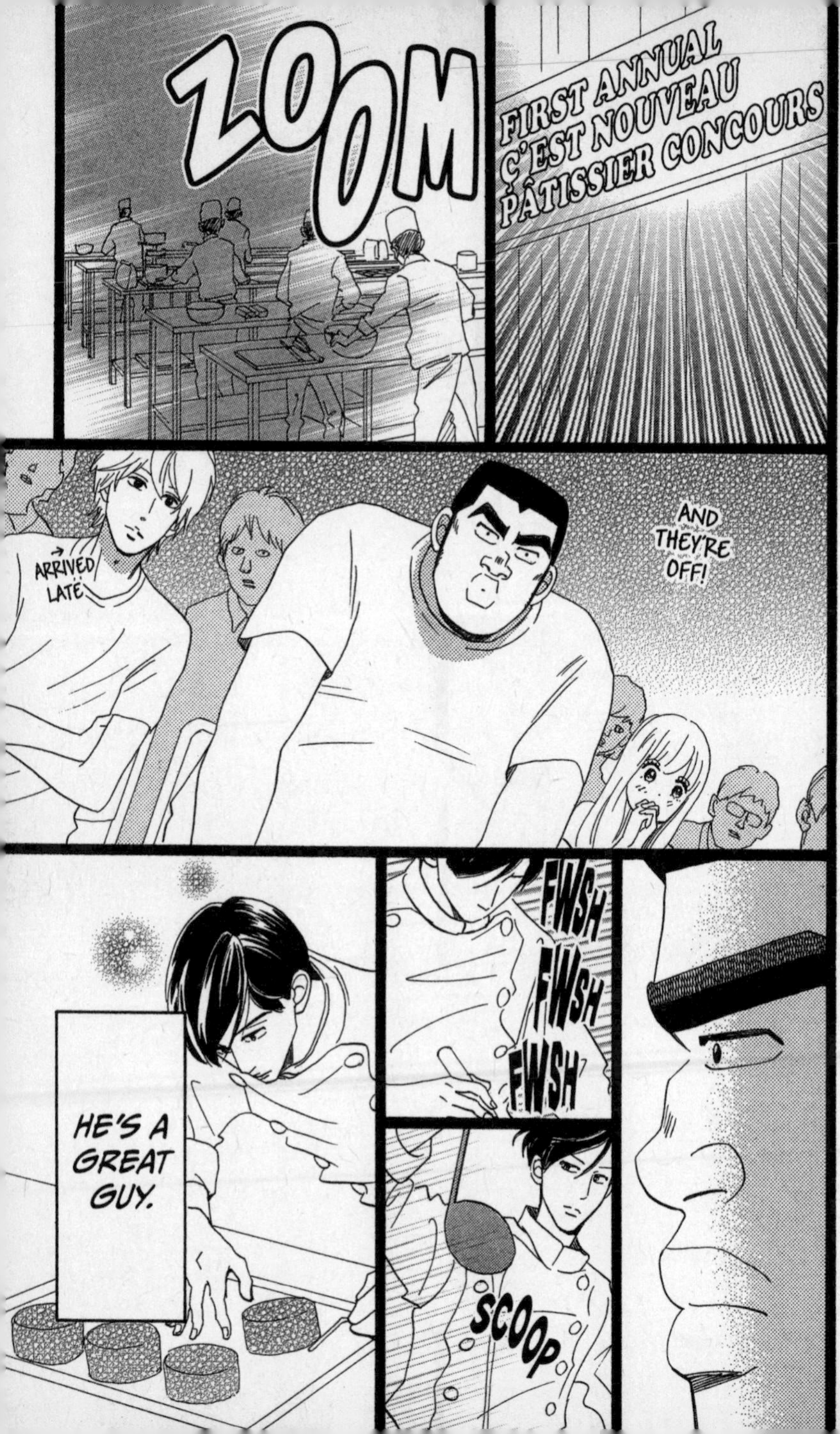
FIRST ANNUAL
Ç'EST NOUVEAU
PÂTISSIER CONCOURS
ZOOM
AND THEY'RE OFF!
ARRIVED LATE
FWSH
FWSH
FWSH
SCOOP
HE'S A GREAT GUY.

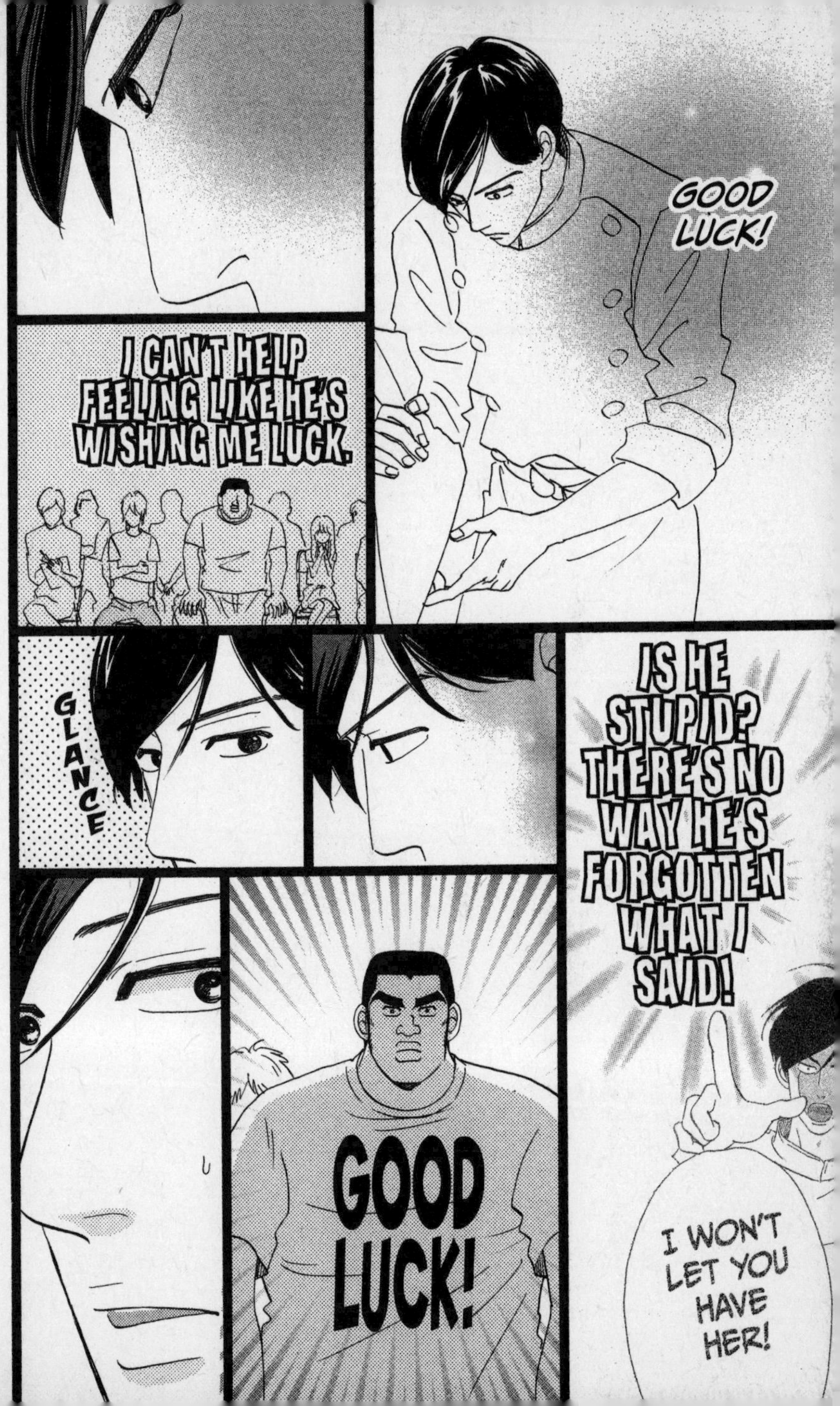
GOOD LUCK!
I CAN'T HELP FEELING LIKE HE'S WISHING ME LUCK.
IS HE STUPID? THERE'S NO WAY HE'S FORGOTTEN WHAT I SAID!
I WON'T LET YOU HAVE HER!
GLANCE
GOOD LUCK!

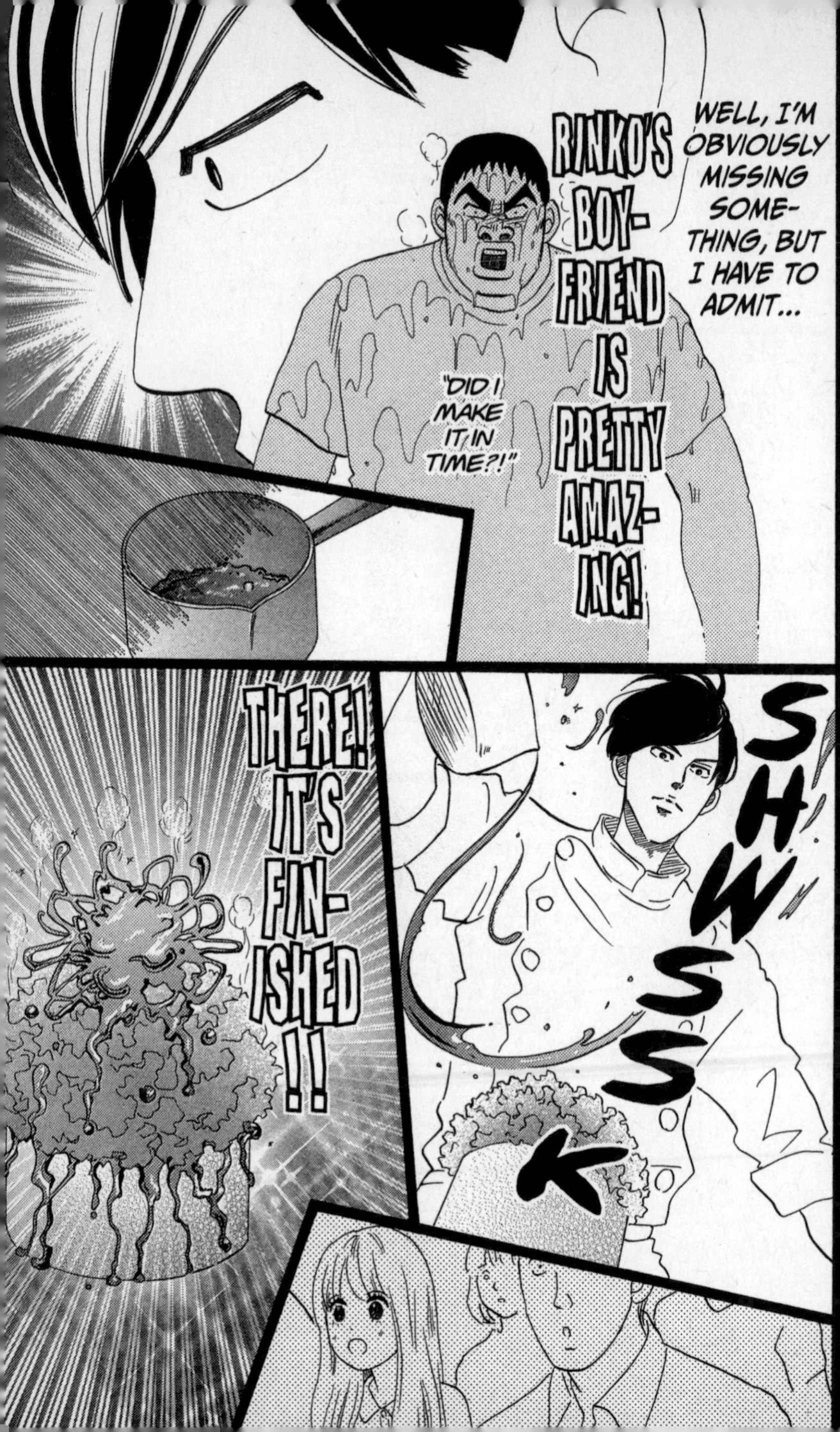
WELL, I'M OBVIOUSLY MISSING SOMETHING, BUT I HAVE TO ADMIT...
RINKO'S BOYFRIEND IS PRETTY AMAZING!
"DID I MAKE IT IN TIME?!"
SHWSSK
THERE! IT'S FINISHED!!

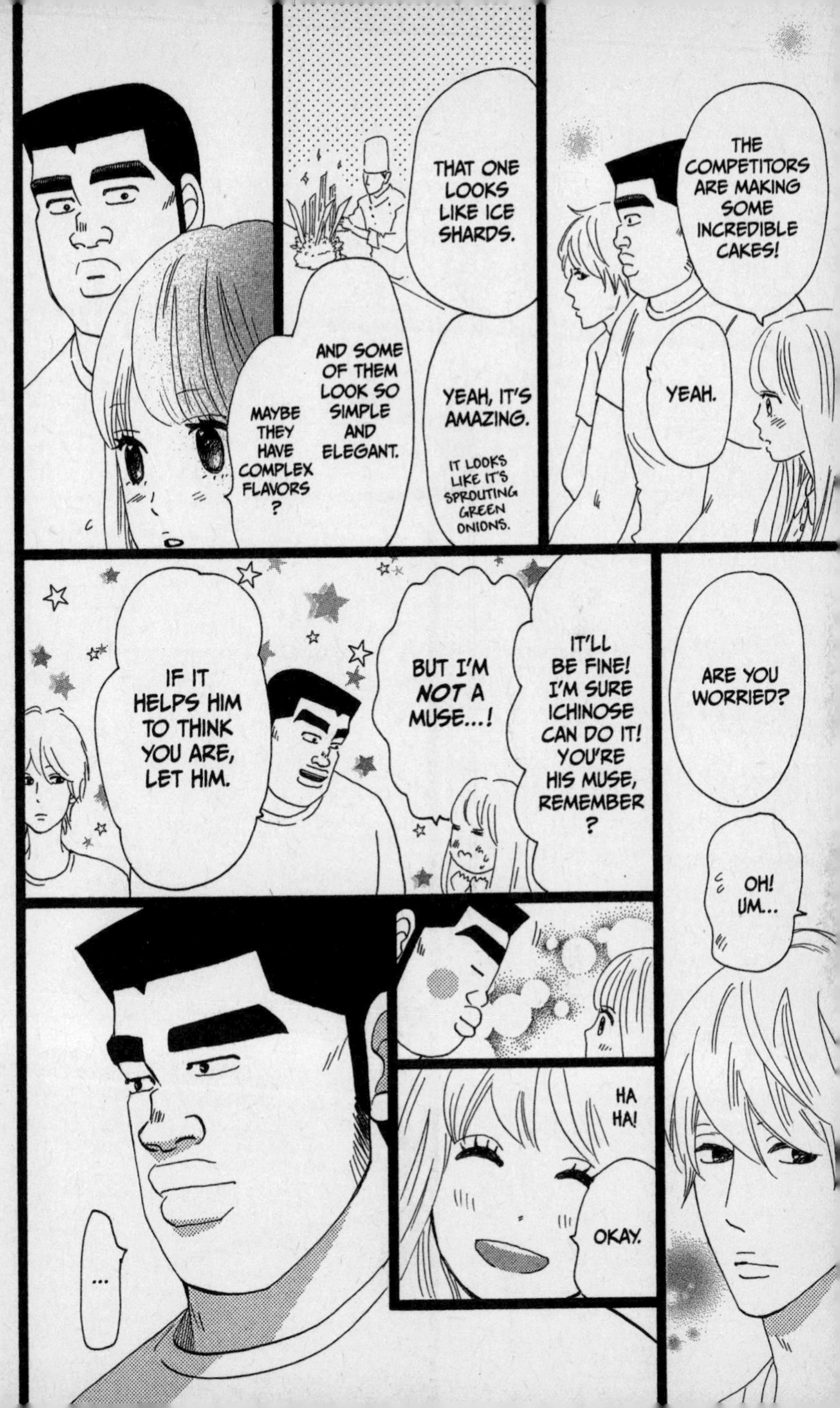
THE COMPETITORS ARE MAKING SOME INCREDIBLE CAKES!
YEAH.
THAT ONE LOOKS LIKE ICE SHARDS.
YEAH, IT'S AMAZING.
IT LOOKS LIKE IT'S SPROUTING GREEN ONIONS.
AND SOME OF THEM LOOK SO SIMPLE AND ELEGANT.
MAYBE THEY HAVE COMPLEX FLAVORS?
ARE YOU WORRIED?
OH! UM...
IT'LL BE FINE! I'M SURE ICHINOSE CAN DO IT! YOU'RE HIS MUSE, REMEMBER?
BUT I'M *NOT* A MUSE...!
IF IT HELPS HIM TO THINK YOU ARE, LET HIM.
HA HA!
OKAY.
...

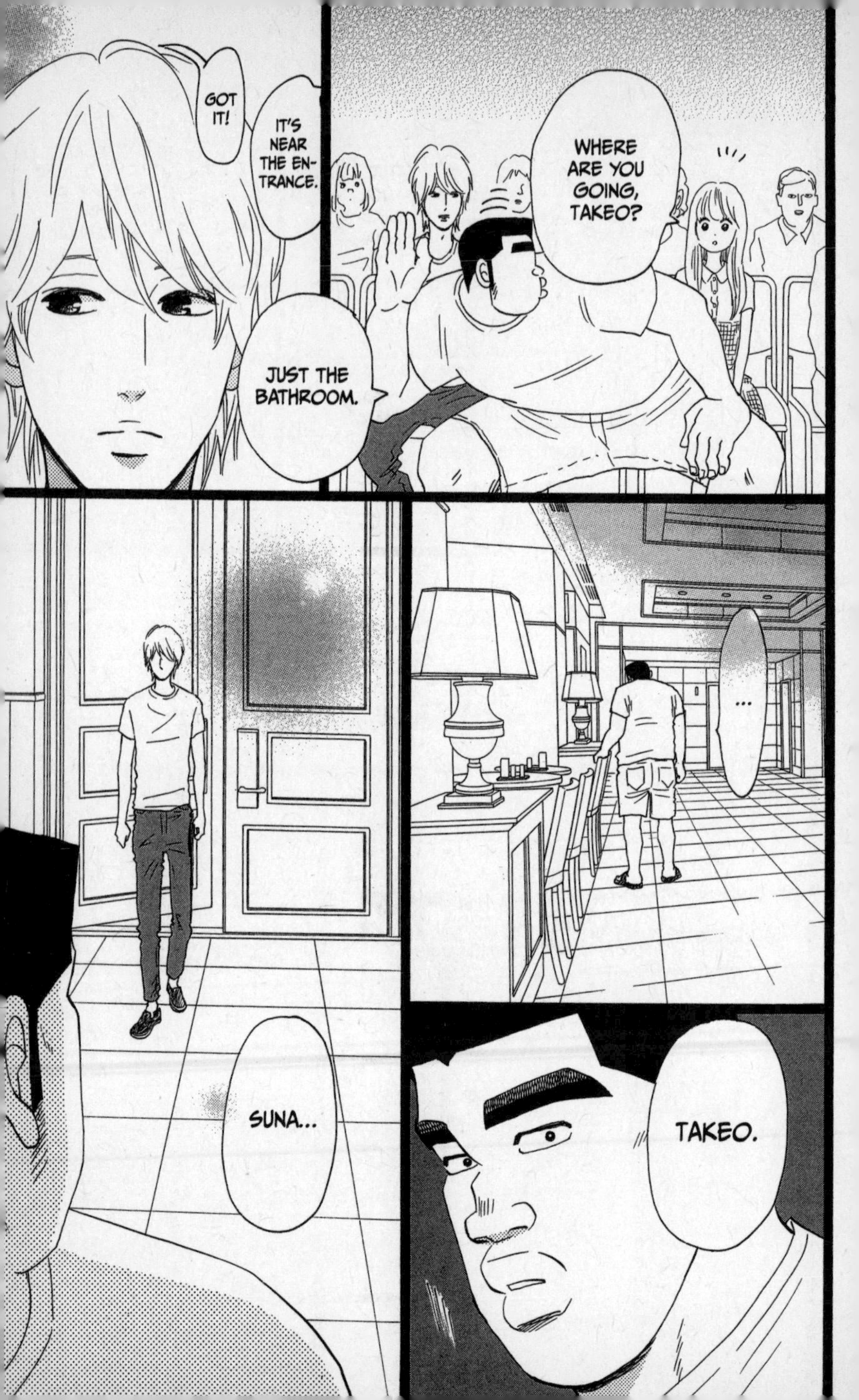
WHERE ARE YOU GOING, TAKEO?
JUST THE BATHROOM.
IT'S NEAR THE EN-TRANCE.
GOT IT!
...
TAKEO.
SUNA...

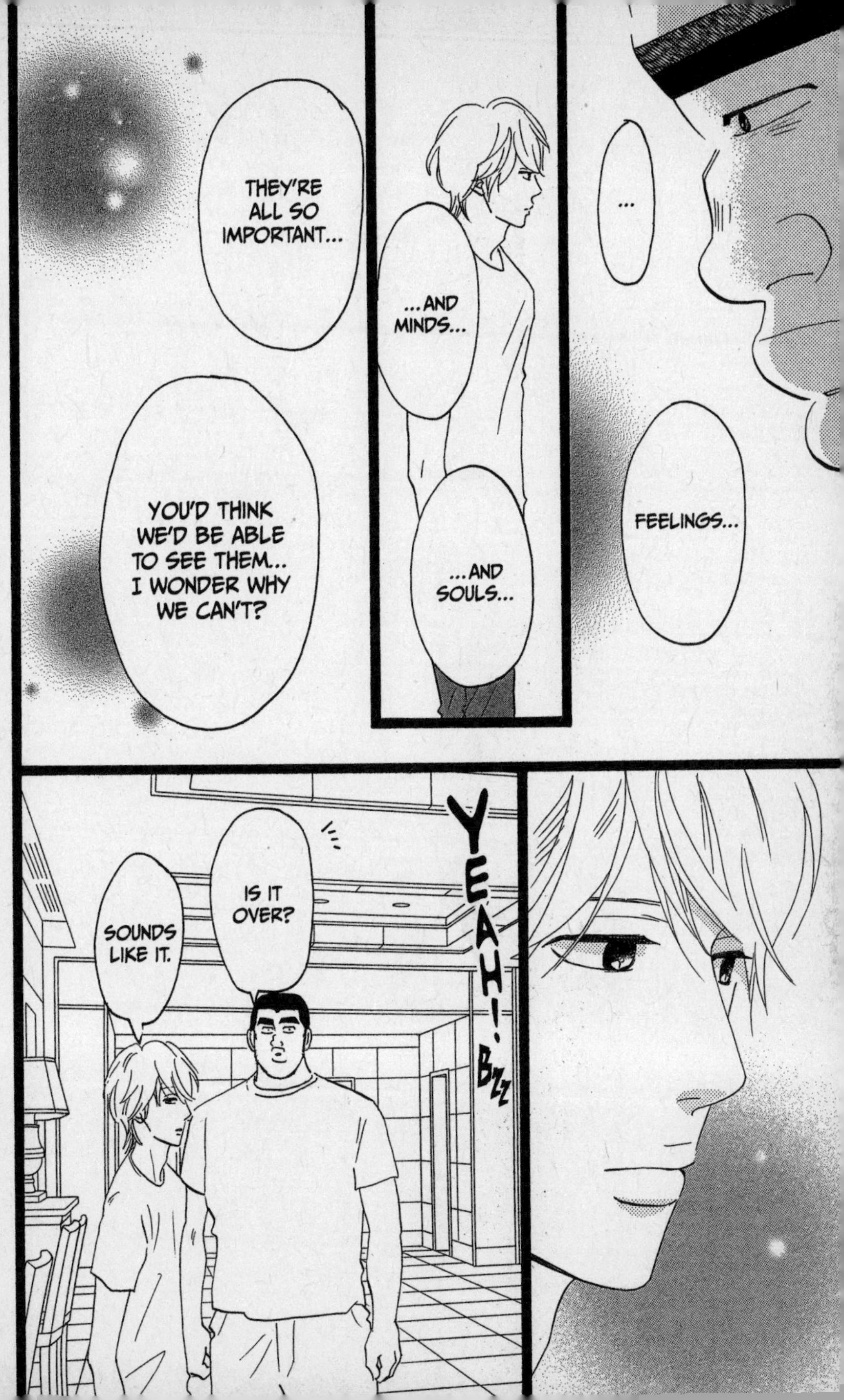
...
FEELINGS...
...AND MINDS...
...AND SOULS...
THEY'RE ALL SO IMPORTANT...
YOU'D THINK WE'D BE ABLE TO SEE THEM... I WONDER WHY WE CAN'T?
YEAH!
BZZ
IS IT OVER?
SOUNDS LIKE IT.

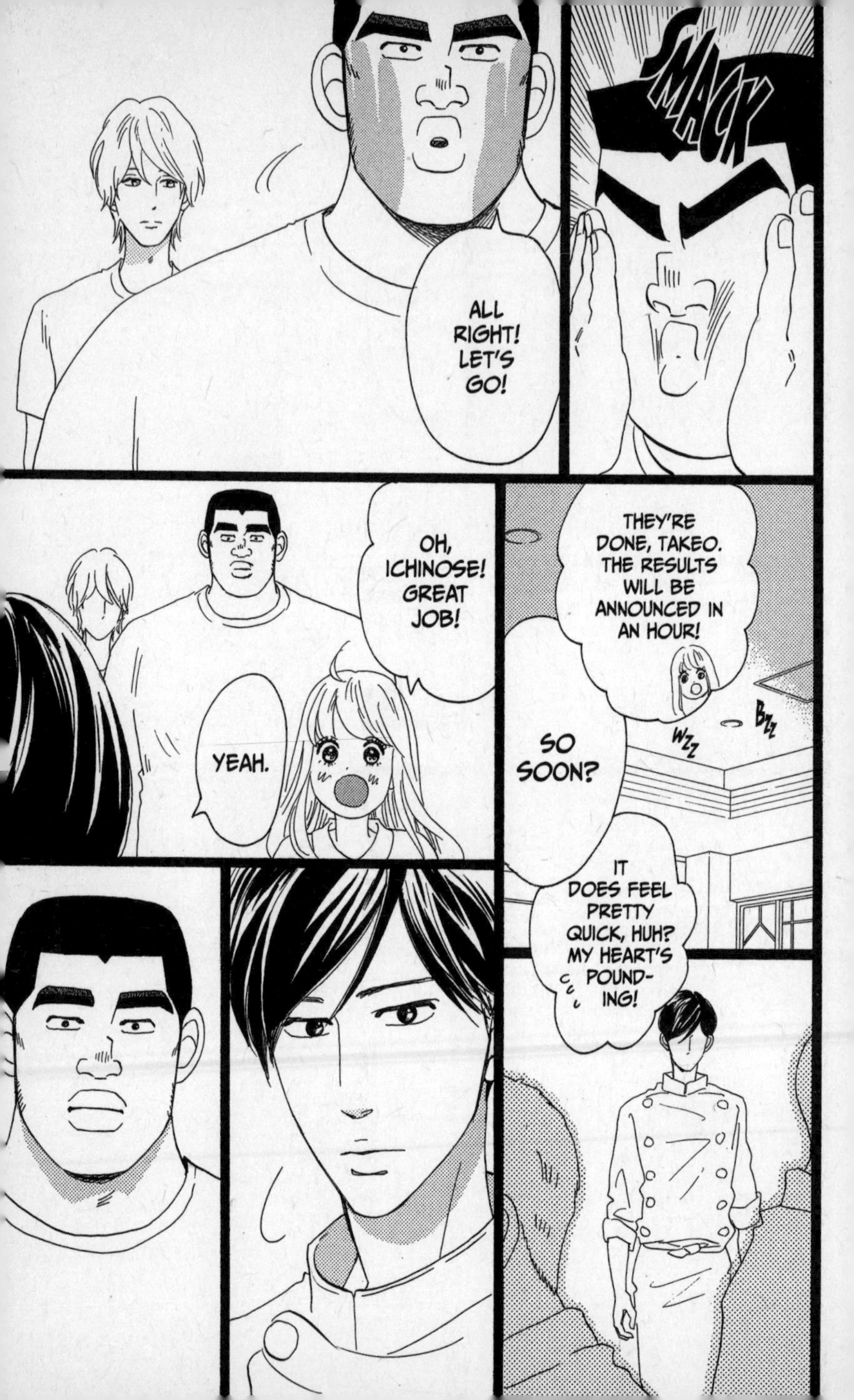
SMACK
ALL RIGHT! LET'S GO!
THEY'RE DONE, TAKEO. THE RESULTS WILL BE ANNOUNCED IN AN HOUR!
BZZ
WZZ
SO SOON?
IT DOES FEEL PRETTY QUICK, HUH? MY HEART'S POUND-ING!
OH, ICHINOSE! GREAT JOB!
YEAH.

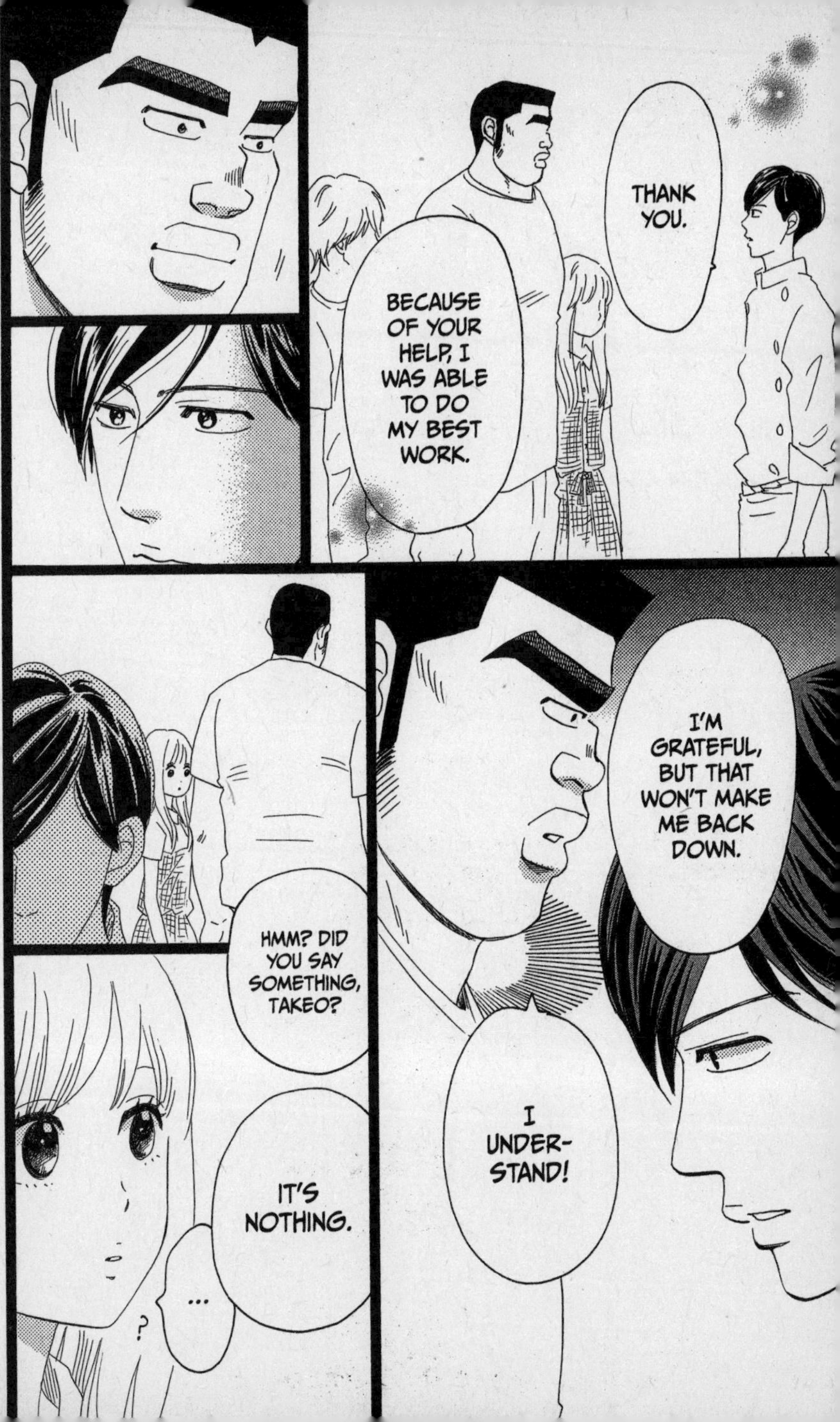
THANK YOU.
BECAUSE OF YOUR HELP, I WAS ABLE TO DO MY BEST WORK.
I'M GRATEFUL, BUT THAT WON'T MAKE ME BACK DOWN.
I UNDER-STAND!
HMM? DID YOU SAY SOMETHING, TAKEO?
IT'S NOTHING.
...
?

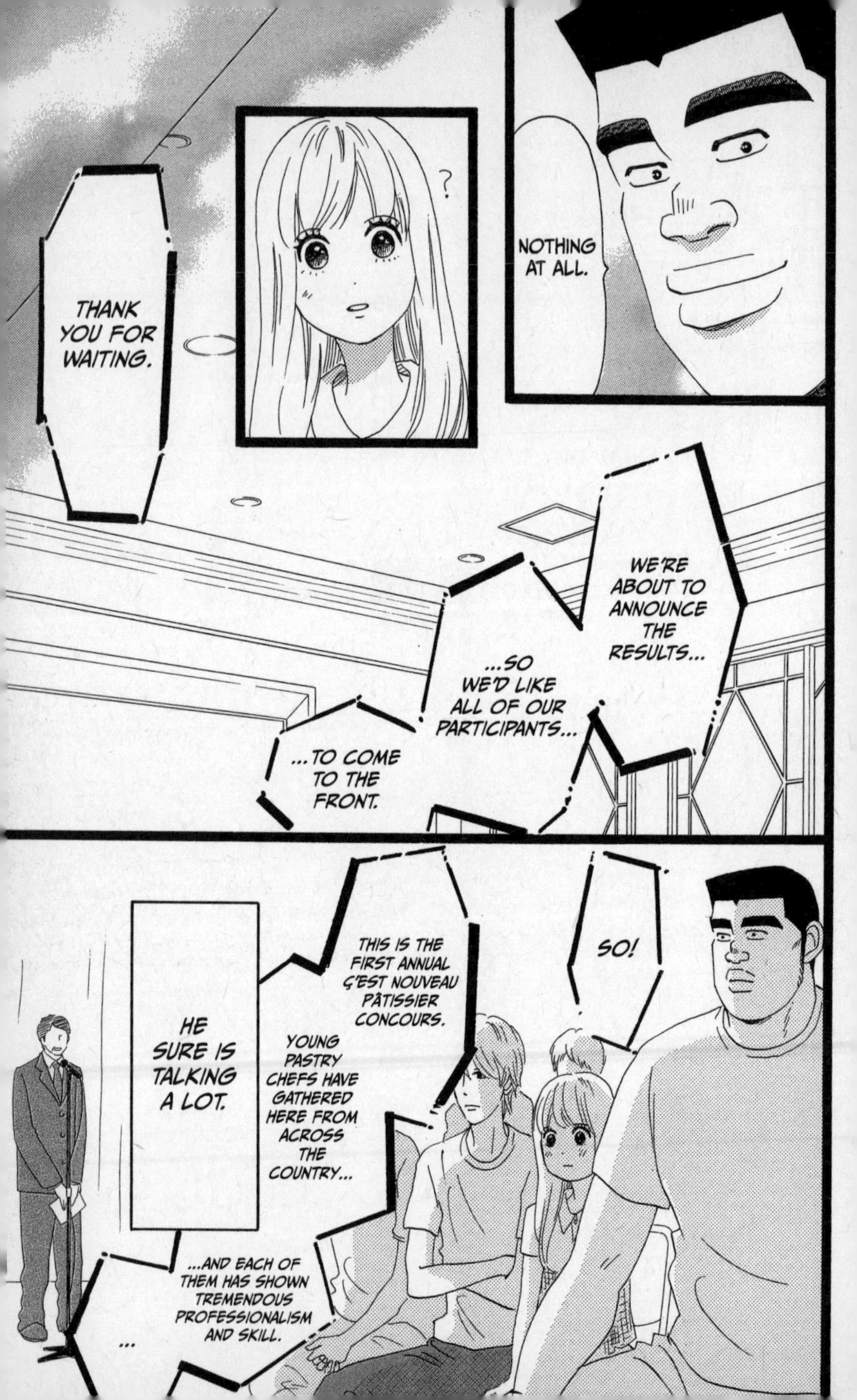
NOTHING AT ALL.
?
THANK YOU FOR WAITING.
WE'RE ABOUT TO ANNOUNCE THE RESULTS...
...SO WE'D LIKE ALL OF OUR PARTICIPANTS...
...TO COME TO THE FRONT.
SO!
THIS IS THE FIRST ANNUAL Ç'EST NOUVEAU PÂTISSIER CONCOURS.
YOUNG PASTRY CHEFS HAVE GATHERED HERE FROM ACROSS THE COUNTRY...
HE SURE IS TALKING A LOT.
...AND EACH OF THEM HAS SHOWN TREMENDOUS PROFESSIONALISM AND SKILL.
...

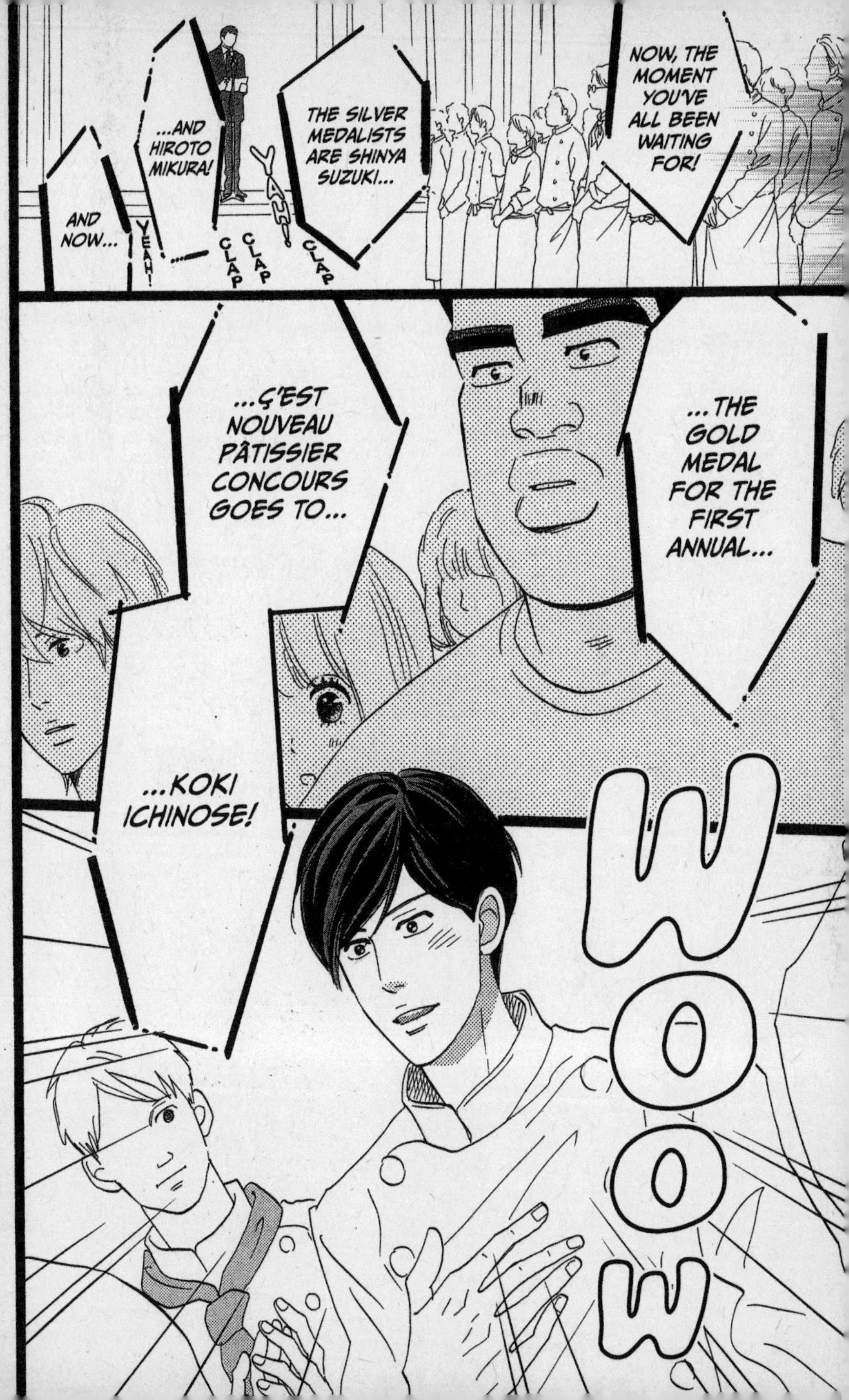
NOW, THE MOMENT YOU'VE ALL BEEN WAITING FOR!
THE SILVER MEDALISTS ARE SHINYA SUZUKI...
CLAP
YAAH!
CLAP
CLAP
...AND HIROTO MIKURA!
YEAH!
AND NOW...
...THE GOLD MEDAL FOR THE FIRST ANNUAL...
...Ç'EST NOUVEAU PÂTISSIER CONCOURS GOES TO...
...KOKI ICHINOSE!
WOOW

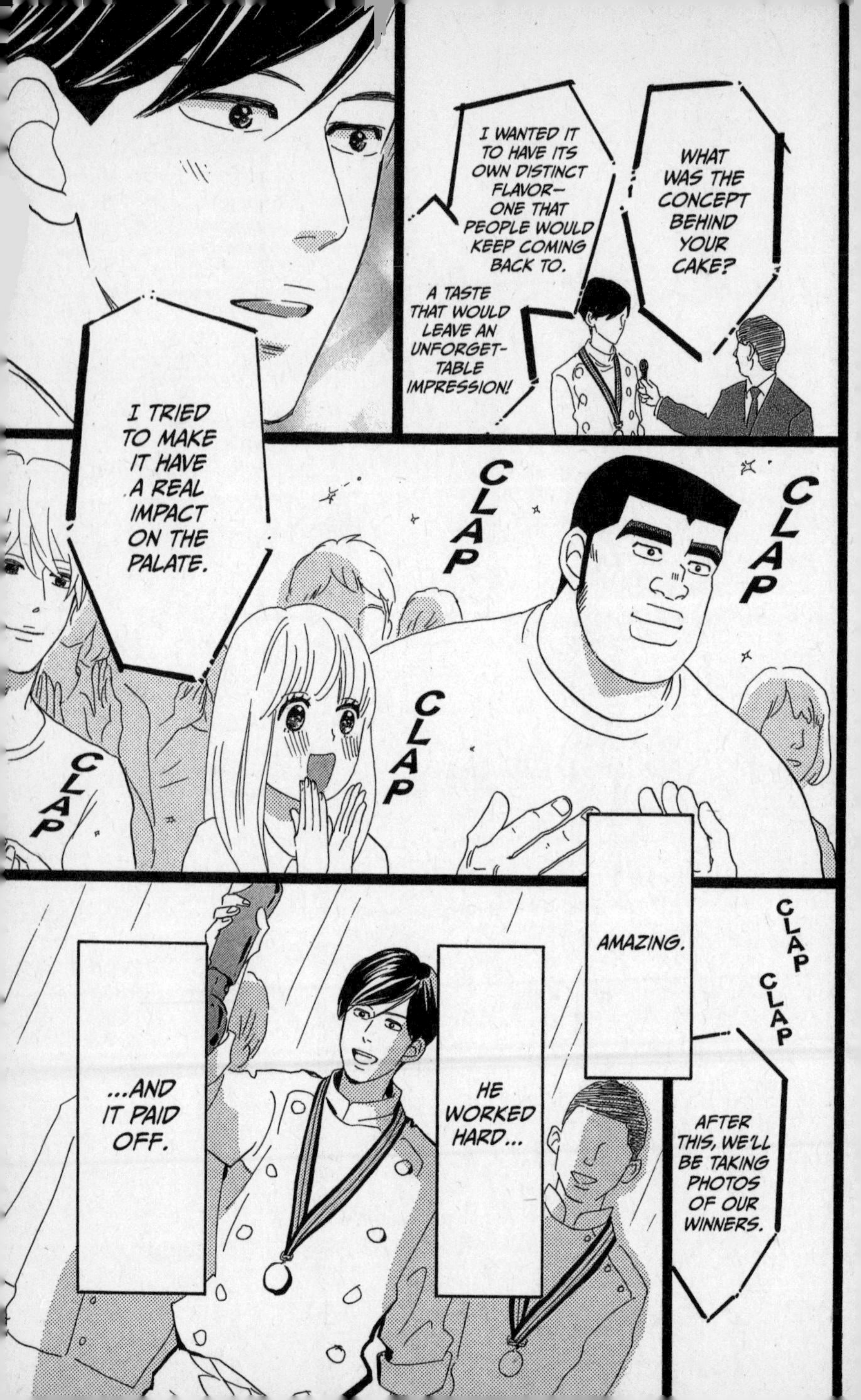
WHAT WAS THE CONCEPT BEHIND YOUR CAKE?
I WANTED IT TO HAVE ITS OWN DISTINCT FLAVOR—ONE THAT PEOPLE WOULD KEEP COMING BACK TO.
A TASTE THAT WOULD LEAVE AN UNFORGETTABLE IMPRESSION!
I TRIED TO MAKE IT HAVE A REAL IMPACT ON THE PALATE.
CLAP
CLAP
CLAP
CLAP
CLAP
CLAP
AMAZING.
AFTER THIS, WE'LL BE TAKING PHOTOS OF OUR WINNERS.
HE WORKED HARD...
...AND IT PAID OFF.

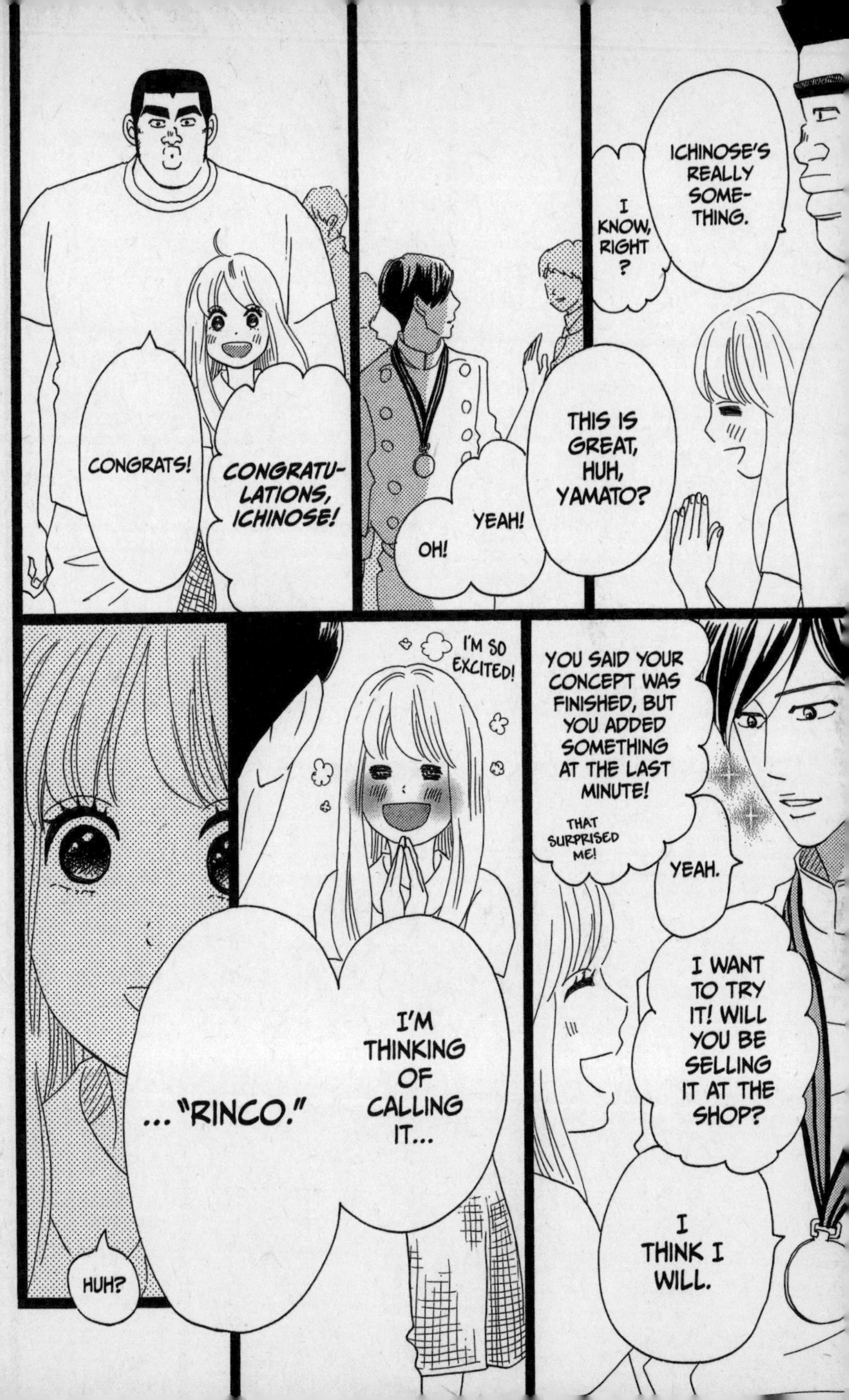
ICHINOSE'S REALLY SOMETHING.
I KNOW, RIGHT?
THIS IS GREAT, HUH, YAMATO?
YEAH!
OH!
CONGRATULATIONS, ICHINOSE!
CONGRATS!
YOU SAID YOUR CONCEPT WAS FINISHED, BUT YOU ADDED SOMETHING AT THE LAST MINUTE!
THAT SURPRISED ME!
YEAH.
I WANT TO TRY IT! WILL YOU BE SELLING IT AT THE SHOP?
I THINK I WILL.
I'M SO EXCITED!
I'M THINKING OF CALLING IT...
..."RINCO."
HUH?

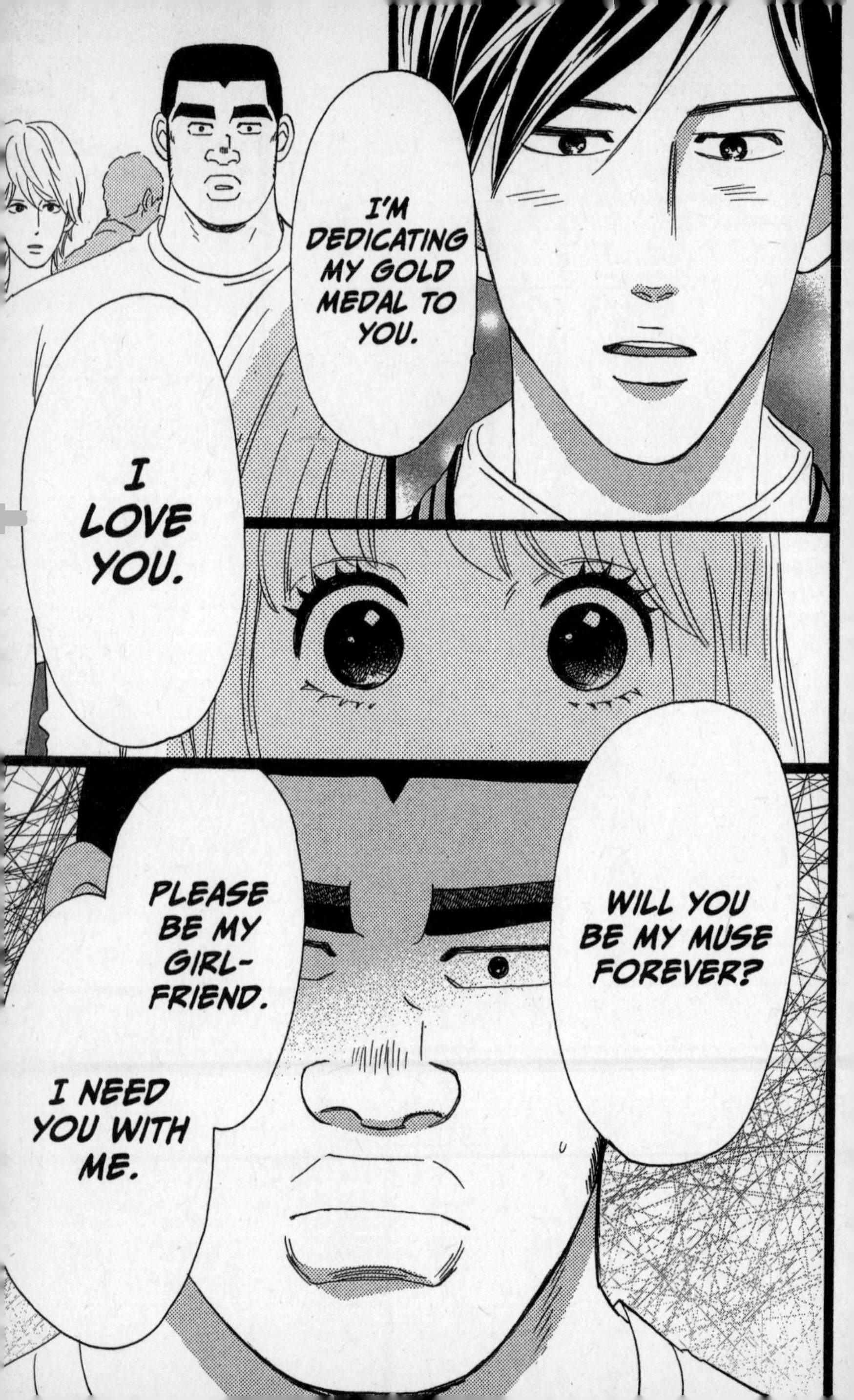
I'M DEDICATING MY GOLD MEDAL TO YOU.
I LOVE YOU.
WILL YOU BE MY MUSE FOREVER?
PLEASE BE MY GIRL-FRIEND.
I NEED YOU WITH ME.

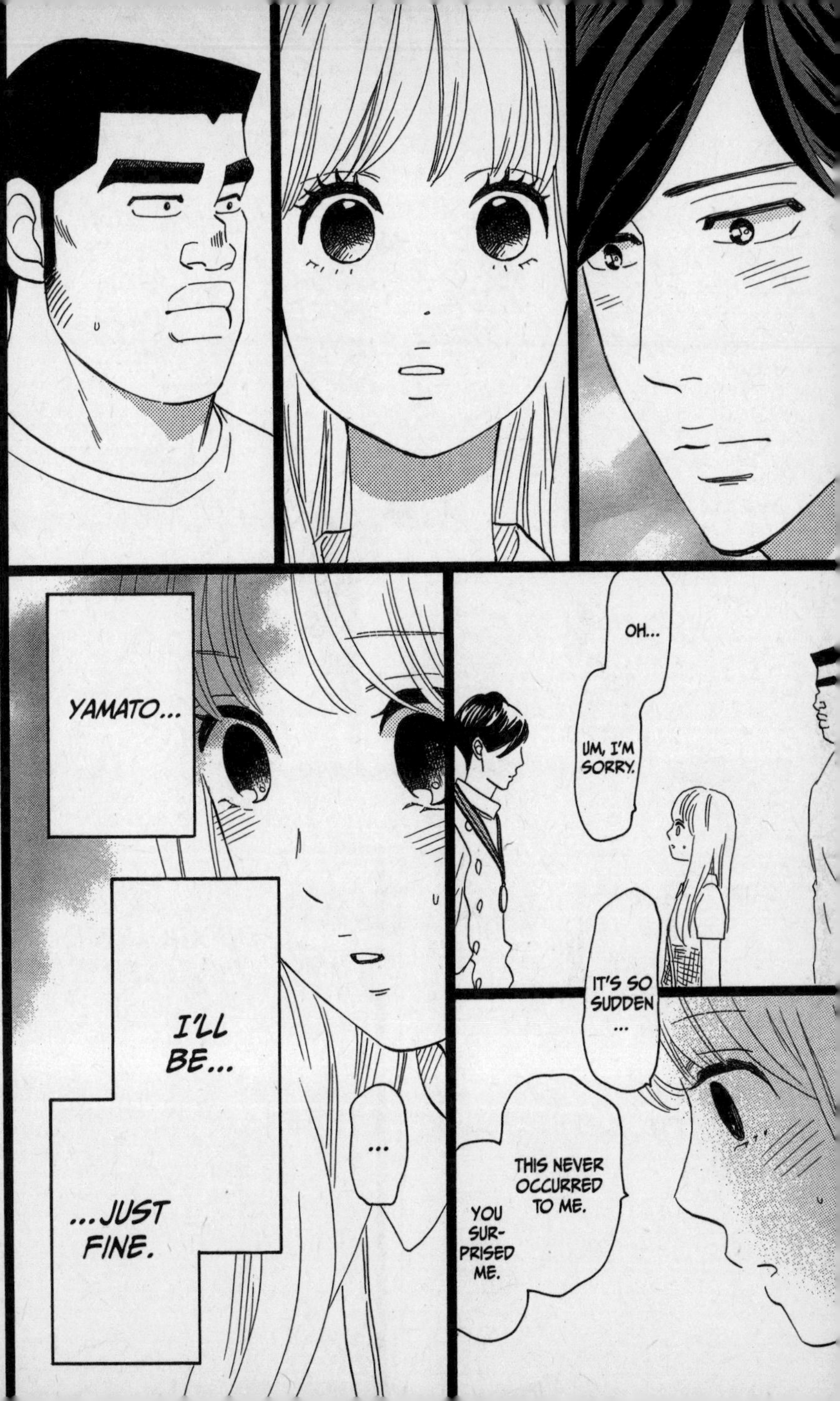
OH...
UM, I'M SORRY.
IT'S SO SUDDEN...
THIS NEVER OCCURRED TO ME.
YOU SURPRISED ME.
YAMATO...
I'LL BE... ...JUST FINE.
...

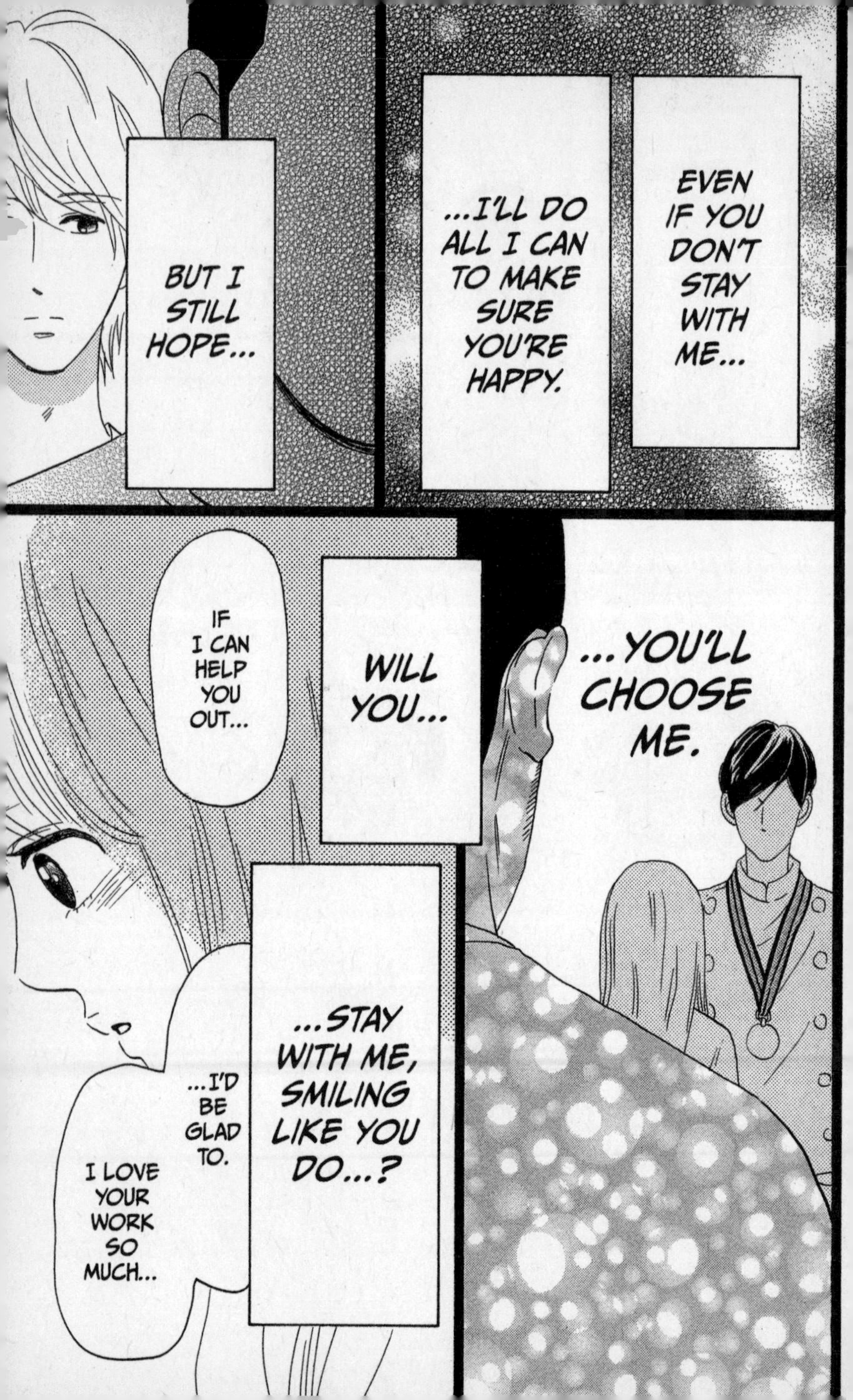
EVEN IF YOU DON'T STAY WITH ME...
...I'LL DO ALL I CAN TO MAKE SURE YOU'RE HAPPY.
BUT I STILL HOPE...
...YOU'LL CHOOSE ME.
WILL YOU...
IF I CAN HELP YOU OUT...
...STAY WITH ME, SMILING LIKE YOU DO...?
...I'D BE GLAD TO.
I LOVE YOUR WORK SO MUCH...

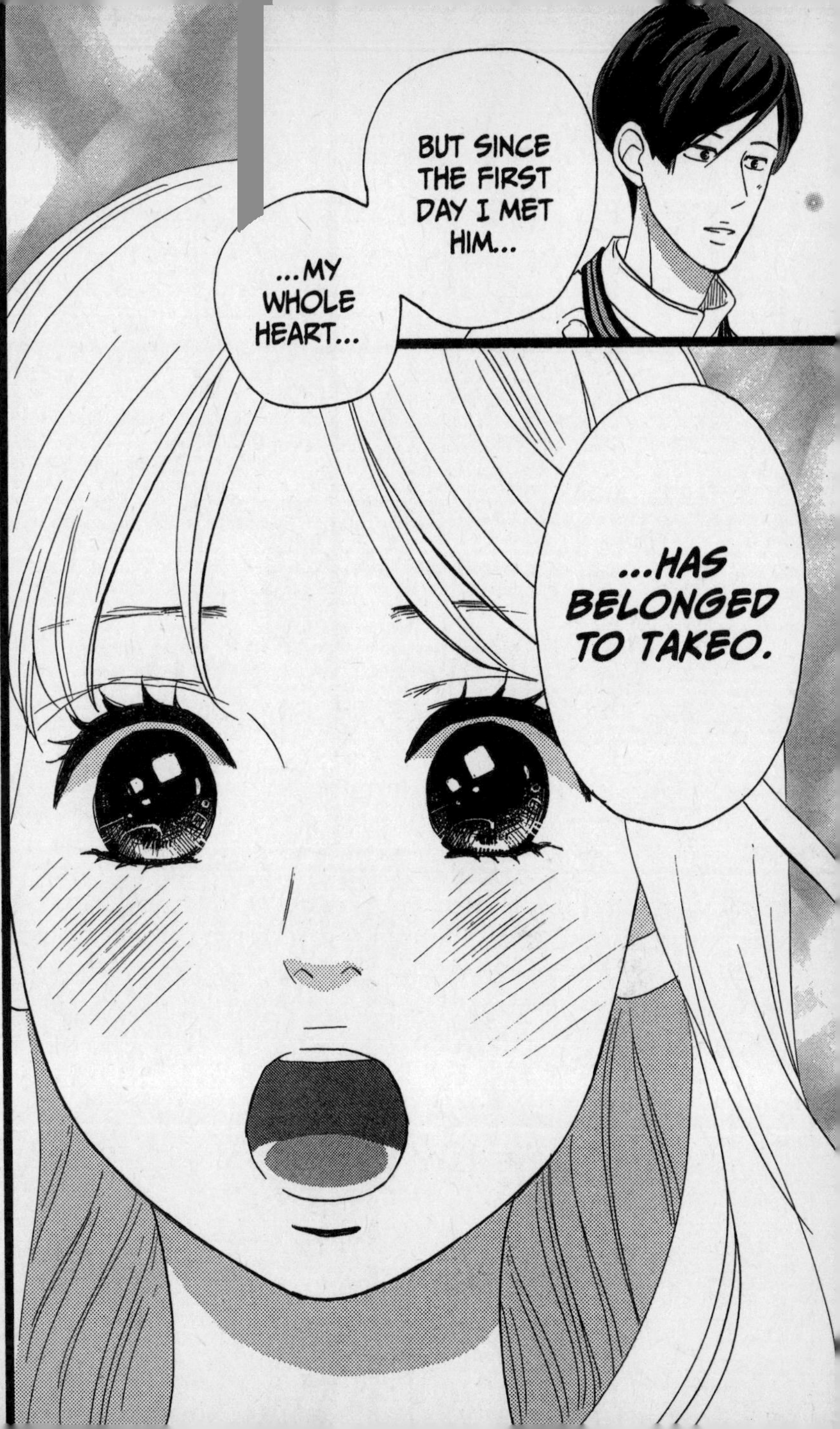
BUT SINCE THE FIRST DAY I MET HIM...
...MY WHOLE HEART...
...HAS BELONGED TO TAKEO.

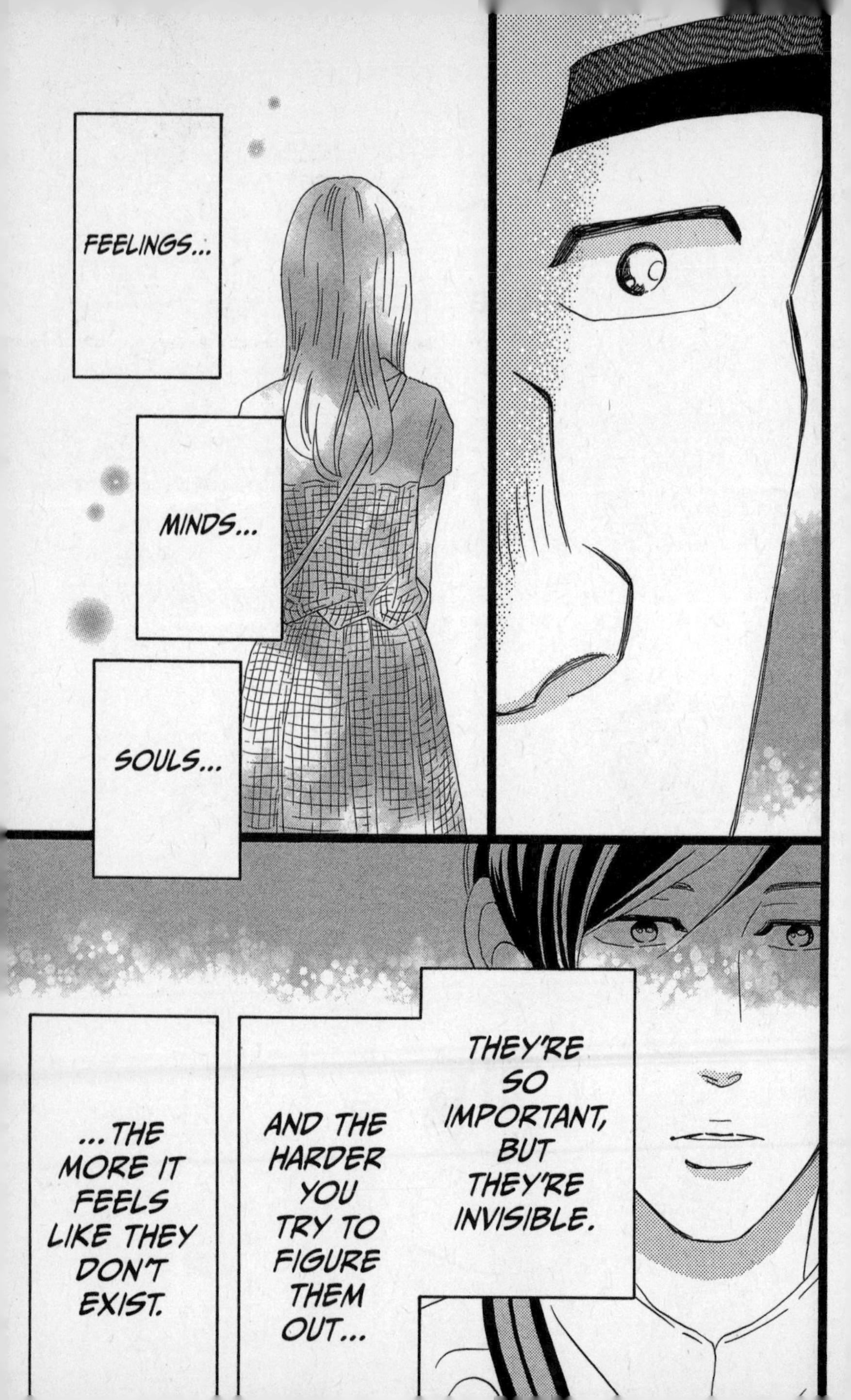
FEELINGS...
MINDS...
SOULS...
THEY'RE SO IMPORTANT, BUT THEY'RE INVISIBLE.
AND THE HARDER YOU TRY TO FIGURE THEM OUT...
...THE MORE IT FEELS LIKE THEY DON'T EXIST.

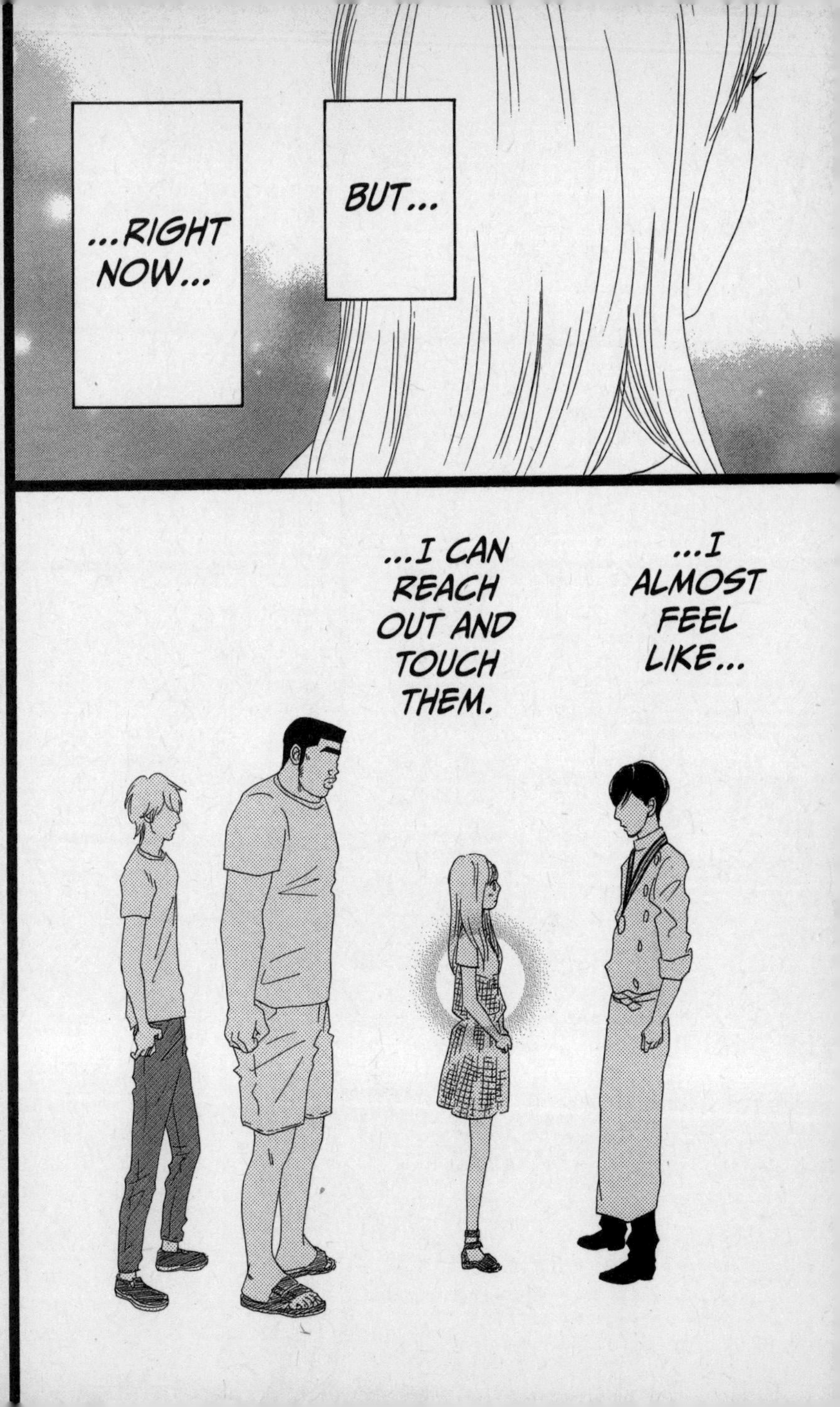
BUT...
...RIGHT NOW...
...I ALMOST FEEL LIKE...
...I CAN REACH OUT AND TOUCH THEM.

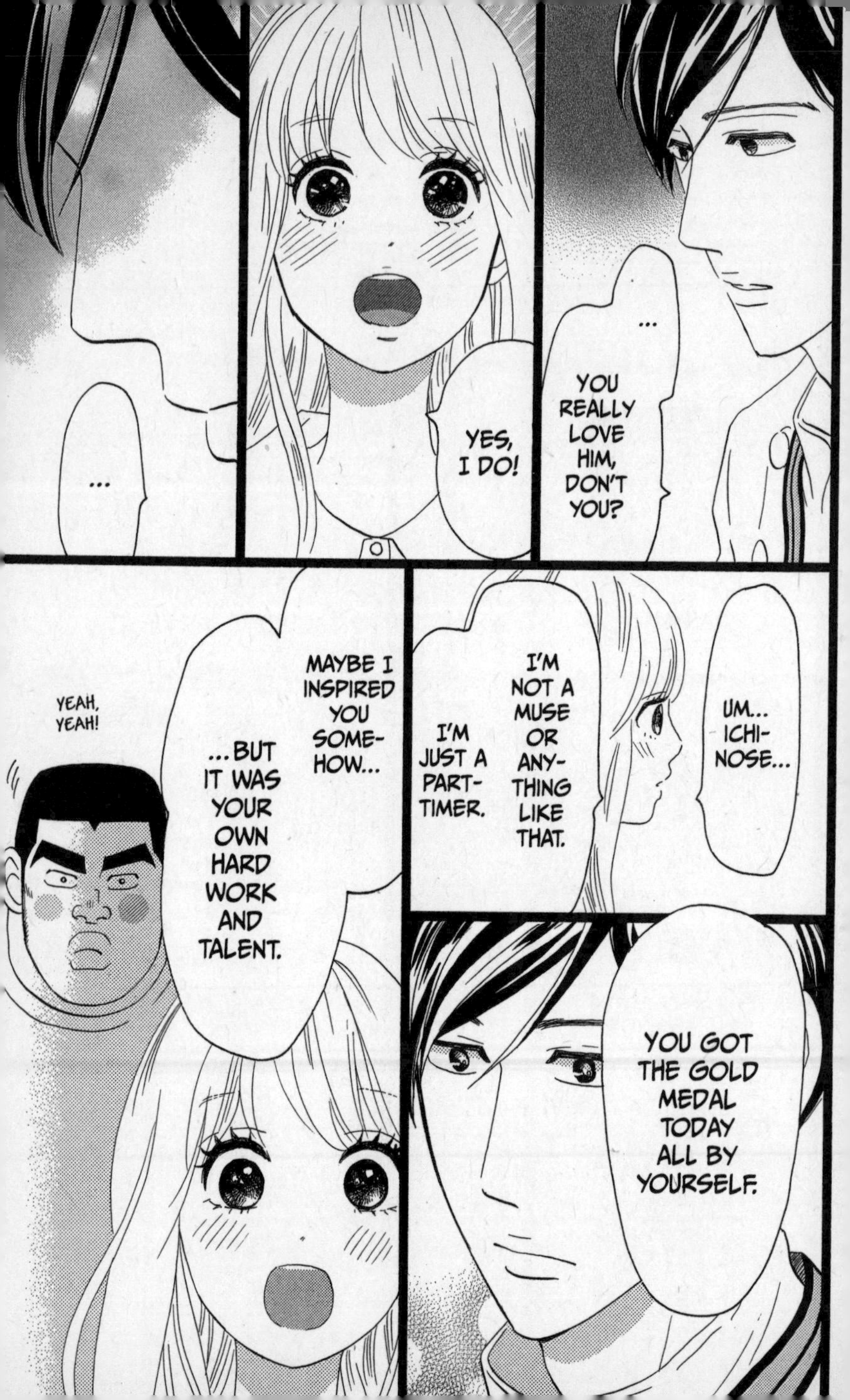
...
YOU REALLY LOVE HIM, DON'T YOU?
YES, I DO!
...
UM... ICHI-NOSE...
I'M NOT A MUSE OR ANY-THING LIKE THAT.
I'M JUST A PART-TIMER.
YOU GOT THE GOLD MEDAL TODAY ALL BY YOURSELF.
MAYBE I INSPIRED YOU SOME-HOW...
...BUT IT WAS YOUR OWN HARD WORK AND TALENT.
YEAH, YEAH!

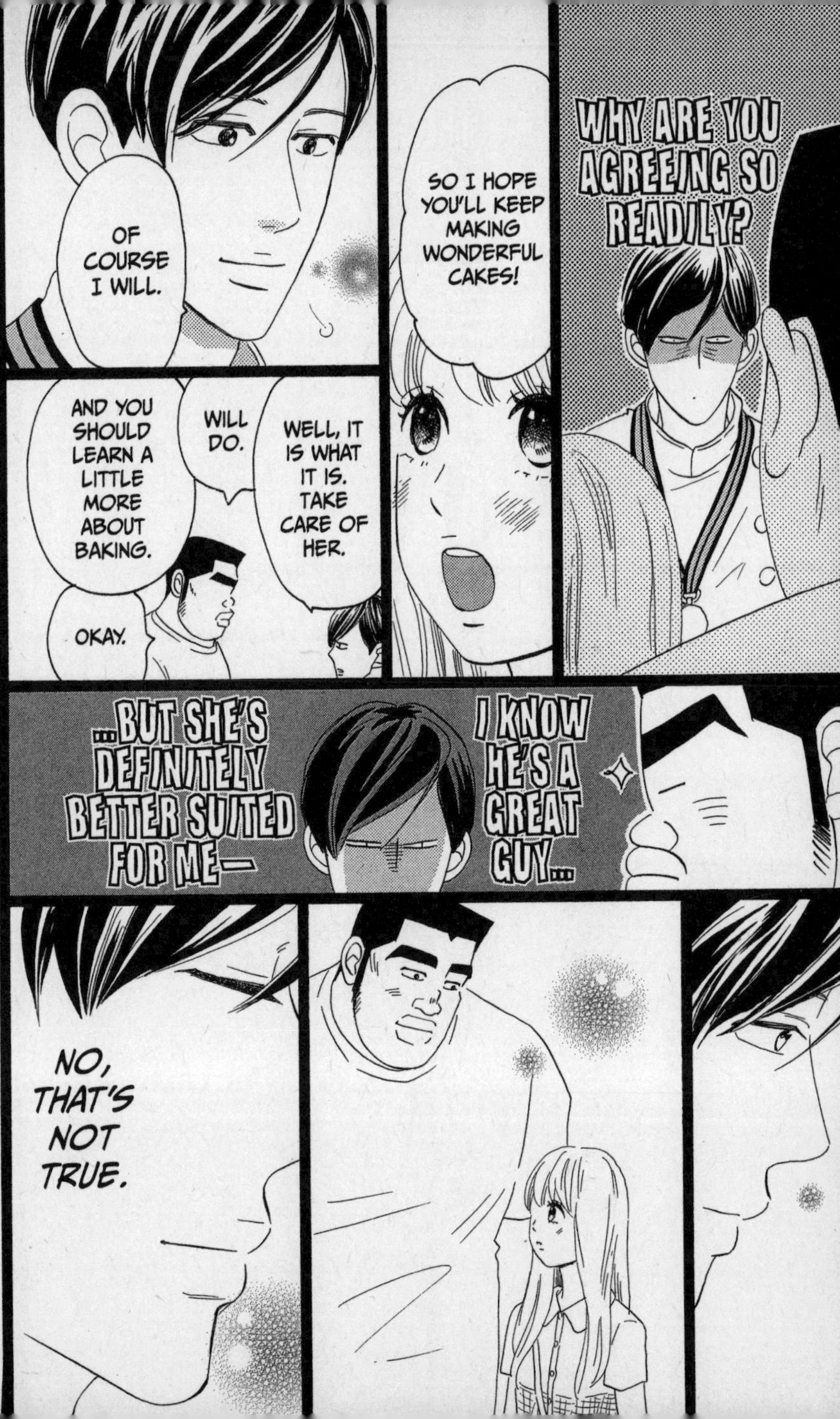
WHY ARE YOU AGREEING SO READILY?
SO I HOPE YOU'LL KEEP MAKING WONDERFUL CAKES!
OF COURSE I WILL.
WELL, IT IS WHAT IT IS. TAKE CARE OF HER.
WILL DO.
AND YOU SHOULD LEARN A LITTLE MORE ABOUT BAKING.
OKAY.
I KNOW HE'S A GREAT GUY...
...BUT SHE'S DEFINITELY BETTER SUITED FOR ME—
NO, THAT'S NOT TRUE.

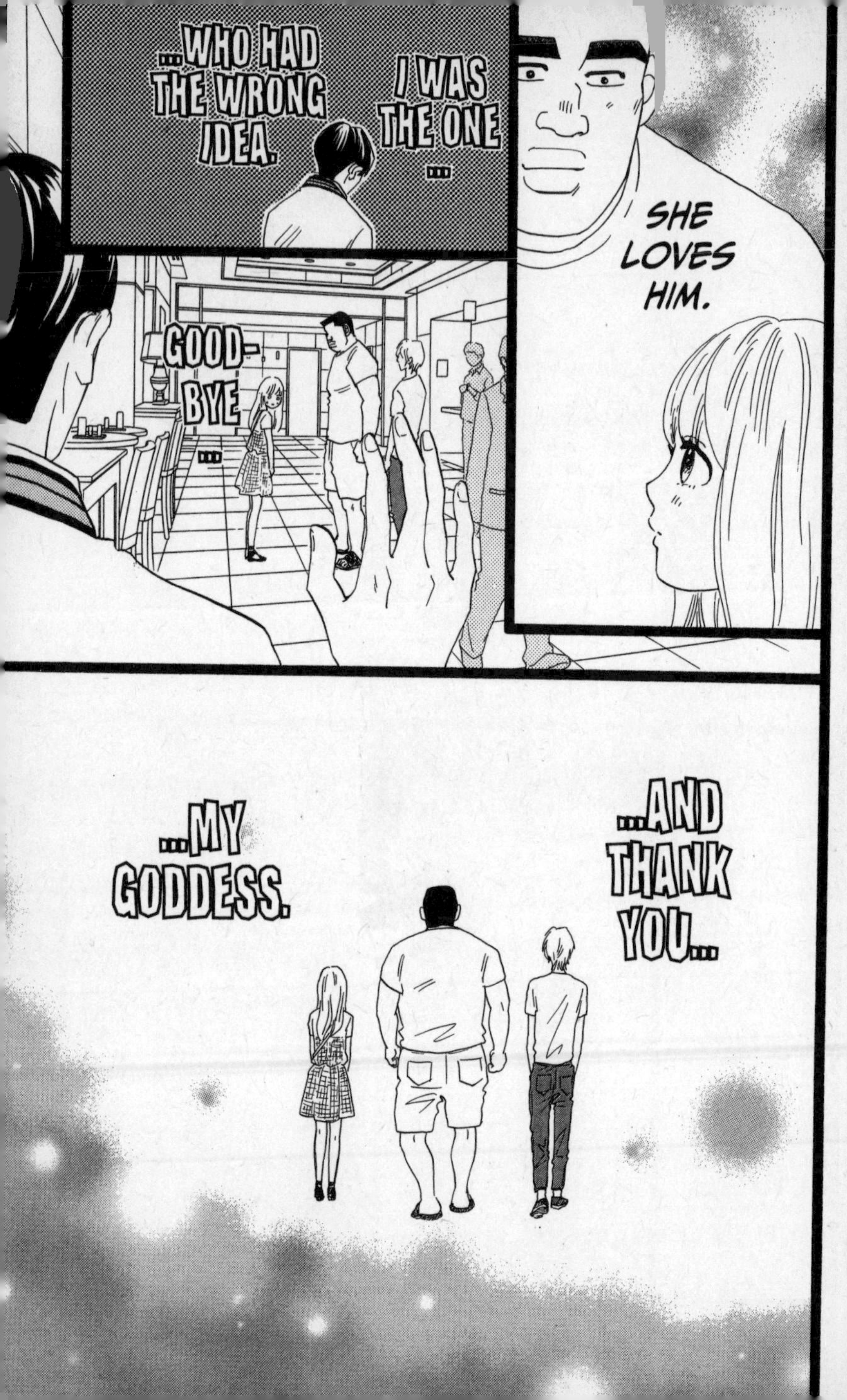
SHE LOVES HIM.
I WAS THE ONE...
...WHO HAD THE WRONG IDEA.
GOOD-BYE...
...AND THANK YOU...
...MY GODDESS.

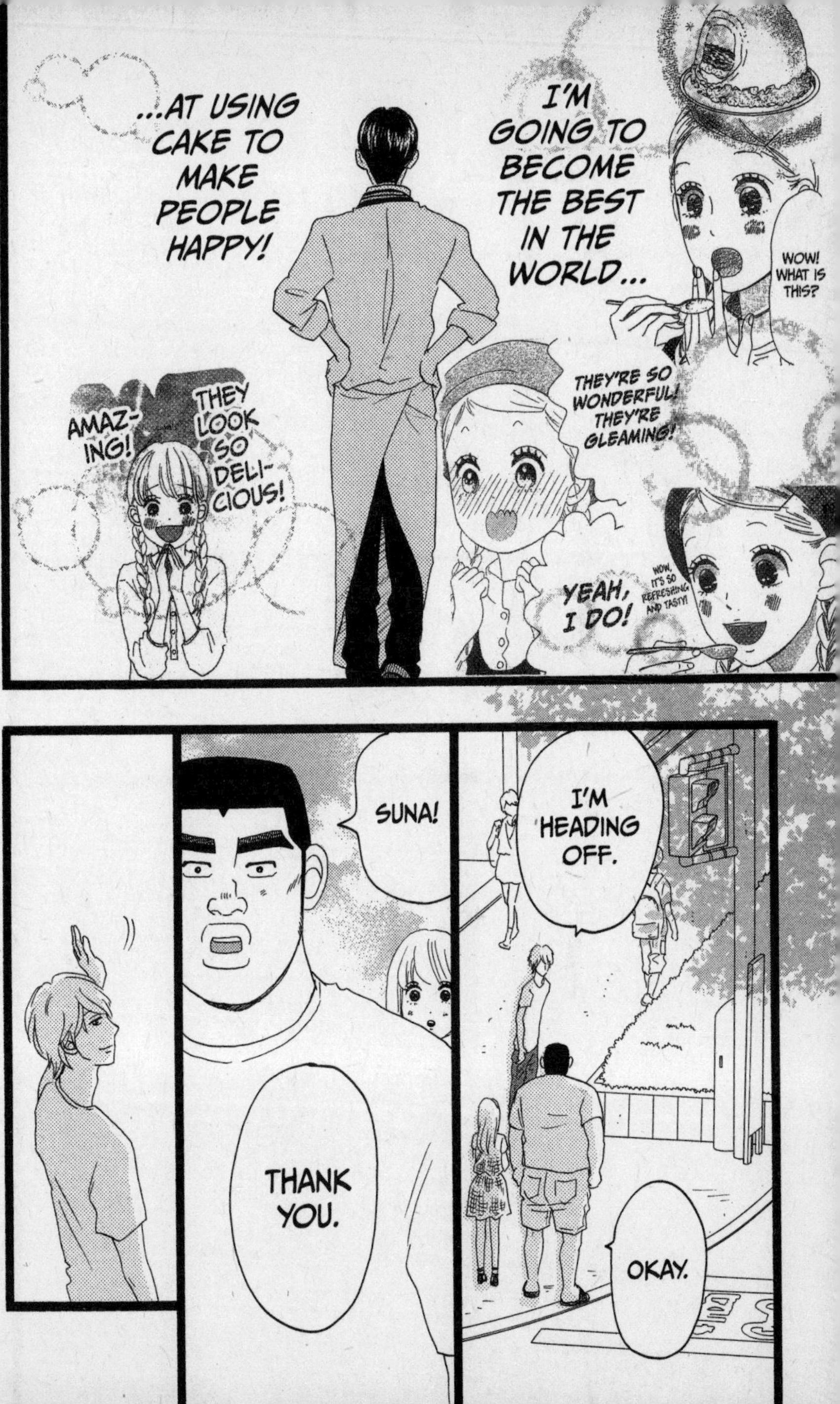
I'M GOING TO BECOME THE BEST IN THE WORLD...
...AT USING CAKE TO MAKE PEOPLE HAPPY!
WOW! WHAT IS THIS?
THEY'RE SO WONDERFUL! THEY'RE GLEAMING!
WOW, IT'S SO REFRESHING AND TASTY!
YEAH, I DO!
THEY LOOK SO DELI-CIOUS!
AMAZ-ING!
I'M HEADING OFF.
OKAY.
SUNA!
THANK YOU.

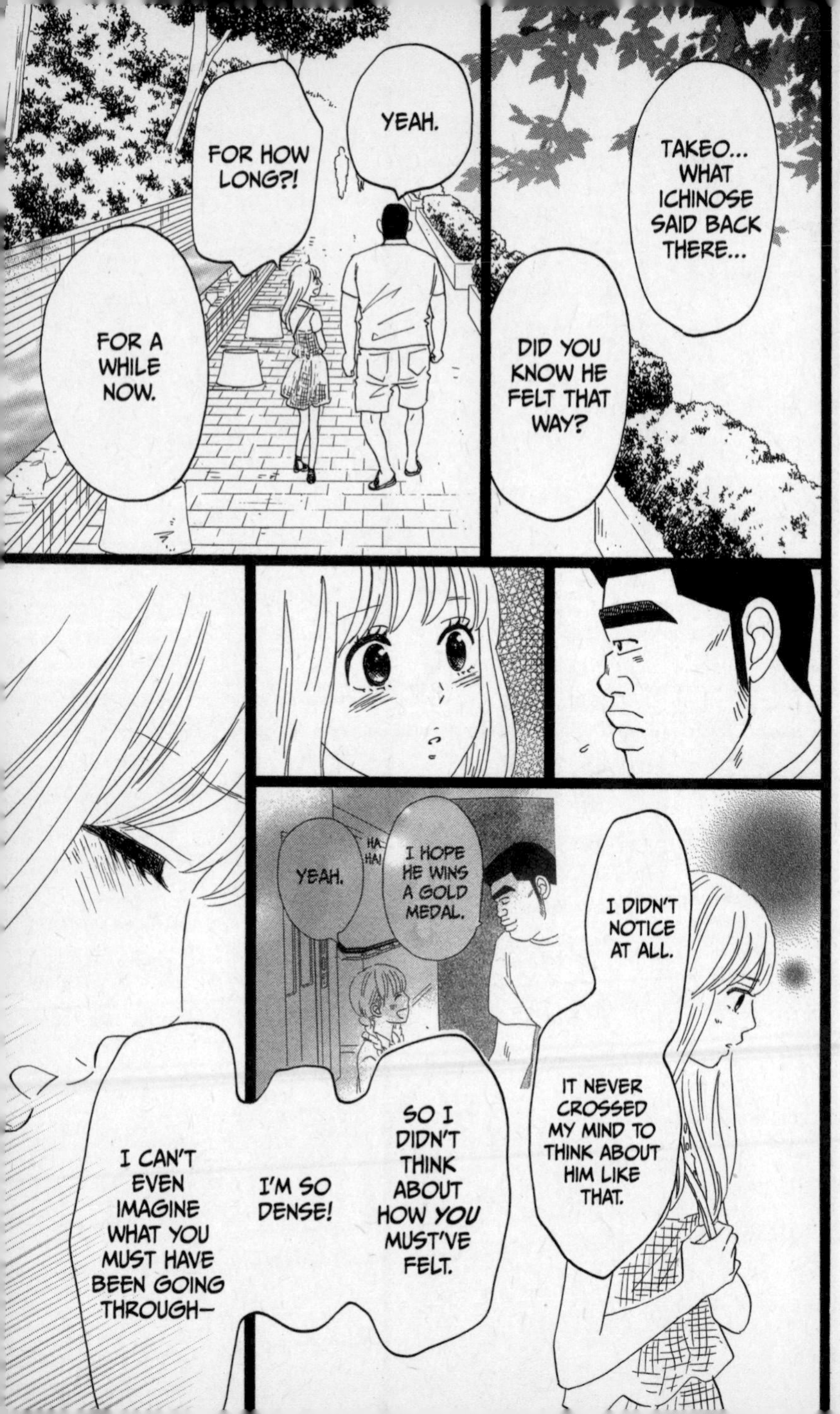
TAKEO... WHAT ICHINOSE SAID BACK THERE...
DID YOU KNOW HE FELT THAT WAY?
YEAH.
FOR HOW LONG?!
FOR A WHILE NOW.
I DIDN'T NOTICE AT ALL.
IT NEVER CROSSED MY MIND TO THINK ABOUT HIM LIKE THAT.
HA HA
I HOPE HE WINS A GOLD MEDAL.
YEAH.
SO I DIDN'T THINK ABOUT HOW *YOU* MUST'VE FELT.
I'M SO DENSE!
I CAN'T EVEN IMAGINE WHAT YOU MUST HAVE BEEN GOING THROUGH—

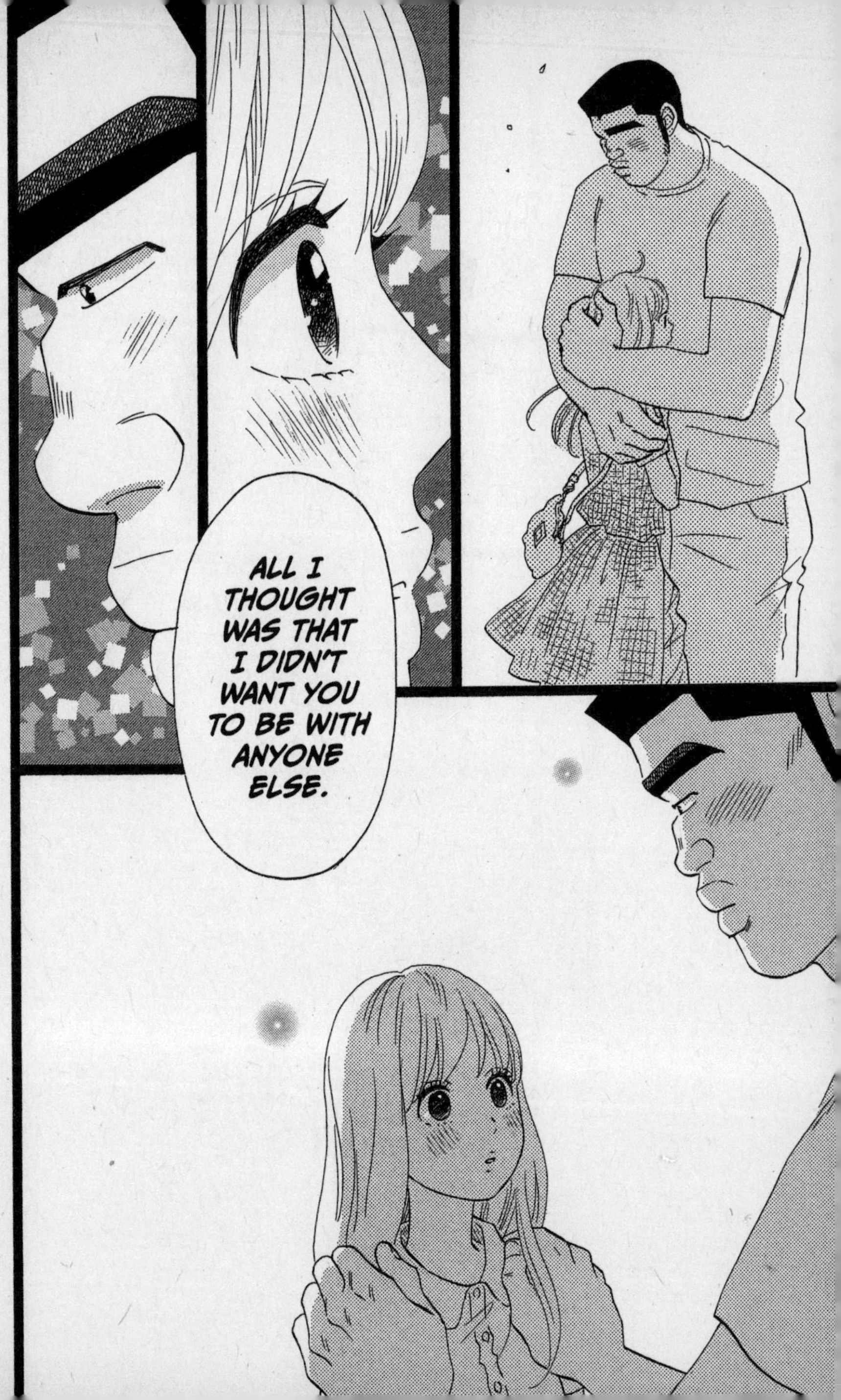
ALL I THOUGHT WAS THAT I DIDN'T WANT YOU TO BE WITH ANYONE ELSE.

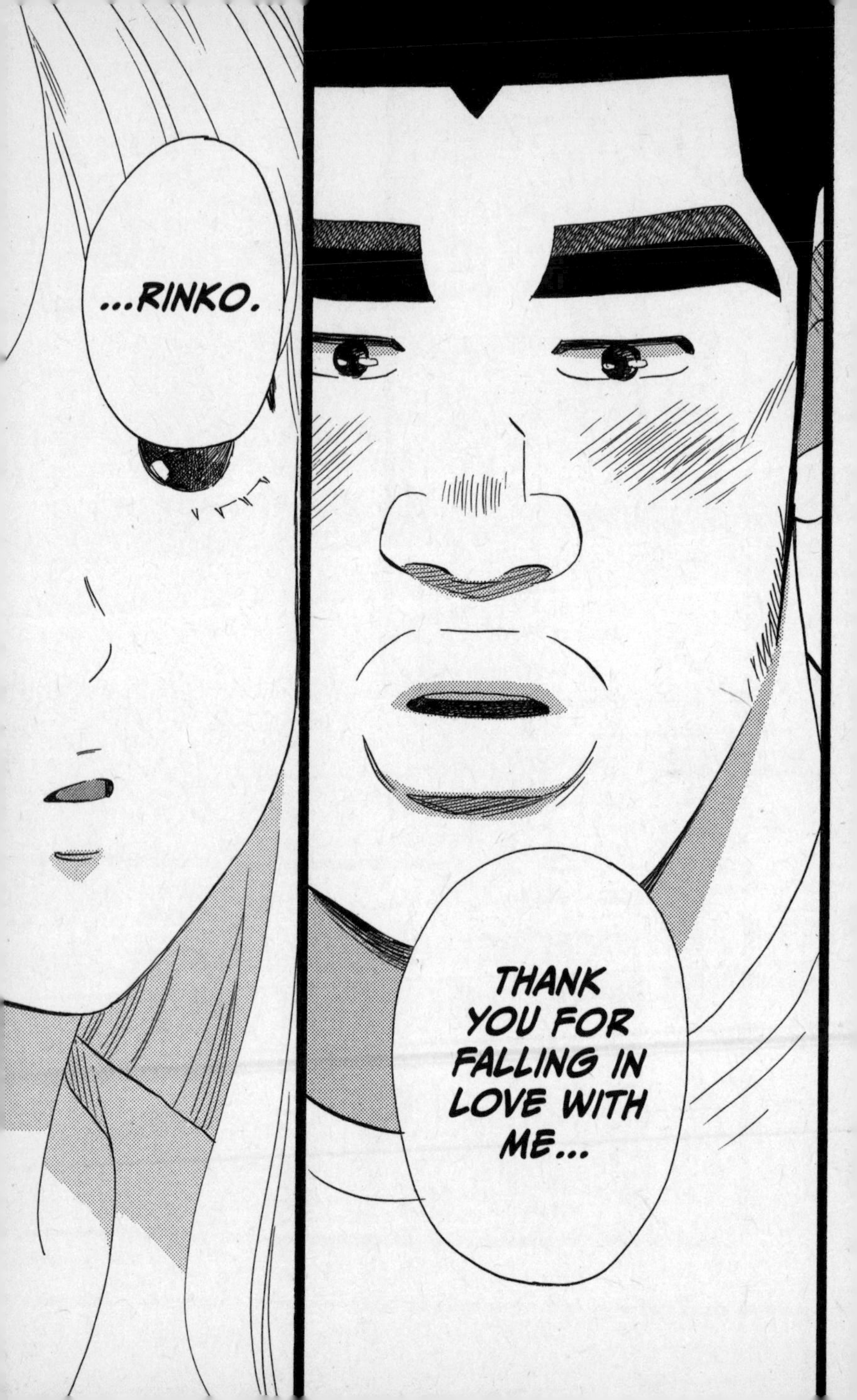
THANK YOU FOR FALLING IN LOVE WITH ME...
...RINKO.

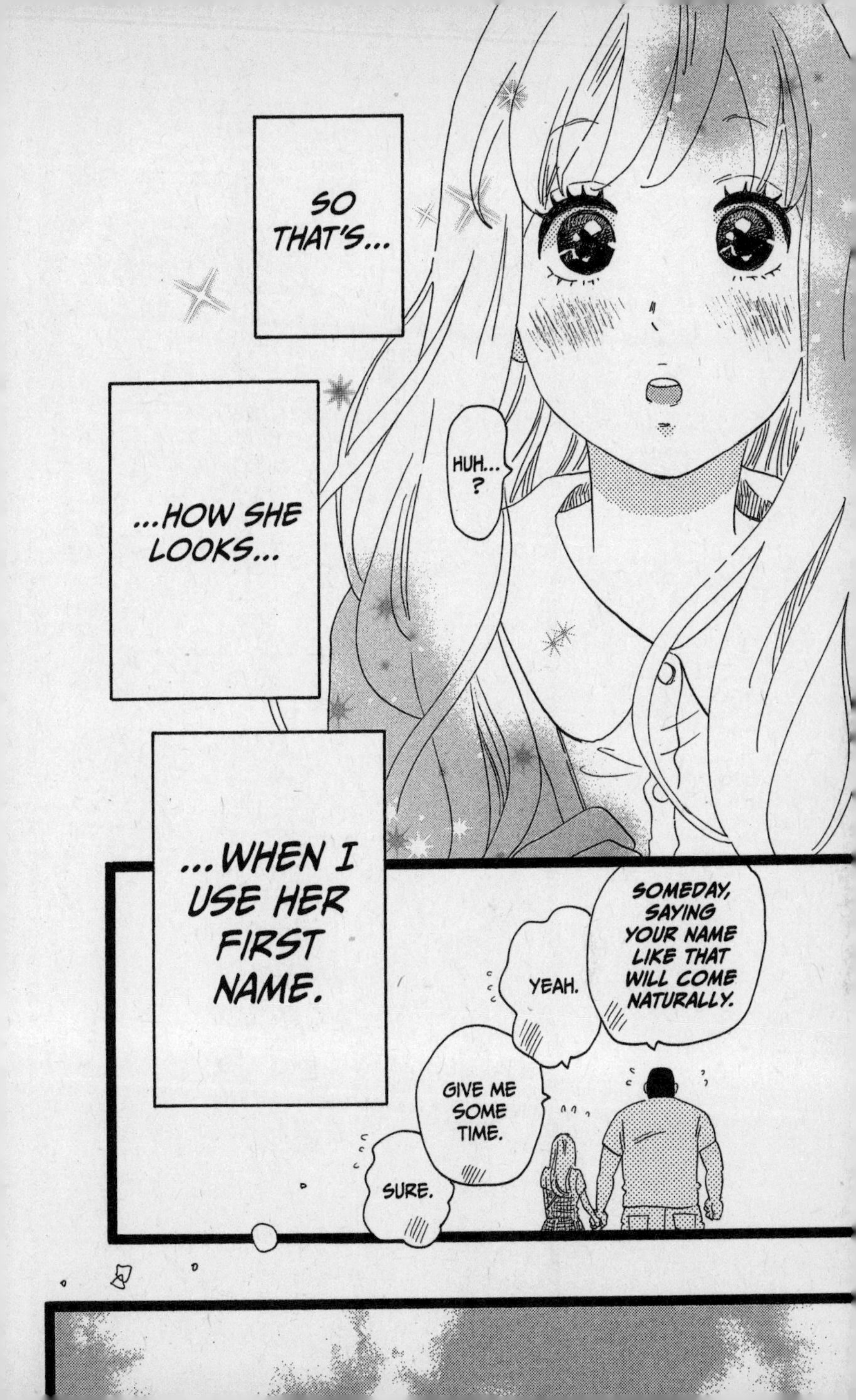
SO THAT'S...
HUH...?
...HOW SHE LOOKS...
...WHEN I USE HER FIRST NAME.
SOMEDAY, SAYING YOUR NAME LIKE THAT WILL COME NATURALLY.
YEAH.
GIVE ME SOME TIME.
SURE.

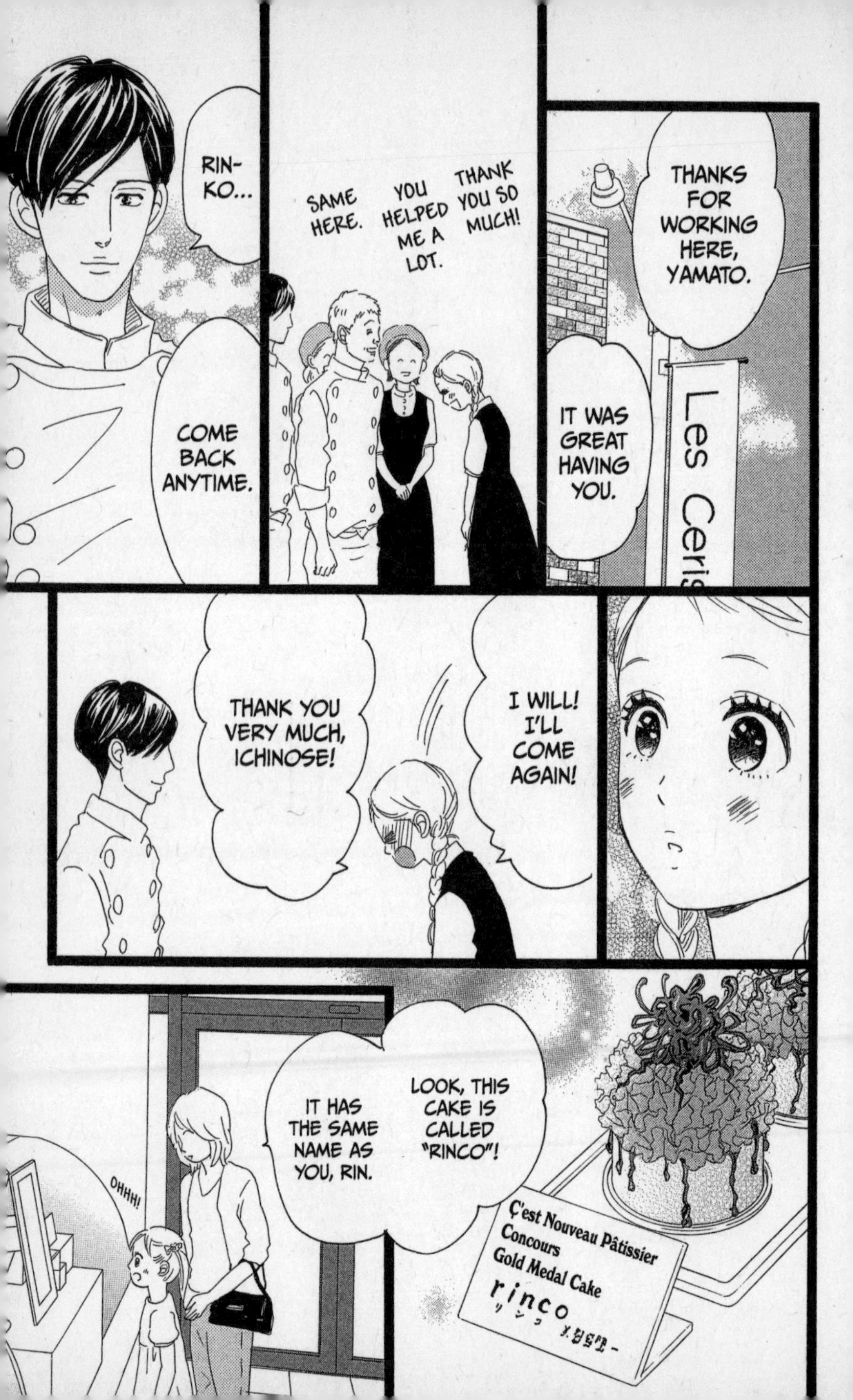
Les Ceris
THANKS FOR WORKING HERE, YAMATO.
IT WAS GREAT HAVING YOU.
THANK YOU SO MUCH!
YOU HELPED ME A LOT.
SAME HERE.
RIN-KO...
COME BACK ANYTIME.
I WILL! I'LL COME AGAIN!
THANK YOU VERY MUCH, ICHINOSE!
Ç'est Nouveau Pâtissier Concours
Gold Medal Cake
rinço
LOOK, THIS CAKE IS CALLED "RINCO"!
IT HAS THE SAME NAME AS YOU, RIN.
OHHH!

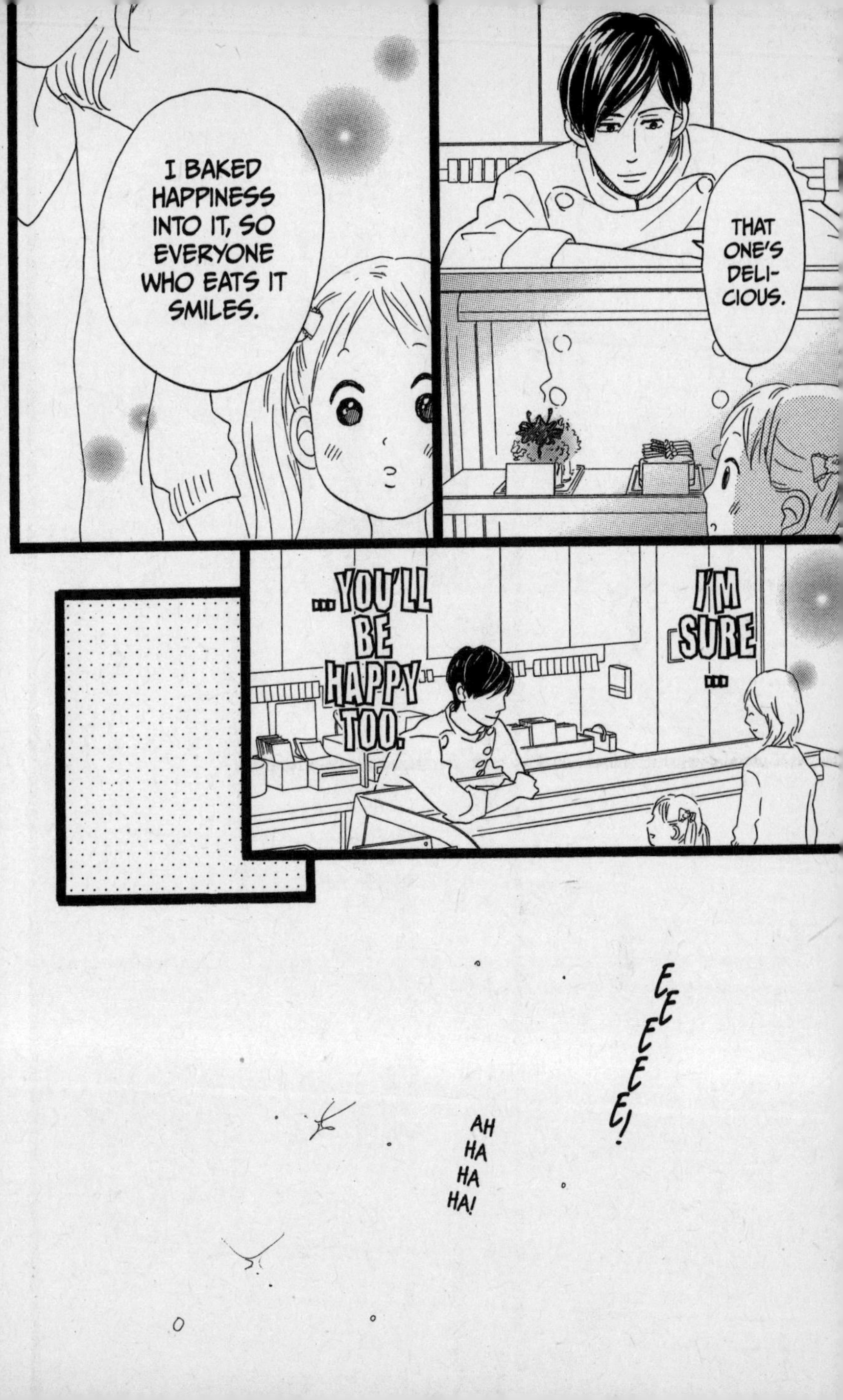
THAT ONE'S DELICIOUS.
I BAKED HAPPINESS INTO IT, SO EVERYONE WHO EATS IT SMILES.
I'M SURE...
...YOU'LL BE HAPPY TOO.
EEEEEE!
AH HA HA HA!

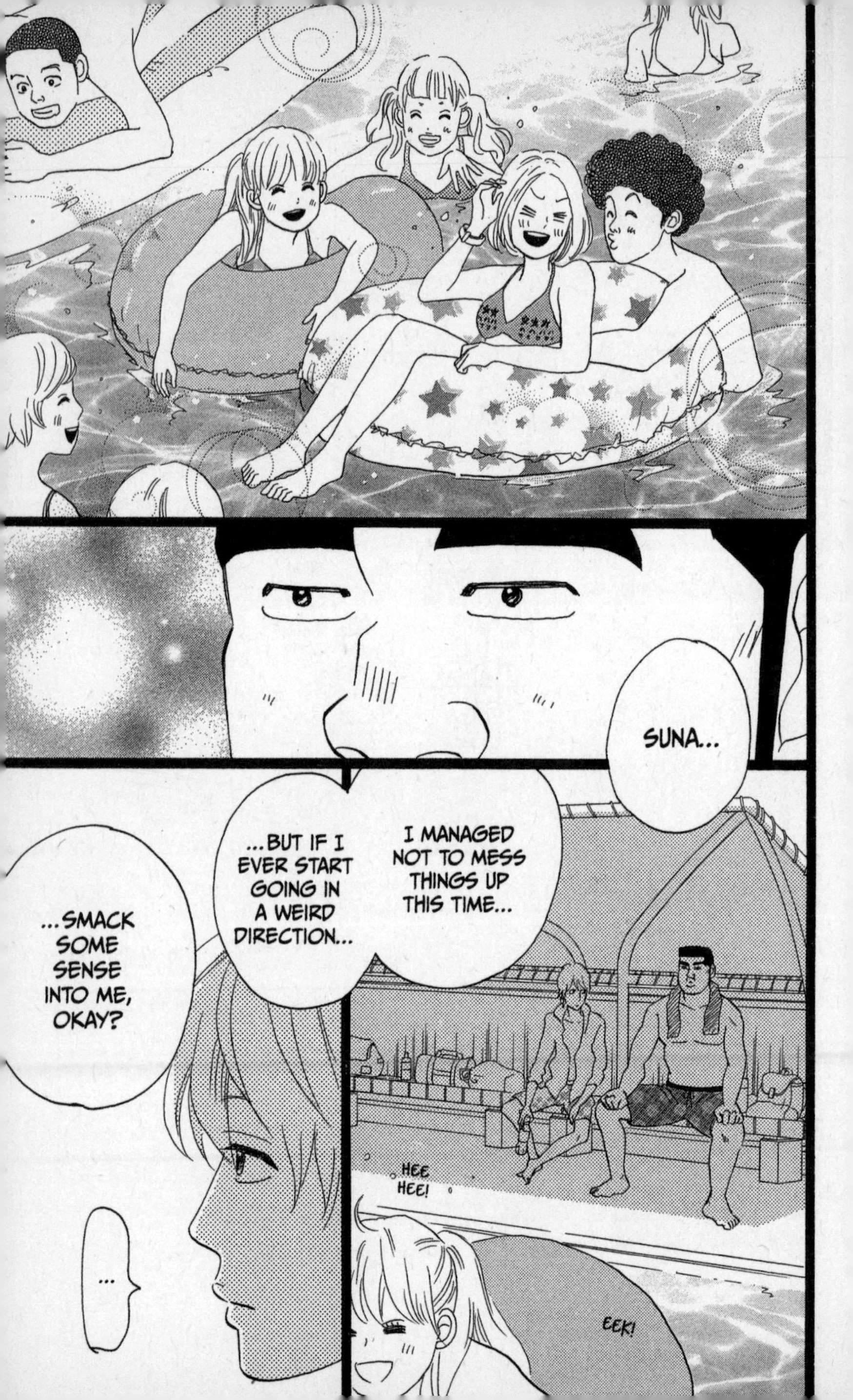
SUNA...
I MANAGED NOT TO MESS THINGS UP THIS TIME...
...BUT IF I EVER START GOING IN A WEIRD DIRECTION...
HEE HEE!
EEK!
...SMACK SOME SENSE INTO ME, OKAY?
...

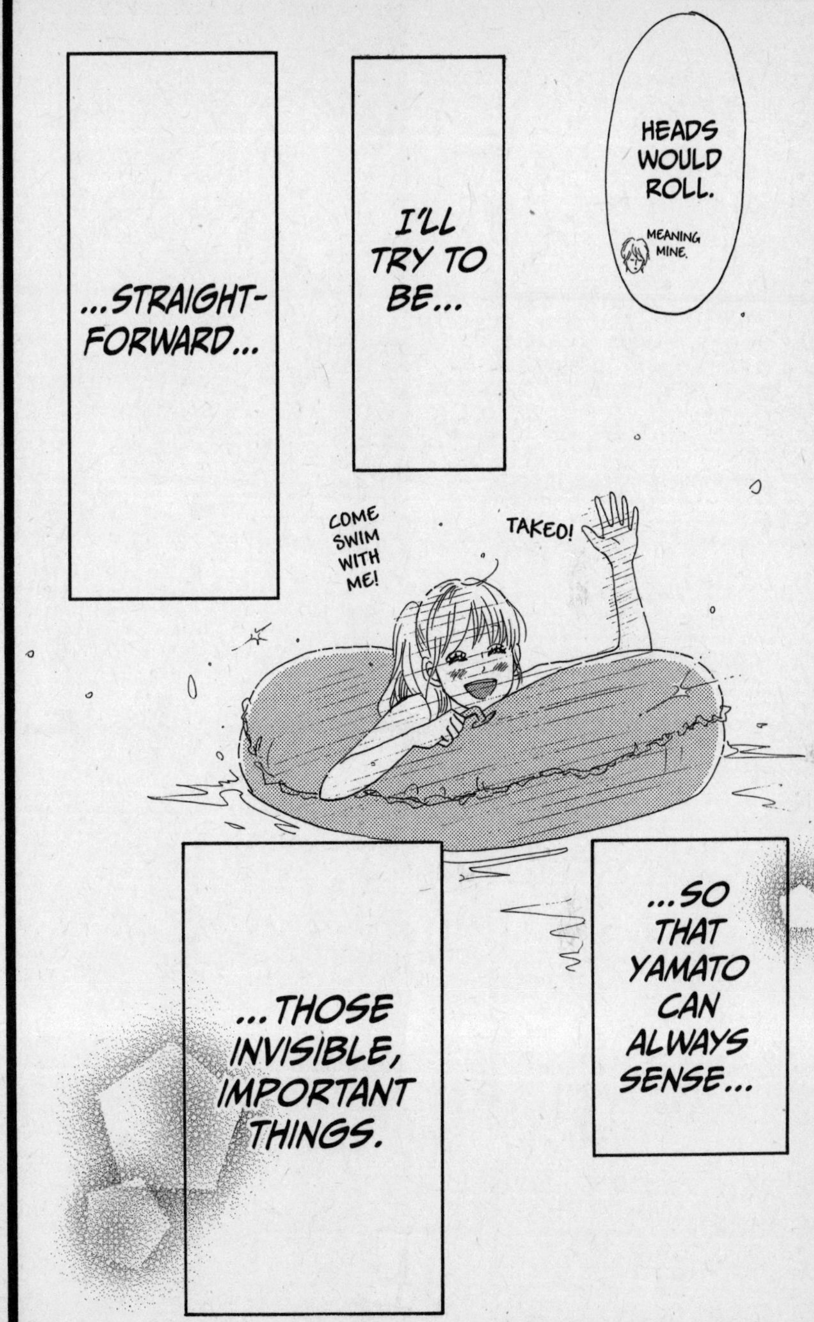
HEADS WOULD ROLL.
MEANING MINE.
I'LL TRY TO BE...
...STRAIGHT-FORWARD...
TAKEO!
COME SWIM WITH ME!
...SO THAT YAMATO CAN ALWAYS SENSE...
...THOSE INVISIBLE, IMPORTANT THINGS.

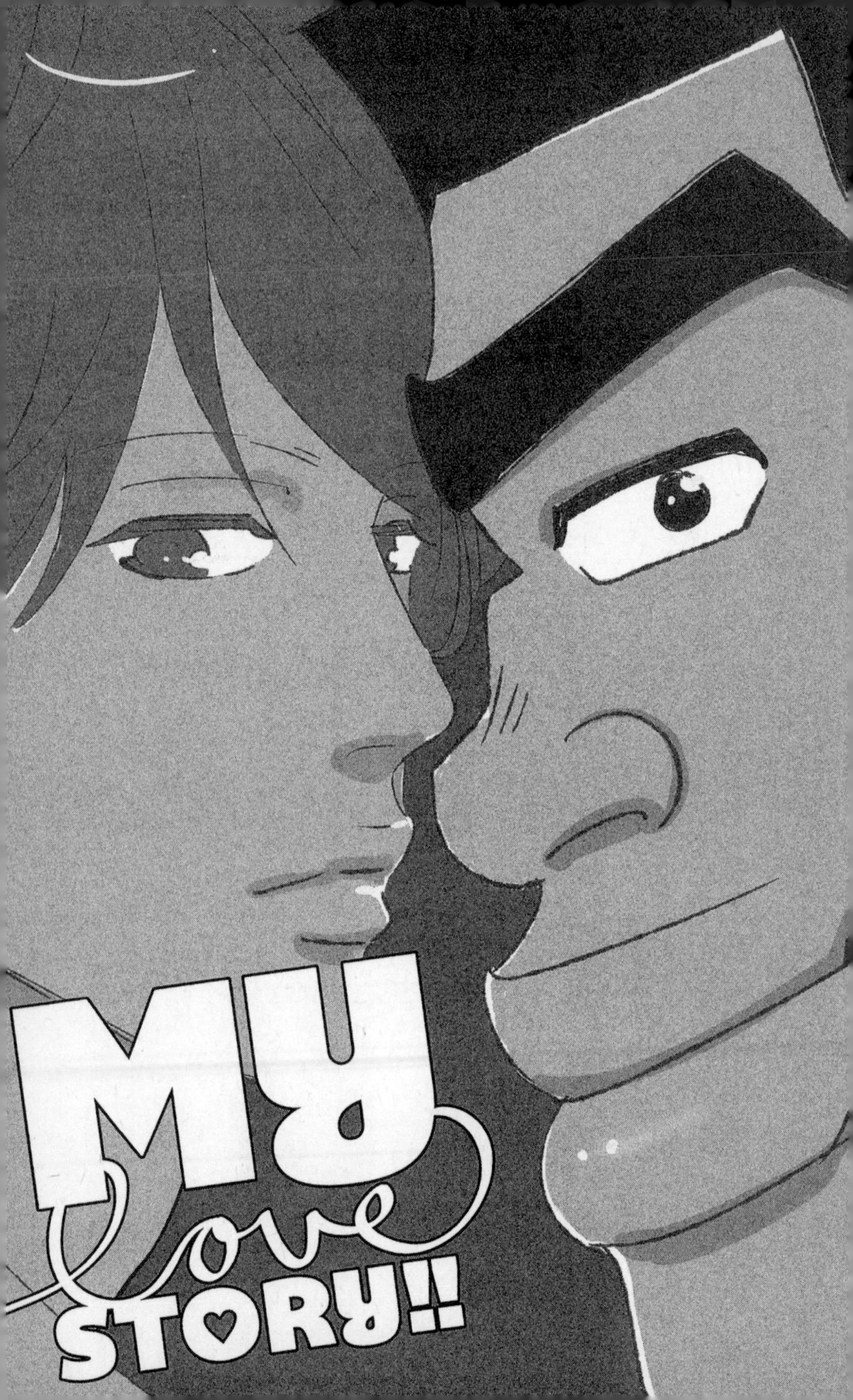
MY Love STORY!!

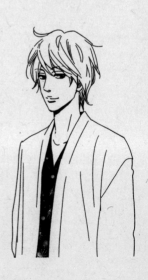

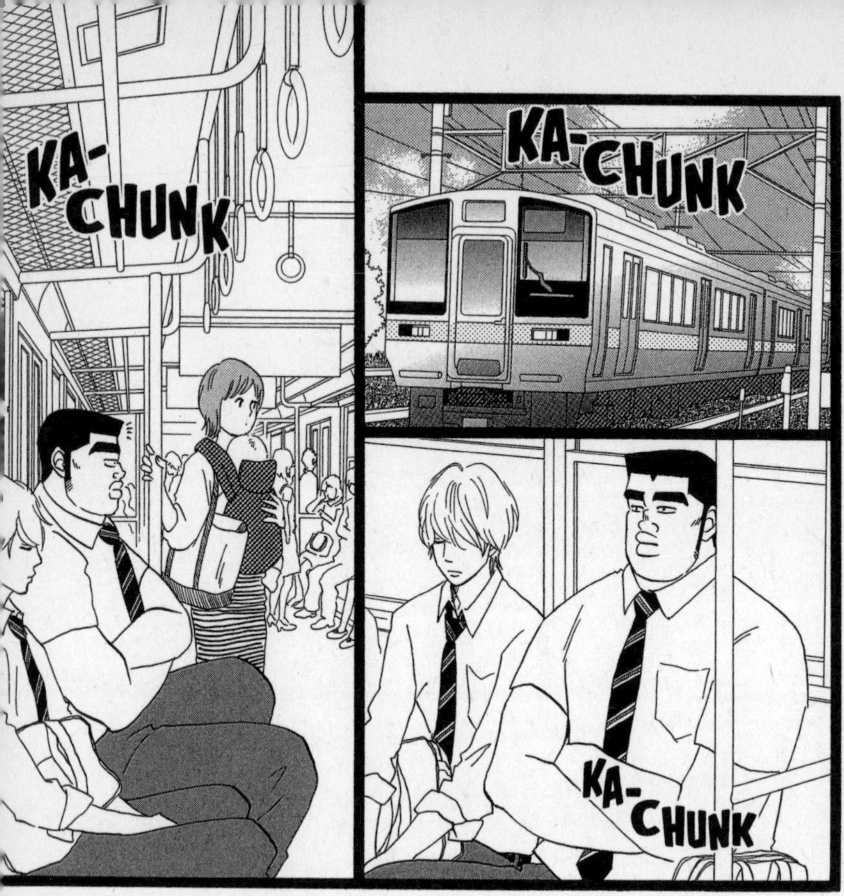
KA-CHUNK
KA-CHUNK
KA-CHUNK

MY love STORY!!

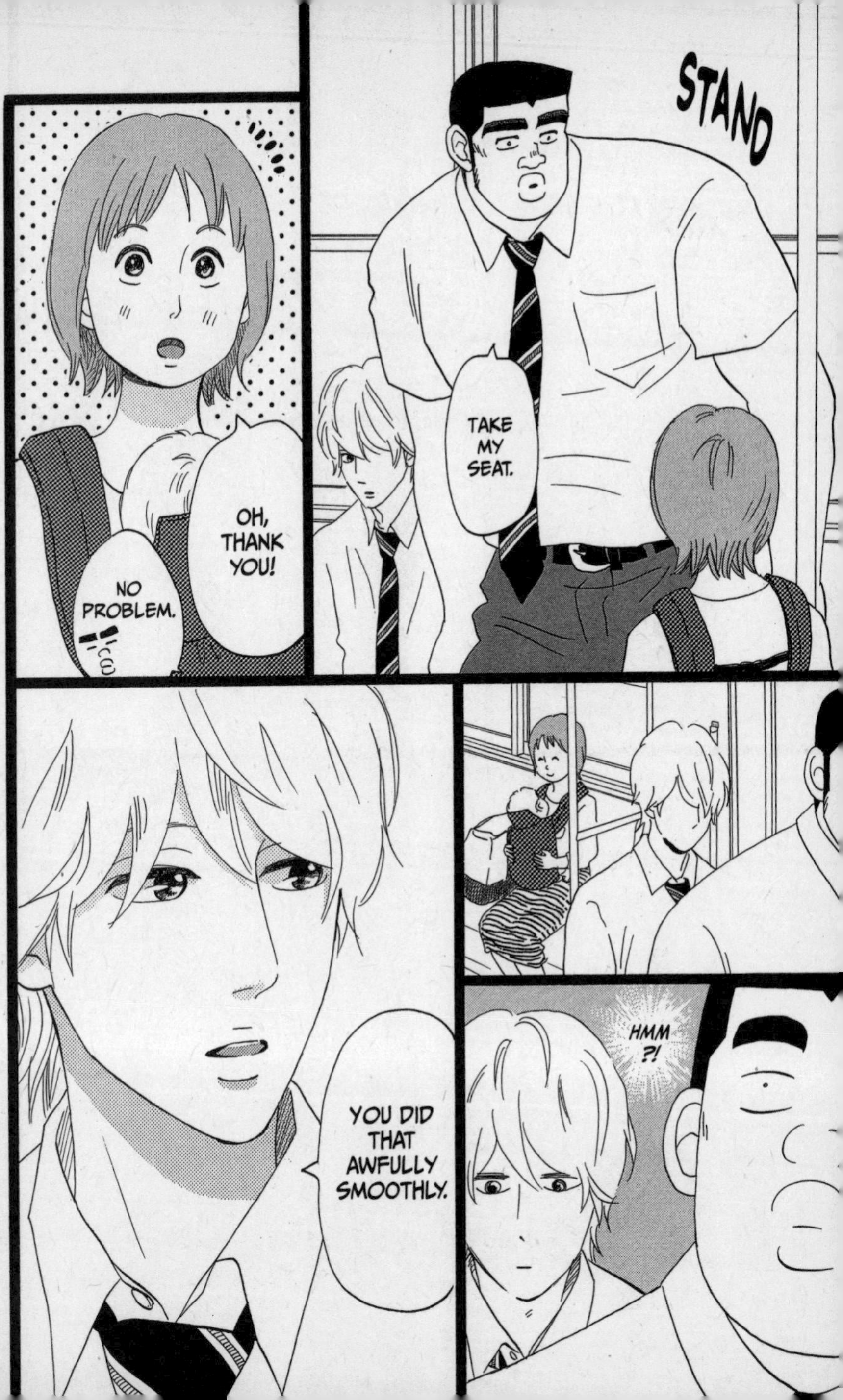
STAND
TAKE MY SEAT.
OH, THANK YOU!
NO PROBLEM.
HMM?!
YOU DID THAT AWFULLY SMOOTHLY.

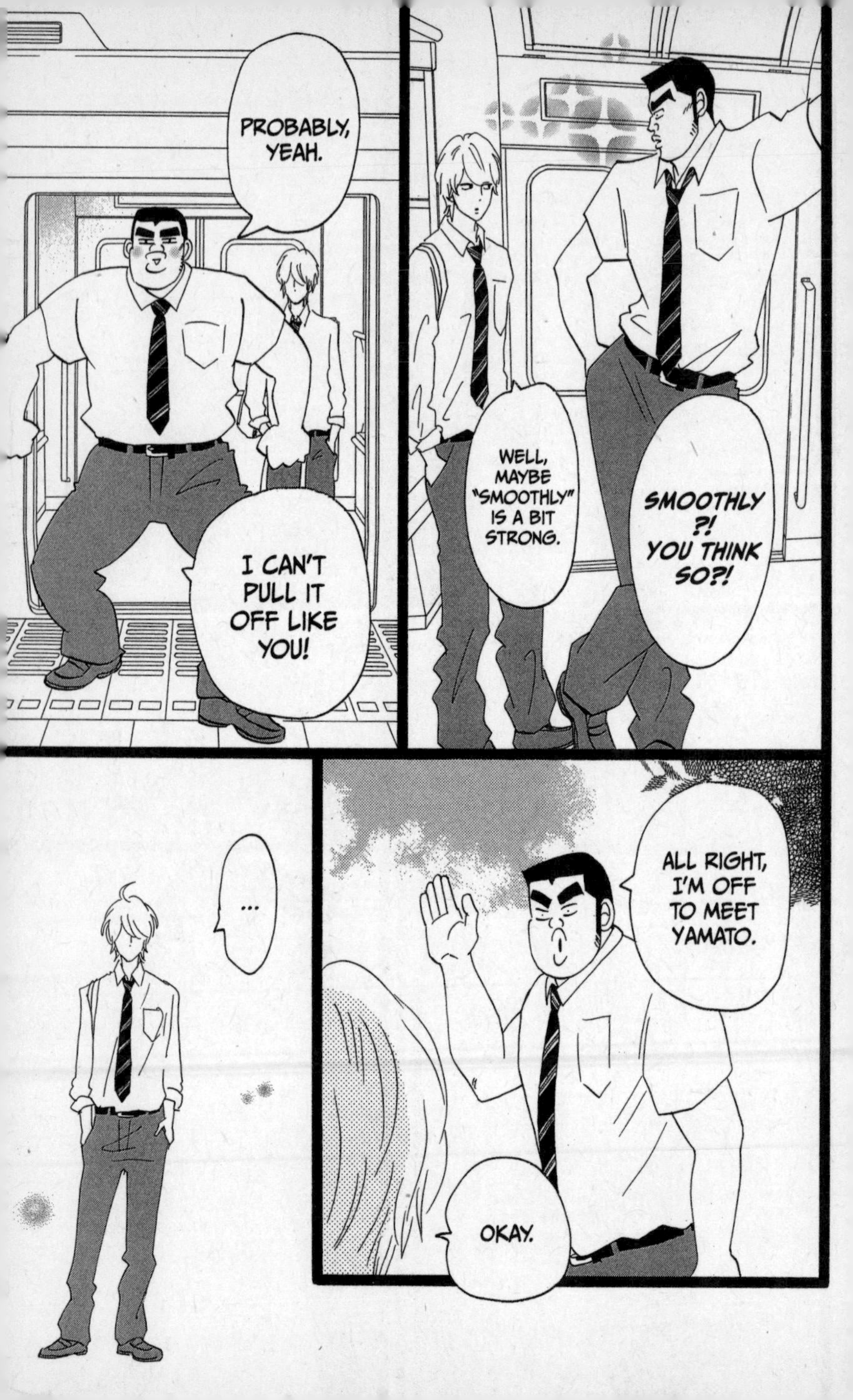
SMOOTHLY?! YOU THINK SO?!
WELL, MAYBE "SMOOTHLY" IS A BIT STRONG.
I CAN'T PULL IT OFF LIKE YOU!
PROBABLY, YEAH.
ALL RIGHT, I'M OFF TO MEET YAMATO.
OKAY.
...

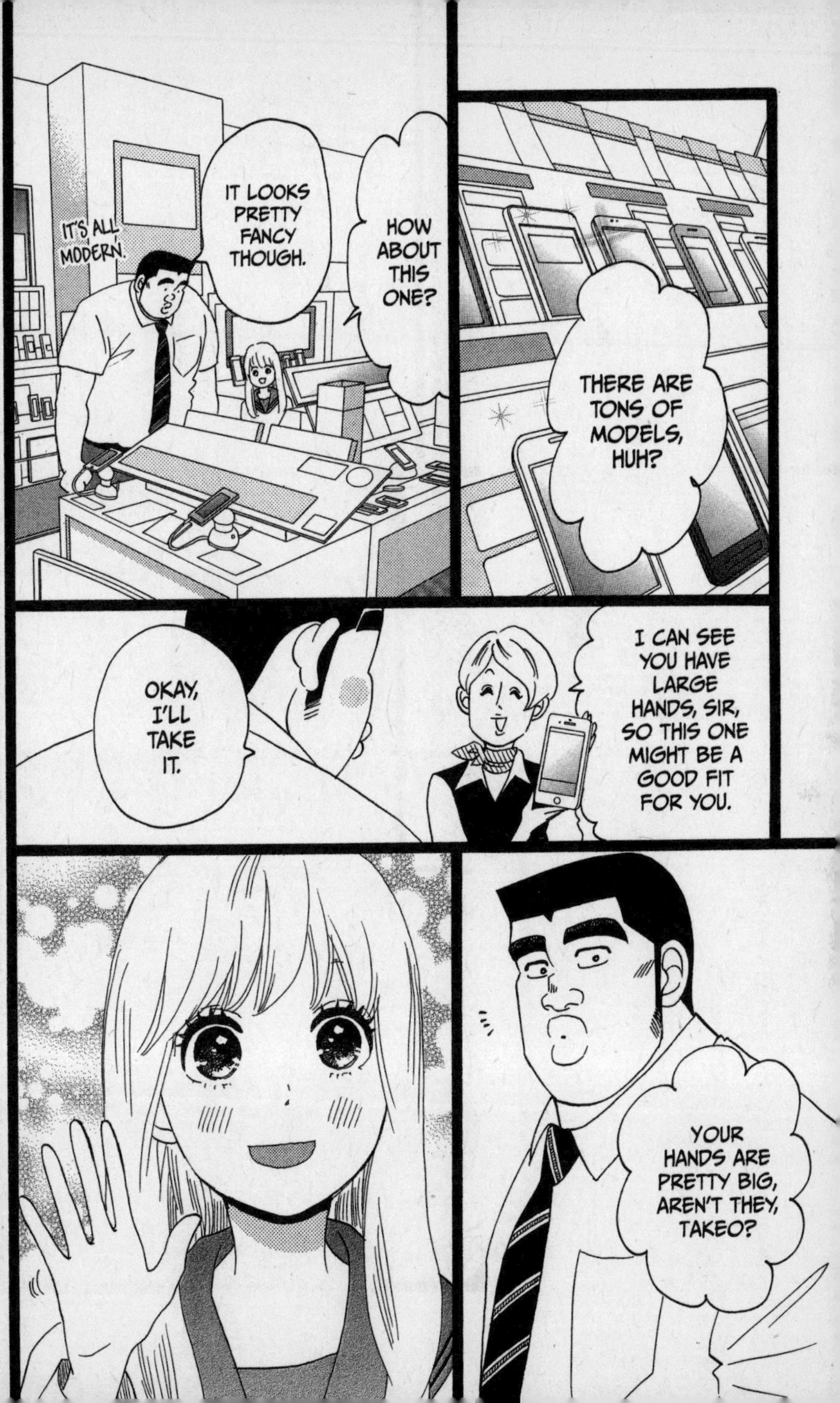
THERE ARE TONS OF MODELS, HUH?
HOW ABOUT THIS ONE?
IT LOOKS PRETTY FANCY THOUGH.
IT'S ALL MODERN.
I CAN SEE YOU HAVE LARGE HANDS, SIR, SO THIS ONE MIGHT BE A GOOD FIT FOR YOU.
OKAY, I'LL TAKE IT.
YOUR HANDS ARE PRETTY BIG, AREN'T THEY, TAKEO?

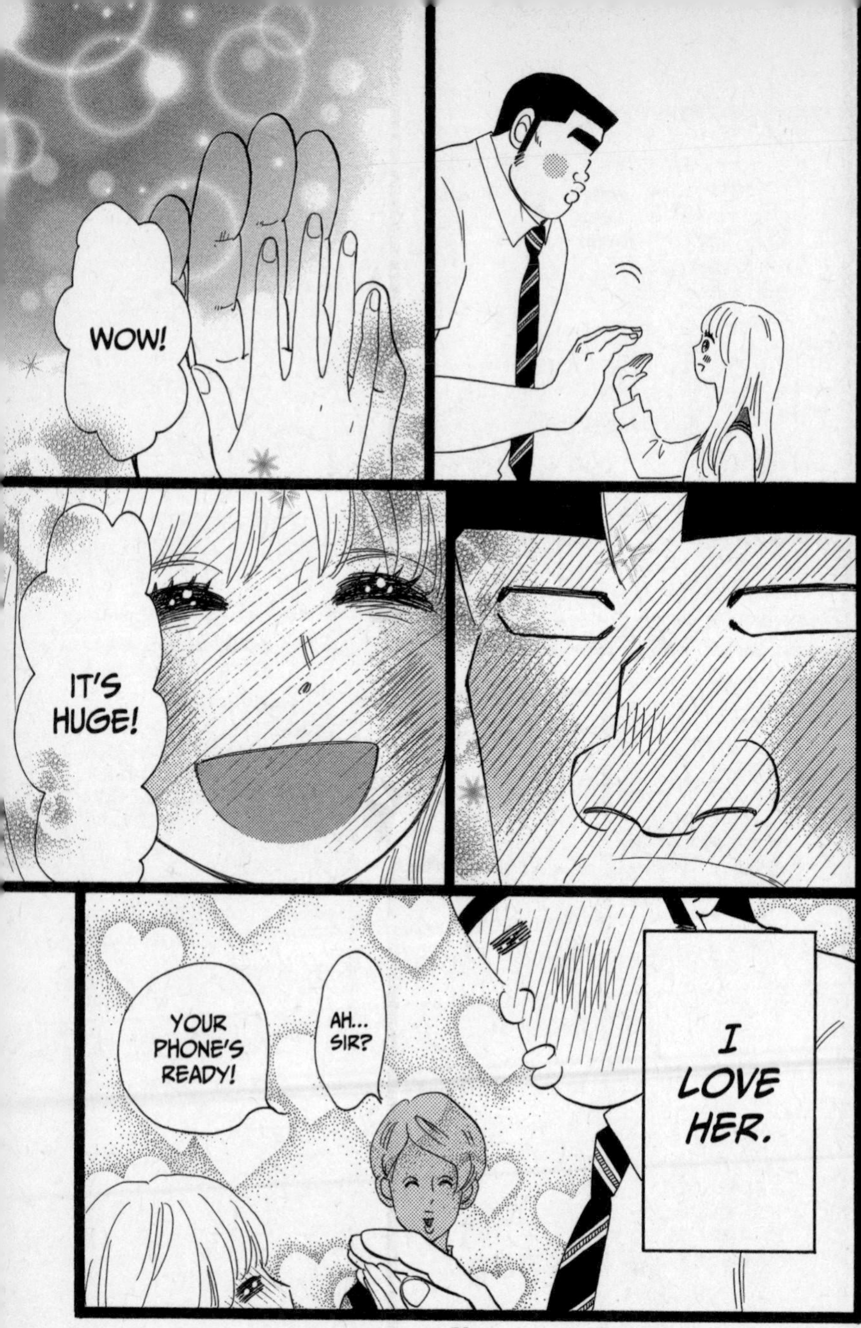
WOW!
IT'S HUGE!
I LOVE HER.
AH... SIR?
YOUR PHONE'S READY!

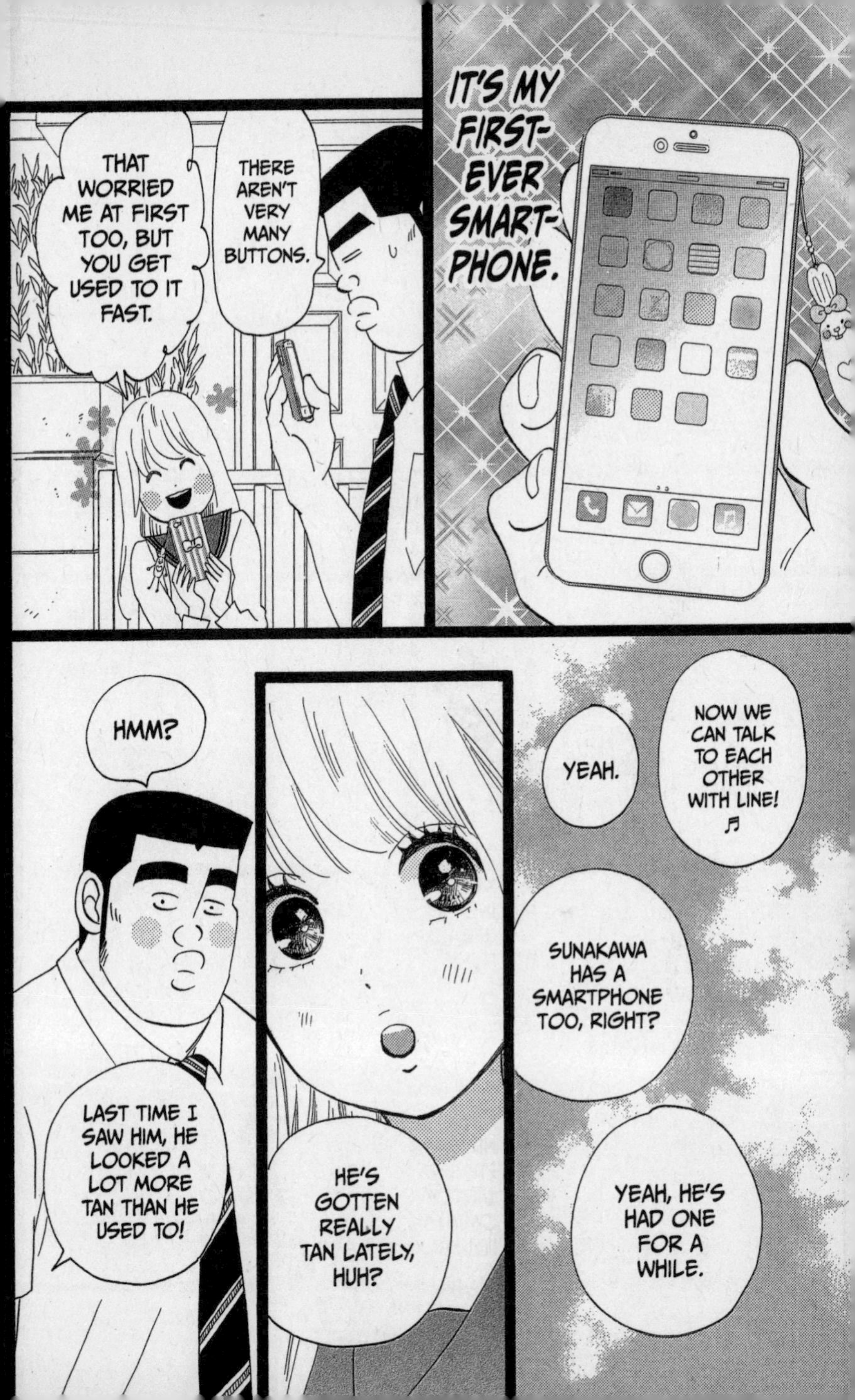
IT'S MY FIRST-EVER SMARTPHONE.
THERE AREN'T VERY MANY BUTTONS.
THAT WORRIED ME AT FIRST TOO, BUT YOU GET USED TO IT FAST.
NOW WE CAN TALK TO EACH OTHER WITH LINE! ♬
YEAH.
SUNAKAWA HAS A SMARTPHONE TOO, RIGHT?
YEAH, HE'S HAD ONE FOR A WHILE.
HE'S GOTTEN REALLY TAN LATELY, HUH?
HMM?
LAST TIME I SAW HIM, HE LOOKED A LOT MORE TAN THAN HE USED TO!

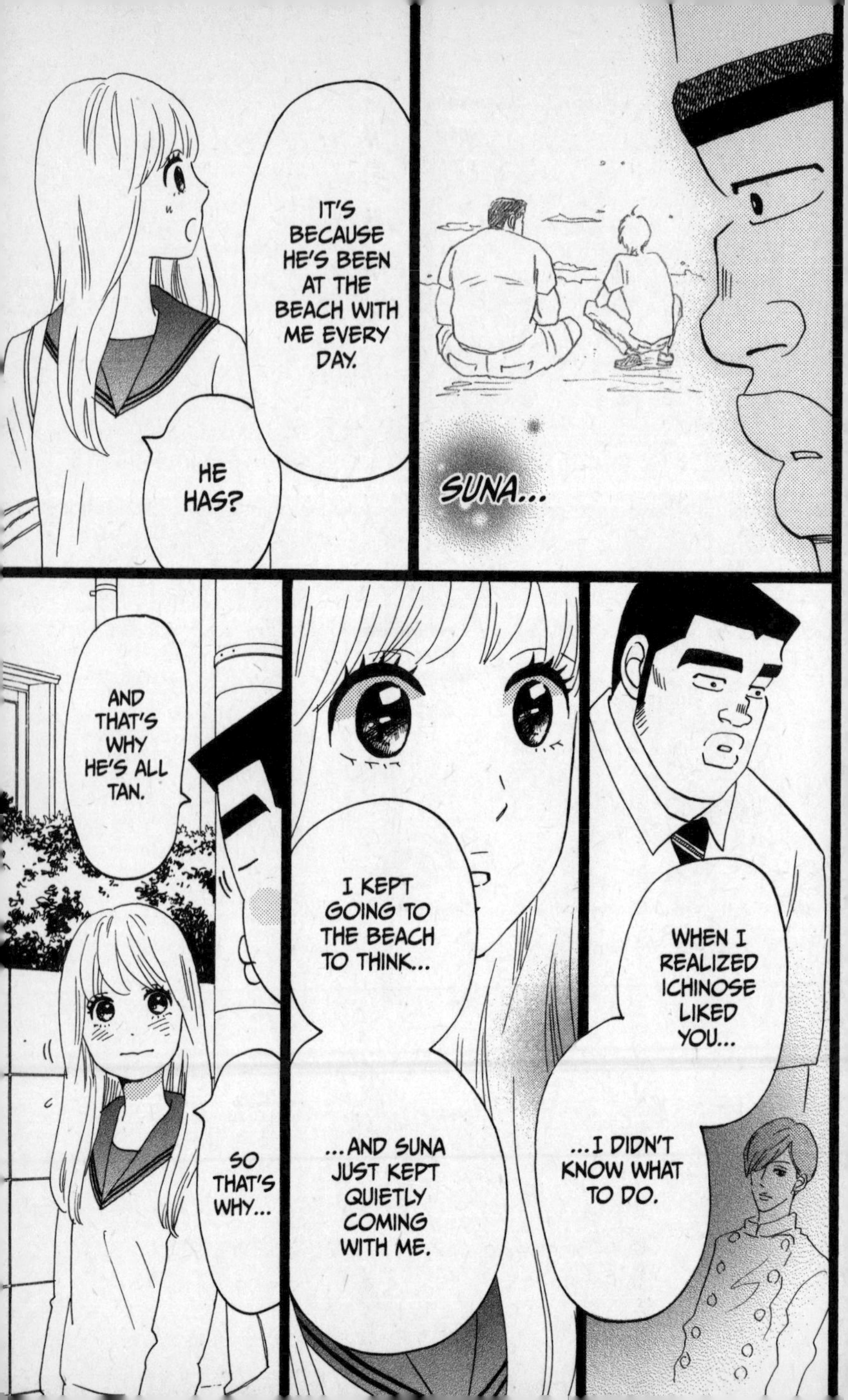
SUNA...
IT'S BECAUSE HE'S BEEN AT THE BEACH WITH ME EVERY DAY.
HE HAS?
WHEN I REALIZED ICHINOSE LIKED YOU...
...I DIDN'T KNOW WHAT TO DO.
I KEPT GOING TO THE BEACH TO THINK...
...AND SUNA JUST KEPT QUIETLY COMING WITH ME.
AND THAT'S WHY HE'S ALL TAN.
SO THAT'S WHY...

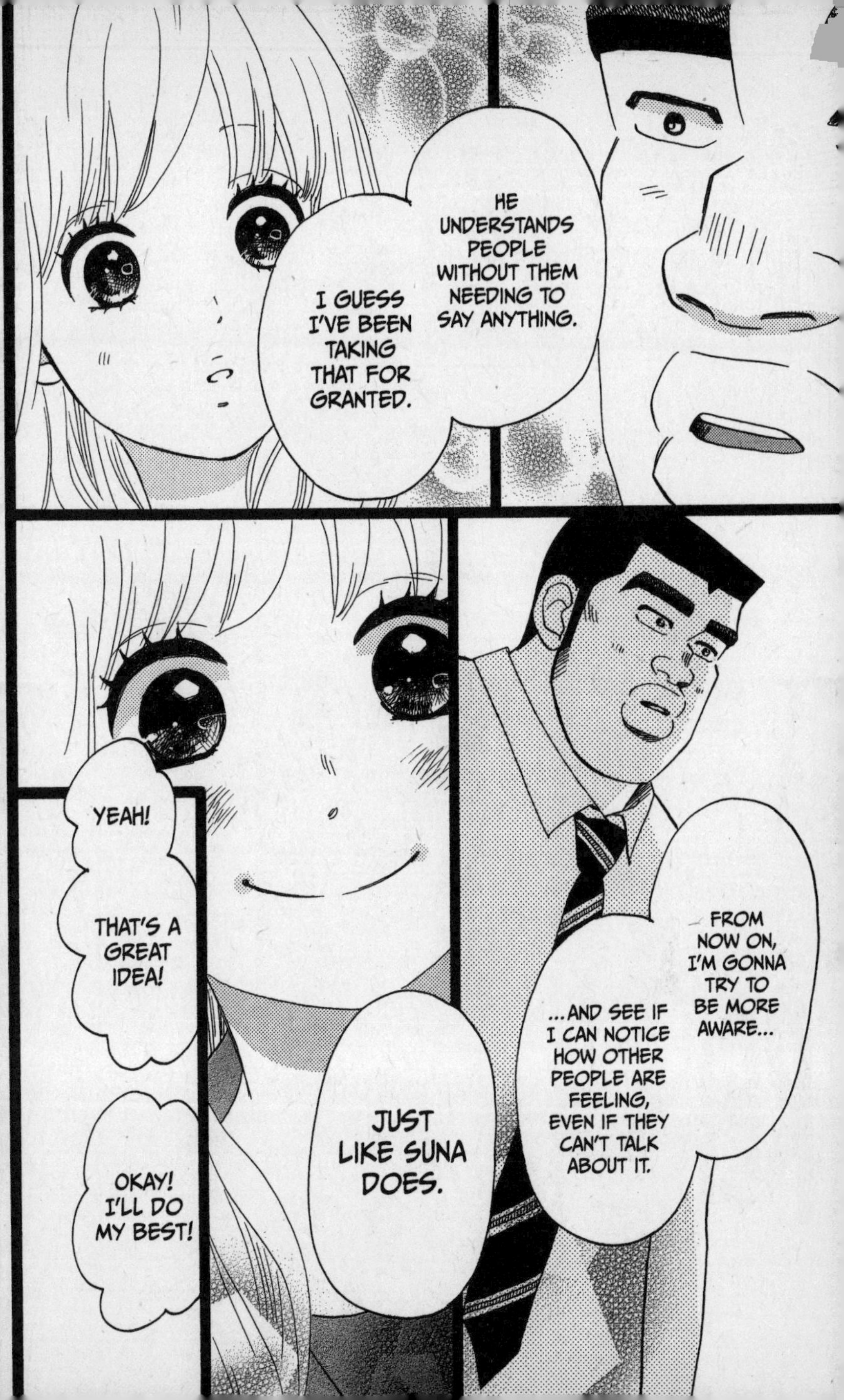
HE UNDERSTANDS PEOPLE WITHOUT THEM NEEDING TO SAY ANYTHING.
I GUESS I'VE BEEN TAKING THAT FOR GRANTED.
FROM NOW ON, I'M GONNA TRY TO BE MORE AWARE...
...AND SEE IF I CAN NOTICE HOW OTHER PEOPLE ARE FEELING, EVEN IF THEY CAN'T TALK ABOUT IT.
JUST LIKE SUNA DOES.
YEAH!
THAT'S A GREAT IDEA!
OKAY! I'LL DO MY BEST!

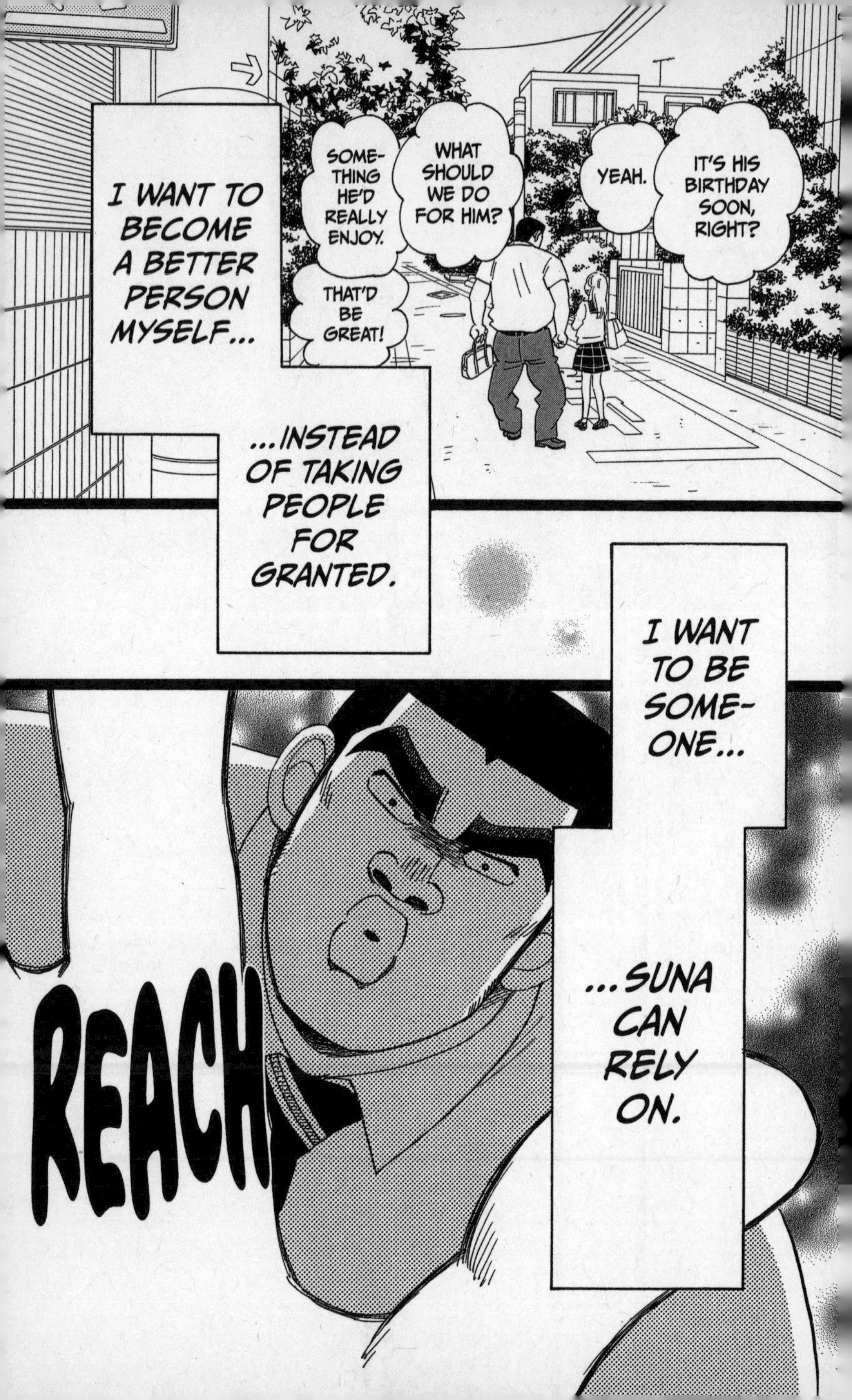
IT'S HIS BIRTHDAY SOON, RIGHT?
YEAH.
WHAT SHOULD WE DO FOR HIM?
SOME-THING HE'D REALLY ENJOY.
THAT'D BE GREAT!
I WANT TO BECOME A BETTER PERSON MYSELF...
...INSTEAD OF TAKING PEOPLE FOR GRANTED.
I WANT TO BE SOME-ONE...
...SUNA CAN RELY ON.
REACH

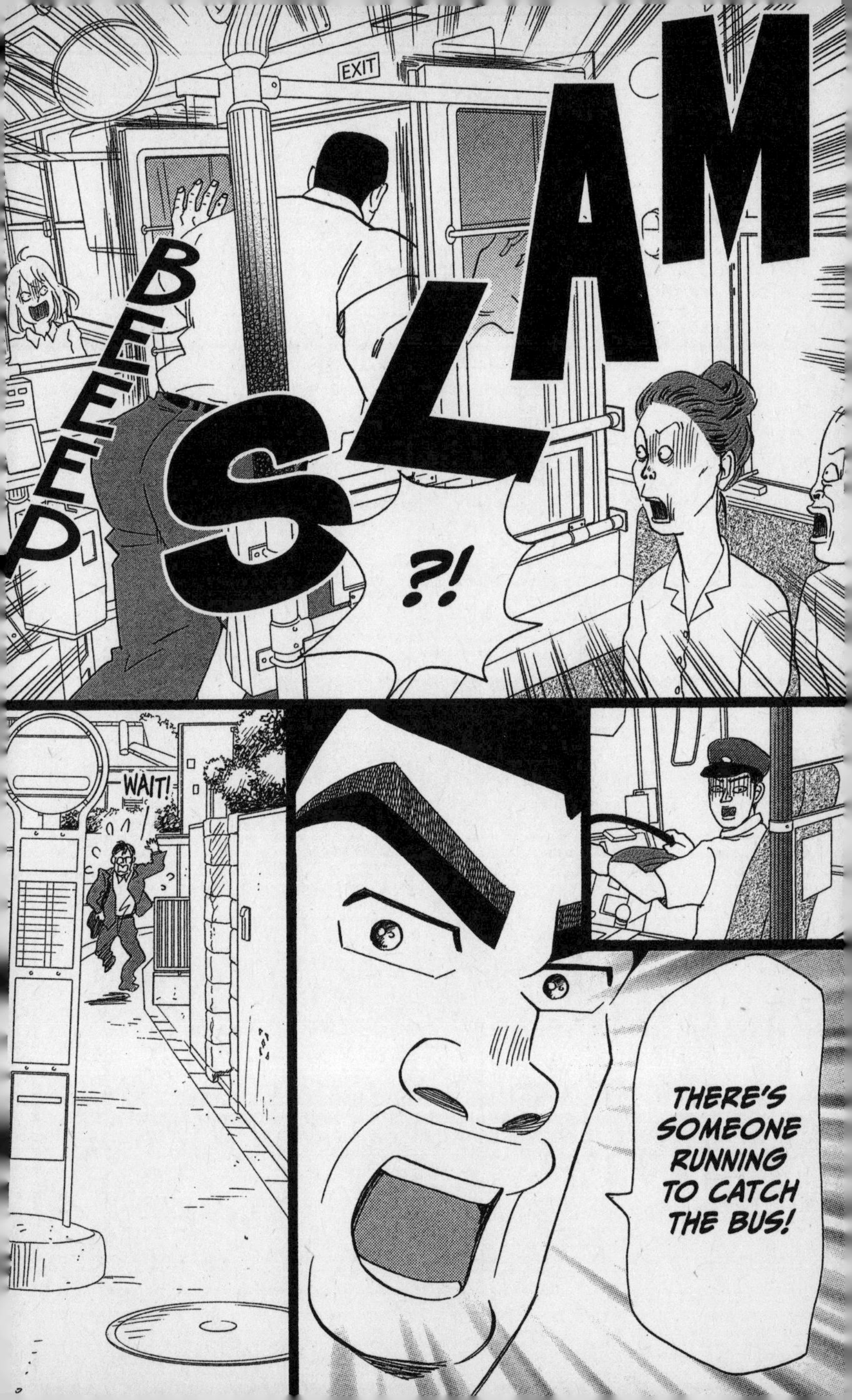
SLAM
BEEEEP
?!
THERE'S SOMEONE RUNNING TO CATCH THE BUS!
WAIT!

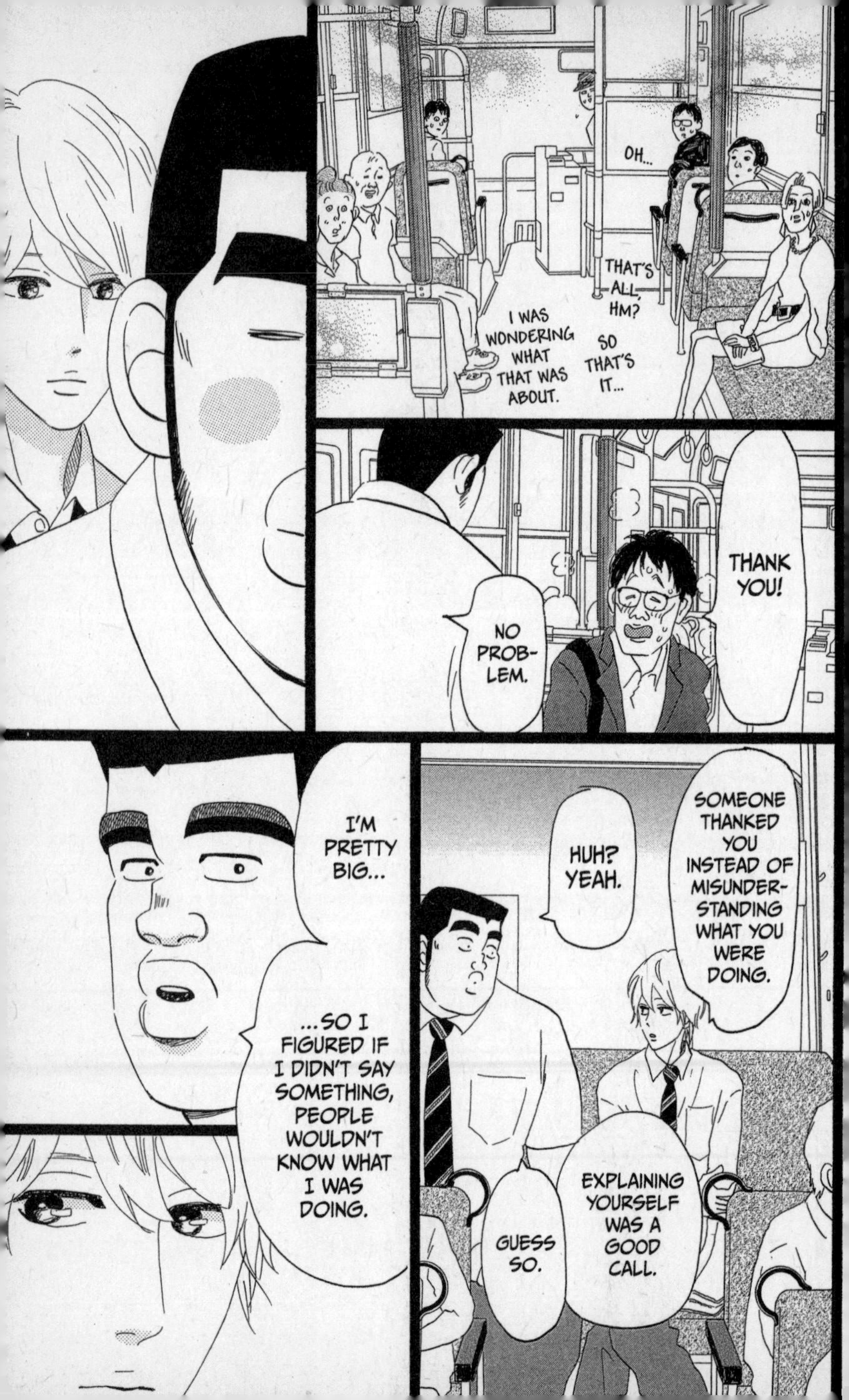
OH...
THAT'S ALL, HM?
SO THAT'S IT...
I WAS WONDERING WHAT THAT WAS ABOUT.
THANK YOU!
NO PROBLEM.
SOMEONE THANKED YOU INSTEAD OF MISUNDERSTANDING WHAT YOU WERE DOING.
HUH? YEAH.
EXPLAINING YOURSELF WAS A GOOD CALL.
GUESS SO.
I'M PRETTY BIG...
...SO I FIGURED IF I DIDN'T SAY SOMETHING, PEOPLE WOULDN'T KNOW WHAT I WAS DOING.

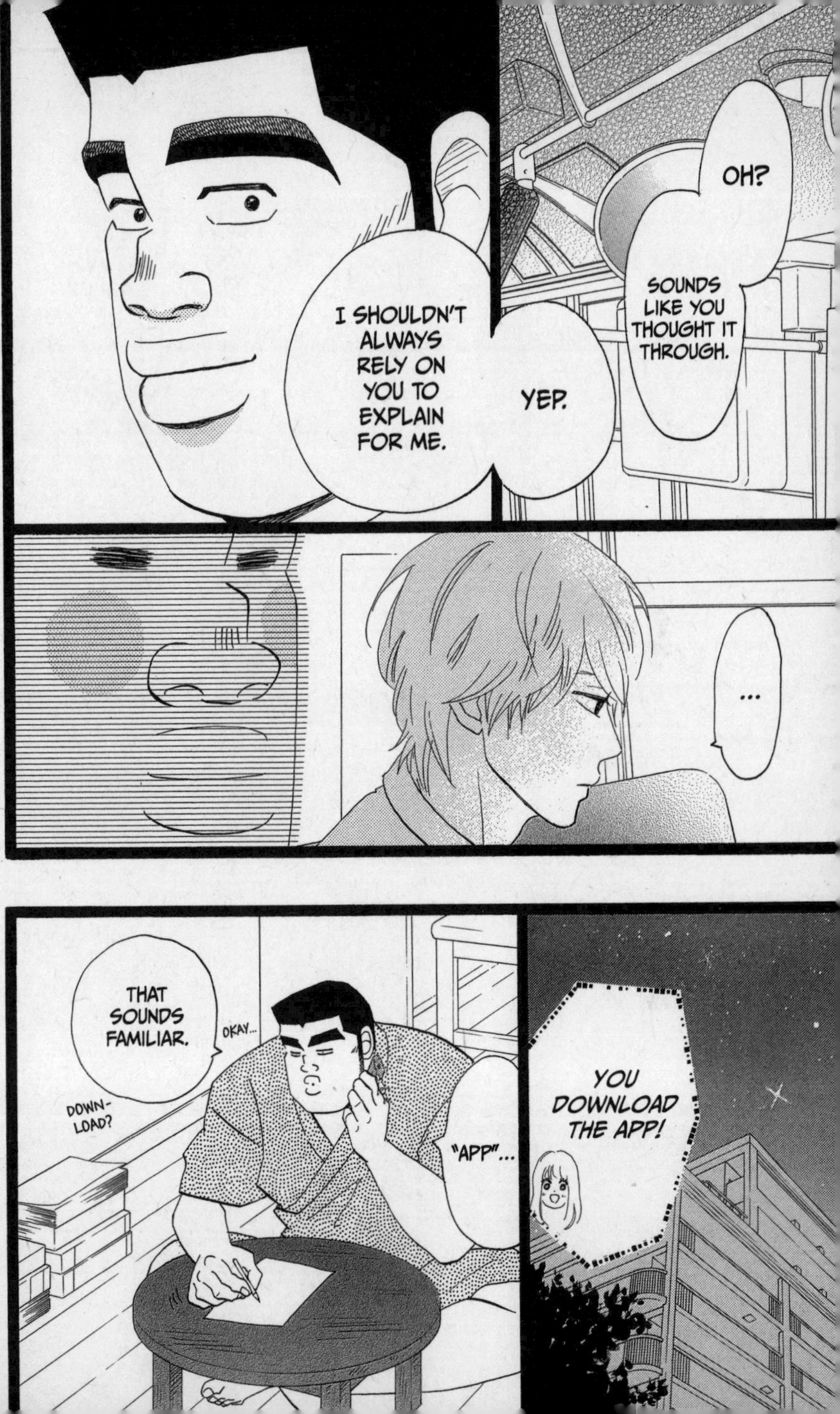
OH?
SOUNDS LIKE YOU THOUGHT IT THROUGH.
YEP.
I SHOULDN'T ALWAYS RELY ON YOU TO EXPLAIN FOR ME.
...
YOU DOWNLOAD THE APP!
"APP"...
OKAY...
THAT SOUNDS FAMILIAR.
DOWN-LOAD?

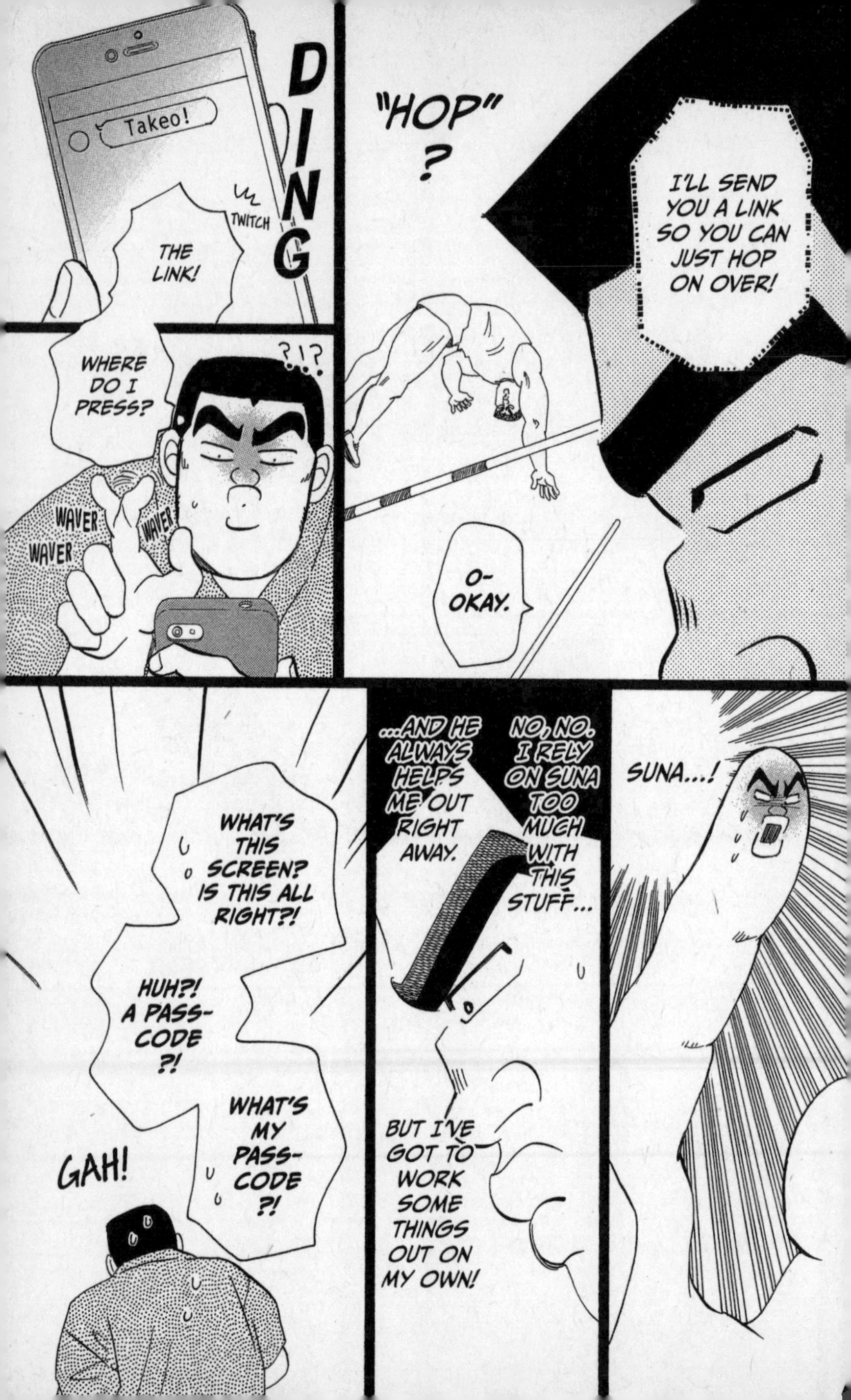
I'LL SEND YOU A LINK SO YOU CAN JUST HOP ON OVER!
"HOP"?
O-OKAY.
DING
Takeo!
TWITCH
THE LINK!
?!?
WHERE DO I PRESS?
WAVER
WAVER
WAVER
SUNA...!
NO, NO. I RELY ON SUNA TOO MUCH WITH THIS STUFF...
...AND HE ALWAYS HELPS ME OUT RIGHT AWAY.
BUT I'VE GOT TO WORK SOME THINGS OUT ON MY OWN!
WHAT'S THIS SCREEN? IS THIS ALL RIGHT?!
HUH?! A PASS-CODE?!
WHAT'S MY PASS-CODE?!
GAH!

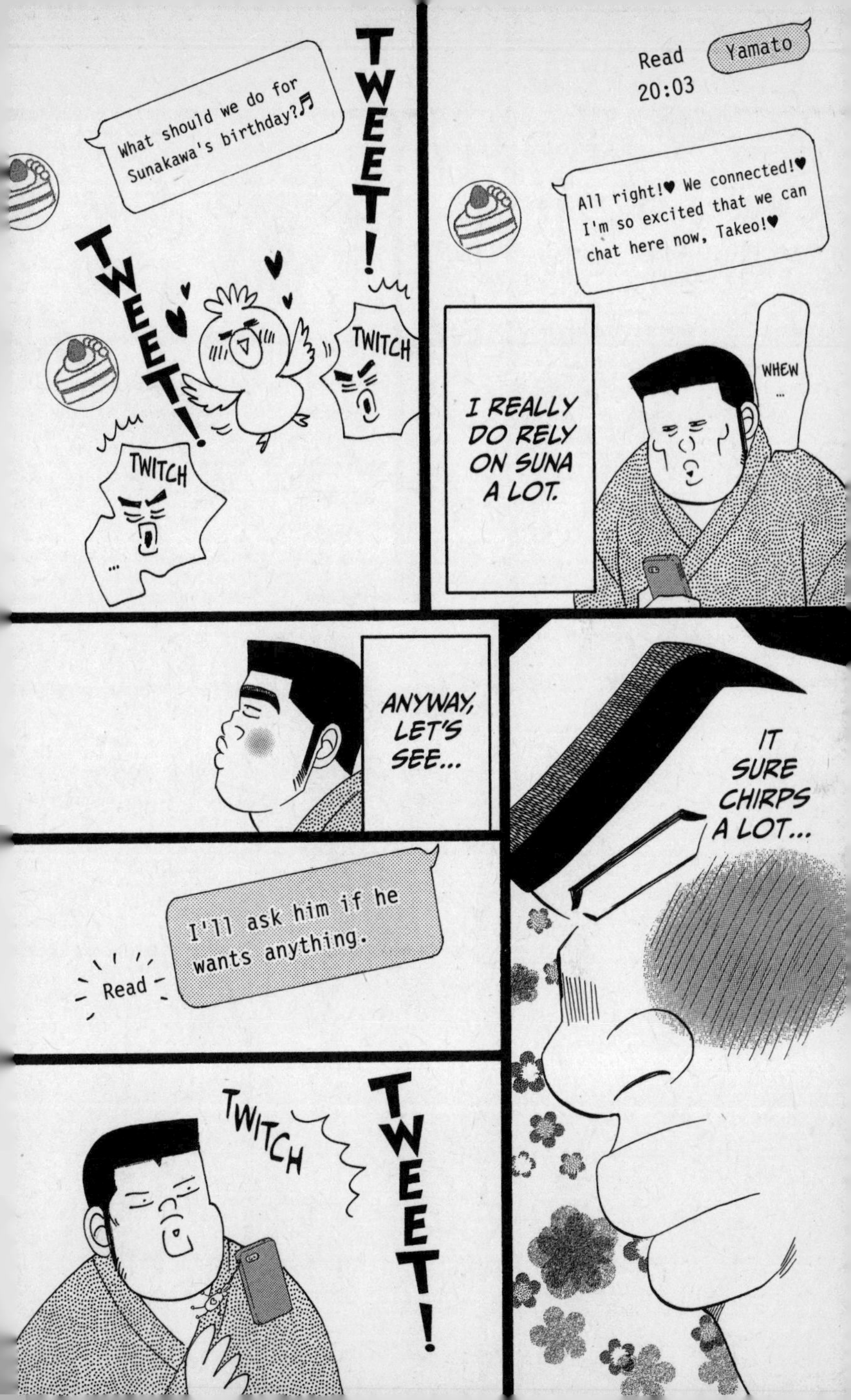

Yamato
Read 20:03
All right!♥ We connected!♥ I'm so excited that we can chat here now, Takeo!♥
WHEW...
I REALLY DO RELY ON SUNA A LOT.
TWEET!
What should we do for Sunakawa's birthday?♬
TWITCH
TWEET!
TWITCH
...
IT SURE CHIRPS A LOT...
ANYWAY, LET'S SEE...
I'll ask him if he wants anything.
Read
TWEET!
TWITCH

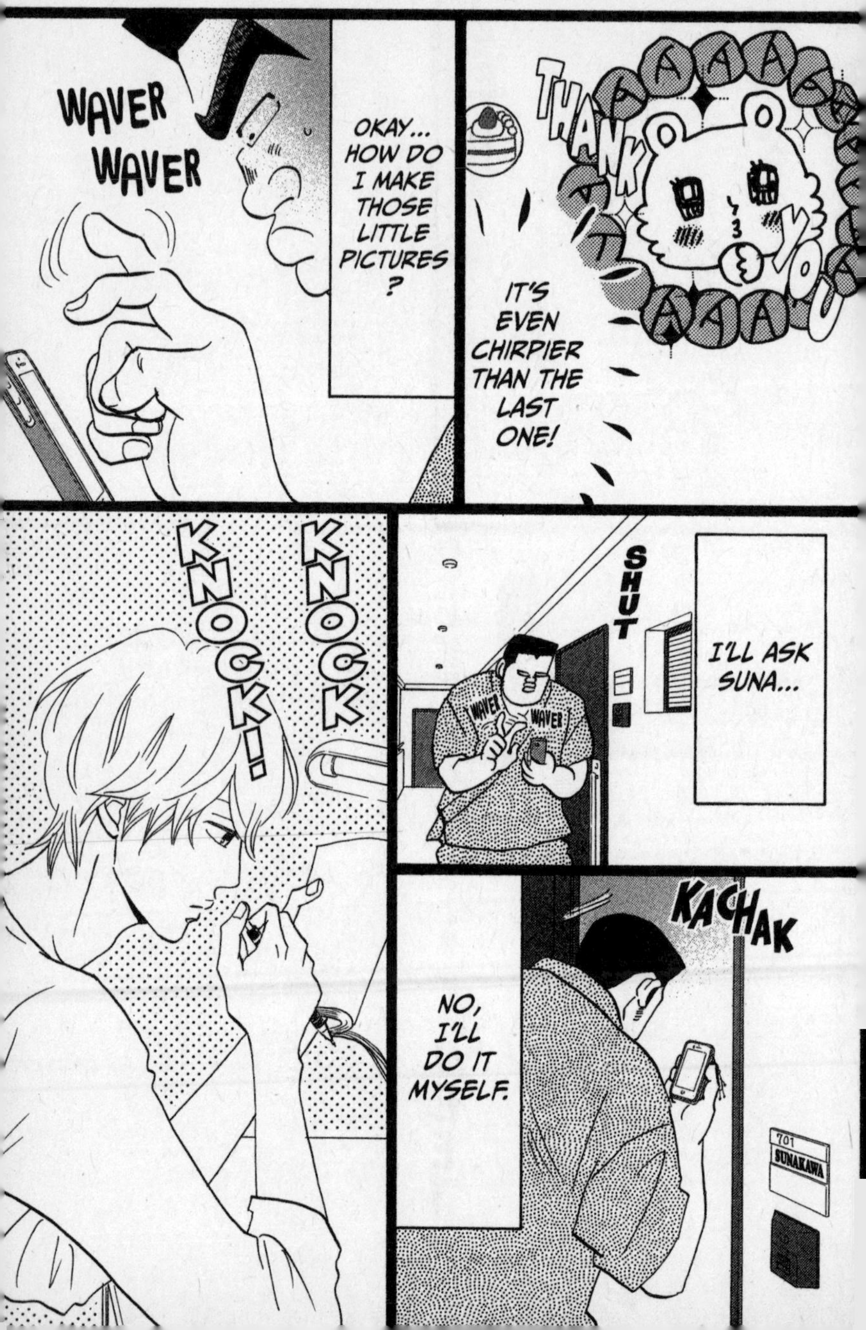
THANK YOU
IT'S EVEN CHIRPIER THAN THE LAST ONE!
OKAY... HOW DO I MAKE THOSE LITTLE PICTURES?
WAVER WAVER
SHUT
I'LL ASK SUNA...
WAVER WAVER
KACHAK
NO, I'LL DO IT MYSELF.
701 SUNAKAWA
KNOCK KNOCK!

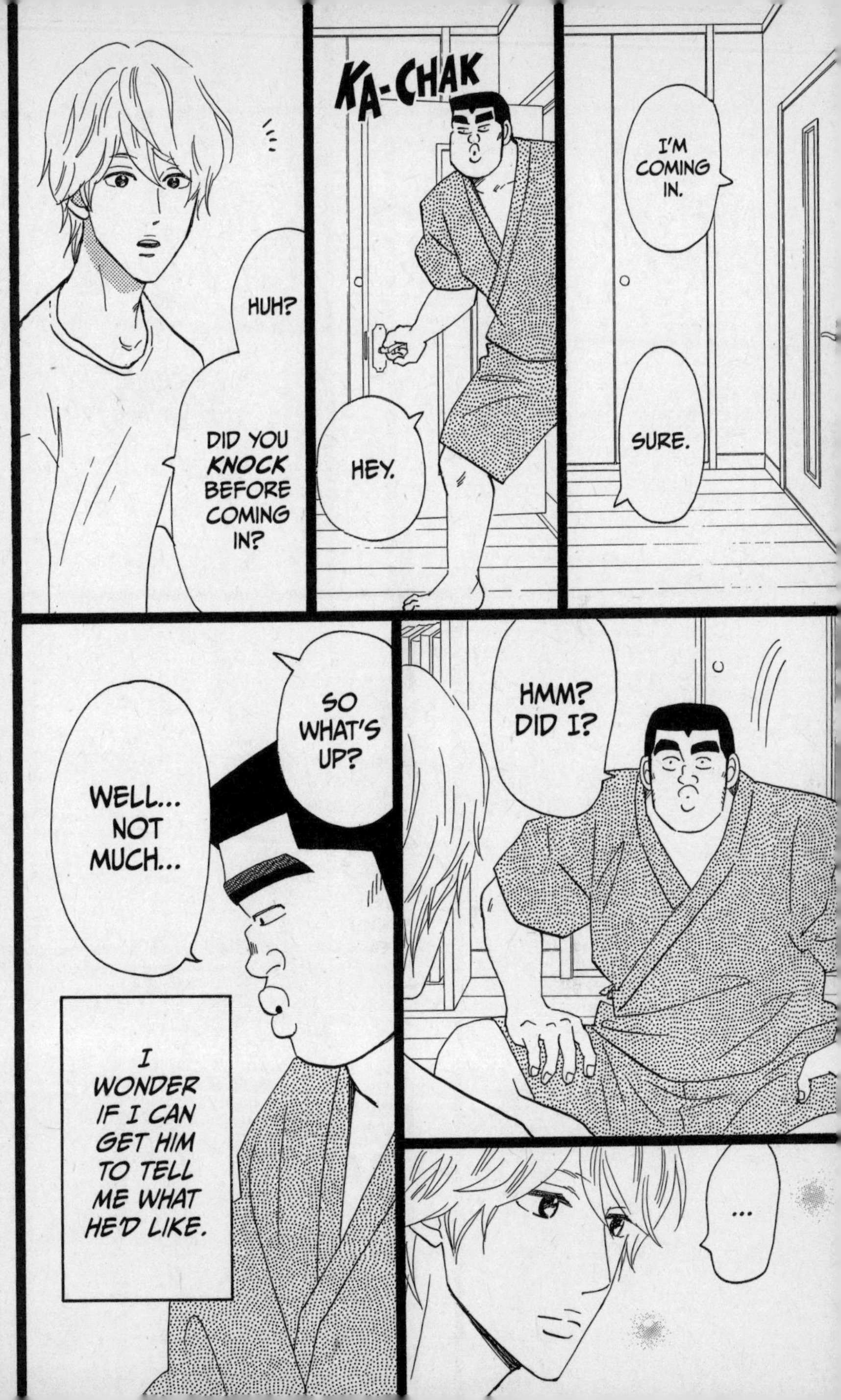
I'M COMING IN.
SURE.
KA-CHAK
HEY.
HUH?
DID YOU KNOCK BEFORE COMING IN?
HMM? DID I?
...
SO WHAT'S UP?
WELL... NOT MUCH...
I WONDER IF I CAN GET HIM TO TELL ME WHAT HE'D LIKE.

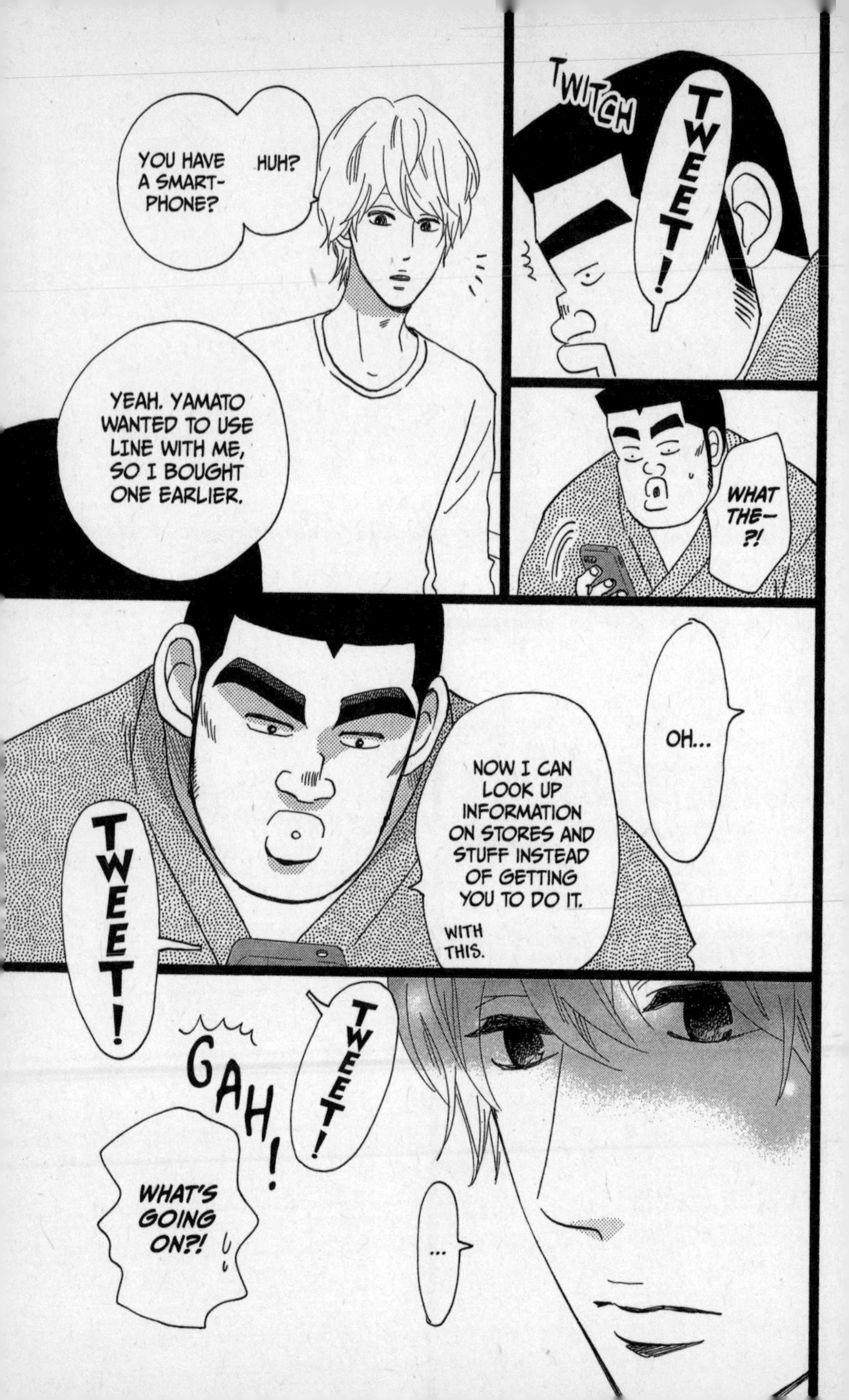
TWITCH
TWEET!
WHAT THE—?!
HUH?
YOU HAVE A SMART-PHONE?
YEAH. YAMATO WANTED TO USE LINE WITH ME, SO I BOUGHT ONE EARLIER.
OH...
NOW I CAN LOOK UP INFORMATION ON STORES AND STUFF INSTEAD OF GETTING YOU TO DO IT.
WITH THIS.
TWEET!
TWEET!
GAH!
WHAT'S GOING ON?!
...

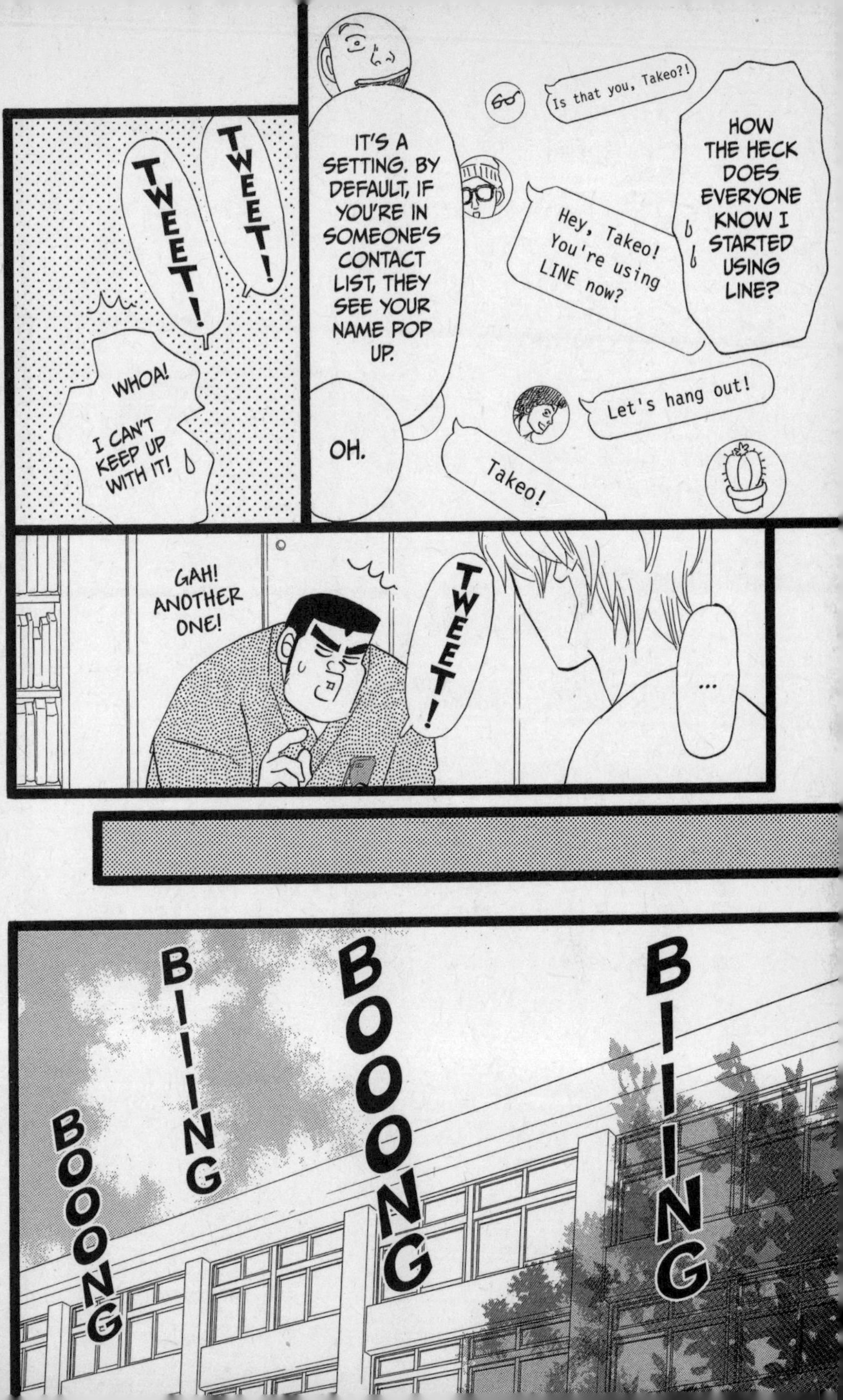
HOW THE HECK DOES EVERYONE KNOW I STARTED USING LINE?
Is that you, Takeo?!
Hey, Takeo! You're using LINE now?
Let's hang out!
Takeo!
IT'S A SETTING. BY DEFAULT, IF YOU'RE IN SOMEONE'S CONTACT LIST, THEY SEE YOUR NAME POP UP.
OH.
TWEET!
TWEET!
WHOA! I CAN'T KEEP UP WITH IT!
...
TWEET!
GAH! ANOTHER ONE!
BIIING
BOOONG
BIIING
BOOONG

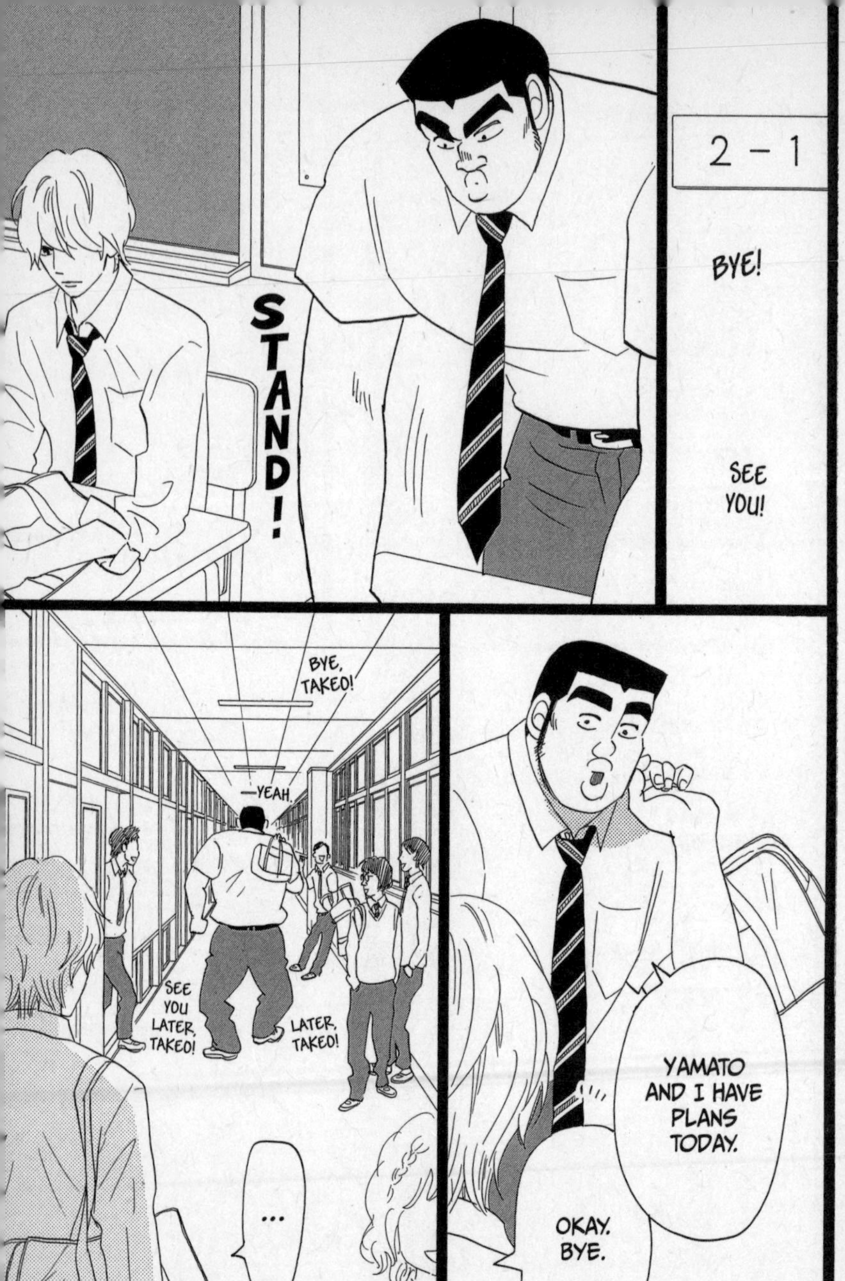
2-1
BYE!
SEE YOU!
STAND!
YAMATO AND I HAVE PLANS TODAY.
OKAY. BYE.
BYE, TAKEO!
—YEAH.
LATER, TAKEO!
SEE YOU LATER, TAKEO!
...

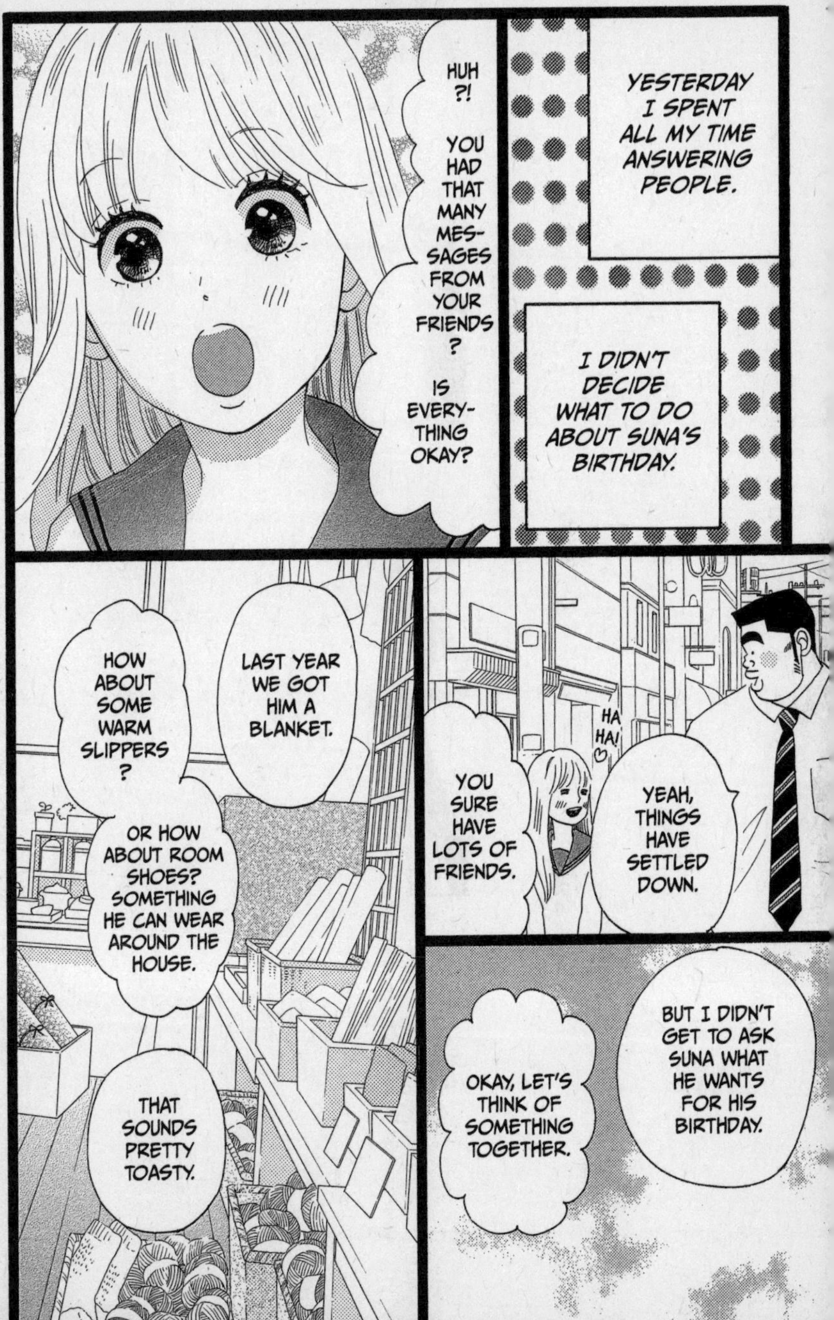
YESTERDAY I SPENT ALL MY TIME ANSWERING PEOPLE.
I DIDN'T DECIDE WHAT TO DO ABOUT SUNA'S BIRTHDAY.
HUH ?! YOU HAD THAT MANY MES-SAGES FROM YOUR FRIENDS ? IS EVERY-THING OKAY?
YEAH, THINGS HAVE SETTLED DOWN.
HA HA!
YOU SURE HAVE LOTS OF FRIENDS.
BUT I DIDN'T GET TO ASK SUNA WHAT HE WANTS FOR HIS BIRTHDAY.
OKAY, LET'S THINK OF SOMETHING TOGETHER.
LAST YEAR WE GOT HIM A BLANKET.
HOW ABOUT SOME WARM SLIPPERS ?
OR HOW ABOUT ROOM SHOES? SOMETHING HE CAN WEAR AROUND THE HOUSE.
THAT SOUNDS PRETTY TOASTY.

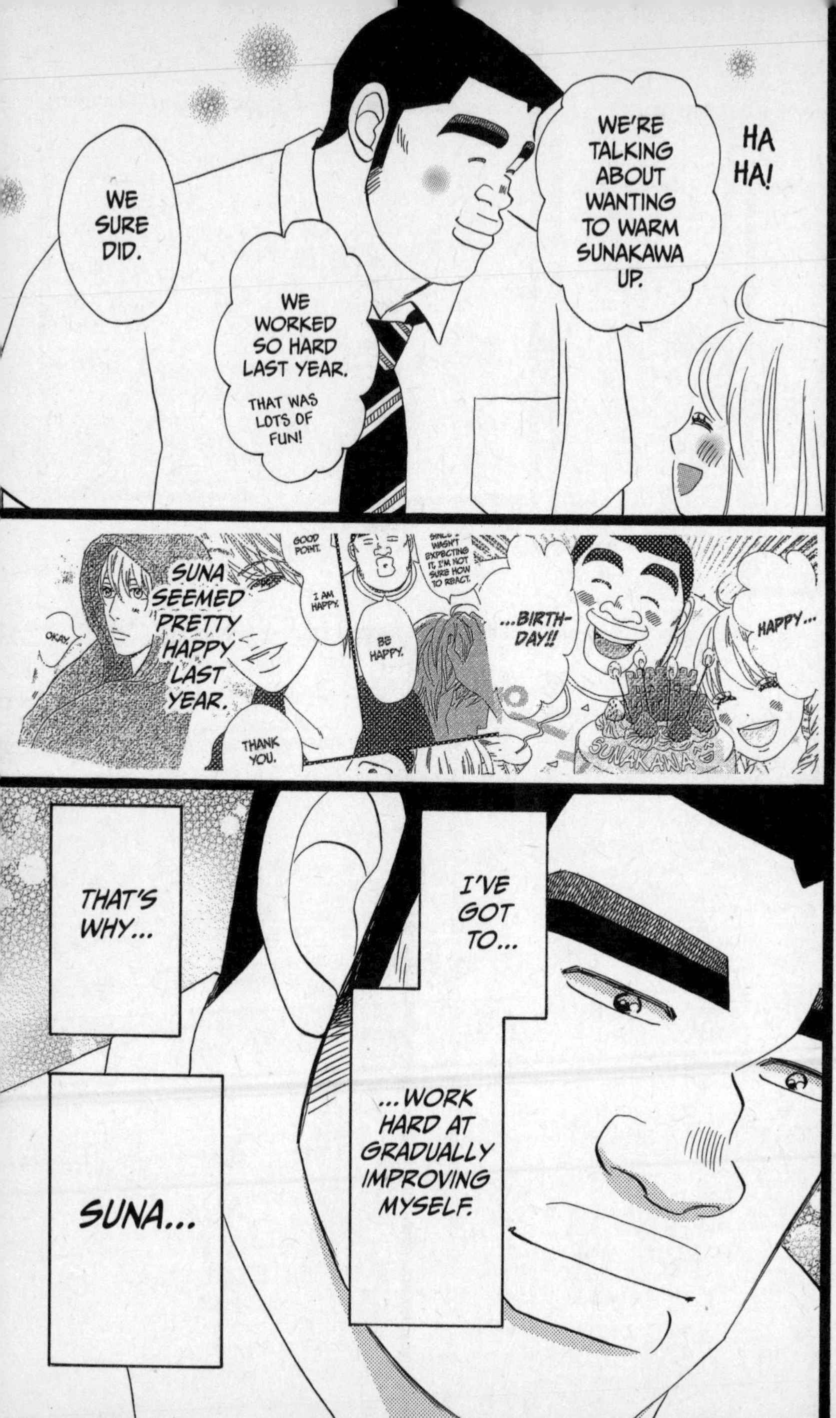
HA HA!
WE'RE TALKING ABOUT WANTING TO WARM SUNAKAWA UP.
WE WORKED SO HARD LAST YEAR.
THAT WAS LOTS OF FUN!
WE SURE DID.
HAPPY...
...BIRTH-DAY!!
SUNAKAWA
WASN'T EXPECTING IT, I'M NOT SURE HOW TO REACT.
BE HAPPY.
GOOD POINT.
I AM HAPPY.
SUNA SEEMED PRETTY HAPPY LAST YEAR.
THANK YOU.
OKAY.
I'VE GOT TO...
...WORK HARD AT GRADUALLY IMPROVING MYSELF.
THAT'S WHY...
SUNA...

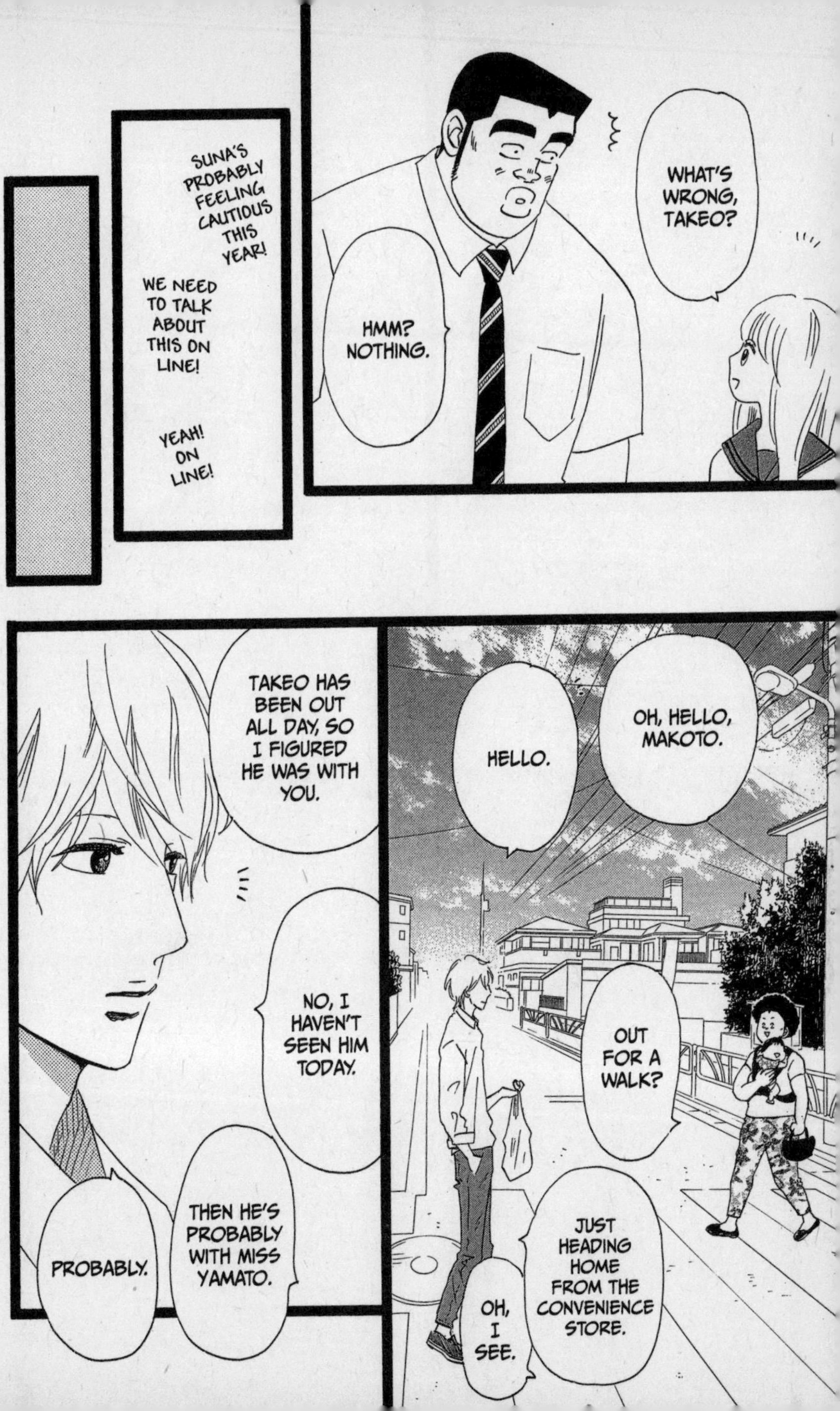
WHAT'S WRONG, TAKEO?
HMM? NOTHING.
SUNA'S PROBABLY FEELING CAUTIOUS THIS YEAR!
WE NEED TO TALK ABOUT THIS ON LINE!
YEAH! ON LINE!
OH, HELLO, MAKOTO.
HELLO.
OUT FOR A WALK?
JUST HEADING HOME FROM THE CONVENIENCE STORE.
OH, I SEE.
TAKEO HAS BEEN OUT ALL DAY, SO I FIGURED HE WAS WITH YOU.
NO, I HAVEN'T SEEN HIM TODAY.
THEN HE'S PROBABLY WITH MISS YAMATO.
PROBABLY.

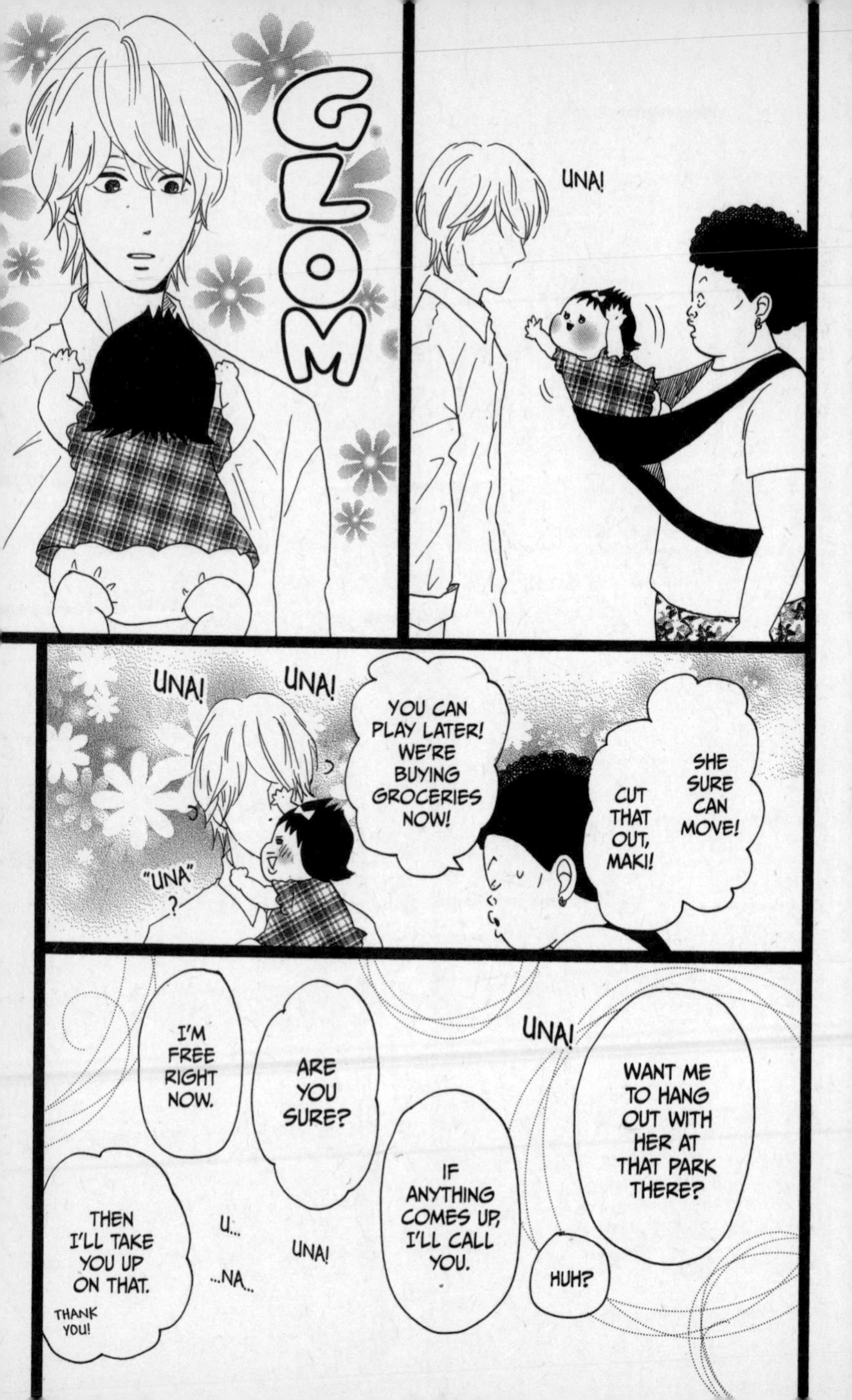
UNA!
GLOM
SHE SURE CAN MOVE!
CUT THAT OUT, MAKI!
YOU CAN PLAY LATER! WE'RE BUYING GROCERIES NOW!
UNA!
UNA!
"UNA" ?
WANT ME TO HANG OUT WITH HER AT THAT PARK THERE?
UNA!
HUH?
ARE YOU SURE?
I'M FREE RIGHT NOW.
IF ANYTHING COMES UP, I'LL CALL YOU.
UNA!
U...
...NA...
THEN I'LL TAKE YOU UP ON THAT.
THANK YOU!

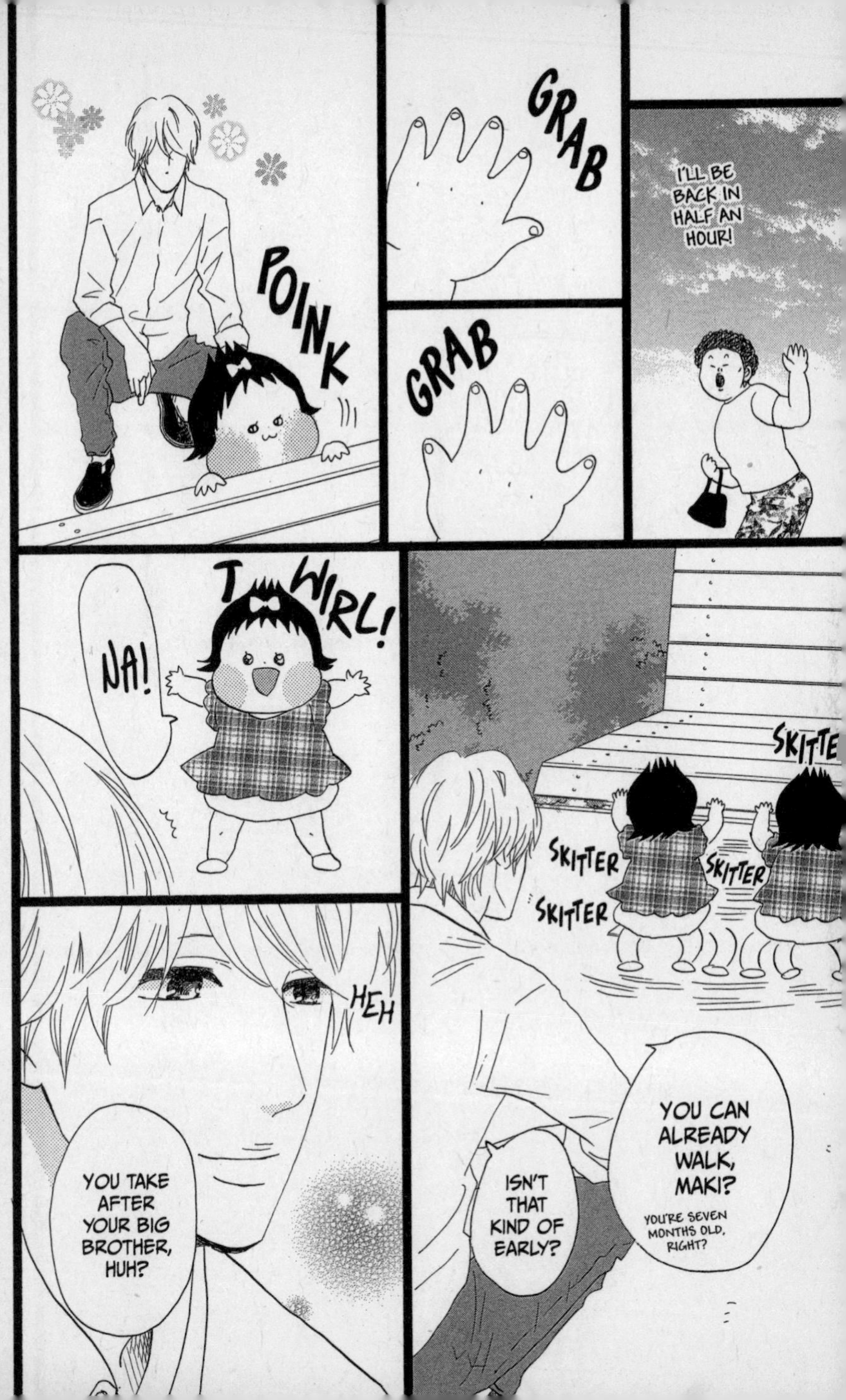
I'LL BE BACK IN HALF AN HOUR!
GRAB
GRAB
POINK
SKITTE
SKITTER
SKITTER
SKITTER
YOU CAN ALREADY WALK, MAKI?
YOU'RE SEVEN MONTHS OLD, RIGHT?
ISN'T THAT KIND OF EARLY?
TWIRL!
NA!
HEH
YOU TAKE AFTER YOUR BIG BROTHER, HUH?

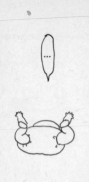

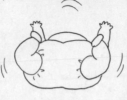

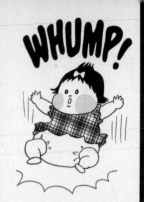

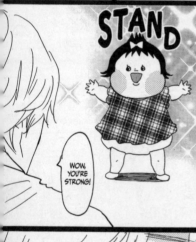

WOW, YOU'RE STRONG!

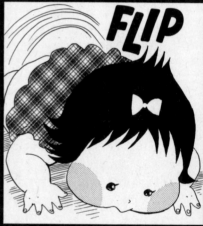

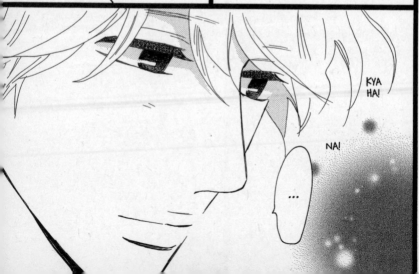

KYA HA!

NA!

...

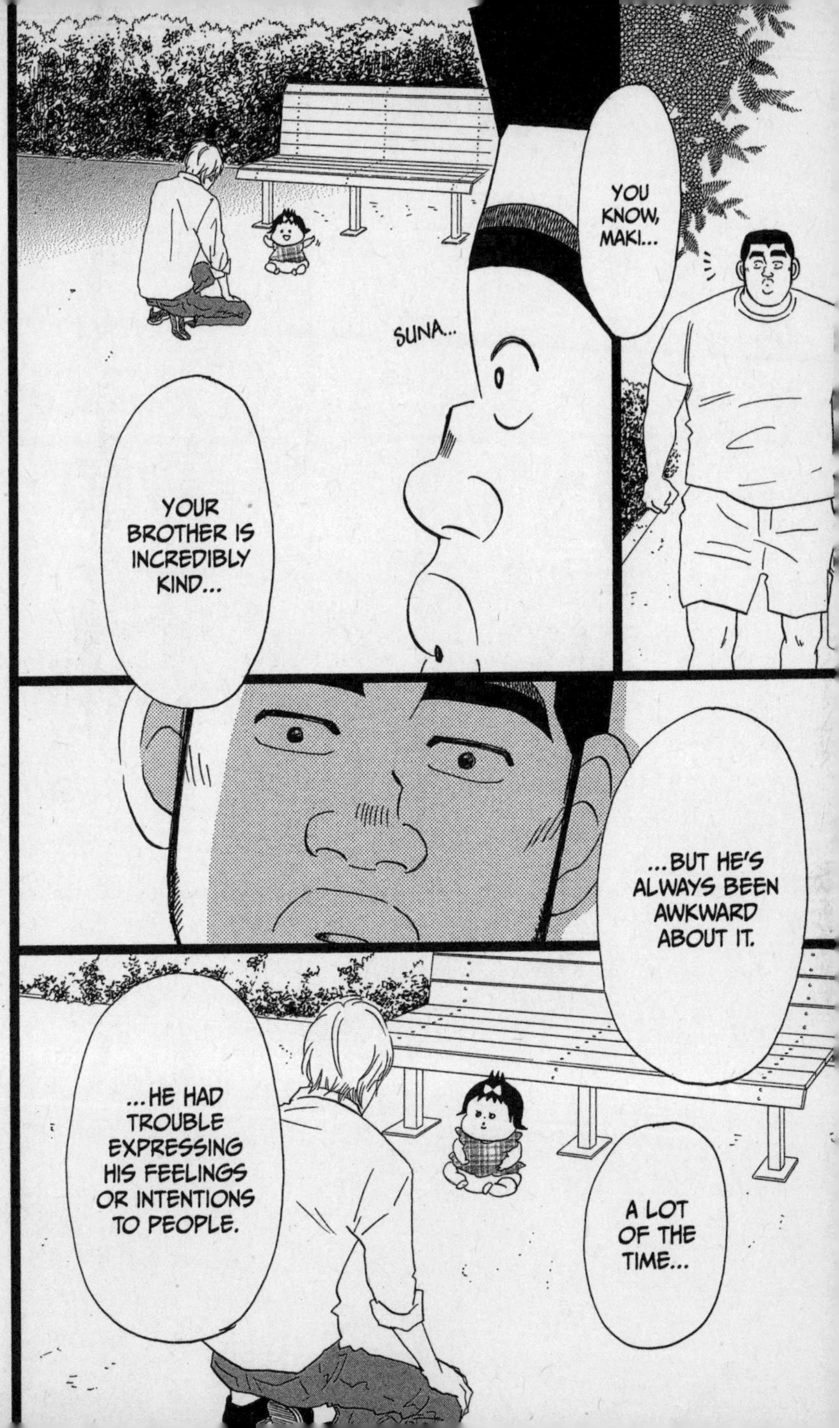
YOU KNOW, MAKI...
SUNA...
YOUR BROTHER IS INCREDIBLY KIND...
...BUT HE'S ALWAYS BEEN AWKWARD ABOUT IT.
A LOT OF THE TIME...
...HE HAD TROUBLE EXPRESSING HIS FEELINGS OR INTENTIONS TO PEOPLE.

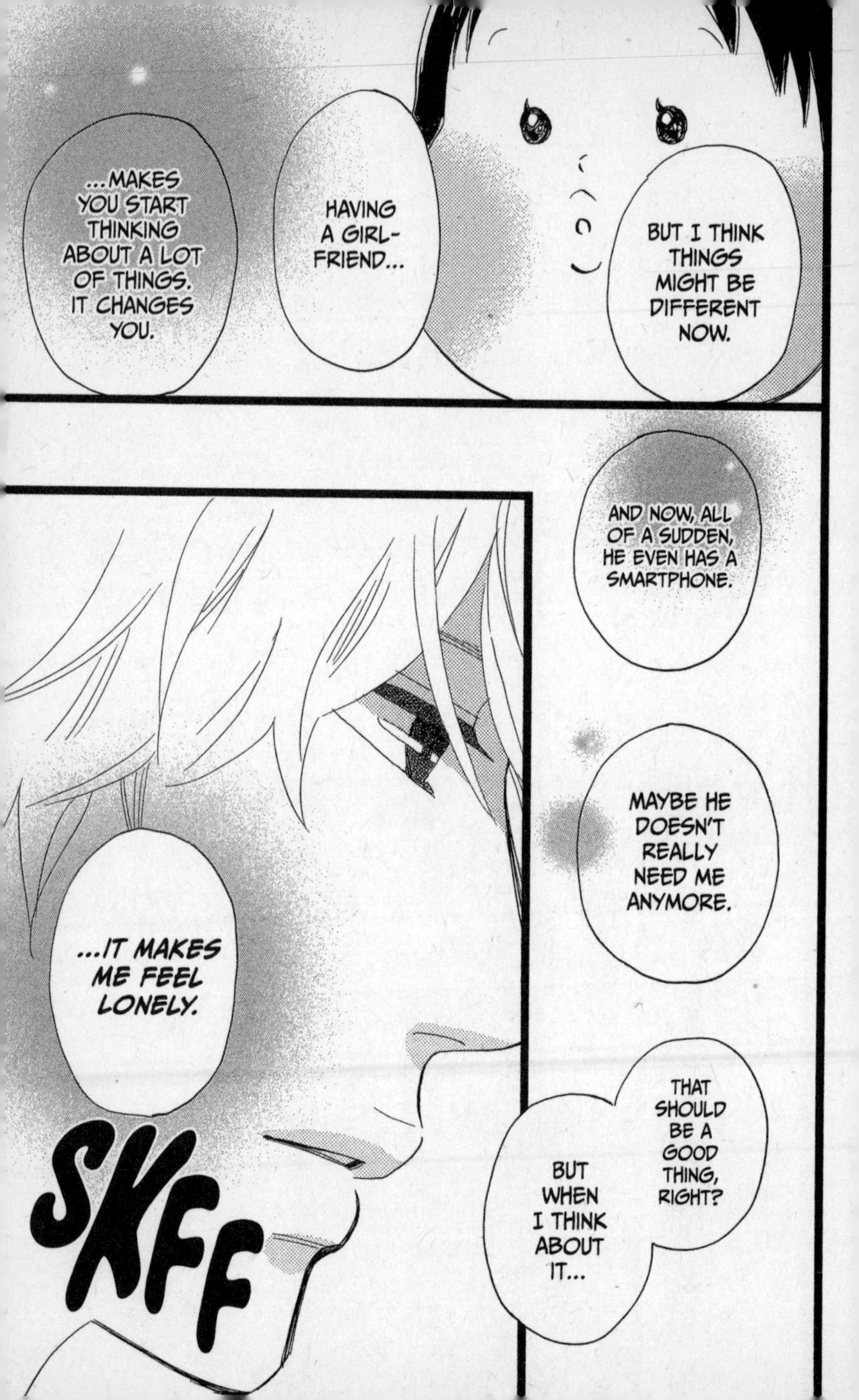
BUT I THINK THINGS MIGHT BE DIFFERENT NOW.
HAVING A GIRL-FRIEND...
...MAKES YOU START THINKING ABOUT A LOT OF THINGS. IT CHANGES YOU.
AND NOW, ALL OF A SUDDEN, HE EVEN HAS A SMARTPHONE.
MAYBE HE DOESN'T REALLY NEED ME ANYMORE.
THAT SHOULD BE A GOOD THING, RIGHT?
BUT WHEN I THINK ABOUT IT...
...IT MAKES ME FEEL LONELY.
SKFF

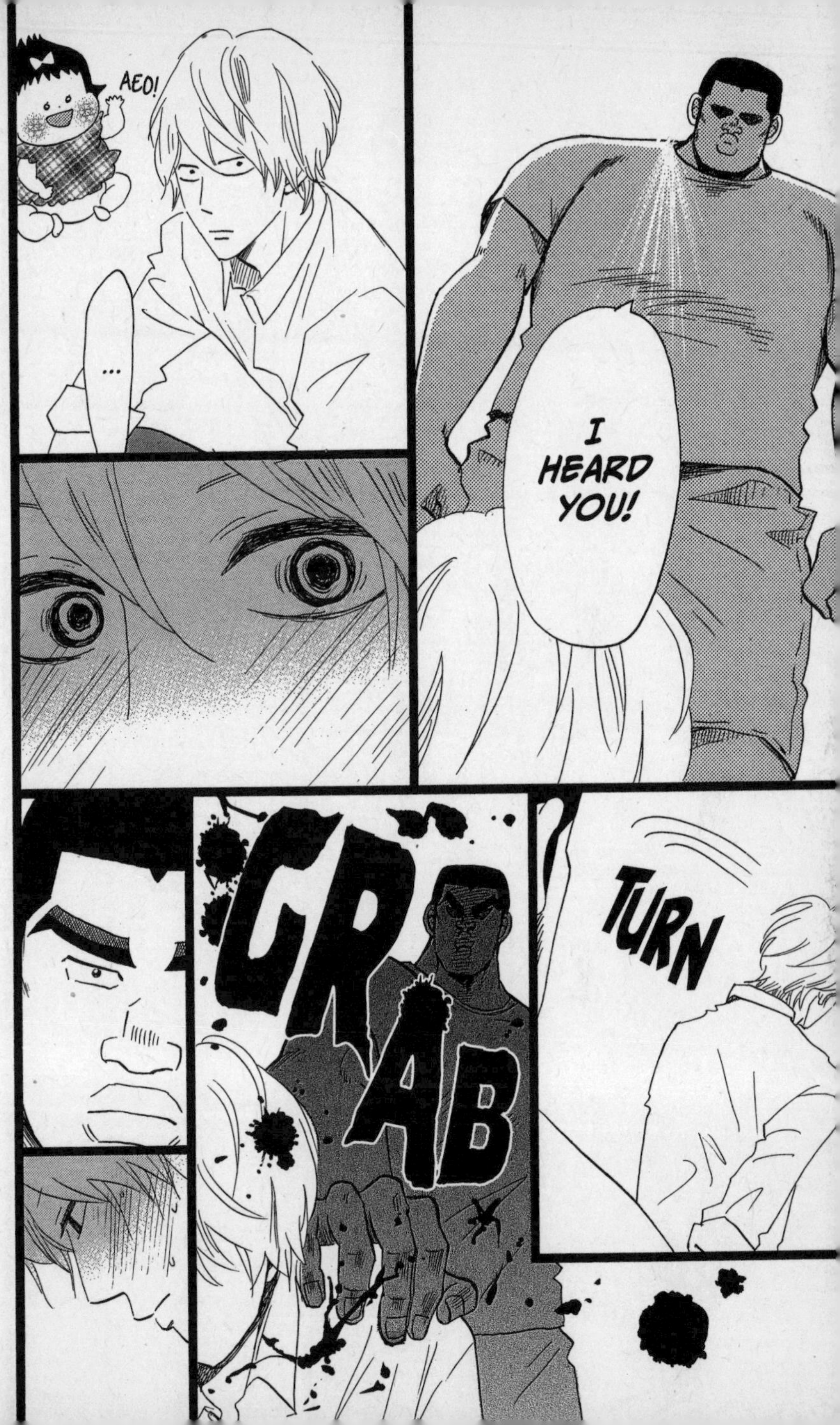
I HEARD YOU!
AEO!
...
TURN
GRAB

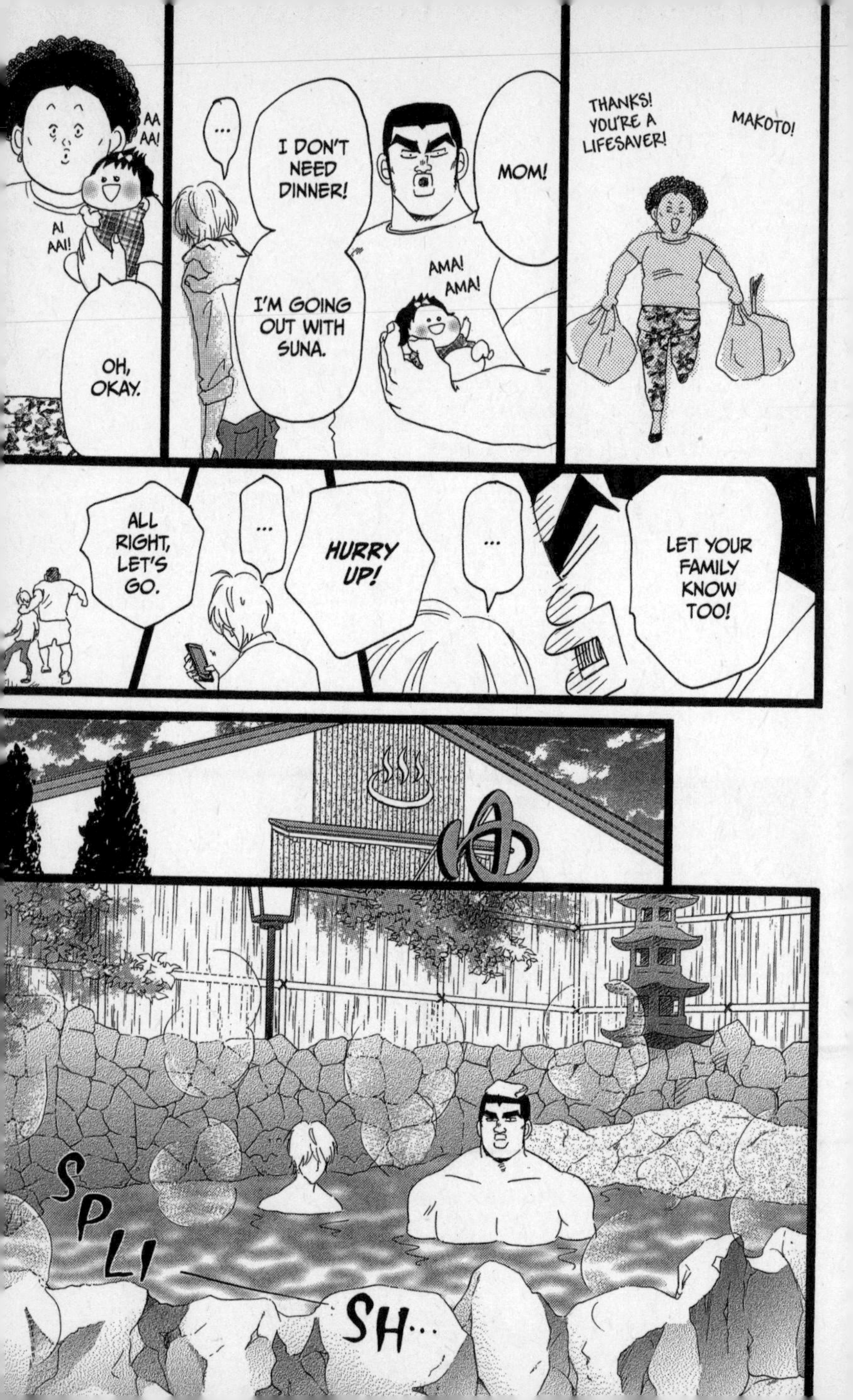
MAKOTO!
THANKS! YOU'RE A LIFESAVER!
MOM!
AMA! AMA!
I DON'T NEED DINNER!
I'M GOING OUT WITH SUNA.
...
AA AA!
AI AAI!
OH, OKAY.
LET YOUR FAMILY KNOW TOO!
...
HURRY UP!
...
ALL RIGHT, LET'S GO.
SPLI
SH...

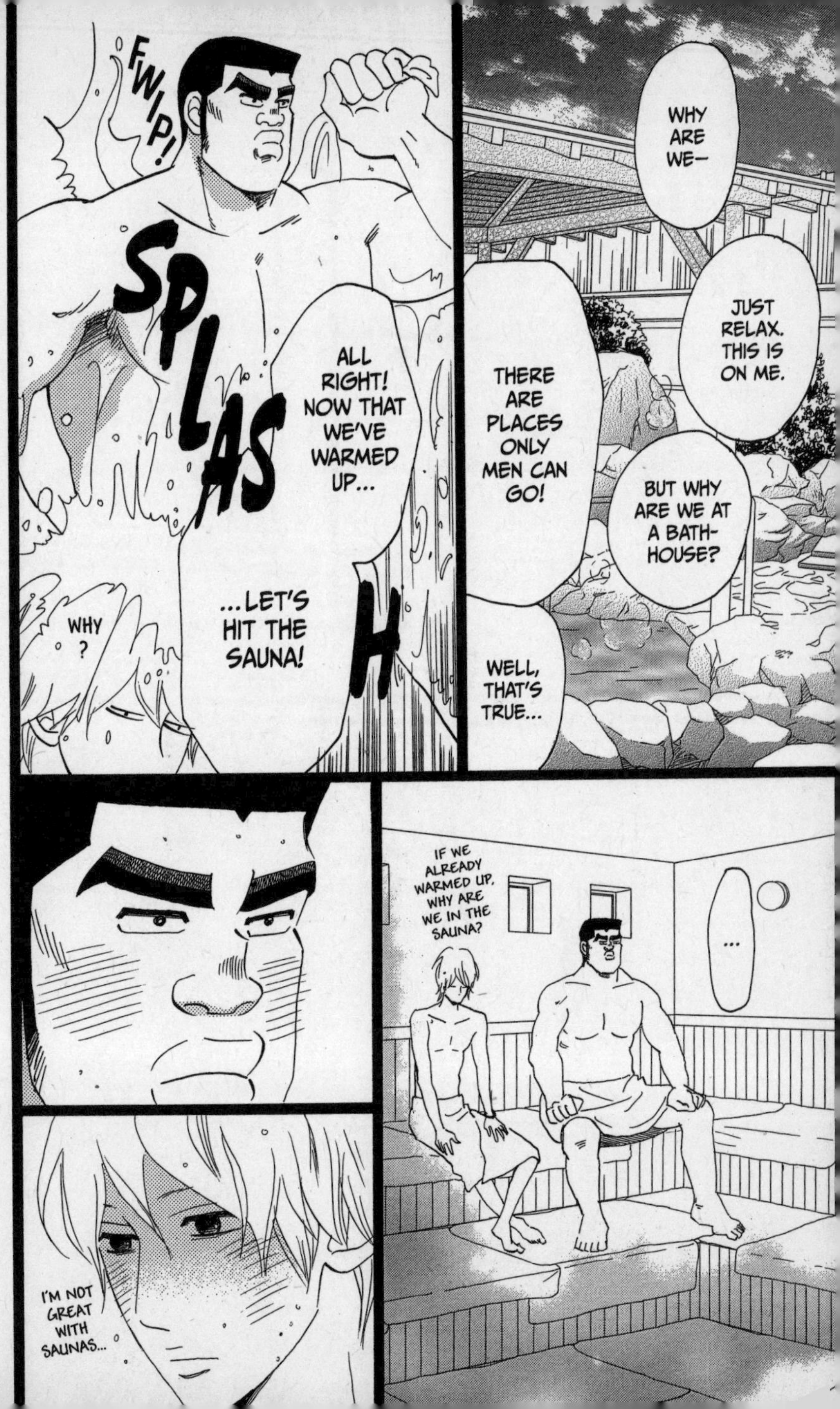
WHY ARE WE—
JUST RELAX. THIS IS ON ME.
BUT WHY ARE WE AT A BATH-HOUSE?
THERE ARE PLACES ONLY MEN CAN GO!
WELL, THAT'S TRUE...
FWIP!
ALL RIGHT! NOW THAT WE'VE WARMED UP...
SPLASH
...LET'S HIT THE SAUNA!
WHY?
...
IF WE ALREADY WARMED UP, WHY ARE WE IN THE SAUNA?
I'M NOT GREAT WITH SAUNAS...

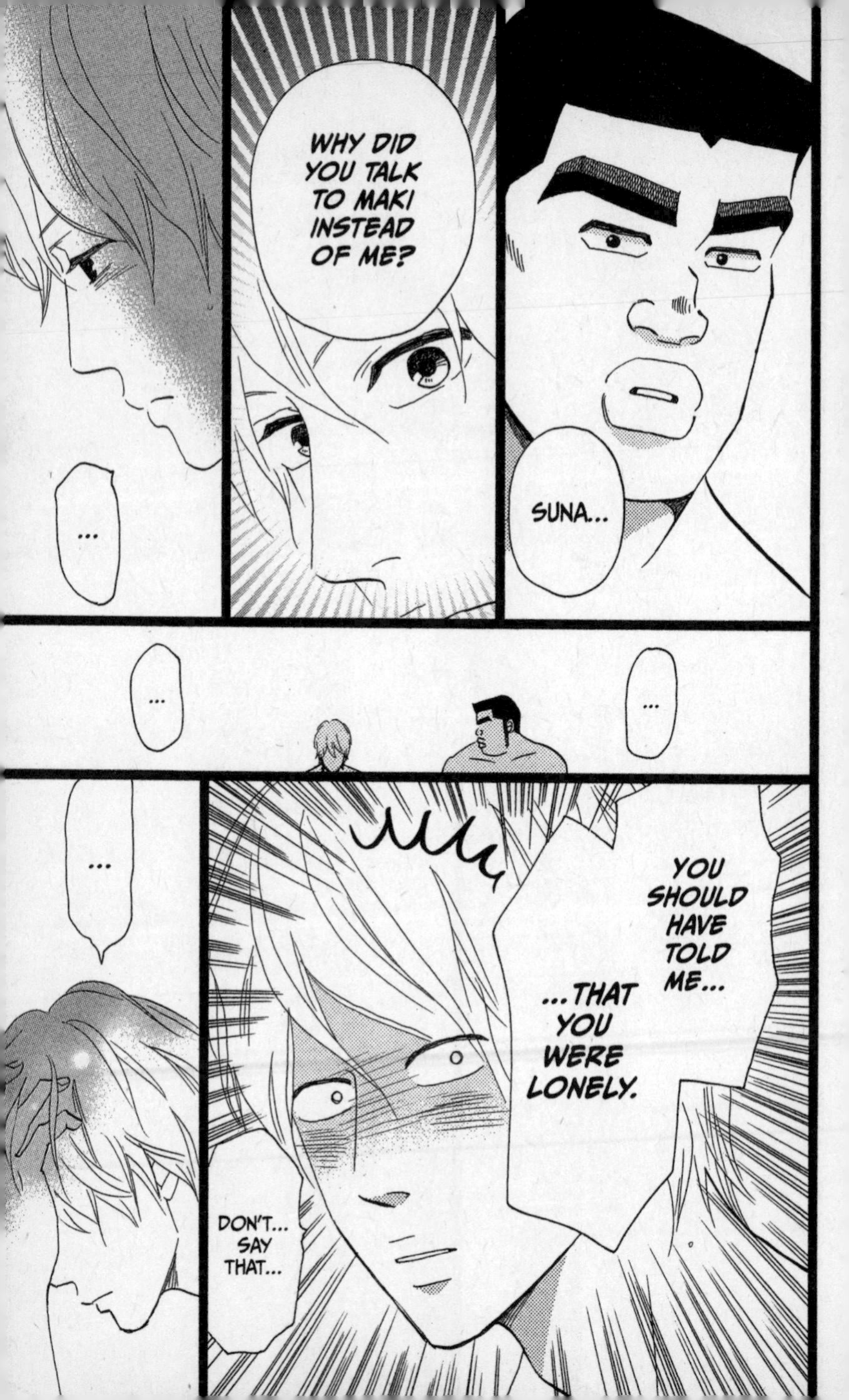
SUNA...
WHY DID YOU TALK TO MAKI INSTEAD OF ME?
...
...
...
YOU SHOULD HAVE TOLD ME...
...THAT YOU WERE LONELY.
...
DON'T... SAY THAT...

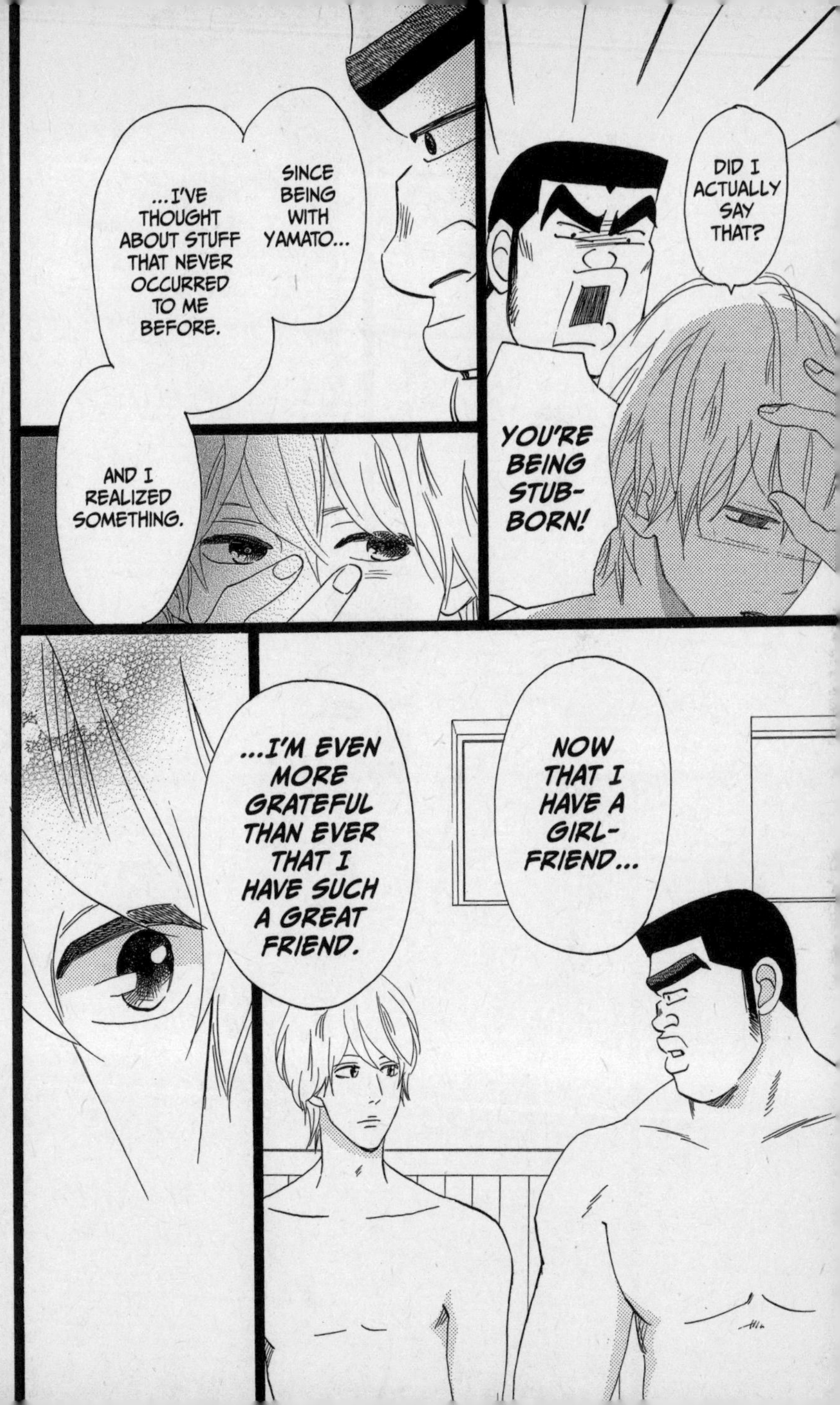
DID I ACTUALLY SAY THAT?
YOU'RE BEING STUB-BORN!
SINCE BEING WITH YAMATO...
...I'VE THOUGHT ABOUT STUFF THAT NEVER OCCURRED TO ME BEFORE.
AND I REALIZED SOMETHING.
NOW THAT I HAVE A GIRL-FRIEND...
...I'M EVEN MORE GRATEFUL THAN EVER THAT I HAVE SUCH A GREAT FRIEND.

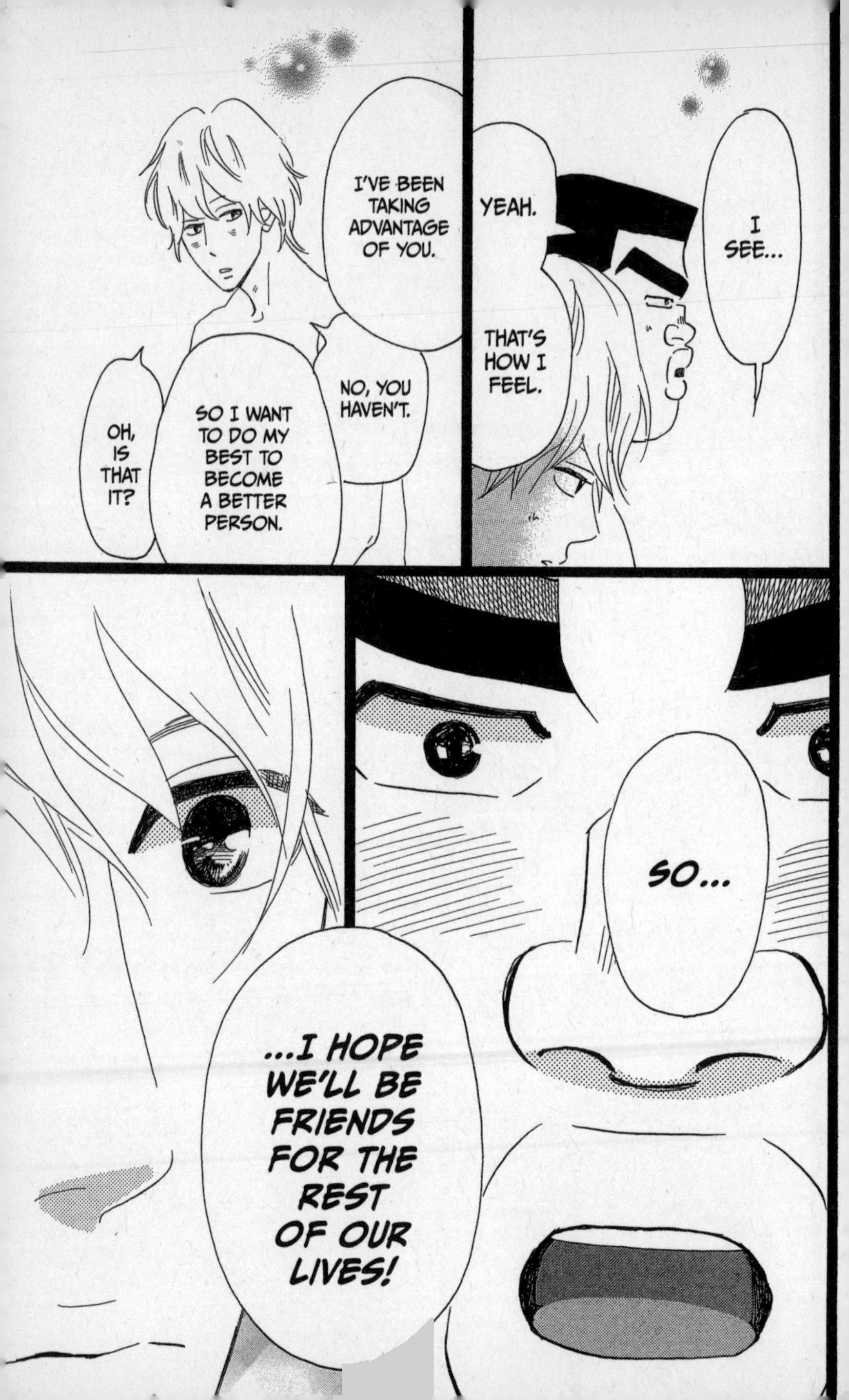
I SEE...
YEAH.
THAT'S HOW I FEEL.
I'VE BEEN TAKING ADVANTAGE OF YOU.
NO, YOU HAVEN'T.
SO I WANT TO DO MY BEST TO BECOME A BETTER PERSON.
OH, IS THAT IT?
SO...
...I HOPE WE'LL BE FRIENDS FOR THE REST OF OUR LIVES!

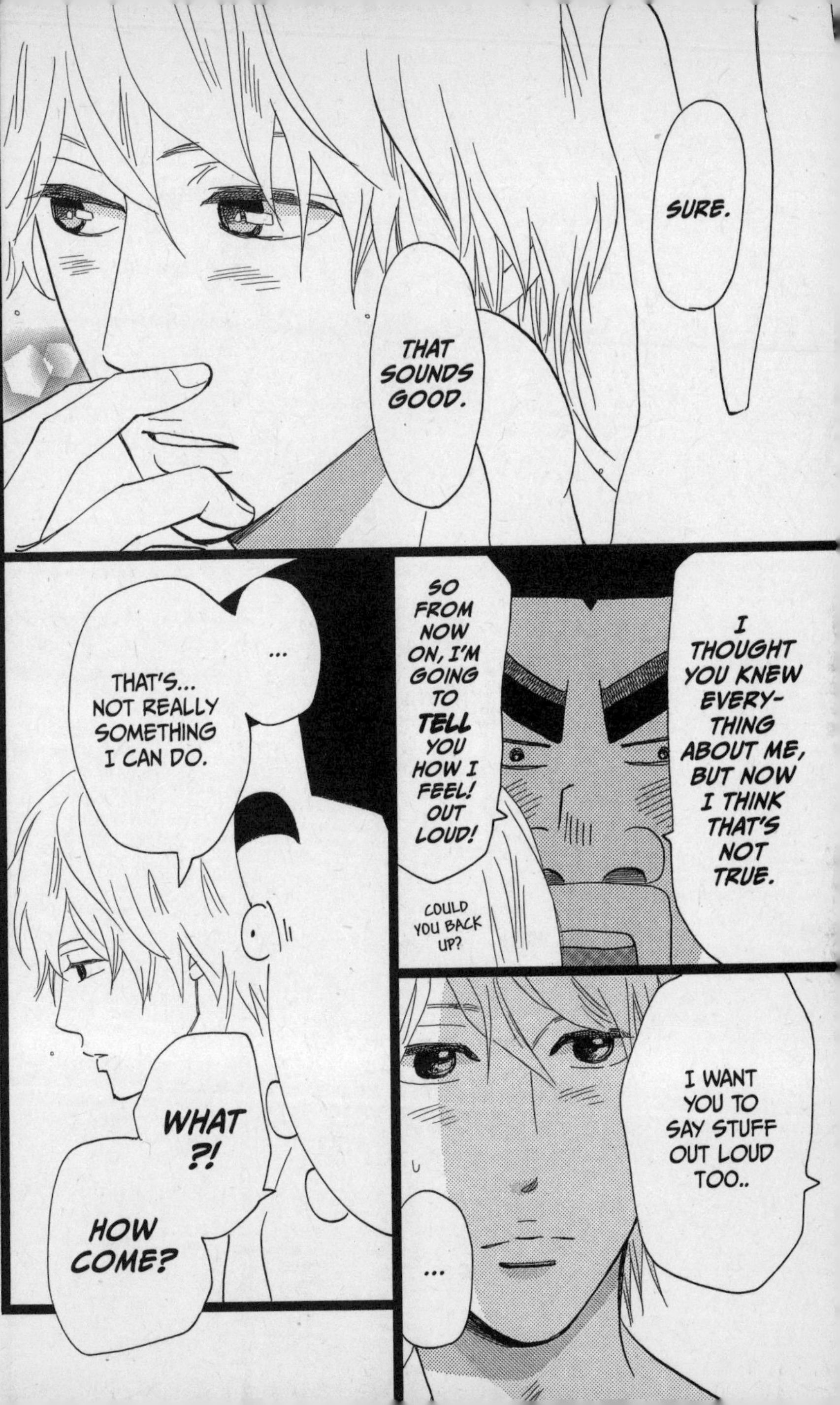
SURE.
THAT SOUNDS GOOD.
I THOUGHT YOU KNEW EVERY-THING ABOUT ME, BUT NOW I THINK THAT'S NOT TRUE.
SO FROM NOW ON, I'M GOING TO TELL YOU HOW I FEEL! OUT LOUD!
COULD YOU BACK UP?
I WANT YOU TO SAY STUFF OUT LOUD TOO..
...
...
THAT'S... NOT REALLY SOMETHING I CAN DO.
WHAT?!
HOW COME?

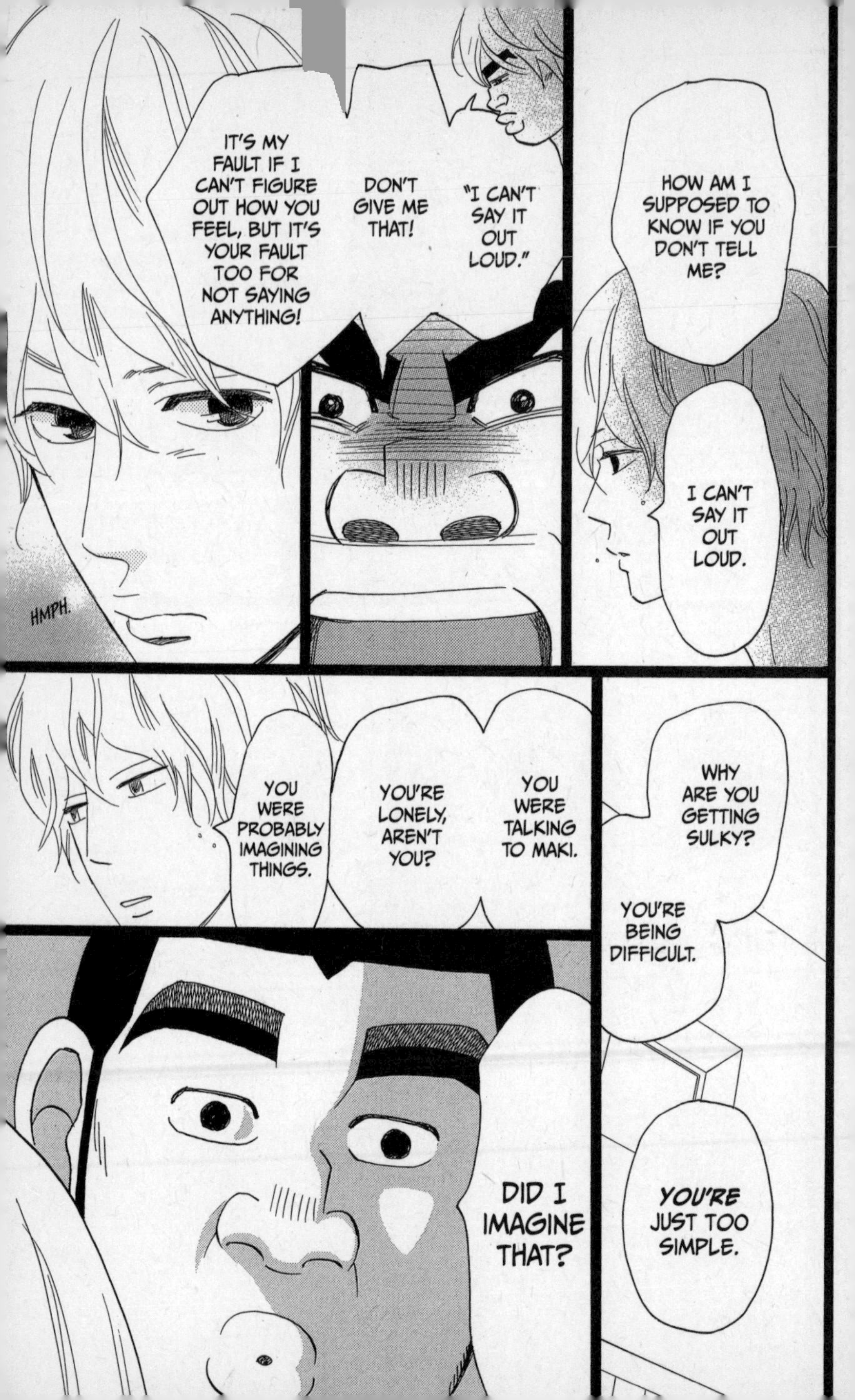
HOW AM I SUPPOSED TO KNOW IF YOU DON'T TELL ME?
I CAN'T SAY IT OUT LOUD.
"I CAN'T SAY IT OUT LOUD."
DON'T GIVE ME THAT!
IT'S MY FAULT IF I CAN'T FIGURE OUT HOW YOU FEEL, BUT IT'S YOUR FAULT TOO FOR NOT SAYING ANYTHING!
HMPH.
WHY ARE YOU GETTING SULKY?
YOU'RE BEING DIFFICULT.
YOU'RE JUST TOO SIMPLE.
YOU WERE TALKING TO MAKI.
YOU'RE LONELY, AREN'T YOU?
YOU WERE PROBABLY IMAGINING THINGS.
DID I IMAGINE THAT?

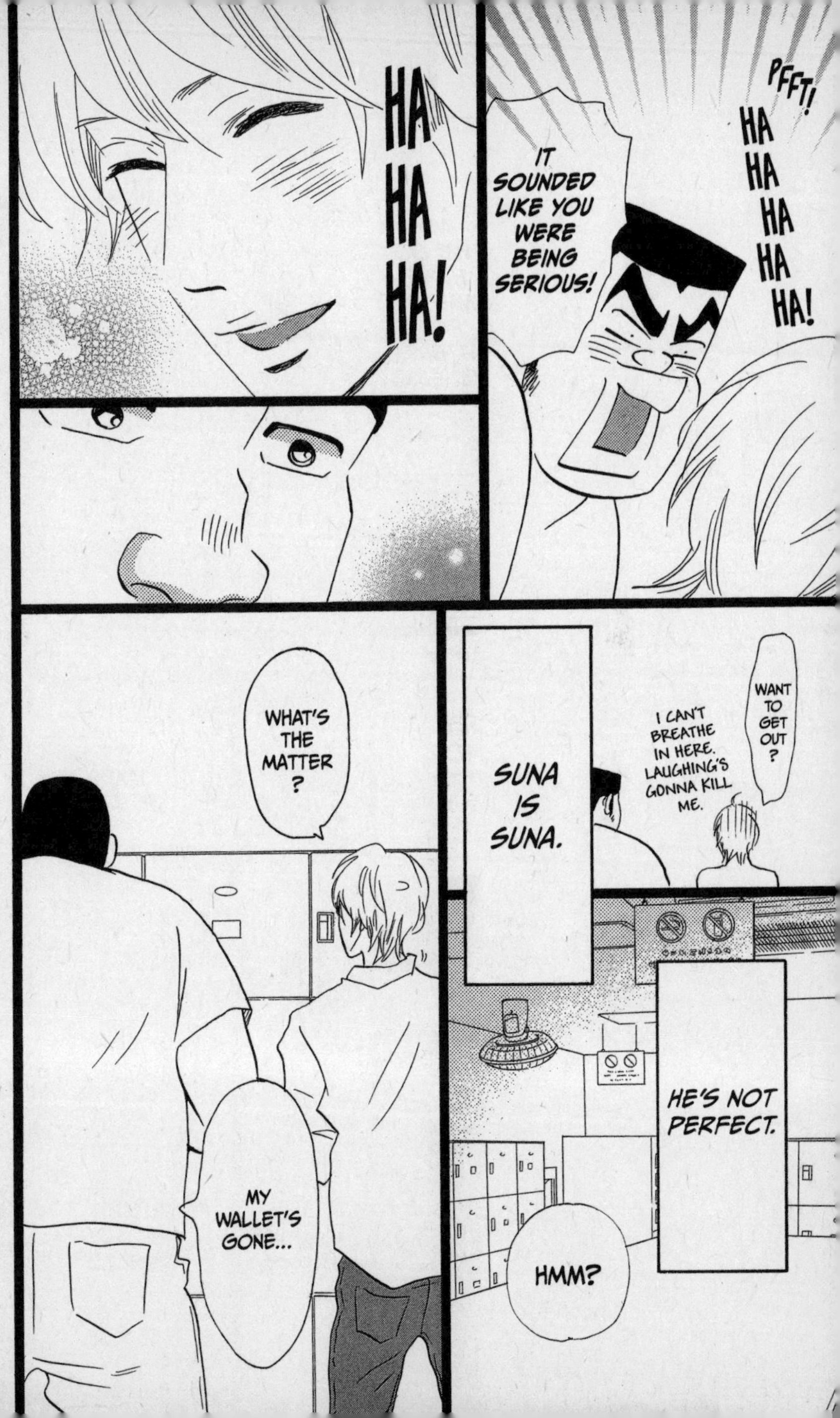
PFFT!
HA HA HA HA HA!
IT SOUNDED LIKE YOU WERE BEING SERIOUS!
HA HA HA!
WANT TO GET OUT?
I CAN'T BREATHE IN HERE. LAUGHING'S GONNA KILL ME.
SUNA IS SUNA.
HE'S NOT PERFECT.
HMM?
WHAT'S THE MATTER?
MY WALLET'S GONE...

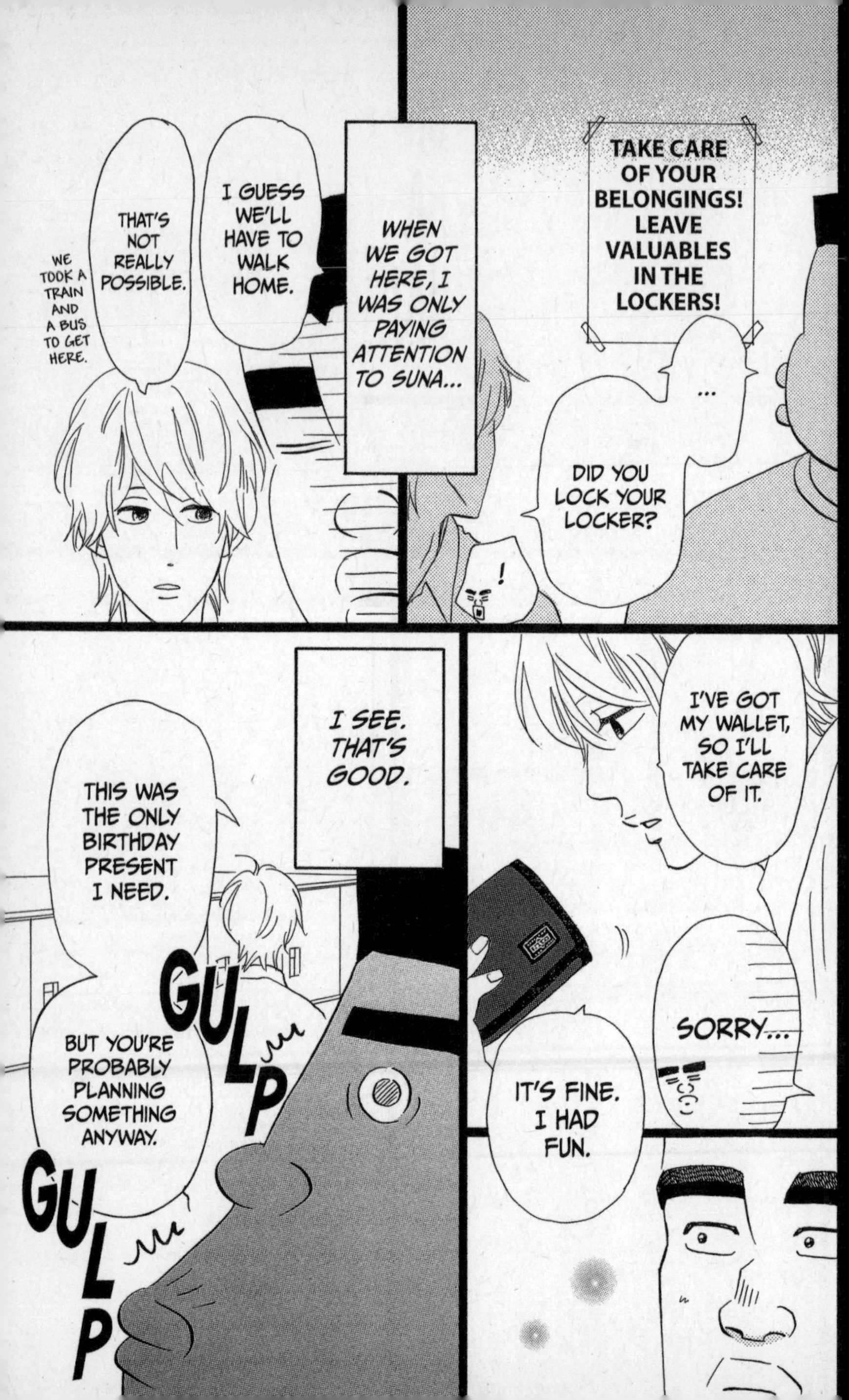
TAKE CARE OF YOUR BELONGINGS! LEAVE VALUABLES IN THE LOCKERS!
...
DID YOU LOCK YOUR LOCKER?
!
WHEN WE GOT HERE, I WAS ONLY PAYING ATTENTION TO SUNA...
I GUESS WE'LL HAVE TO WALK HOME.
THAT'S NOT REALLY POSSIBLE.
WE TOOK A TRAIN AND A BUS TO GET HERE.
I'VE GOT MY WALLET, SO I'LL TAKE CARE OF IT.
SORRY...
IT'S FINE. I HAD FUN.
I SEE. THAT'S GOOD.
THIS WAS THE ONLY BIRTHDAY PRESENT I NEED.
BUT YOU'RE PROBABLY PLANNING SOMETHING ANYWAY.
GULP
GULP

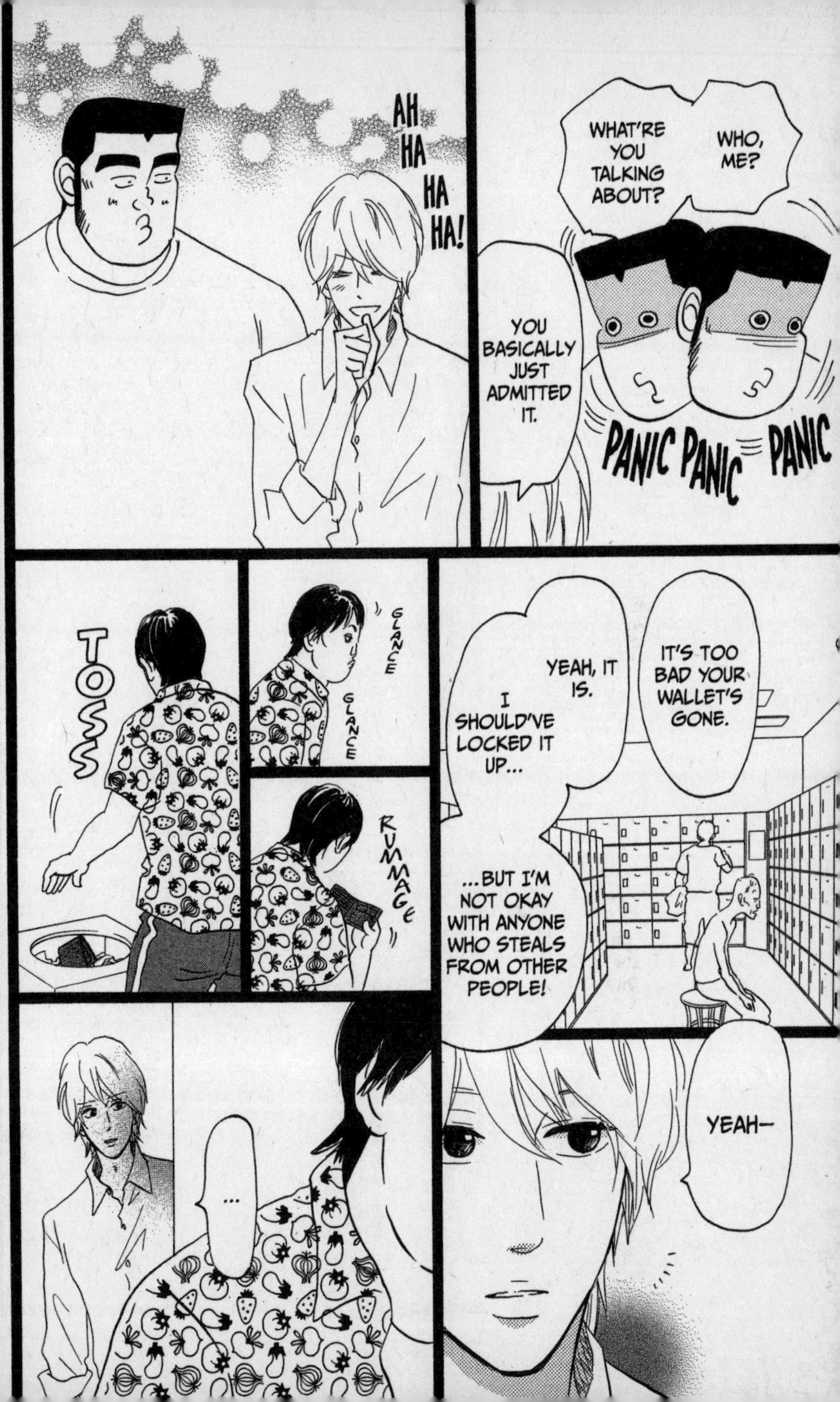
WHO, ME?
WHAT'RE YOU TALKING ABOUT?
YOU BASICALLY JUST ADMITTED IT.
PANIC PANIC PANIC
AH HA HA HA!
IT'S TOO BAD YOUR WALLET'S GONE.
YEAH, IT IS.
I SHOULD'VE LOCKED IT UP...
...BUT I'M NOT OKAY WITH ANYONE WHO STEALS FROM OTHER PEOPLE!
GLANCE
GLANCE
RUMMAGE
TOSS
YEAH—
...

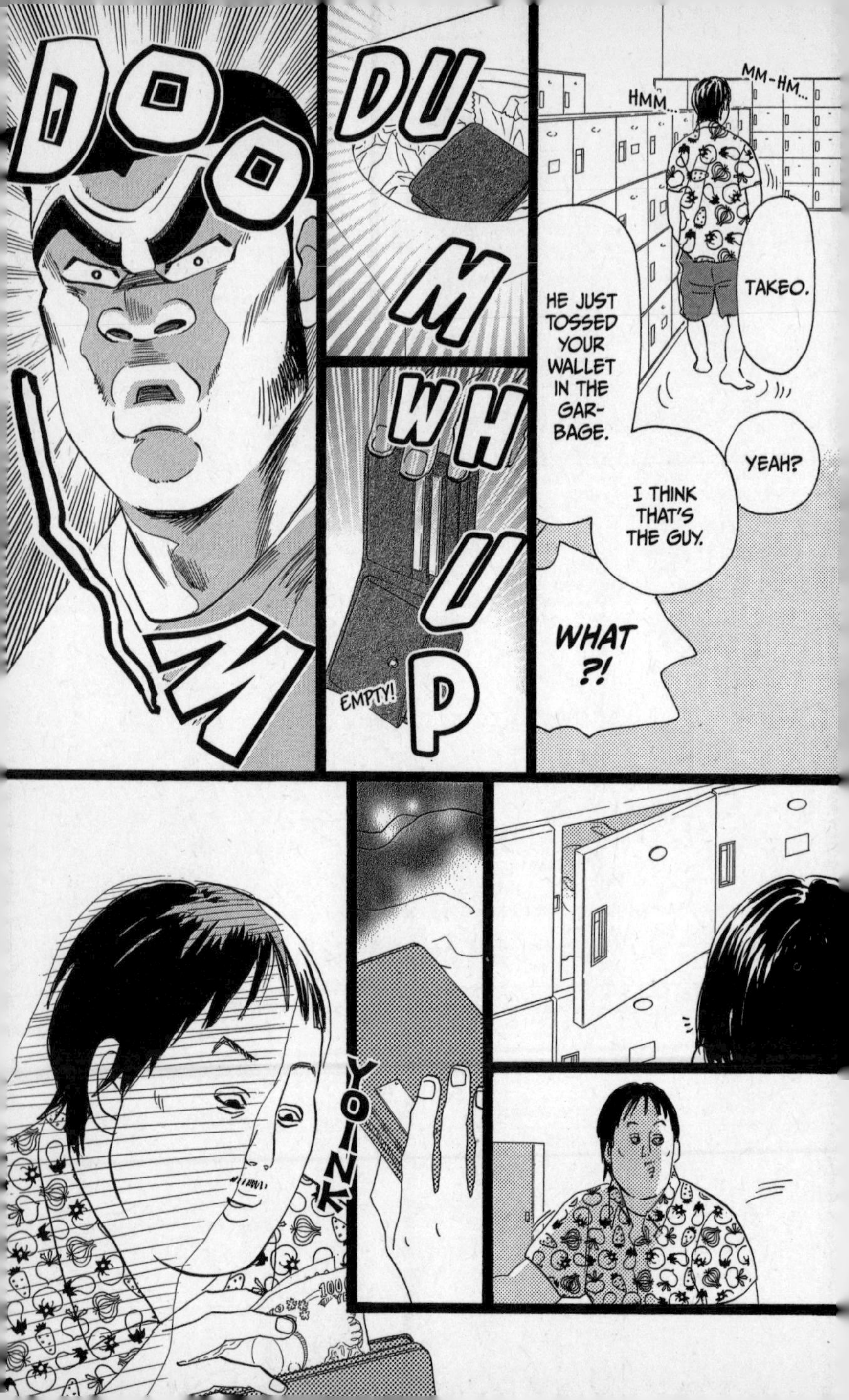
MM-HM...
HMM...
TAKEO.
HE JUST TOSSED YOUR WALLET IN THE GARBAGE.
YEAH?
I THINK THAT'S THE GUY.
WHAT ?!
DU
M
WH
U
P
EMPTY!
DOOO
M
YOINK

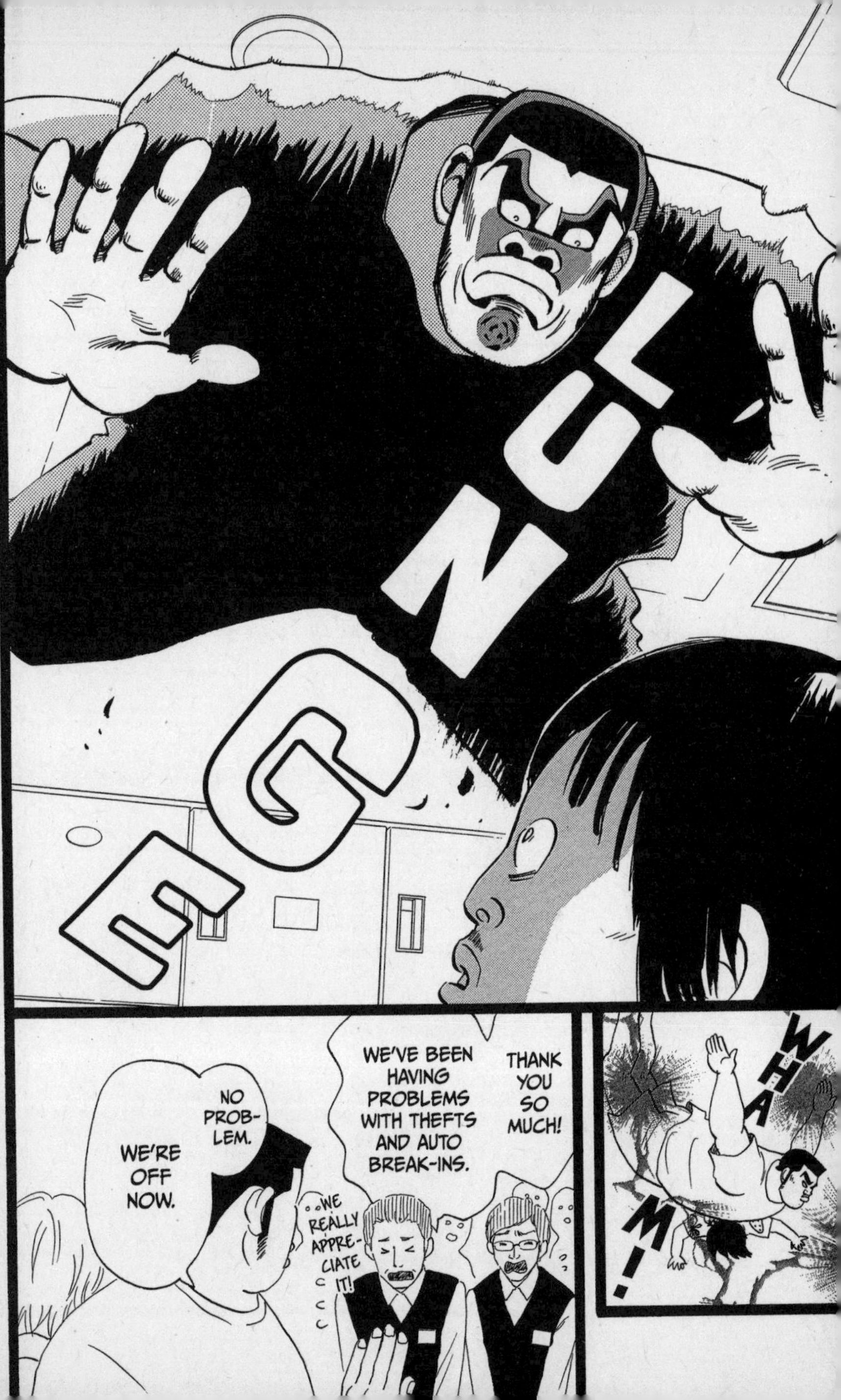
LUNGE
WHAM!
THANK YOU SO MUCH!
WE'VE BEEN HAVING PROBLEMS WITH THEFTS AND AUTO BREAK-INS.
WE REALLY APPRECIATE IT!
NO PROBLEM.
WE'RE OFF NOW.

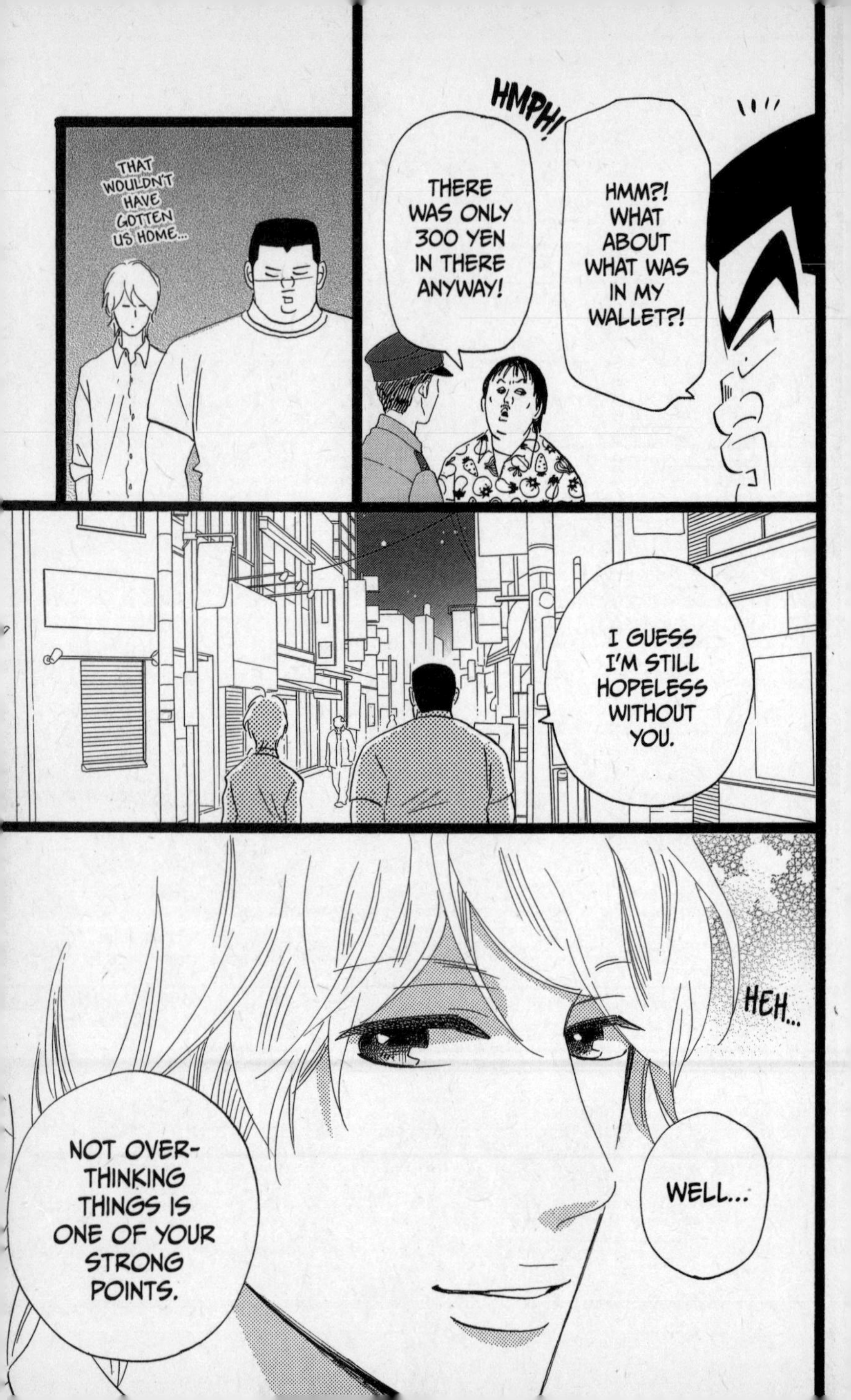
HMM?! WHAT ABOUT WHAT WAS IN MY WALLET?!
HMPH!
THERE WAS ONLY 300 YEN IN THERE ANYWAY!
THAT WOULDN'T HAVE GOTTEN US HOME...
I GUESS I'M STILL HOPELESS WITHOUT YOU.
HEH...
WELL...
NOT OVER-THINKING THINGS IS ONE OF YOUR STRONG POINTS.

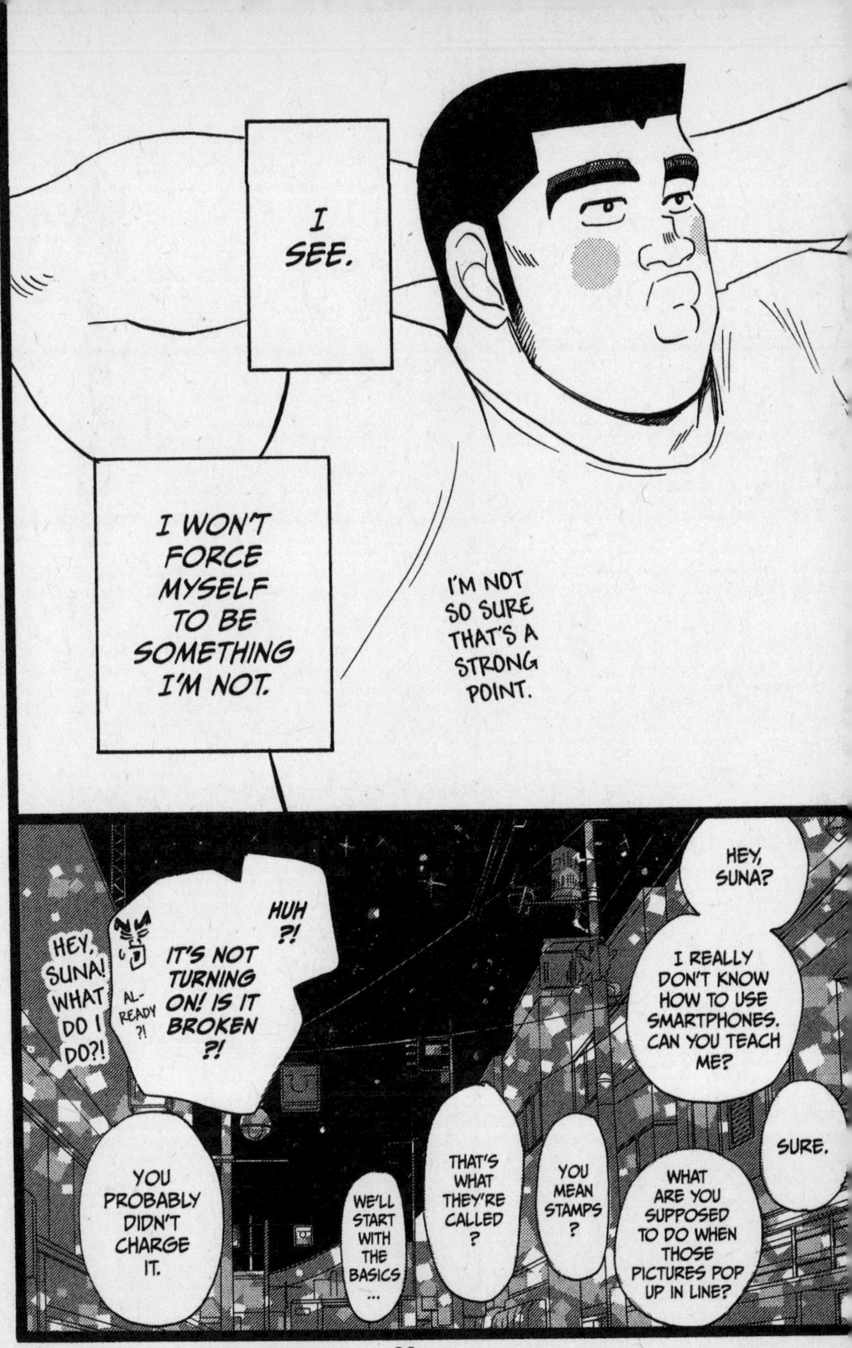
I SEE.
I WON'T FORCE MYSELF TO BE SOMETHING I'M NOT.
I'M NOT SO SURE THAT'S A STRONG POINT.
HEY, SUNA?
I REALLY DON'T KNOW HOW TO USE SMARTPHONES. CAN YOU TEACH ME?
SURE.
WHAT ARE YOU SUPPOSED TO DO WHEN THOSE PICTURES POP UP IN LINE?
YOU MEAN STAMPS?
THAT'S WHAT THEY'RE CALLED?
WE'LL START WITH THE BASICS...
HUH?!
IT'S NOT TURNING ON! IS IT BROKEN?!
AL-READY?!
HEY, SUNA! WHAT DO I DO?!
YOU PROBABLY DIDN'T CHARGE IT.

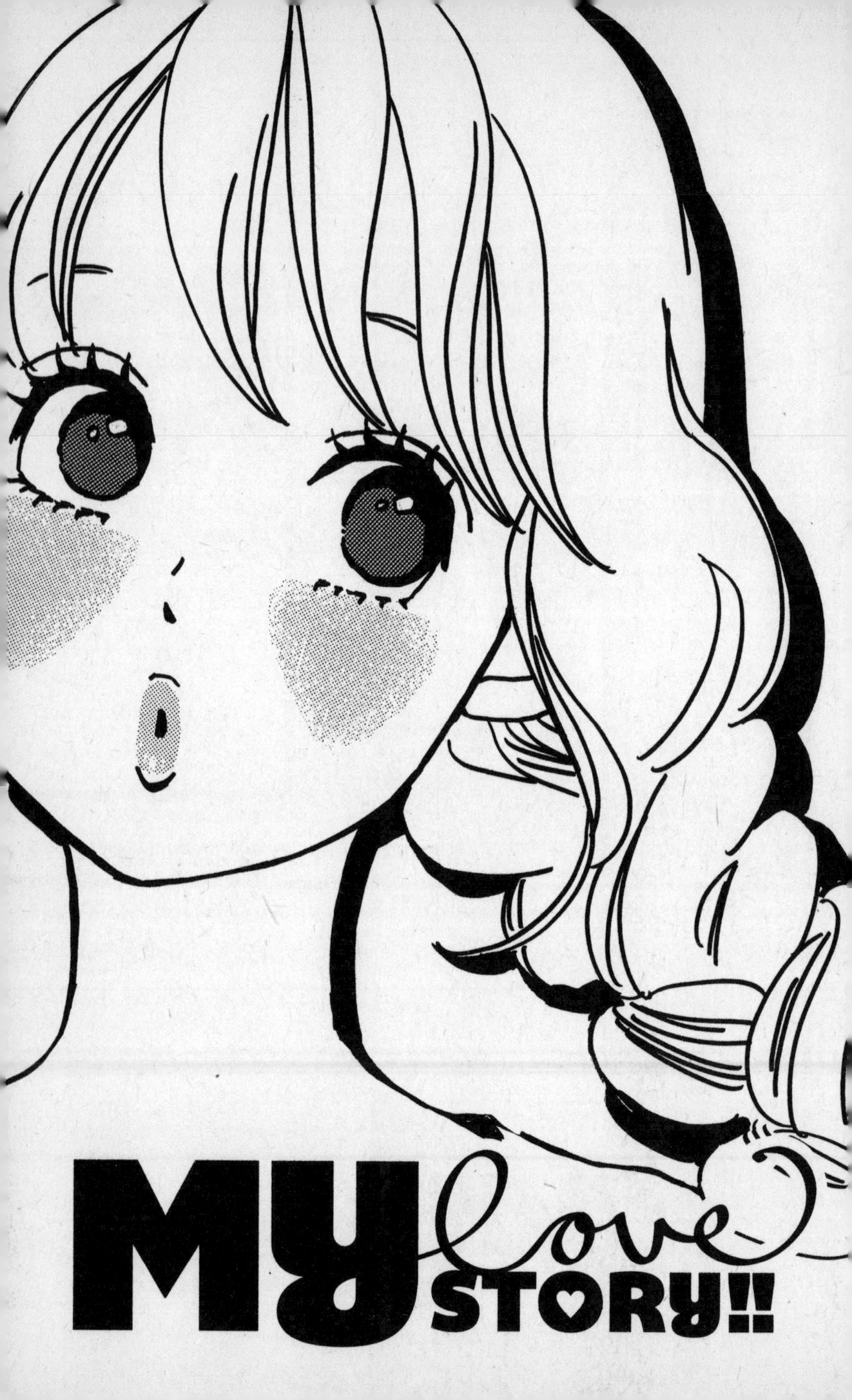
MY love STORY!!

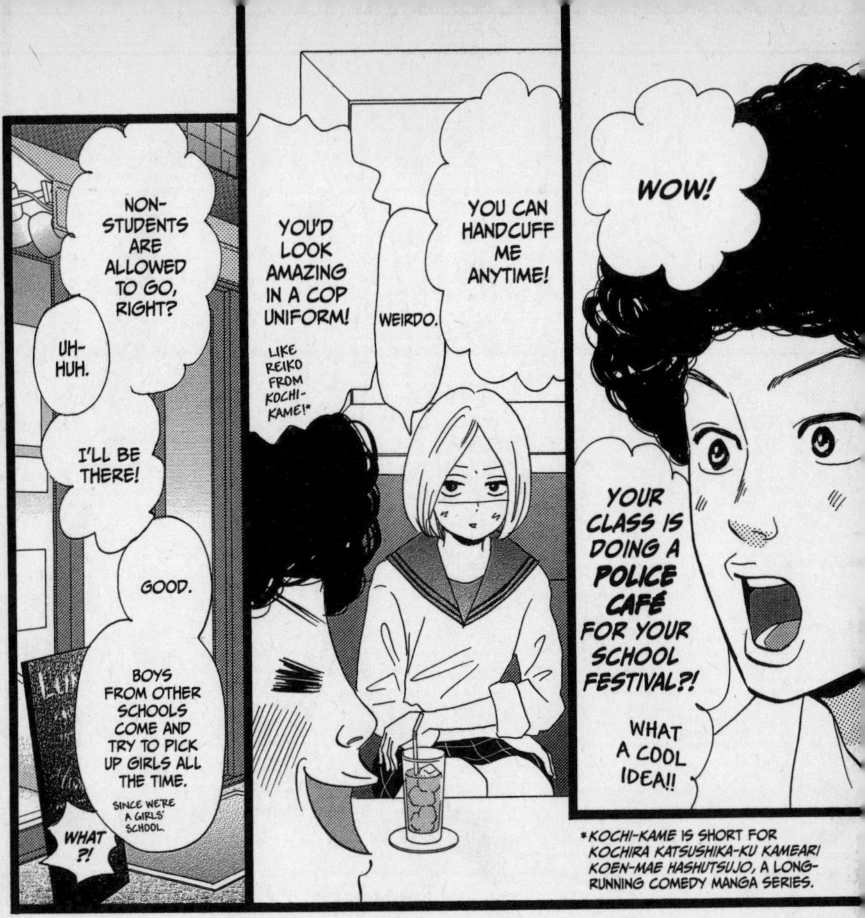
WOW!
YOUR CLASS IS DOING A POLICE CAFÉ FOR YOUR SCHOOL FESTIVAL?!
WHAT A COOL IDEA!!
YOU CAN HANDCUFF ME ANYTIME!
YOU'D LOOK AMAZING IN A COP UNIFORM!
WEIRDO.
LIKE REIKO FROM KOCHI-KAME!*
NON-STUDENTS ARE ALLOWED TO GO, RIGHT?
UH-HUH.
I'LL BE THERE!
GOOD.
BOYS FROM OTHER SCHOOLS COME AND TRY TO PICK UP GIRLS ALL THE TIME.
SINCE WE'RE A GIRLS' SCHOOL.
WHAT?!

*KOCHI-KAME IS SHORT FOR KOCHIRA KATSUSHIKA-KU KAMEARI KOEN-MAE HASHUTSUJO, A LONG-RUNNING COMEDY MANGA SERIES.

MY love STORY!!

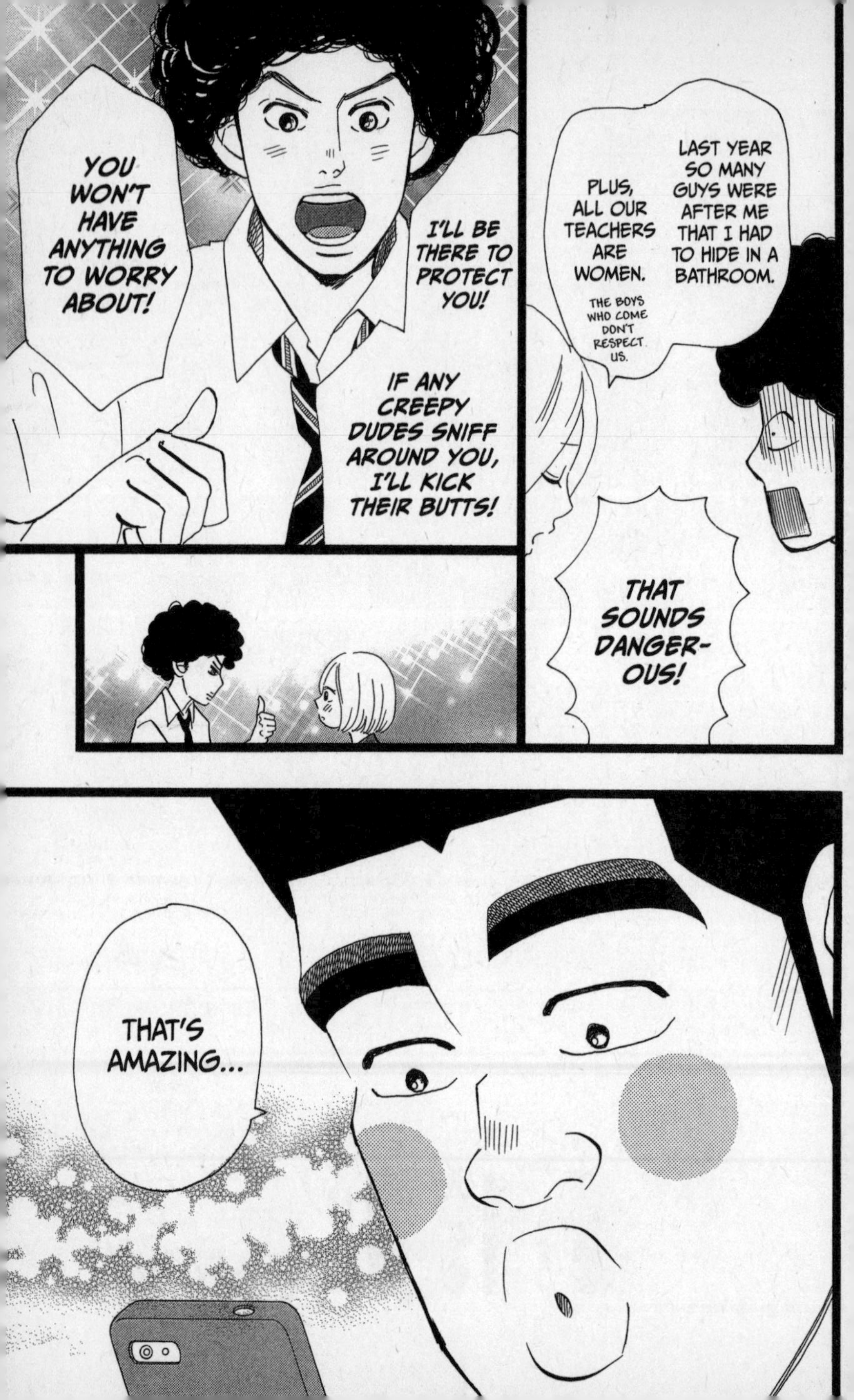
PLUS, ALL OUR TEACHERS ARE WOMEN.
THE BOYS WHO COME DON'T RESPECT US.
LAST YEAR SO MANY GUYS WERE AFTER ME THAT I HAD TO HIDE IN A BATHROOM.
THAT SOUNDS DANGER-OUS!
I'LL BE THERE TO PROTECT YOU!
IF ANY CREEPY DUDES SNIFF AROUND YOU, I'LL KICK THEIR BUTTS!
YOU WON'T HAVE ANYTHING TO WORRY ABOUT!
THAT'S AMAZING...

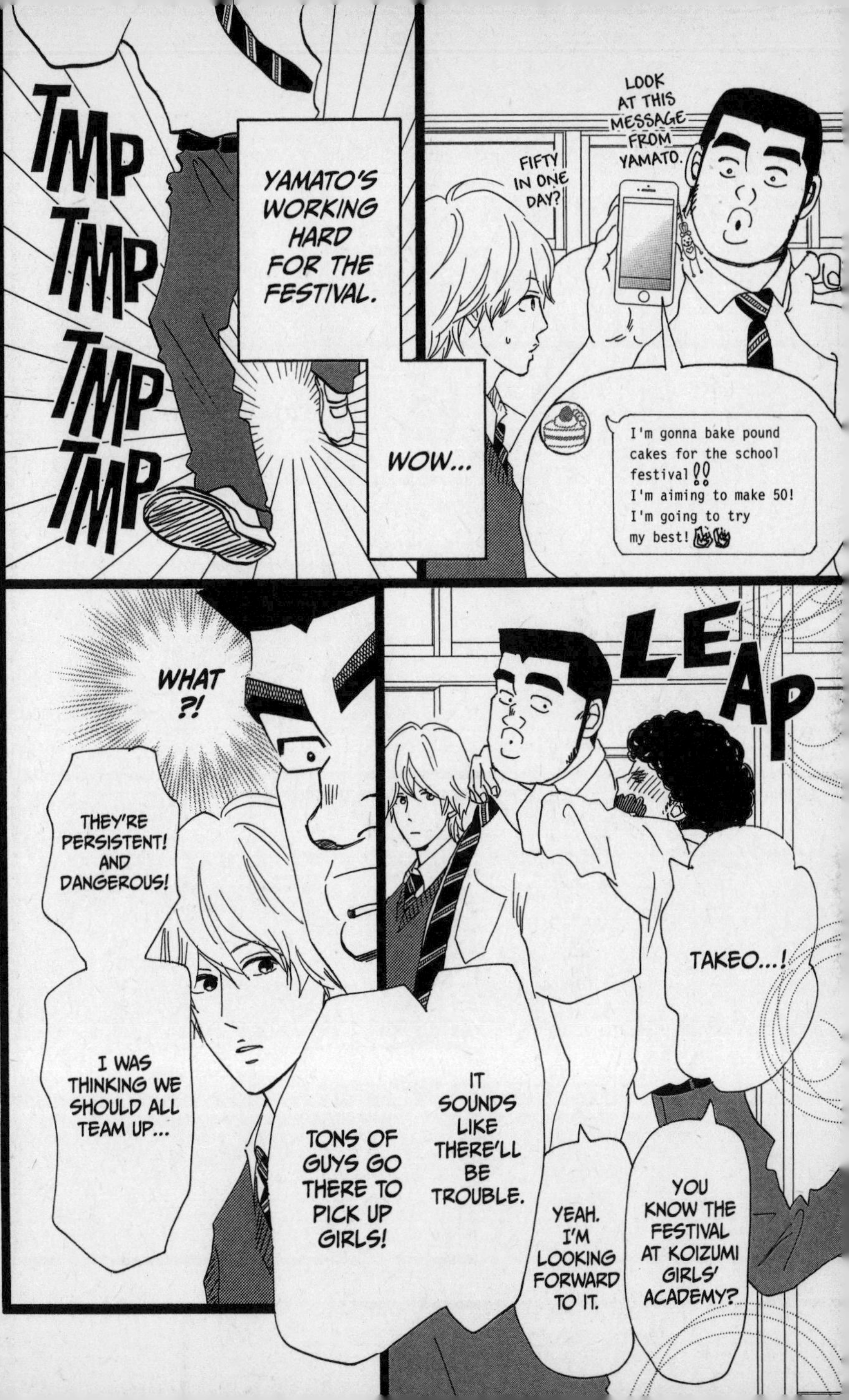
LOOK AT THIS MESSAGE FROM YAMATO.
I'm gonna bake pound cakes for the school festival!! I'm aiming to make 50! I'm going to try my best!
FIFTY IN ONE DAY?
WOW...
YAMATO'S WORKING HARD FOR THE FESTIVAL.
TMP TMP TMP TMP
LEAP
TAKEO...!
YOU KNOW THE FESTIVAL AT KOIZUMI GIRLS' ACADEMY?
YEAH. I'M LOOKING FORWARD TO IT.
IT SOUNDS LIKE THERE'LL BE TROUBLE.
TONS OF GUYS GO THERE TO PICK UP GIRLS!
WHAT?!
THEY'RE PERSISTENT! AND DANGEROUS!
I WAS THINKING WE SHOULD ALL TEAM UP...

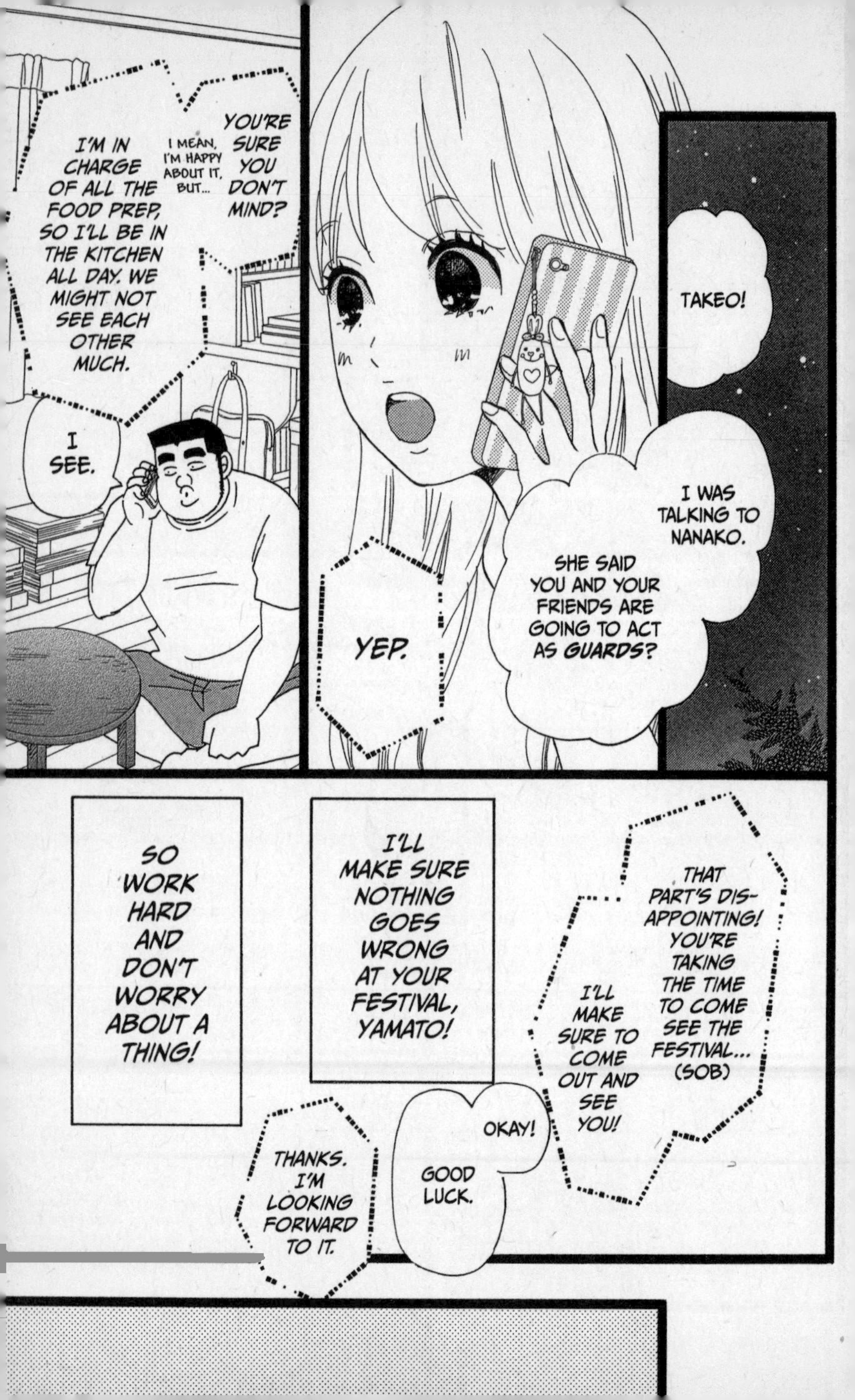
TAKEO!
I WAS TALKING TO NANAKO.
SHE SAID YOU AND YOUR FRIENDS ARE GOING TO ACT AS GUARDS?
YEP.
YOU'RE SURE YOU DON'T MIND?
I MEAN, I'M HAPPY ABOUT IT, BUT...
I'M IN CHARGE OF ALL THE FOOD PREP, SO I'LL BE IN THE KITCHEN ALL DAY. WE MIGHT NOT SEE EACH OTHER MUCH.
I SEE.
THAT PART'S DIS-APPOINTING! YOU'RE TAKING THE TIME TO COME SEE THE FESTIVAL... (SOB)
I'LL MAKE SURE TO COME OUT AND SEE YOU!
I'LL MAKE SURE NOTHING GOES WRONG AT YOUR FESTIVAL, YAMATO!
SO WORK HARD AND DON'T WORRY ABOUT A THING!
OKAY!
GOOD LUCK.
THANKS. I'M LOOKING FORWARD TO IT.

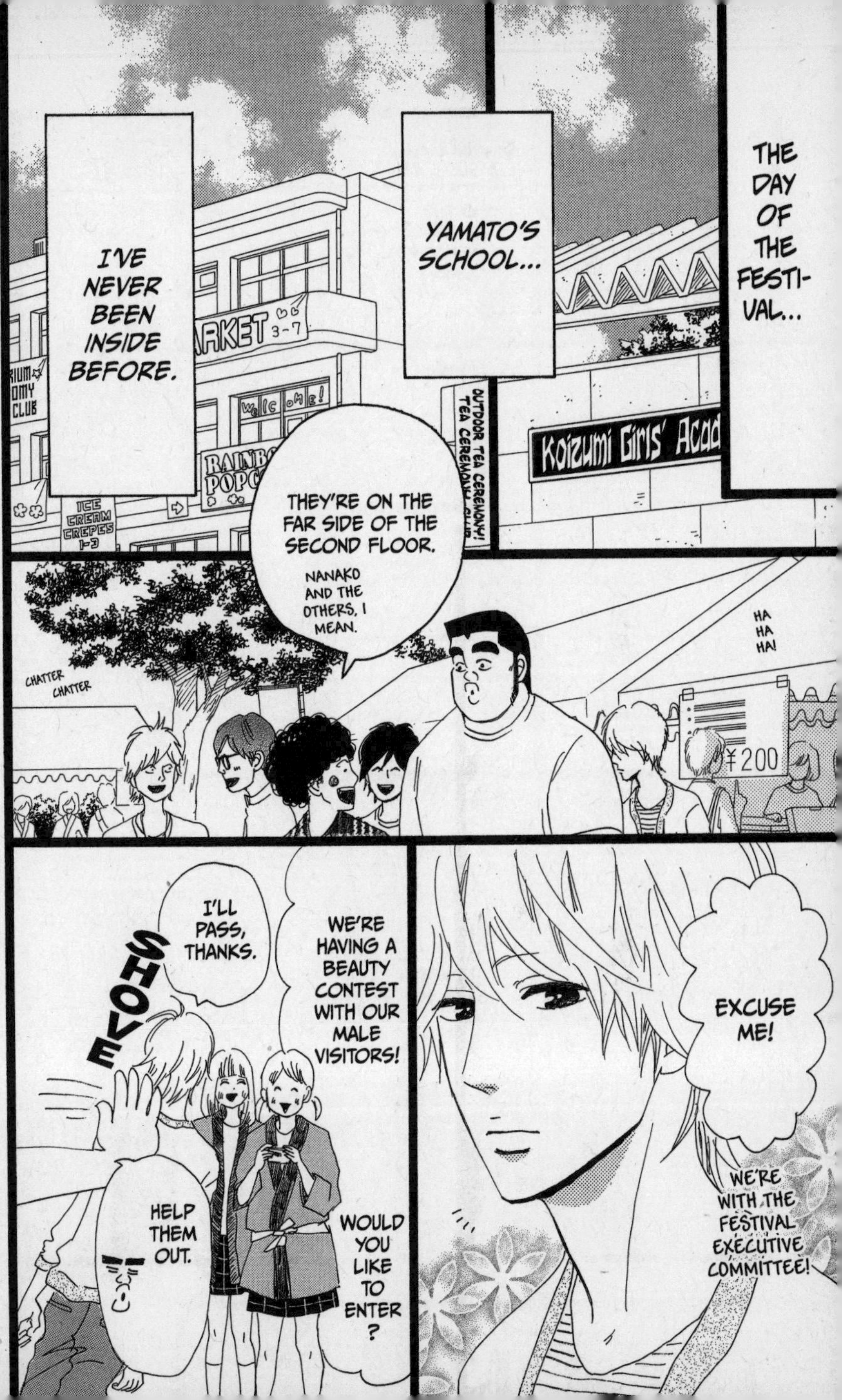
THE DAY OF THE FESTIVAL...
Koizumi Girls' Acad
OUTDOOR TEA CEREMONY!
YAMATO'S SCHOOL...
I'VE NEVER BEEN INSIDE BEFORE.
ARKET 3-7
WELCOME!
ICE CREAM CREPES 1-3
HA HA HA!
¥200
THEY'RE ON THE FAR SIDE OF THE SECOND FLOOR.
NANAKO AND THE OTHERS, I MEAN.
CHATTER CHATTER
EXCUSE ME!
WE'RE WITH THE FESTIVAL EXECUTIVE COMMITTEE!
WE'RE HAVING A BEAUTY CONTEST WITH OUR MALE VISITORS!
WOULD YOU LIKE TO ENTER?
I'LL PASS, THANKS.
SHOVE
HELP THEM OUT.

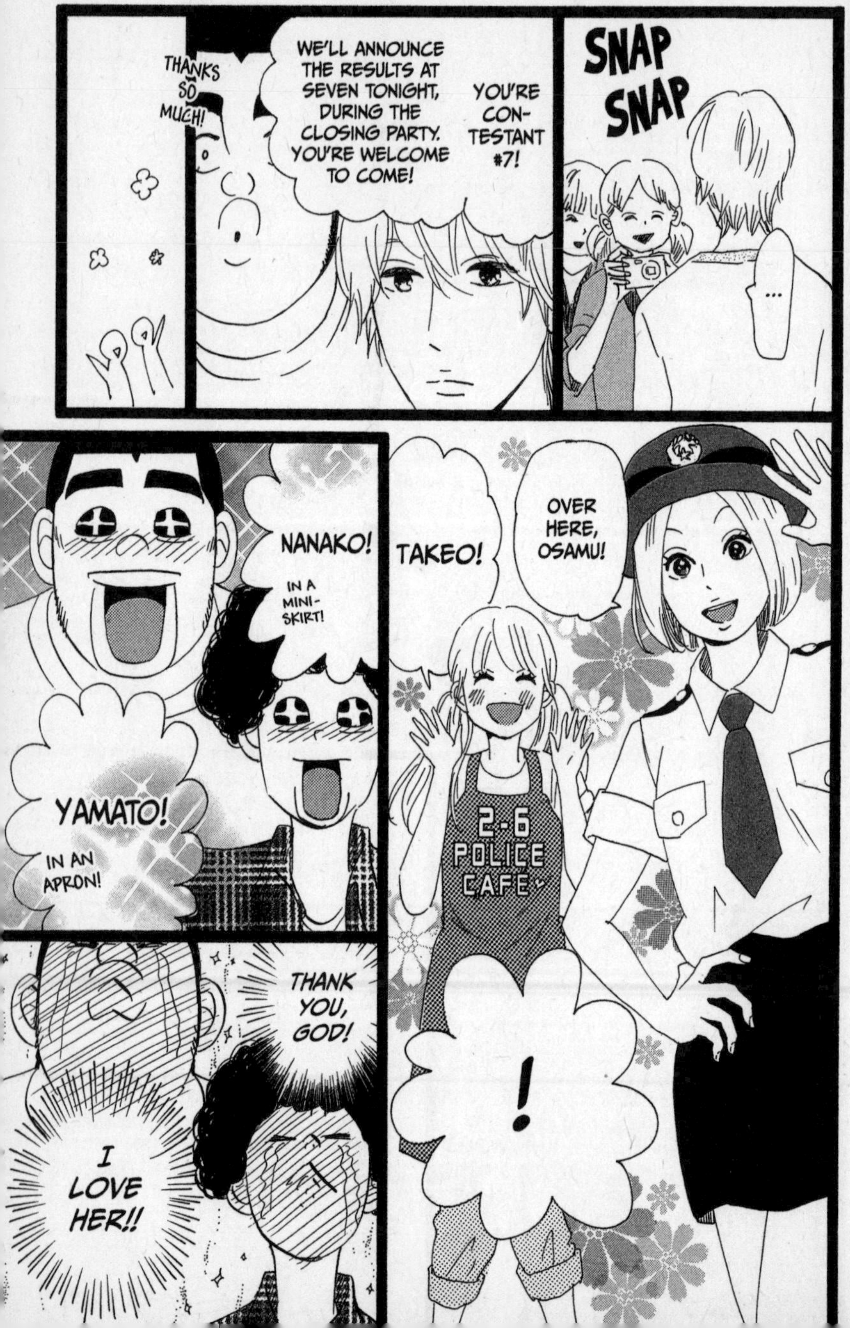
SNAP
SNAP
...
YOU'RE CONTESTANT #7!
WE'LL ANNOUNCE THE RESULTS AT SEVEN TONIGHT, DURING THE CLOSING PARTY. YOU'RE WELCOME TO COME!
THANKS SO MUCH!
OVER HERE, OSAMU!
TAKEO!
!
NANAKO!
IN A MINI-SKIRT!
YAMATO!
IN AN APRON!
THANK YOU, GOD!
I LOVE HER!!

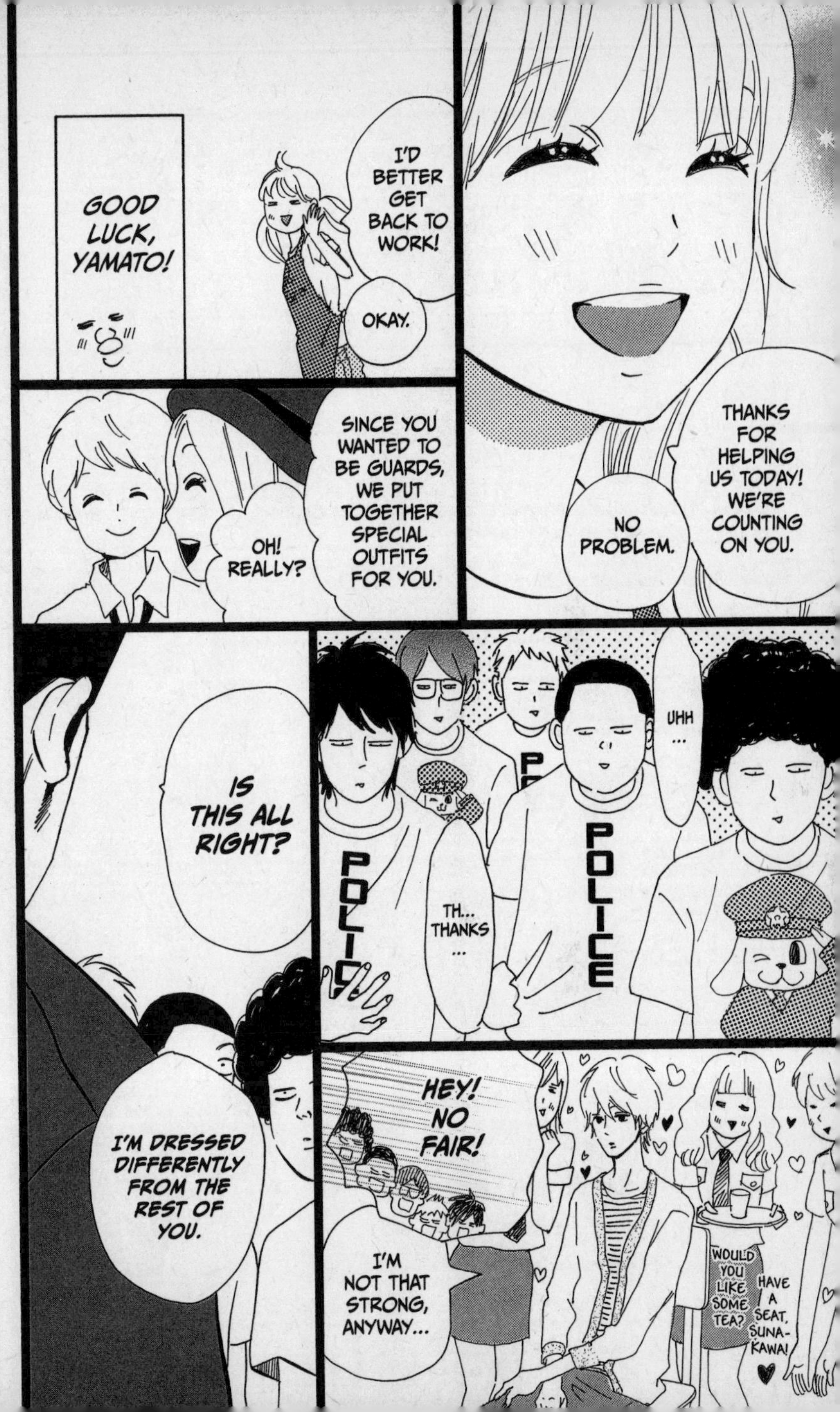
THANKS FOR HELPING US TODAY! WE'RE COUNTING ON YOU.
NO PROBLEM.
I'D BETTER GET BACK TO WORK!
OKAY.
GOOD LUCK, YAMATO!
SINCE YOU WANTED TO BE GUARDS, WE PUT TOGETHER SPECIAL OUTFITS FOR YOU.
OH! REALLY?
UHH...
POLICE
POLICE
TH... THANKS...
HAVE A SEAT, SUNAKAWA!
WOULD YOU LIKE SOME TEA?
HEY! NO FAIR!
I'M NOT THAT STRONG, ANYWAY...
IS THIS ALL RIGHT?
I'M DRESSED DIFFERENTLY FROM THE REST OF YOU.

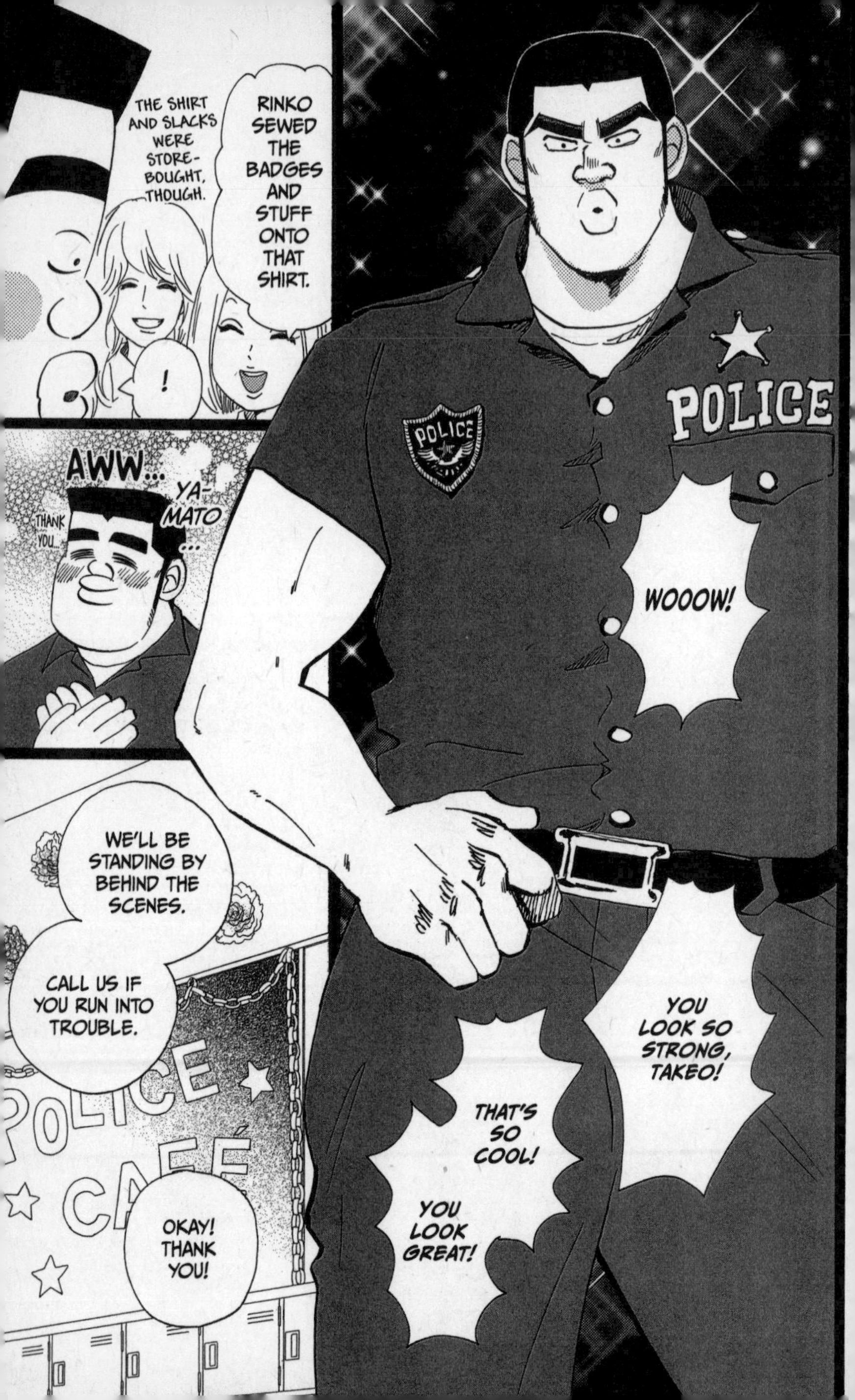
POLICE
POLICE
WOOOW!
YOU LOOK SO STRONG, TAKEO!
THAT'S SO COOL!
YOU LOOK GREAT!
RINKO SEWED THE BADGES AND STUFF ONTO THAT SHIRT.
THE SHIRT AND SLACKS WERE STORE-BOUGHT, THOUGH.
!
YA-MATO...
AWW...
THANK YOU...
WE'LL BE STANDING BY BEHIND THE SCENES.
CALL US IF YOU RUN INTO TROUBLE.
POLICE CAFÉ
OKAY! THANK YOU!

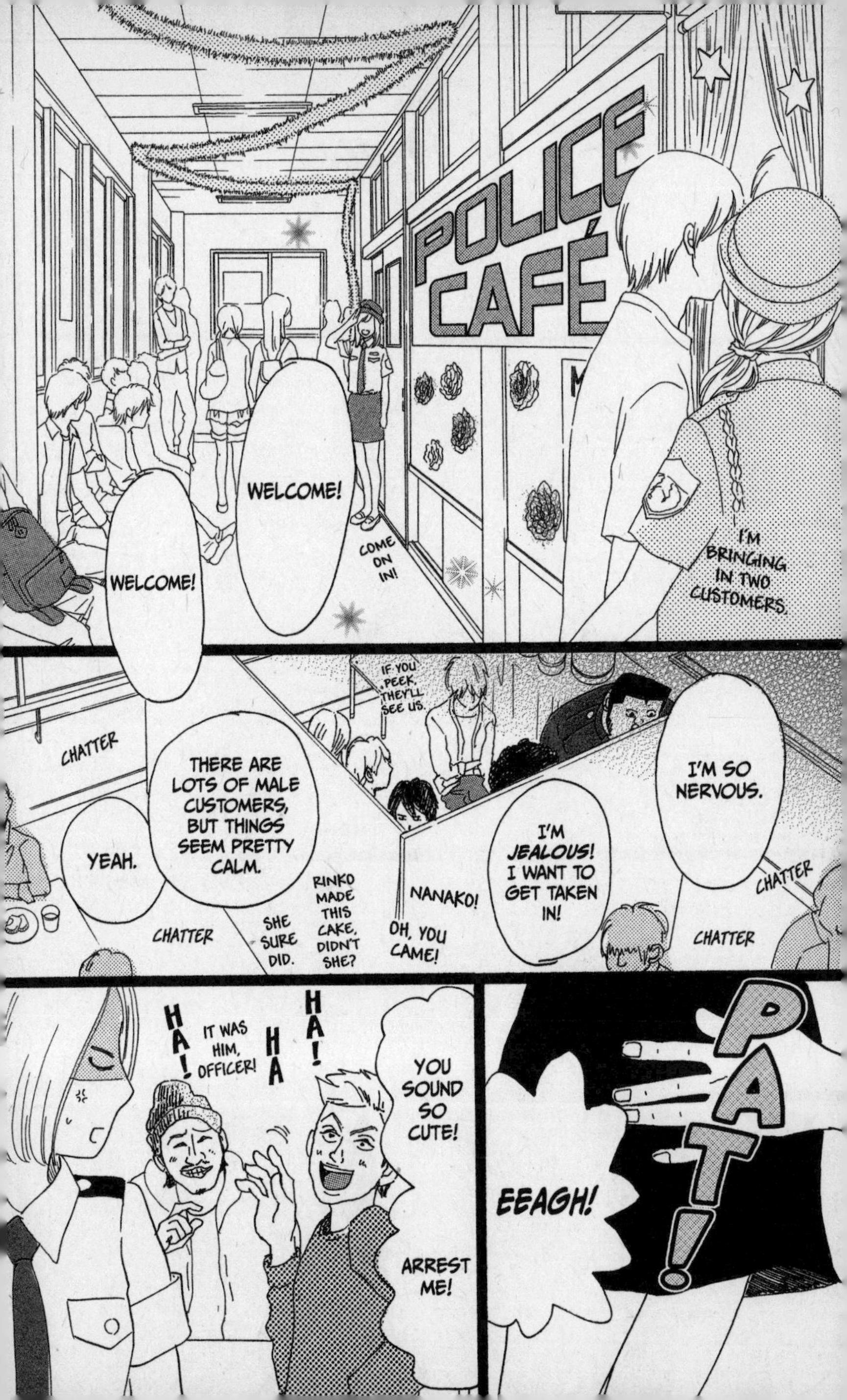
POLICE CAFÉ
I'M BRINGING IN TWO CUSTOMERS.
WELCOME!
COME ON IN!
WELCOME!
I'M SO NERVOUS.
CHATTER
I'M JEALOUS! I WANT TO GET TAKEN IN!
IF YOU PEEK, THEY'LL SEE US.
NANAKO!
OH, YOU CAME!
CHATTER
THERE ARE LOTS OF MALE CUSTOMERS, BUT THINGS SEEM PRETTY CALM.
RINKO MADE THIS CAKE, DIDN'T SHE?
SHE SURE DID.
YEAH.
CHATTER
CHATTER
PAT!
EEAGH!
YOU SOUND SO CUTE!
ARREST ME!
HA!
HA
IT WAS HIM, OFFICER!
HA!

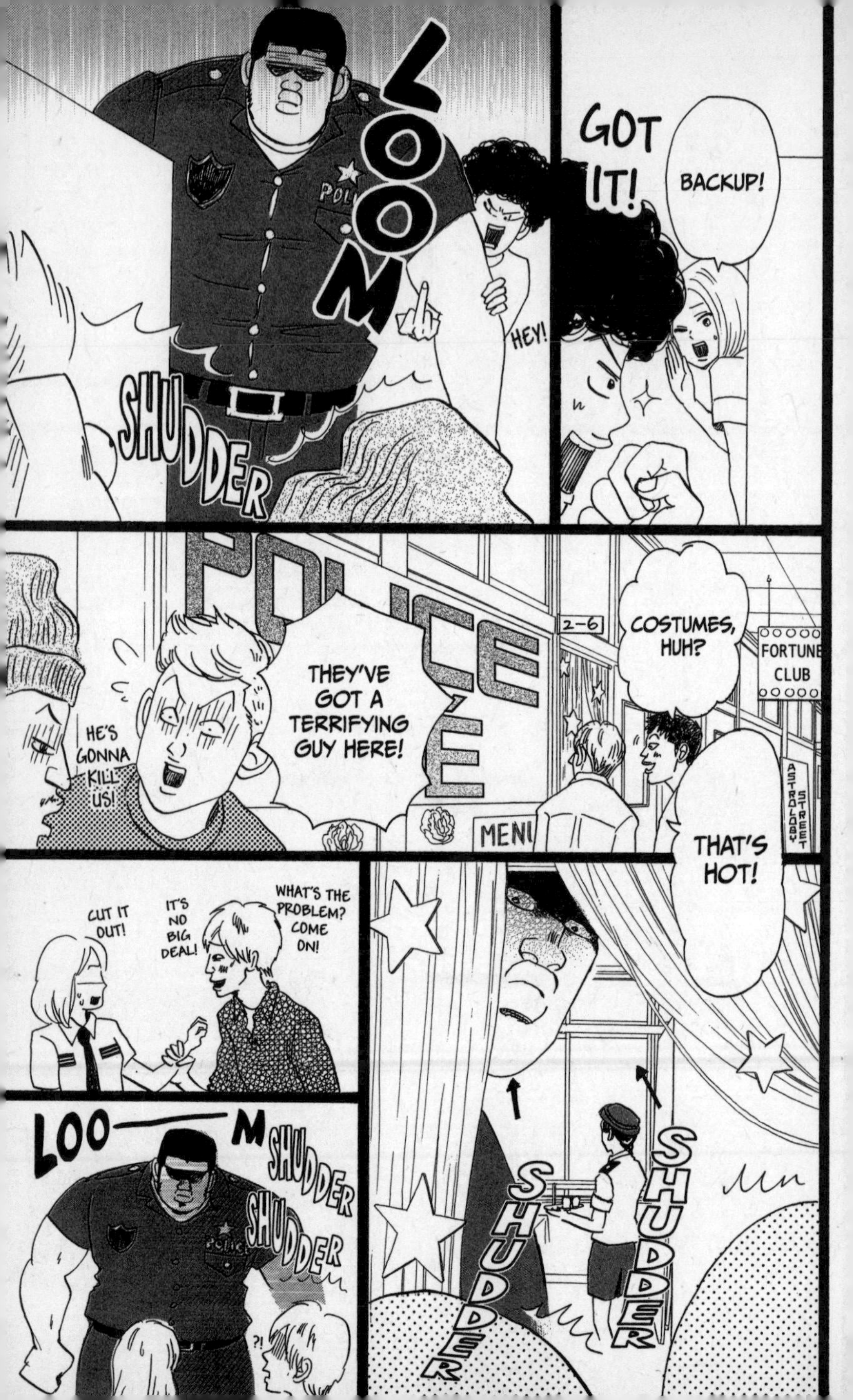
BACKUP!
GOT IT!
LOOM
HEY!
SHUDDER
COSTUMES, HUH?
FORTUNE CLUB
2-6
THAT'S HOT!
ASTROLOGY STREET
THEY'VE GOT A TERRIFYING GUY HERE!
HE'S GONNA KILL US!
SHUDDER
SHUDDER
WHAT'S THE PROBLEM? COME ON!
IT'S NO BIG DEAL!
CUT IT OUT!
LOO——M
SHUDDER
SHUDDER
?!

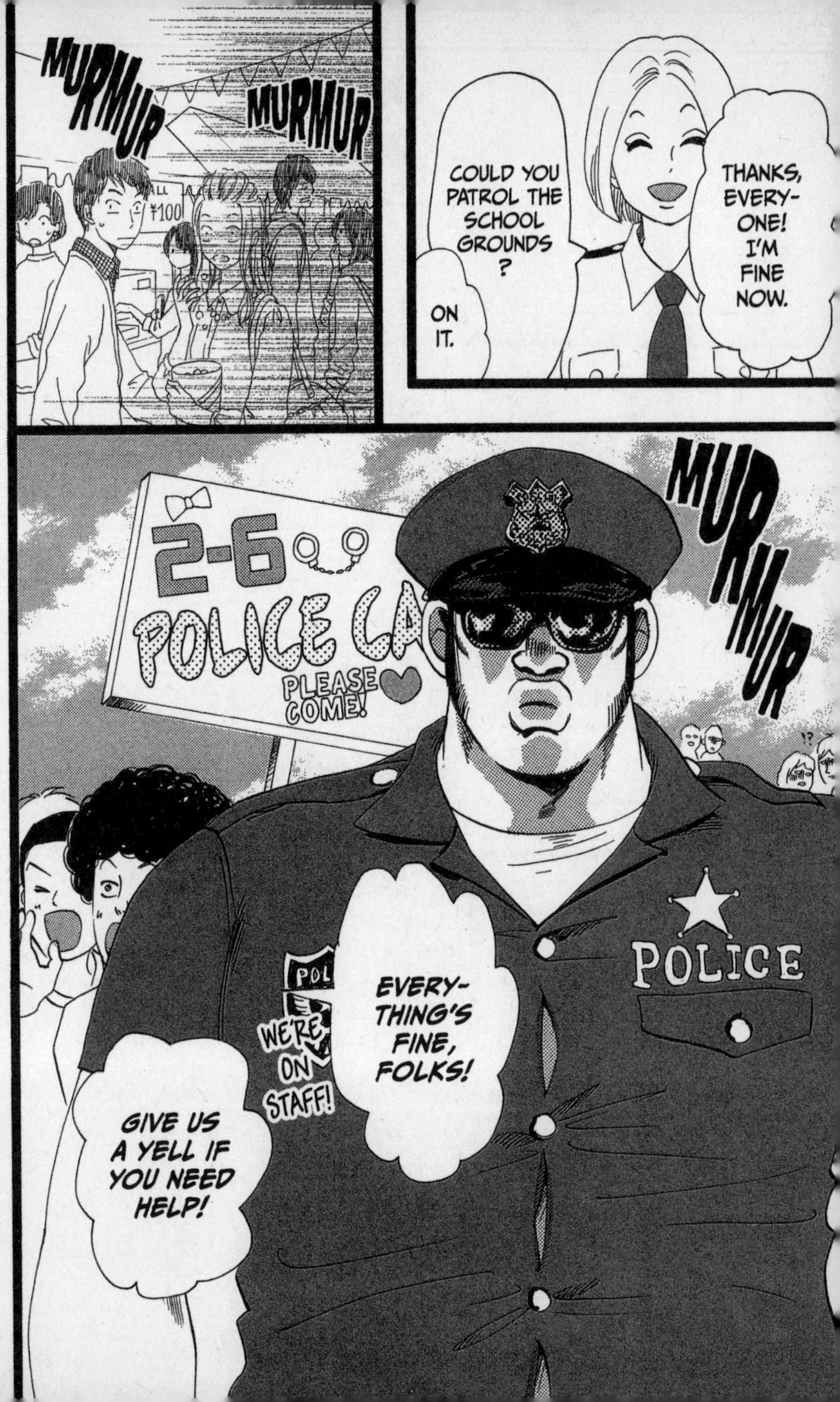
THANKS, EVERYONE! I'M FINE NOW.
COULD YOU PATROL THE SCHOOL GROUNDS?
ON IT.
MURMUR
MURMUR
¥100
2-6
POLICE CA
PLEASE COME!
MURMUR
POLICE
POL
EVERYTHING'S FINE, FOLKS!
WE'RE ON STAFF!
GIVE US A YELL IF YOU NEED HELP!

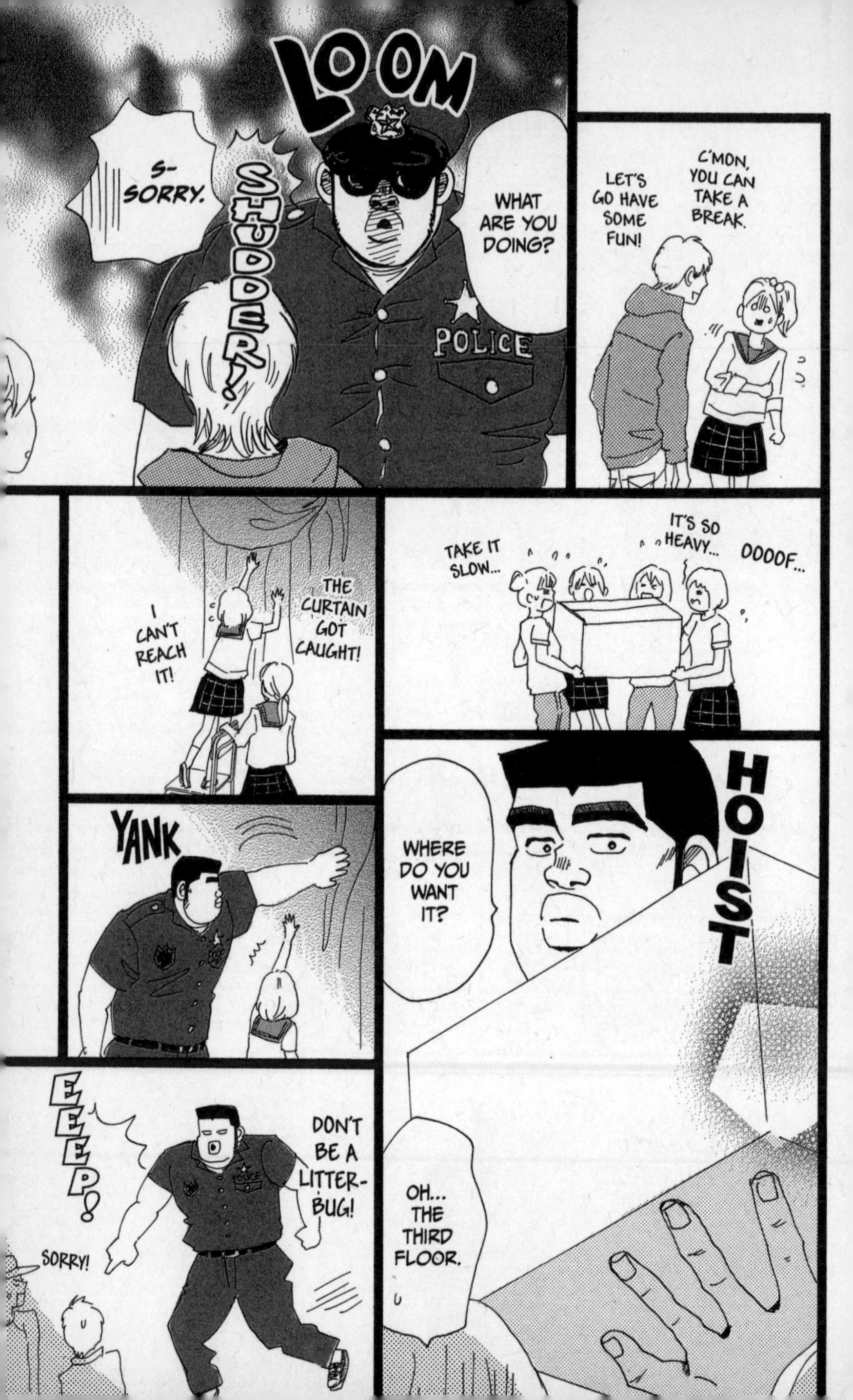
C'MON, YOU CAN TAKE A BREAK.
LET'S GO HAVE SOME FUN!
LOOM
WHAT ARE YOU DOING?
SHUDDER!
S-SORRY.
OOOOF...
IT'S SO HEAVY...
TAKE IT SLOW...
THE CURTAIN GOT CAUGHT!
I CAN'T REACH IT!
HOIST
WHERE DO YOU WANT IT?
OH... THE THIRD FLOOR.
YANK
DON'T BE A LITTER-BUG!
EEEP!
SORRY!

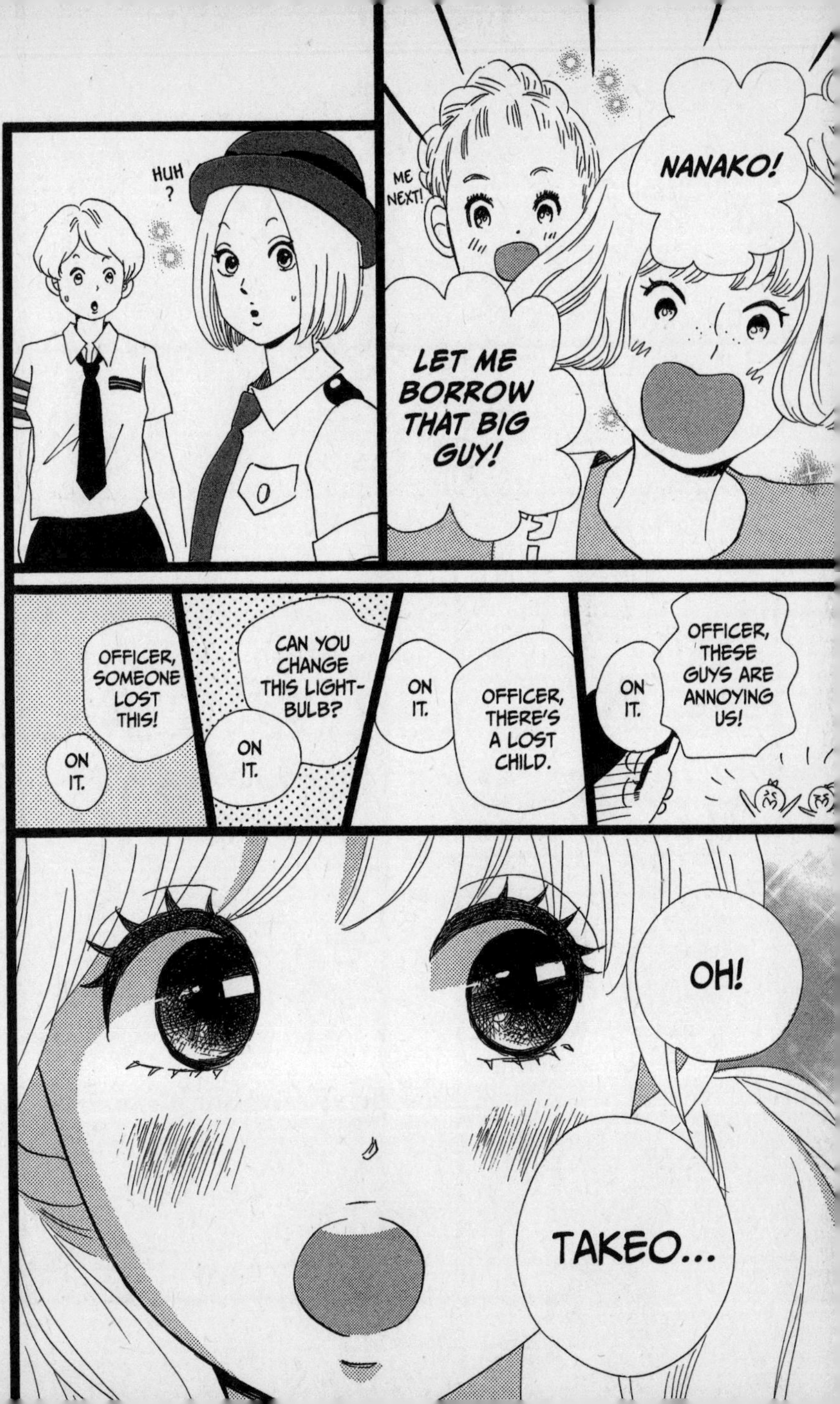
NANAKO!
ME NEXT!
LET ME BORROW THAT BIG GUY!
HUH?
OFFICER, THESE GUYS ARE ANNOYING US!
ON IT.
OFFICER, THERE'S A LOST CHILD.
ON IT.
CAN YOU CHANGE THIS LIGHT-BULB?
ON IT.
OFFICER, SOMEONE LOST THIS!
ON IT.
OH!
TAKEO...

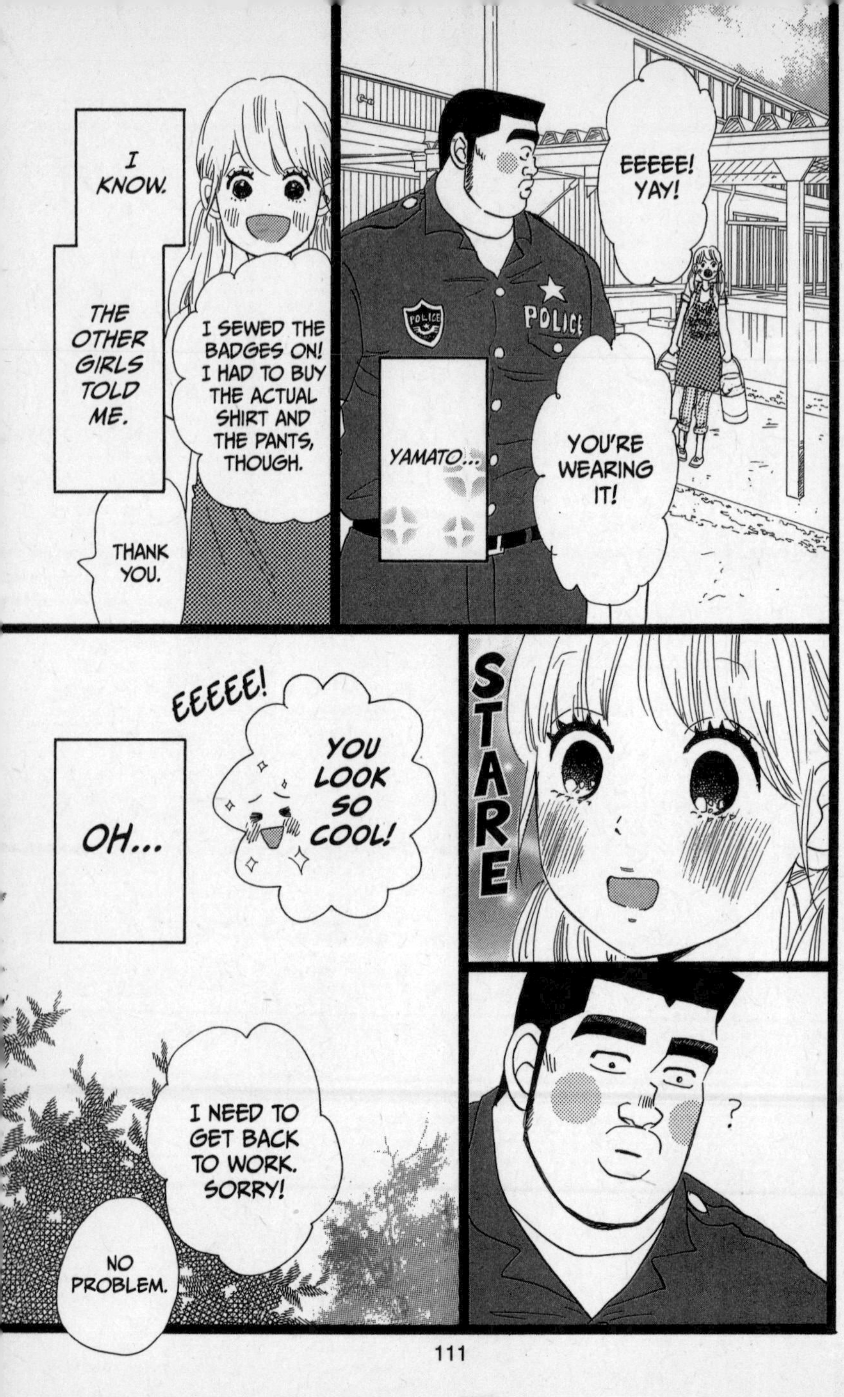
EEEEE! YAY!
YOU'RE WEARING IT!
YAMATO...
I SEWED THE BADGES ON! I HAD TO BUY THE ACTUAL SHIRT AND THE PANTS, THOUGH.
I KNOW.
THE OTHER GIRLS TOLD ME.
THANK YOU.
STARE
EEEEE!
YOU LOOK SO COOL!
OH...
?
I NEED TO GET BACK TO WORK. SORRY!
NO PROBLEM.

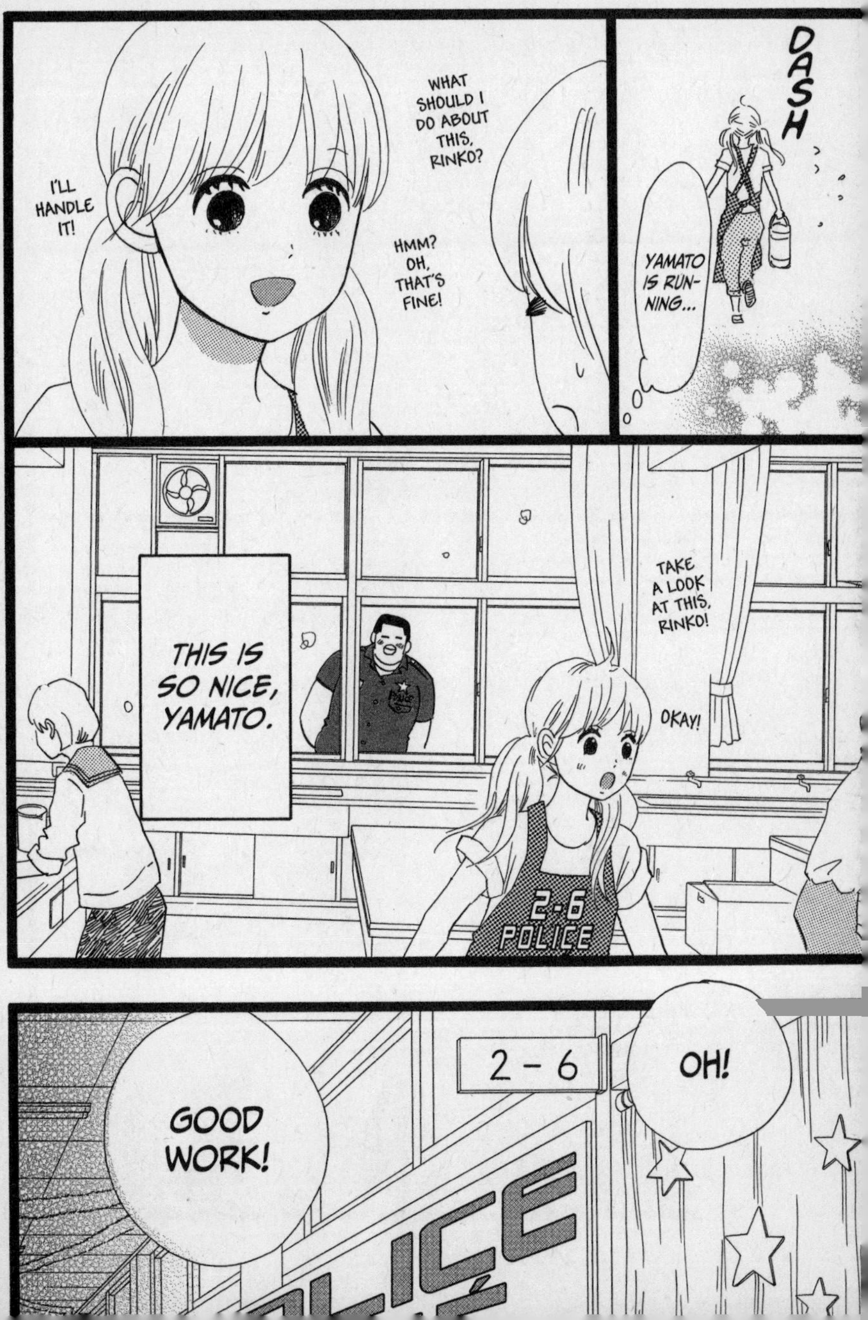
DASH
YAMATO IS RUNNING...
WHAT SHOULD I DO ABOUT THIS, RINKO?
HMM? OH, THAT'S FINE!
I'LL HANDLE IT!
TAKE A LOOK AT THIS, RINKO!
OKAY!
THIS IS SO NICE, YAMATO.
2-6 POLICE
OH!
2 - 6
GOOD WORK!

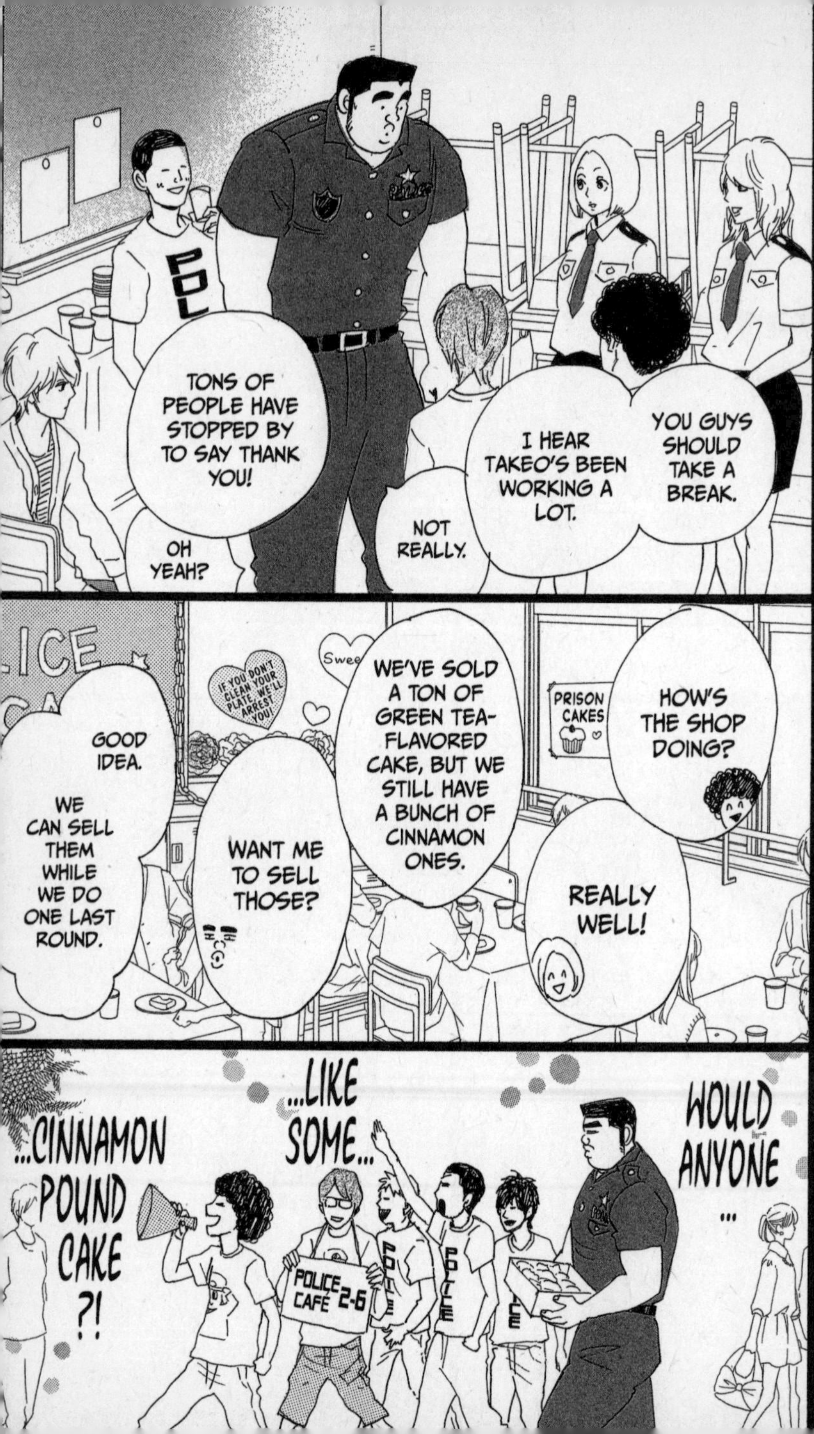
YOU GUYS SHOULD TAKE A BREAK.
I HEAR TAKEO'S BEEN WORKING A LOT.
NOT REALLY.
TONS OF PEOPLE HAVE STOPPED BY TO SAY THANK YOU!
OH YEAH?
PRISON CAKES
HOW'S THE SHOP DOING?
REALLY WELL!
WE'VE SOLD A TON OF GREEN TEA-FLAVORED CAKE, BUT WE STILL HAVE A BUNCH OF CINNAMON ONES.
IF YOU DON'T CLEAN YOUR PLATE, WE'LL ARREST YOU!
WANT ME TO SELL THOSE?
GOOD IDEA.
WE CAN SELL THEM WHILE WE DO ONE LAST ROUND.
WOULD ANYONE...
...LIKE SOME...
...CINNAMON POUND CAKE?!
POLICE CAFÉ 2-6

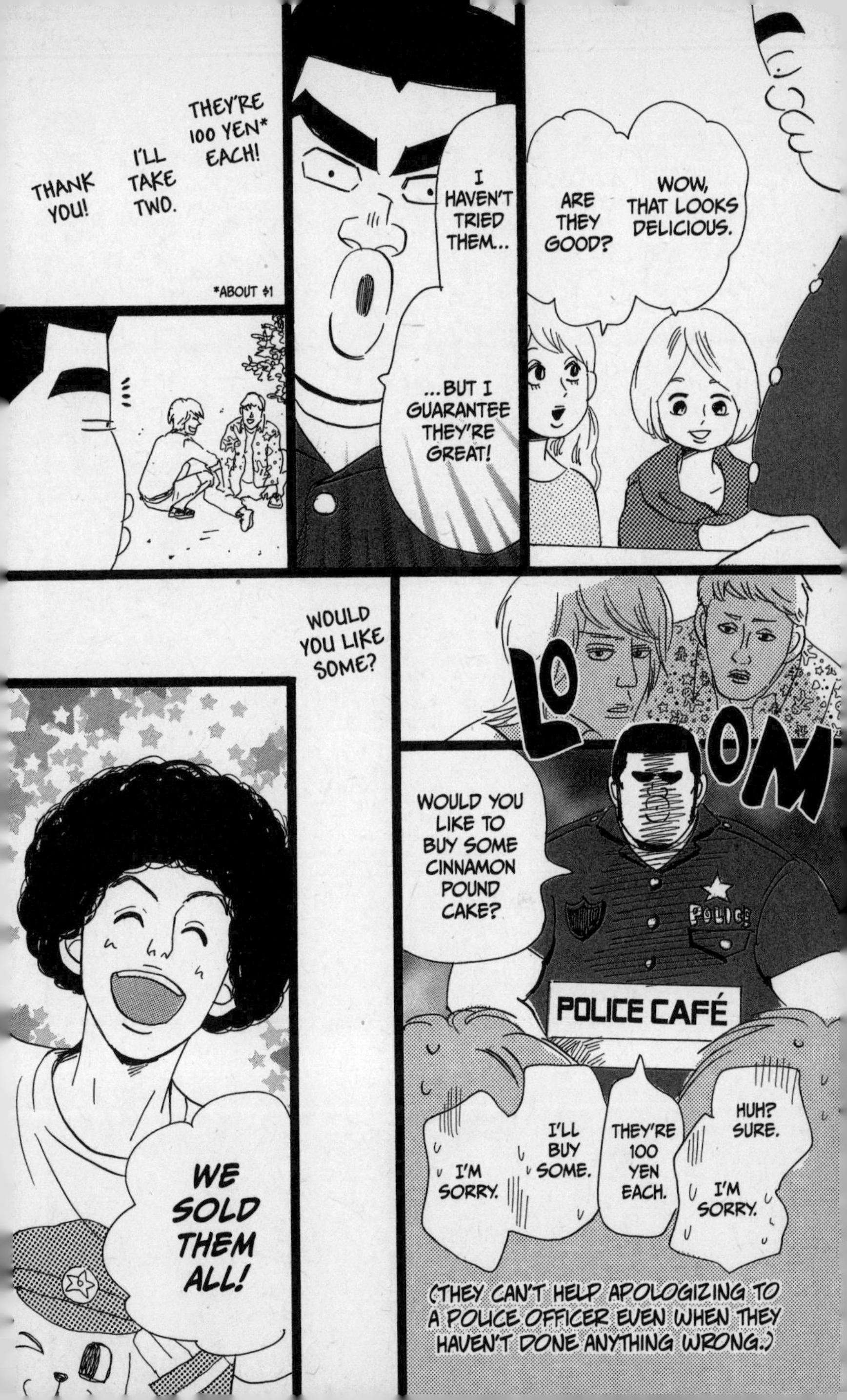
WOW, THAT LOOKS DELICIOUS.
ARE THEY GOOD?
I HAVEN'T TRIED THEM...
...BUT I GUARANTEE THEY'RE GREAT!
THEY'RE 100 YEN* EACH!
I'LL TAKE TWO.
THANK YOU!
*ABOUT $1
LOOM
POLICE
WOULD YOU LIKE TO BUY SOME CINNAMON POUND CAKE?
POLICE CAFÉ
HUH? SURE.
I'M SORRY.
THEY'RE 100 YEN EACH.
I'LL BUY SOME.
I'M SORRY.
(THEY CAN'T HELP APOLOGIZING TO A POLICE OFFICER EVEN WHEN THEY HAVEN'T DONE ANYTHING WRONG.)
WOULD YOU LIKE SOME?
WE SOLD THEM ALL!

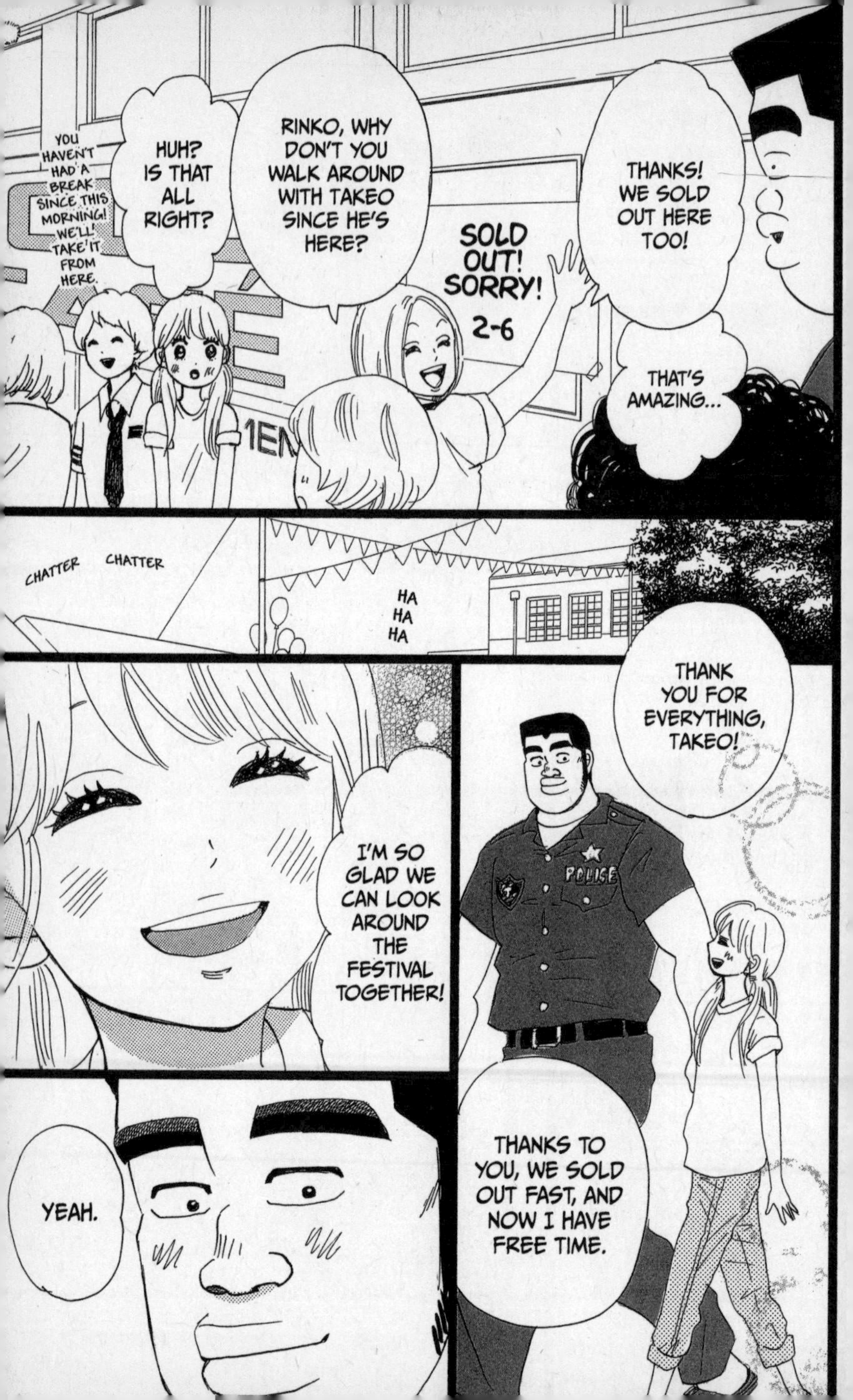
THANKS! WE SOLD OUT HERE TOO!
THAT'S AMAZING...
SOLD OUT! SORRY! 2-6
RINKO, WHY DON'T YOU WALK AROUND WITH TAKEO SINCE HE'S HERE?
HUH? IS THAT ALL RIGHT?
YOU HAVEN'T HAD A BREAK SINCE THIS MORNING! WE'LL TAKE IT FROM HERE.
HA HA HA
CHATTER CHATTER
THANK YOU FOR EVERYTHING, TAKEO!
THANKS TO YOU, WE SOLD OUT FAST, AND NOW I HAVE FREE TIME.
I'M SO GLAD WE CAN LOOK AROUND THE FESTIVAL TOGETHER!
YEAH.

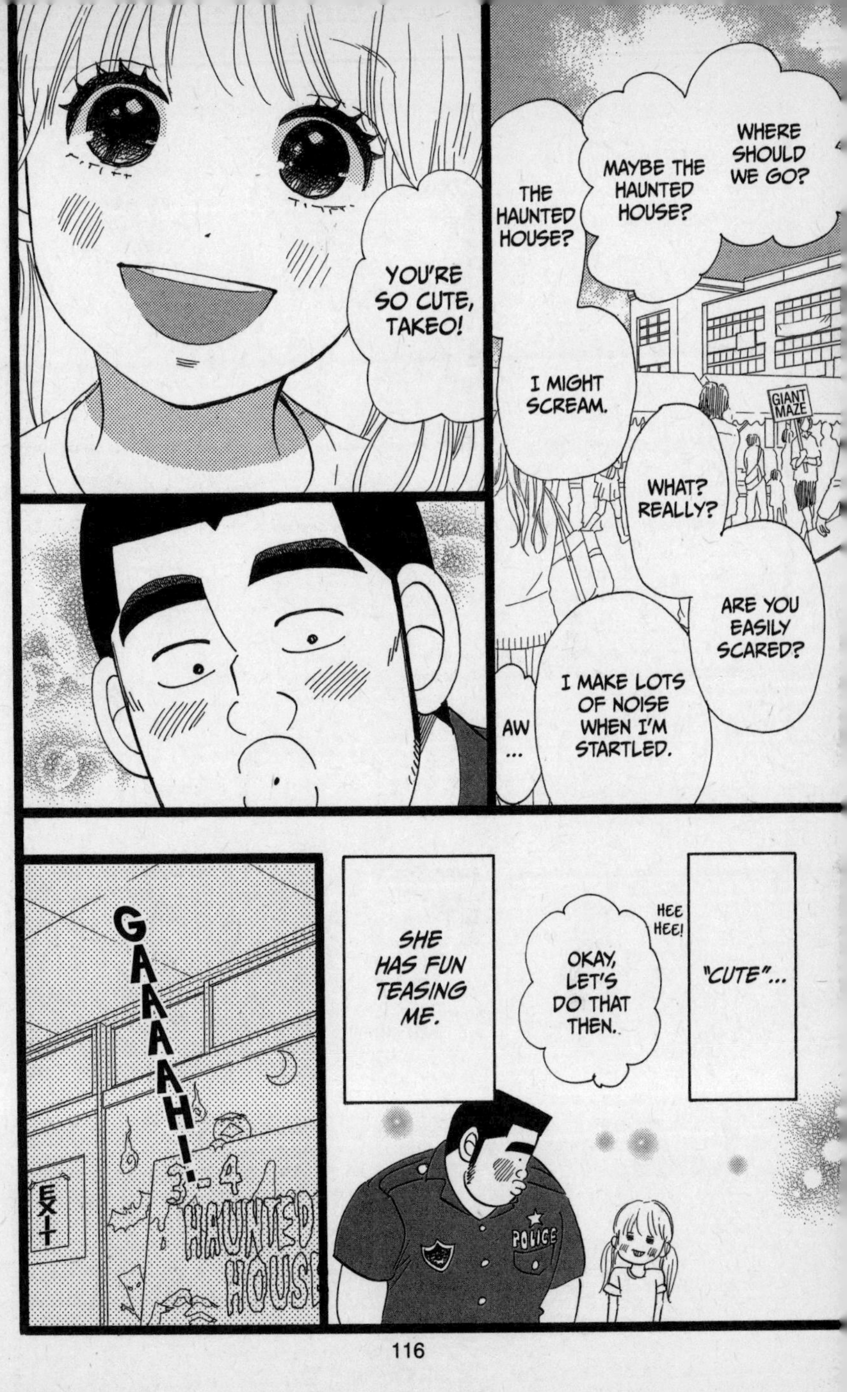
WHERE SHOULD WE GO?
MAYBE THE HAUNTED HOUSE?
THE HAUNTED HOUSE?
GIANT MAZE
I MIGHT SCREAM.
WHAT? REALLY?
ARE YOU EASILY SCARED?
I MAKE LOTS OF NOISE WHEN I'M STARTLED.
AW...
YOU'RE SO CUTE, TAKEO!
"CUTE"...
HEE HEE!
OKAY, LET'S DO THAT THEN.
SHE HAS FUN TEASING ME.
GAAAAH!!
EXIT
3-4
HAUNTED HOUSE

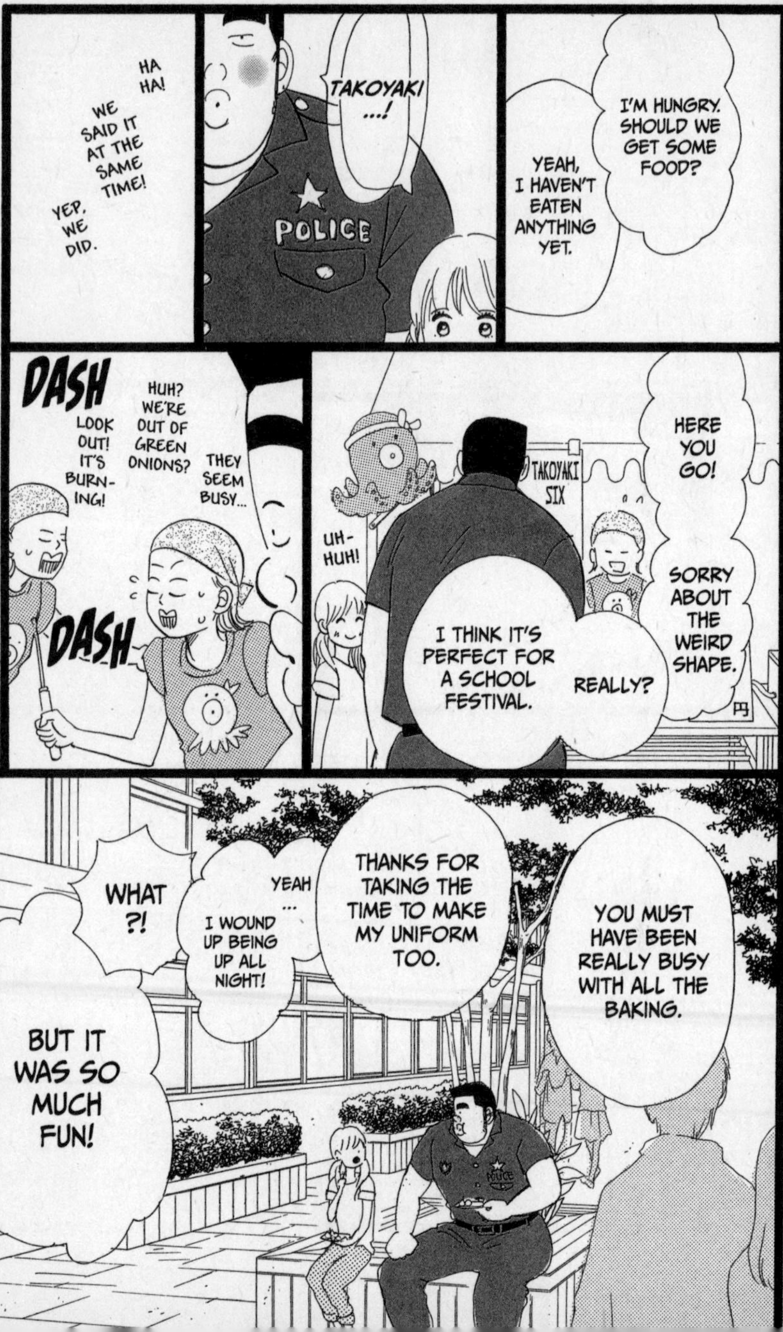
I'M HUNGRY. SHOULD WE GET SOME FOOD?
YEAH, I HAVEN'T EATEN ANYTHING YET.
TAKOYAKI ...!
POLICE
HA HA!
WE SAID IT AT THE SAME TIME!
YEP, WE DID.
HERE YOU GO!
SORRY ABOUT THE WEIRD SHAPE.
円
TAKOYAKI SIX
REALLY?
I THINK IT'S PERFECT FOR A SCHOOL FESTIVAL.
UH-HUH!
THEY SEEM BUSY...
HUH? WE'RE OUT OF GREEN ONIONS?
DASH
LOOK OUT! IT'S BURNING!
DASH
YOU MUST HAVE BEEN REALLY BUSY WITH ALL THE BAKING.
THANKS FOR TAKING THE TIME TO MAKE MY UNIFORM TOO.
YEAH...
I WOUND UP BEING UP ALL NIGHT!
WHAT?!
BUT IT WAS SO MUCH FUN!

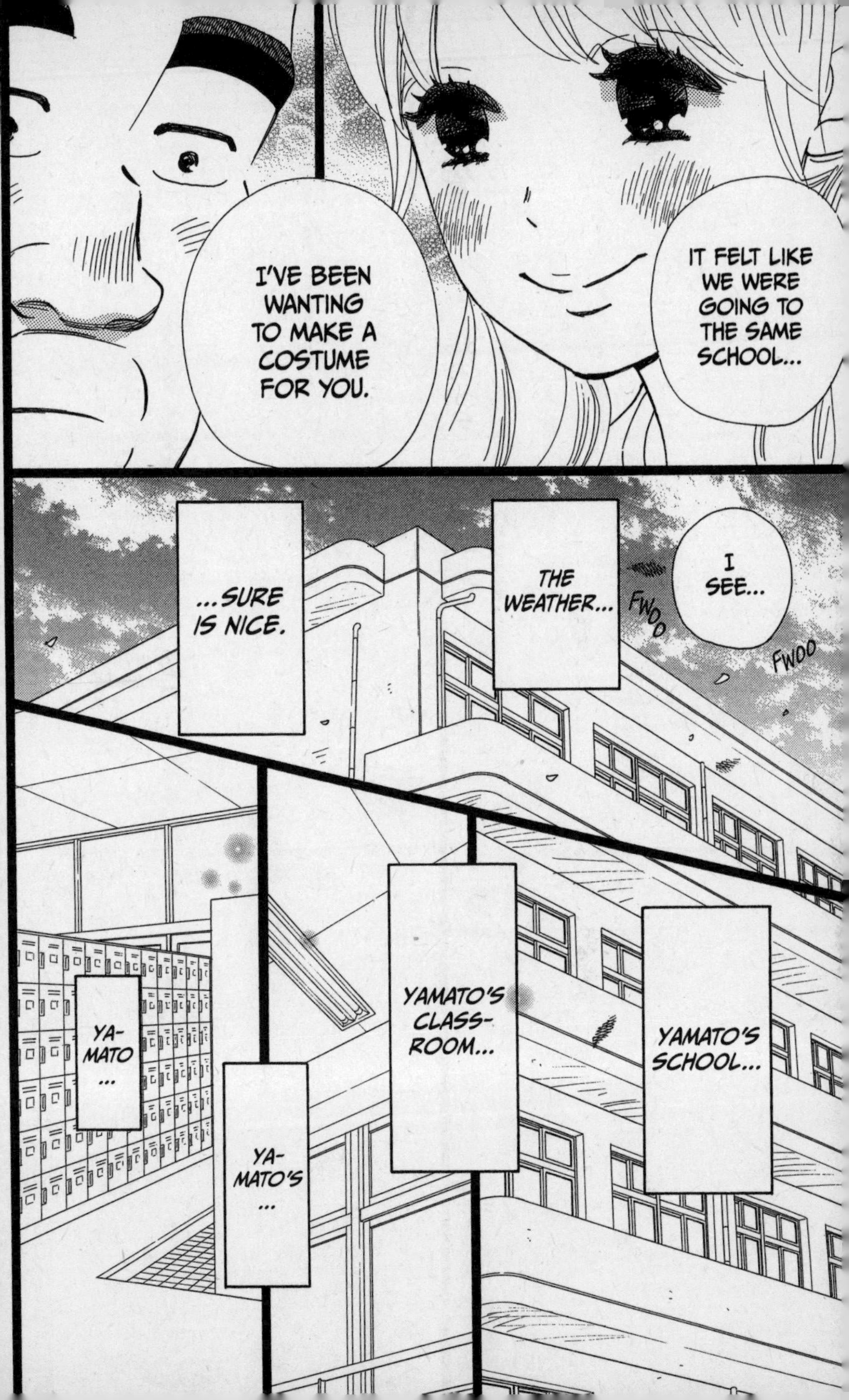
IT FELT LIKE WE WERE GOING TO THE SAME SCHOOL...
I'VE BEEN WANTING TO MAKE A COSTUME FOR YOU.
I SEE...
FWOO
FWOO
THE WEATHER...
...SURE IS NICE.
YAMATO'S SCHOOL...
YAMATO'S CLASS-ROOM...
YA-MATO'S...
YA-MATO...

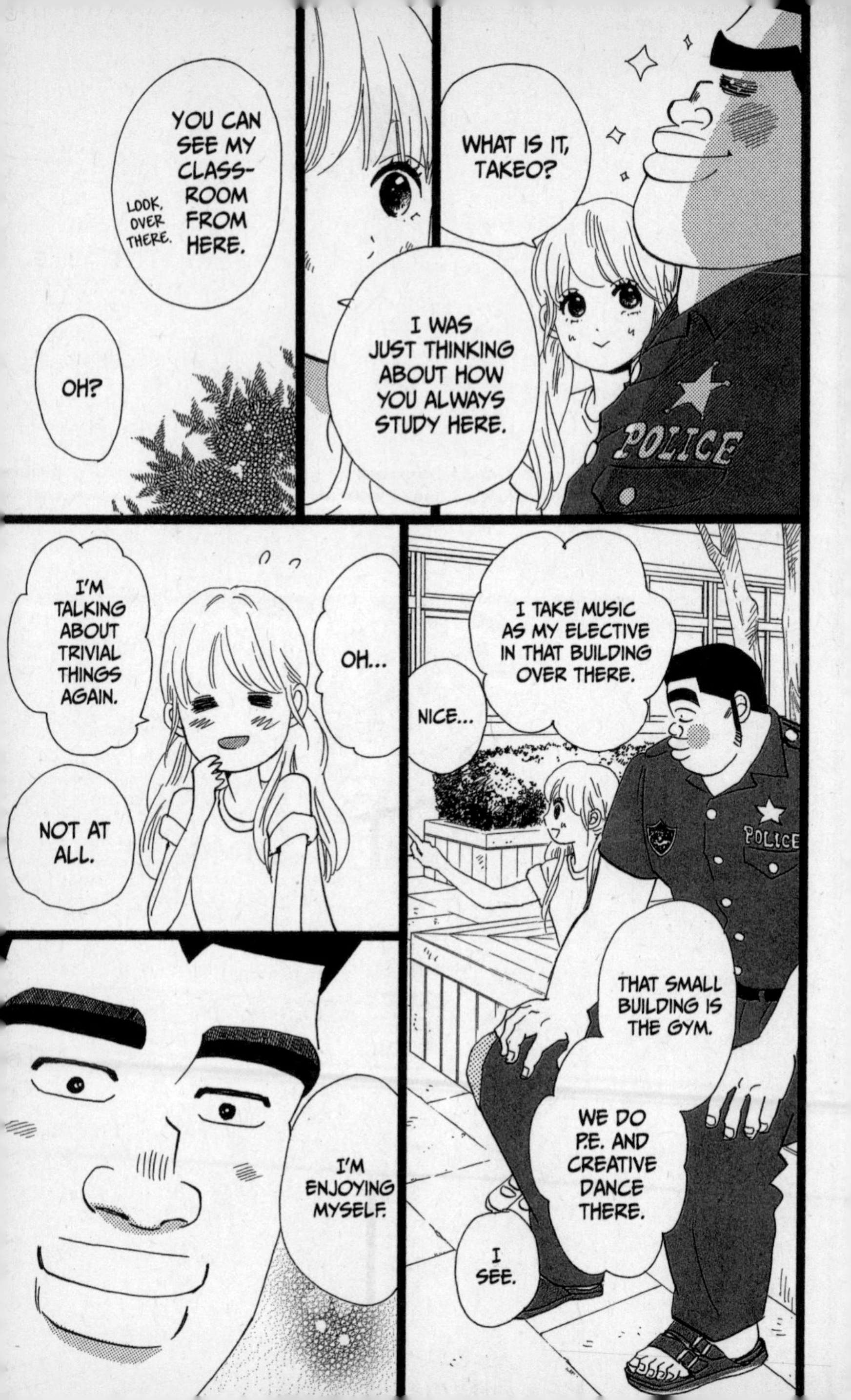
WHAT IS IT, TAKEO?
I WAS JUST THINKING ABOUT HOW YOU ALWAYS STUDY HERE.
YOU CAN SEE MY CLASS-ROOM FROM HERE.
LOOK, OVER THERE.
OH?
I TAKE MUSIC AS MY ELECTIVE IN THAT BUILDING OVER THERE.
NICE...
THAT SMALL BUILDING IS THE GYM.
WE DO P.E. AND CREATIVE DANCE THERE.
I SEE.
OH...
I'M TALKING ABOUT TRIVIAL THINGS AGAIN.
NOT AT ALL.
I'M ENJOYING MYSELF.

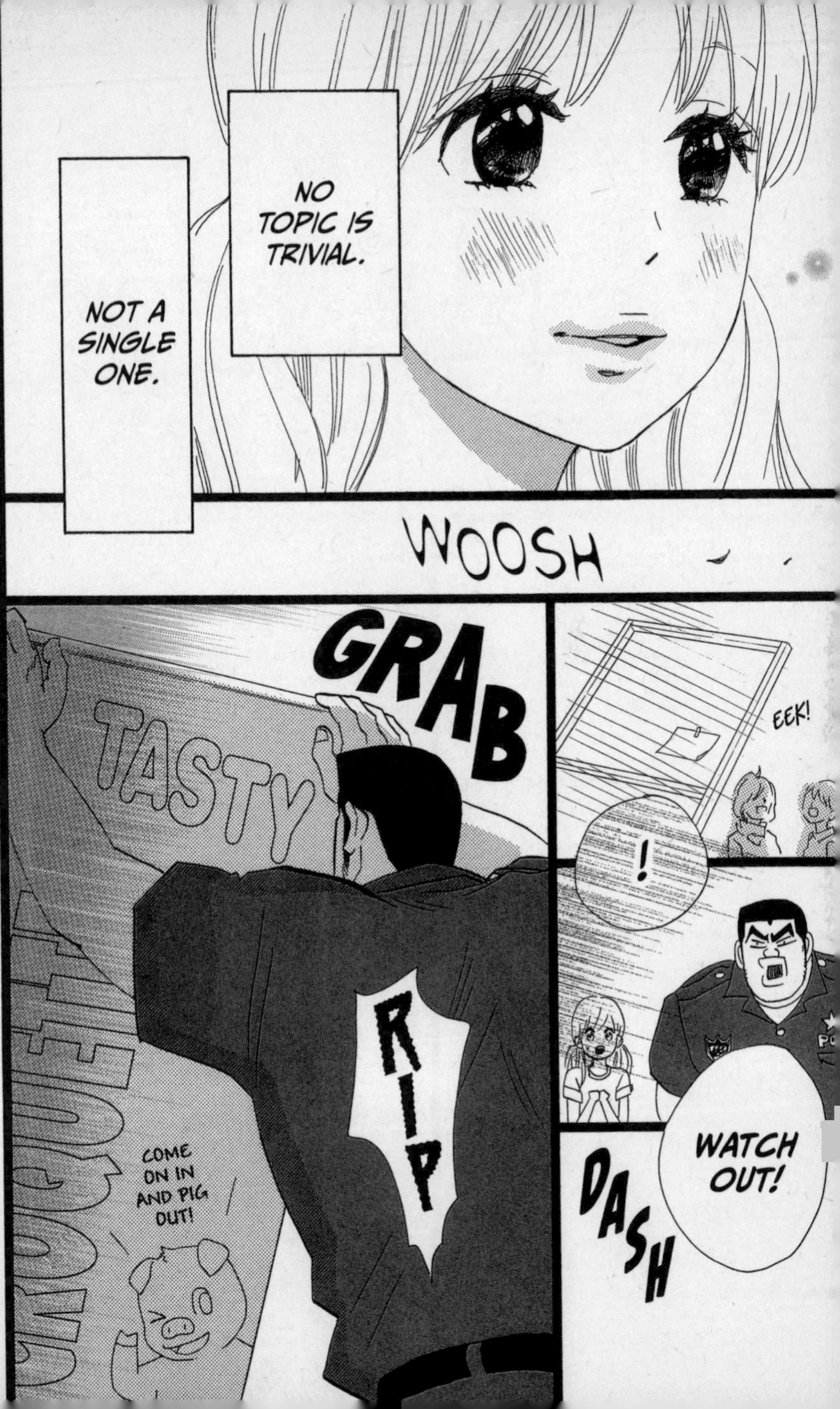
NO TOPIC IS TRIVIAL.
NOT A SINGLE ONE.
WOOSH
EEK!
!
WATCH OUT!
DASH
GRAB
TASTY
RIP
COME ON IN AND PIG OUT!

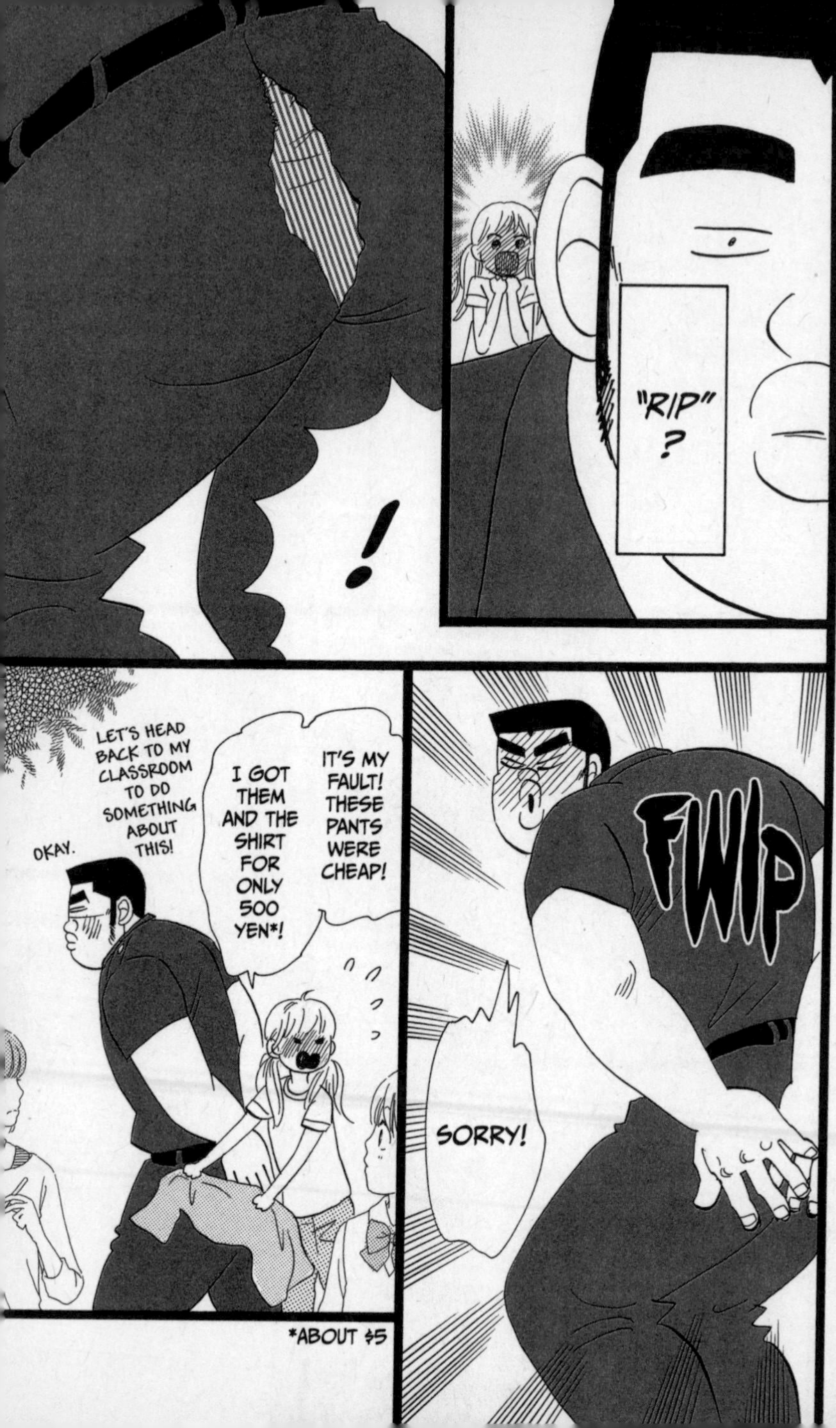
"RIP"?
!
FWIP
SORRY!
IT'S MY FAULT! THESE PANTS WERE CHEAP!
I GOT THEM AND THE SHIRT FOR ONLY 500 YEN*!
LET'S HEAD BACK TO MY CLASSROOM TO DO SOMETHING ABOUT THIS!
OKAY.

*ABOUT $5

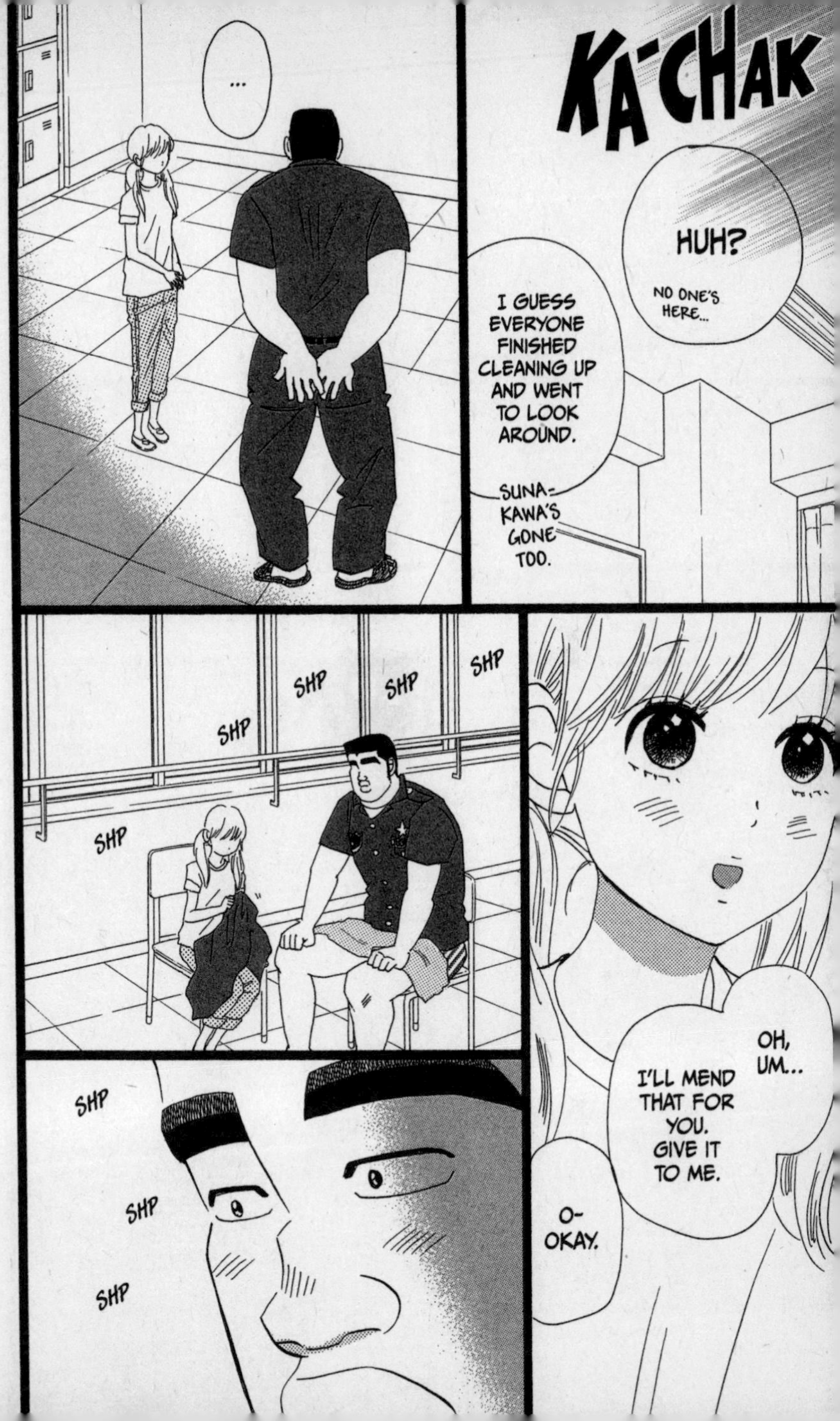
KA-CHAK
HUH?
NO ONE'S HERE...
I GUESS EVERYONE FINISHED CLEANING UP AND WENT TO LOOK AROUND.
SUNAKAWA'S GONE TOO.
...
OH, UM...
I'LL MEND THAT FOR YOU. GIVE IT TO ME.
O-OKAY.
SHP
SHP
SHP
SHP
SHP
SHP
SHP
SHP

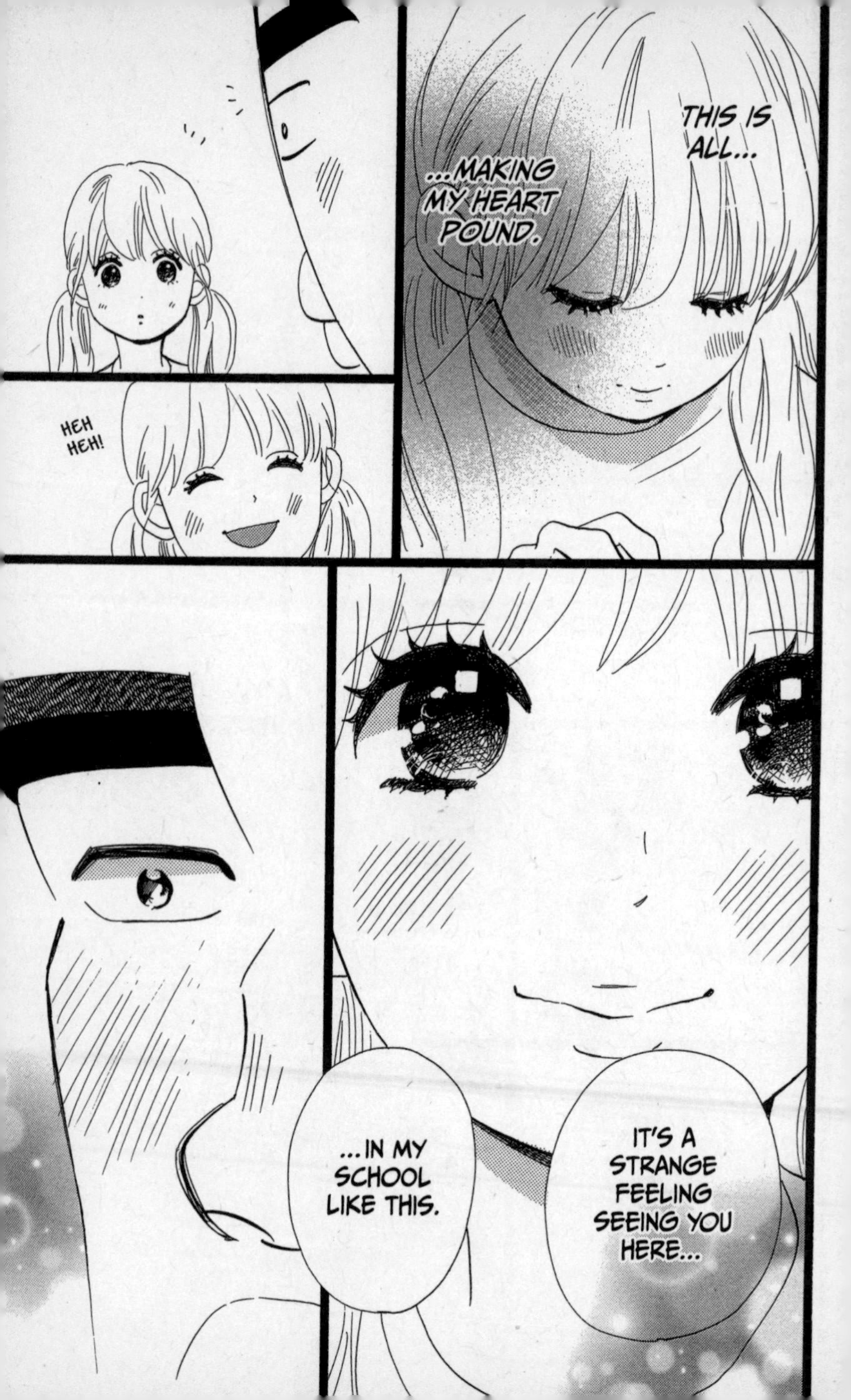
THIS IS ALL...
...MAKING MY HEART POUND.
HEH HEH!
IT'S A STRANGE FEELING SEEING YOU HERE...
...IN MY SCHOOL LIKE THIS.

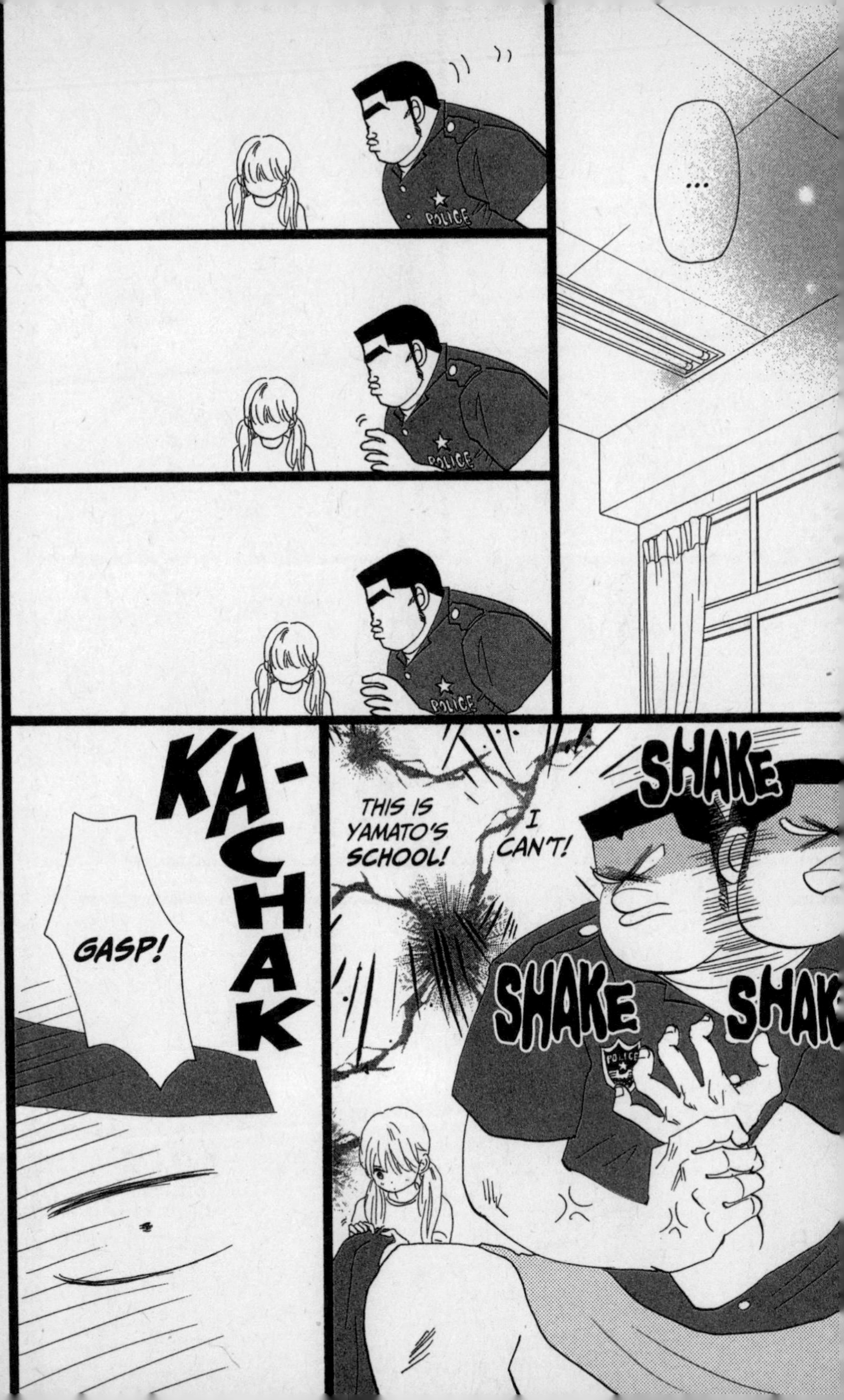
...
SHAKE
I CAN'T!
THIS IS YAMATO'S SCHOOL!
SHAK
SHAKE
KA-CHAK
GASP!

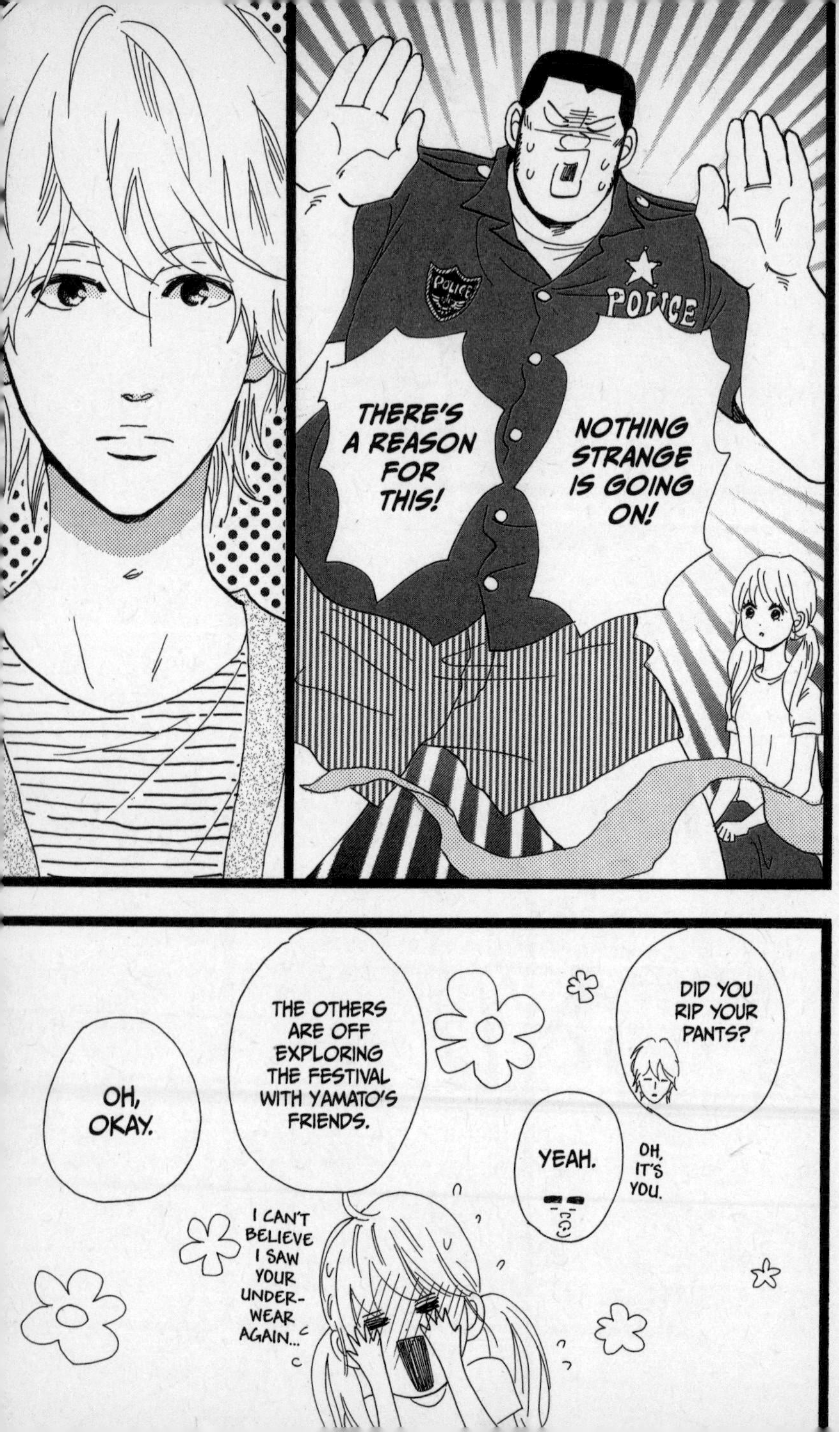
NOTHING STRANGE IS GOING ON!
THERE'S A REASON FOR THIS!
DID YOU RIP YOUR PANTS?
OH, IT'S YOU.
YEAH.
THE OTHERS ARE OFF EXPLORING THE FESTIVAL WITH YAMATO'S FRIENDS.
OH, OKAY.
I CAN'T BELIEVE I SAW YOUR UNDER-WEAR AGAIN...

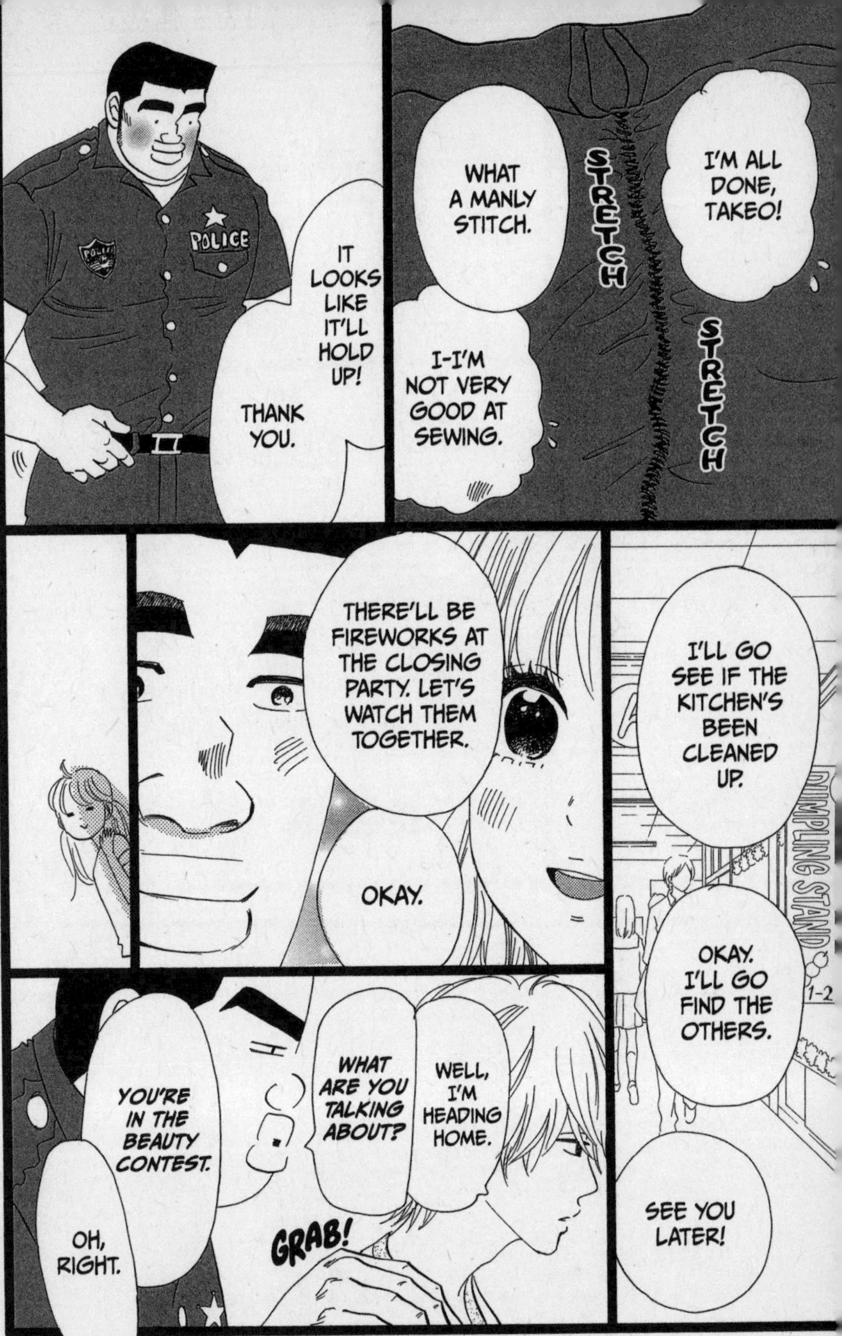
I'M ALL DONE, TAKEO!
STRETCH
STRETCH
WHAT A MANLY STITCH.
I-I'M NOT VERY GOOD AT SEWING.
IT LOOKS LIKE IT'LL HOLD UP!
THANK YOU.
POLICE
DUMPLING STAND
1-2
I'LL GO SEE IF THE KITCHEN'S BEEN CLEANED UP.
OKAY. I'LL GO FIND THE OTHERS.
SEE YOU LATER!
THERE'LL BE FIREWORKS AT THE CLOSING PARTY. LET'S WATCH THEM TOGETHER.
OKAY.
WELL, I'M HEADING HOME.
WHAT ARE YOU TALKING ABOUT?
GRAB!
YOU'RE IN THE BEAUTY CONTEST.
OH, RIGHT.

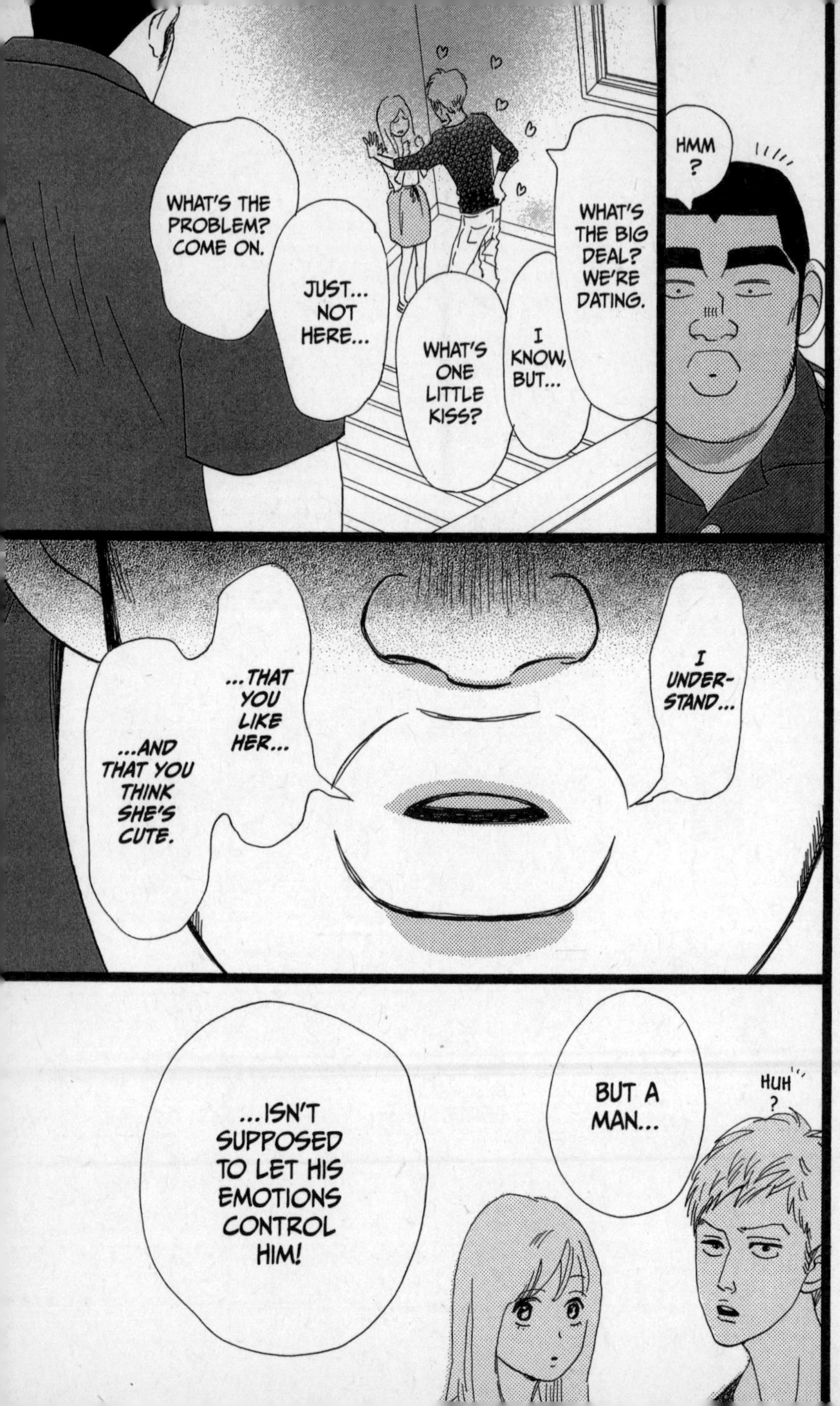
HMM ?
WHAT'S THE BIG DEAL? WE'RE DATING.
I KNOW, BUT...
WHAT'S ONE LITTLE KISS?
JUST... NOT HERE...
WHAT'S THE PROBLEM? COME ON.
I UNDERSTAND...
...THAT YOU LIKE HER...
...AND THAT YOU THINK SHE'S CUTE.
HUH ?
BUT A MAN...
...ISN'T SUPPOSED TO LET HIS EMOTIONS CONTROL HIM!

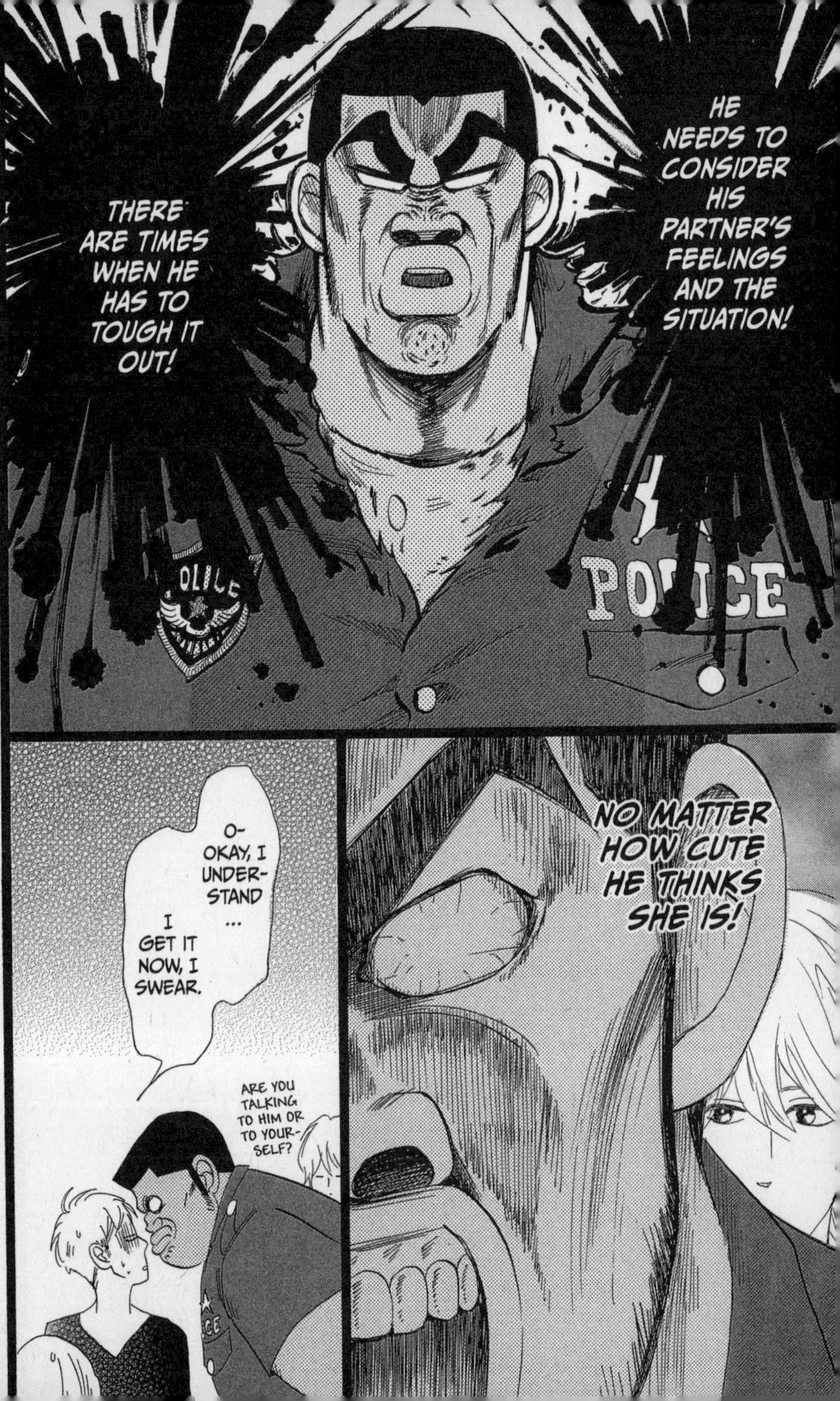
HE NEEDS TO CONSIDER HIS PARTNER'S FEELINGS AND THE SITUATION!
THERE ARE TIMES WHEN HE HAS TO TOUGH IT OUT!
NO MATTER HOW CUTE HE THINKS SHE IS!
O-OKAY, I UNDERSTAND... I GET IT NOW, I SWEAR.
ARE YOU TALKING TO HIM OR TO YOURSELF?

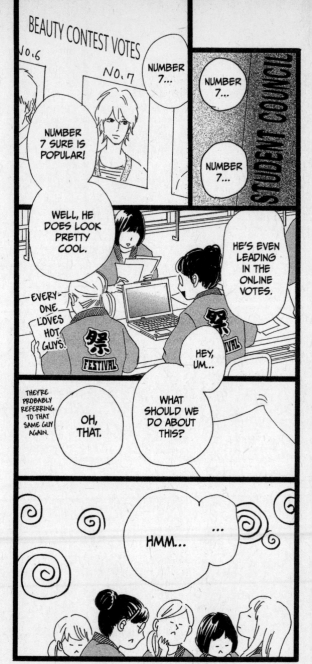

STUDENT COUNCIL
NUMBER 7...
NUMBER 7...
BEAUTY CONTEST VOTES
NO.6
NO.7
NUMBER 7...
NUMBER 7 SURE IS POPULAR!
WELL, HE DOES LOOK PRETTY COOL.
HE'S EVEN LEADING IN THE ONLINE VOTES.
EVERY-ONE LOVES HOT GUYS.
FESTIVAL
FESTIVAL
HEY, UM...
WHAT SHOULD WE DO ABOUT THIS?
OH, THAT.
THEY'RE PROBABLY REFERRING TO THAT SAME GUY AGAIN.
...
HMM...

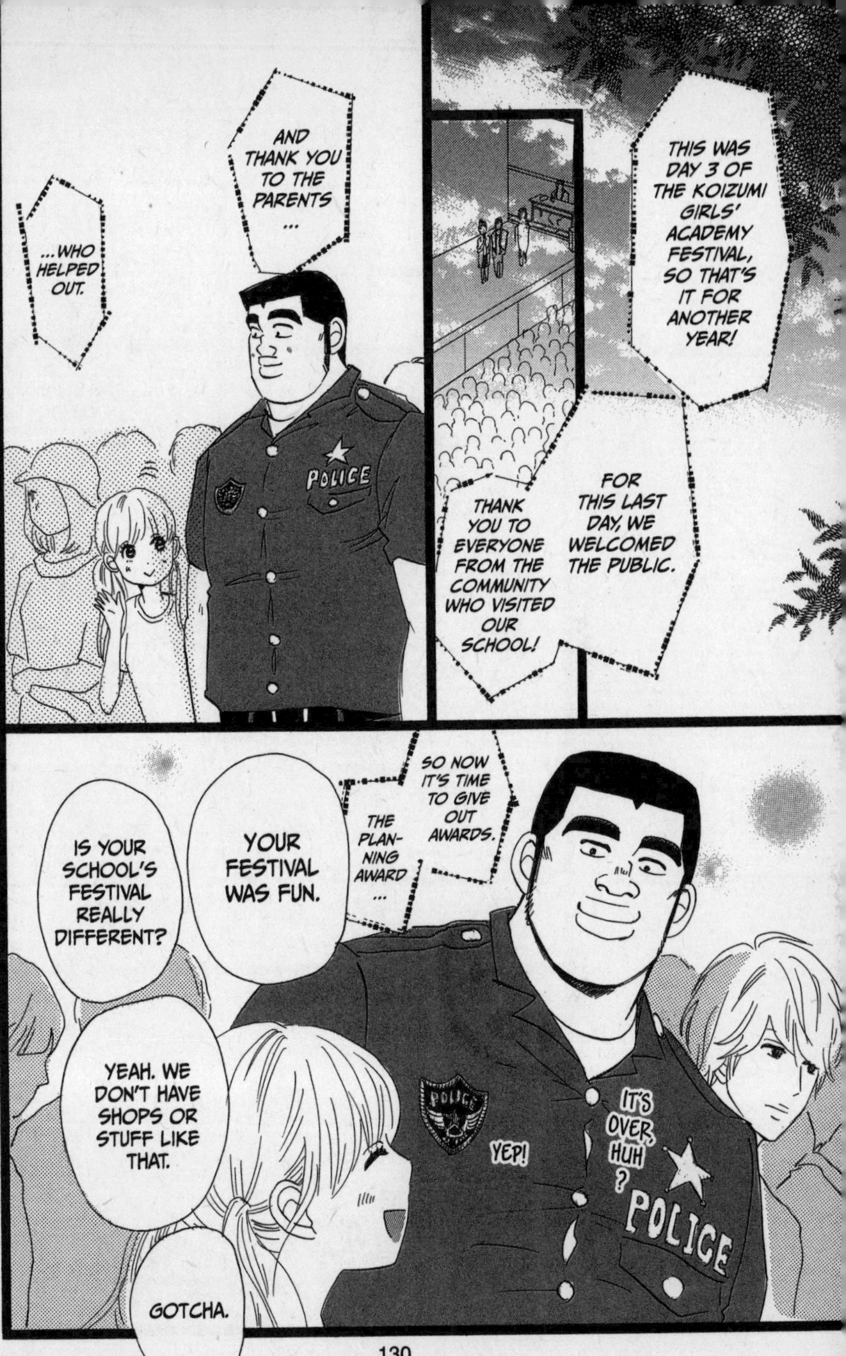
THIS WAS DAY 3 OF THE KOIZUMI GIRLS' ACADEMY FESTIVAL, SO THAT'S IT FOR ANOTHER YEAR!
FOR THIS LAST DAY, WE WELCOMED THE PUBLIC.
THANK YOU TO EVERYONE FROM THE COMMUNITY WHO VISITED OUR SCHOOL!
AND THANK YOU TO THE PARENTS ...
...WHO HELPED OUT.
POLICE
SO NOW IT'S TIME TO GIVE OUT AWARDS.
THE PLAN-NING AWARD ...
IT'S OVER, HUH?
YEP!
POLICE
YOUR FESTIVAL WAS FUN.
IS YOUR SCHOOL'S FESTIVAL REALLY DIFFERENT?
YEAH. WE DON'T HAVE SHOPS OR STUFF LIKE THAT.
GOTCHA.

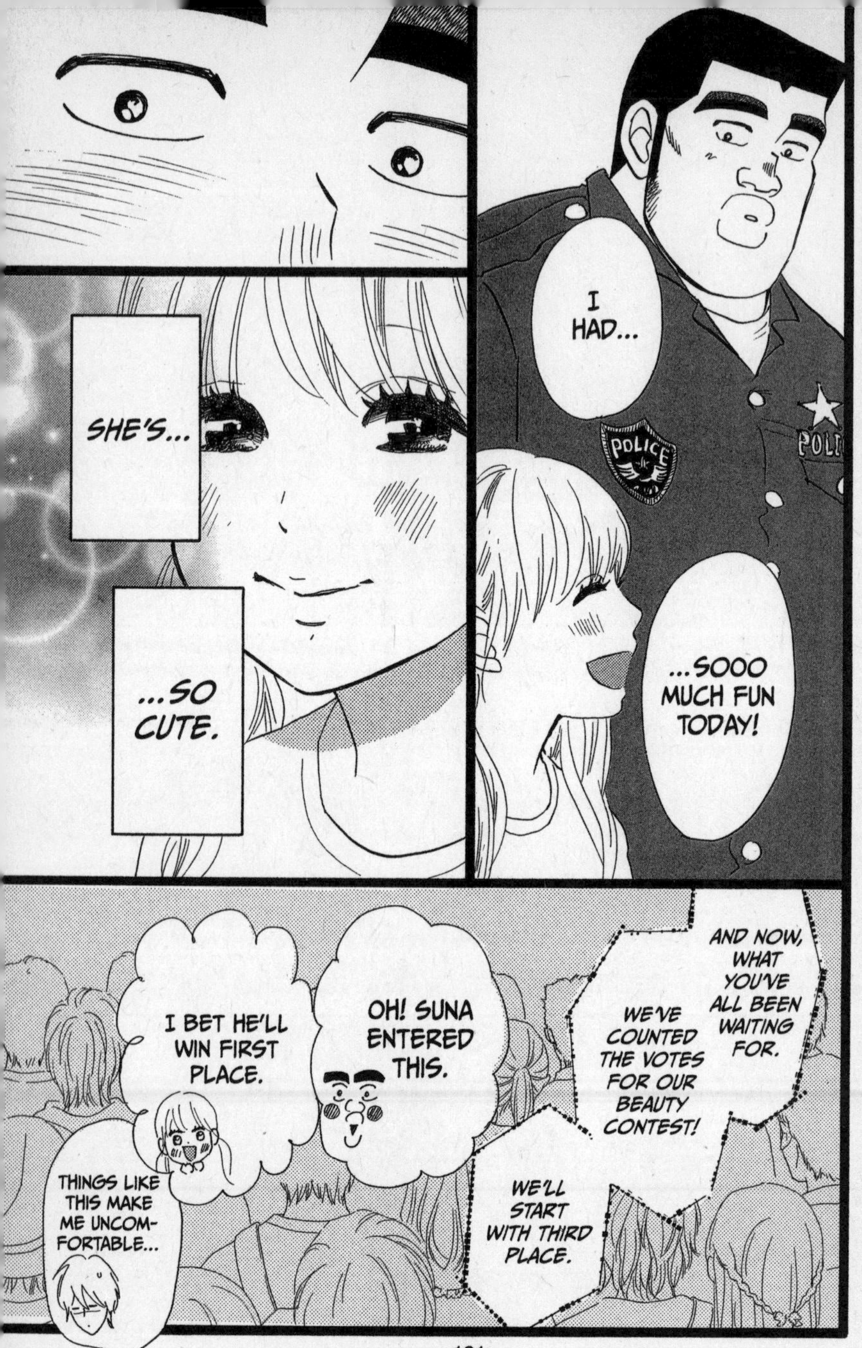
POLICE
I HAD...
...SOOO MUCH FUN TODAY!
SHE'S...
...SO CUTE.
AND NOW, WHAT YOU'VE ALL BEEN WAITING FOR.
WE'VE COUNTED THE VOTES FOR OUR BEAUTY CONTEST!
WE'LL START WITH THIRD PLACE.
OH! SUNA ENTERED THIS.
I BET HE'LL WIN FIRST PLACE.
THINGS LIKE THIS MAKE ME UNCOMFORTABLE...

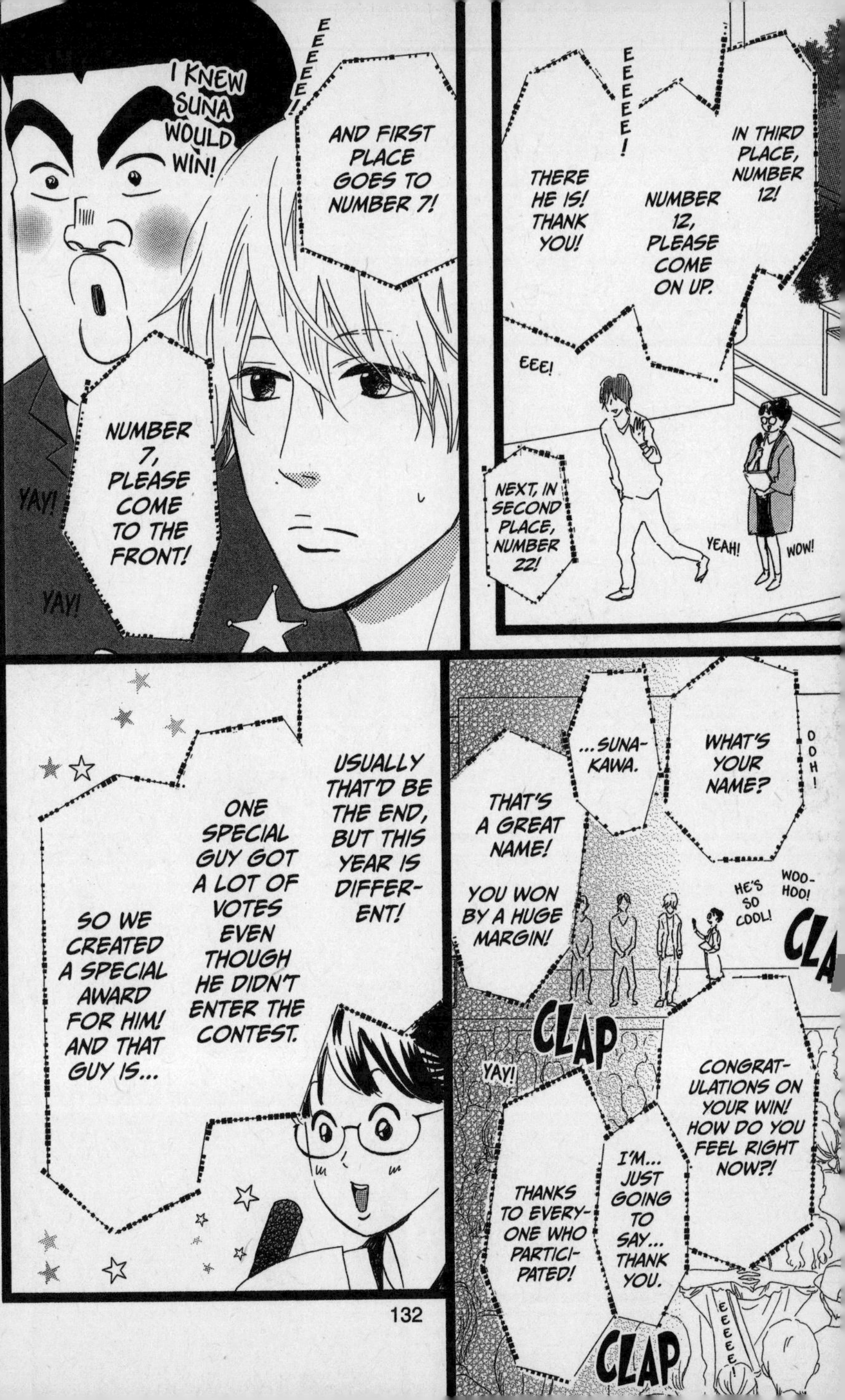
IN THIRD PLACE, NUMBER 12!
NUMBER 12, PLEASE COME ON UP.
EEEEE!
THERE HE IS! THANK YOU!
EEE!
YEAH!
WOW!
NEXT, IN SECOND PLACE, NUMBER 22!
EEEEE!
AND FIRST PLACE GOES TO NUMBER 7!
I KNEW SUNA WOULD WIN!
NUMBER 7, PLEASE COME TO THE FRONT!
YAY!
YAY!
WHAT'S YOUR NAME?
OOH!
...SUNA-KAWA.
THAT'S A GREAT NAME!
YOU WON BY A HUGE MARGIN!
WOO-HOO!
HE'S SO COOL!
CLA
CLAP
YAY!
CONGRAT-ULATIONS ON YOUR WIN! HOW DO YOU FEEL RIGHT NOW?!
I'M... JUST GOING TO SAY... THANK YOU.
THANKS TO EVERY-ONE WHO PARTICI-PATED!
CLAP
EEEEE!
USUALLY THAT'D BE THE END, BUT THIS YEAR IS DIFFER-ENT!
ONE SPECIAL GUY GOT A LOT OF VOTES EVEN THOUGH HE DIDN'T ENTER THE CONTEST.
SO WE CREATED A SPECIAL AWARD FOR HIM! AND THAT GUY IS...

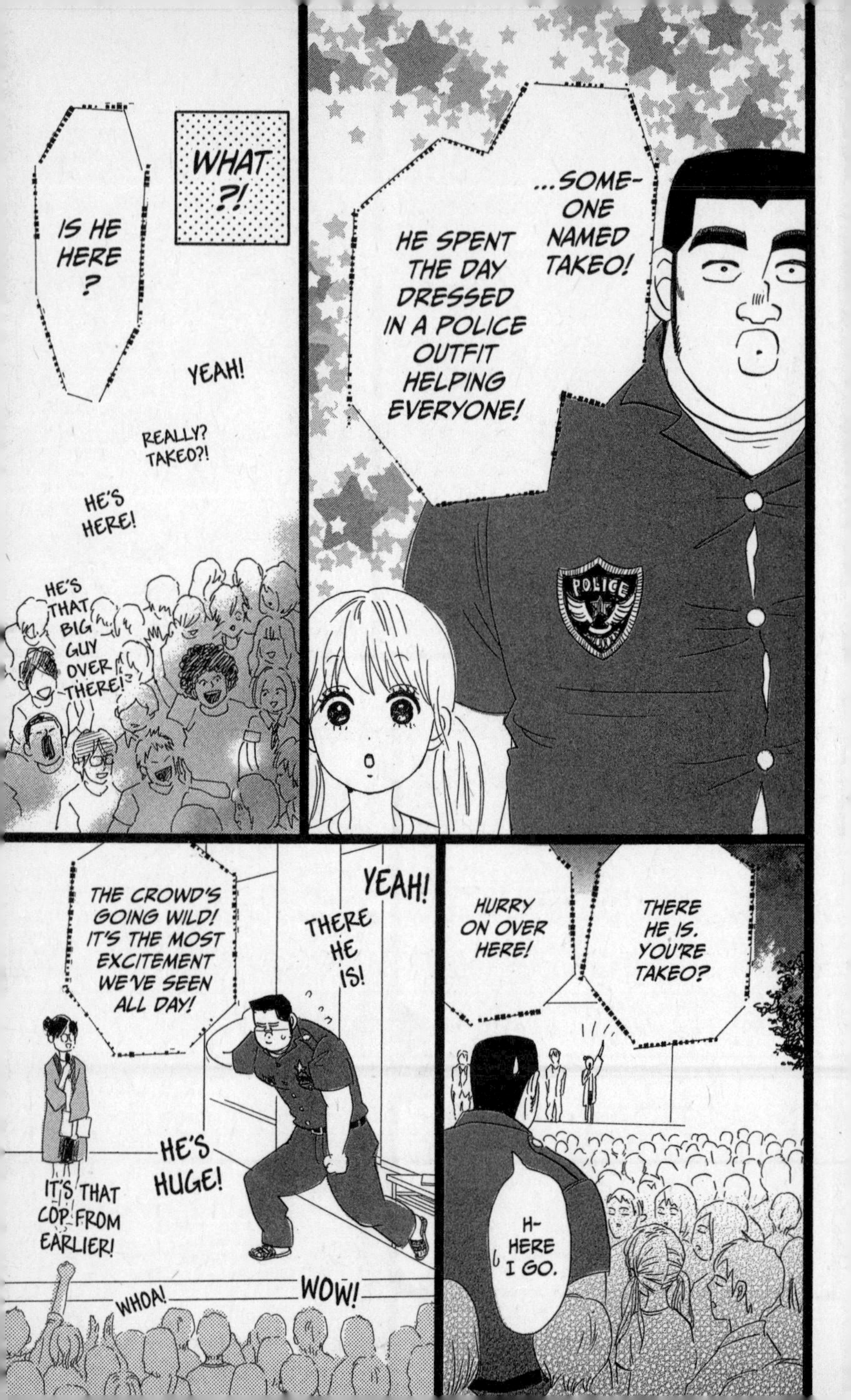
...SOMEONE NAMED TAKEO!
HE SPENT THE DAY DRESSED IN A POLICE OUTFIT HELPING EVERYONE!
WHAT?!
IS HE HERE?
YEAH!
REALLY? TAKEO?!
HE'S HERE!
HE'S THAT BIG GUY OVER THERE!
THERE HE IS. YOU'RE TAKEO?
HURRY ON OVER HERE!
H-HERE I GO.
YEAH!
THERE HE IS!
THE CROWD'S GOING WILD! IT'S THE MOST EXCITEMENT WE'VE SEEN ALL DAY!
HE'S HUGE!
IT'S THAT COP FROM EARLIER!
WOW!
WHOA!

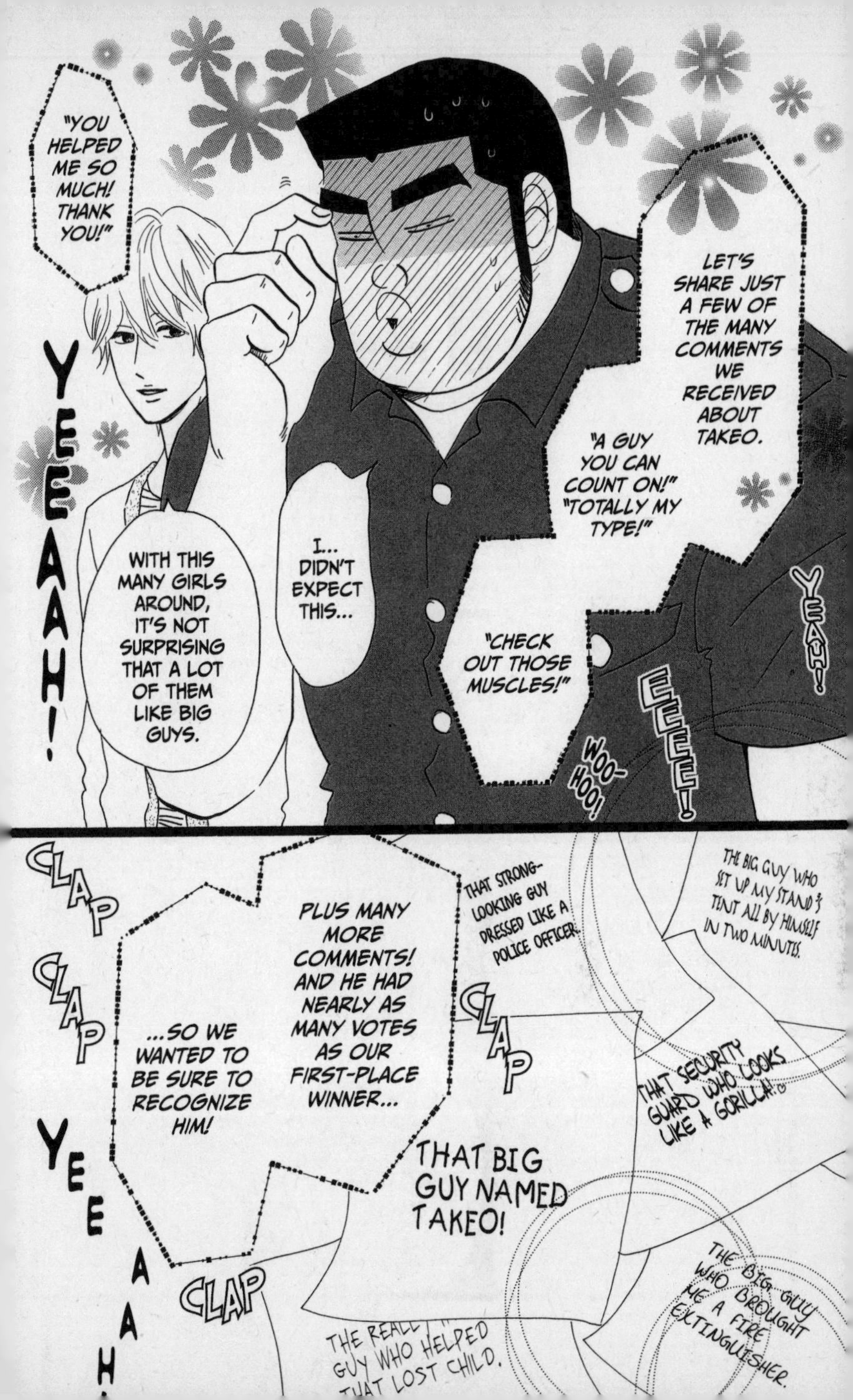
LET'S SHARE JUST A FEW OF THE MANY COMMENTS WE RECEIVED ABOUT TAKEO.
"A GUY YOU CAN COUNT ON!" "TOTALLY MY TYPE!"
YEAAH!
"CHECK OUT THOSE MUSCLES!"
EEEEE!
WOO-HOO!
"YOU HELPED ME SO MUCH! THANK YOU!"
I... DIDN'T EXPECT THIS...
WITH THIS MANY GIRLS AROUND, IT'S NOT SURPRISING THAT A LOT OF THEM LIKE BIG GUYS.
YEEAAH!
THE BIG GUY WHO SET UP MY STAND & TENT ALL BY HIMSELF IN TWO MINUTES.
THAT STRONG-LOOKING GUY DRESSED LIKE A POLICE OFFICER.
PLUS MANY MORE COMMENTS! AND HE HAD NEARLY AS MANY VOTES AS OUR FIRST-PLACE WINNER...
...SO WE WANTED TO BE SURE TO RECOGNIZE HIM!
CLAP
CLAP
CLAP
THAT SECURITY GUARD WHO LOOKS LIKE A GORILLA!
THAT BIG GUY NAMED TAKEO!
THE BIG GUY WHO BROUGHT ME A FIRE EXTINGUISHER.
GUY WHO HELPED THAT LOST CHILD.
CLAP
YEEEAAH!

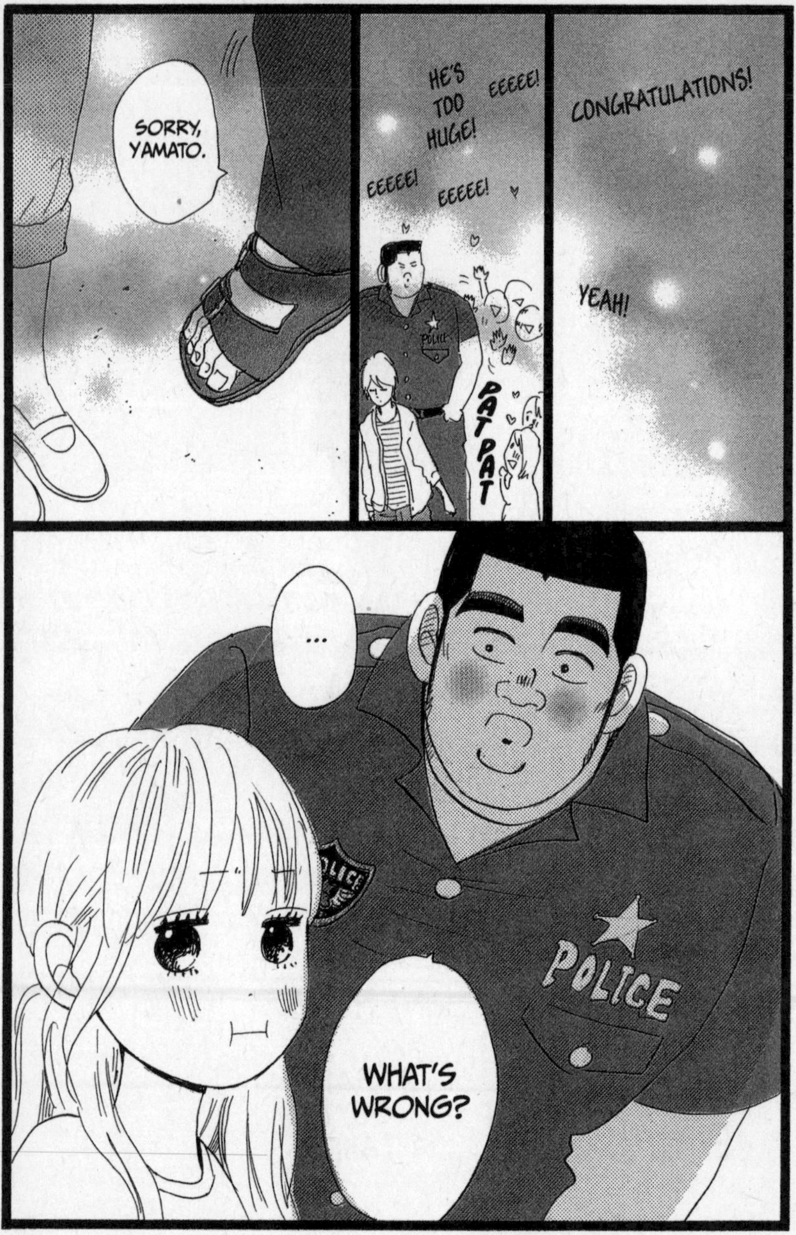
CONGRATULATIONS!
YEAH!
EEEEE!
HE'S TOO HUGE!
EEEEE!
EEEEE!
PAT PAT
SORRY, YAMATO.
...
WHAT'S WRONG?

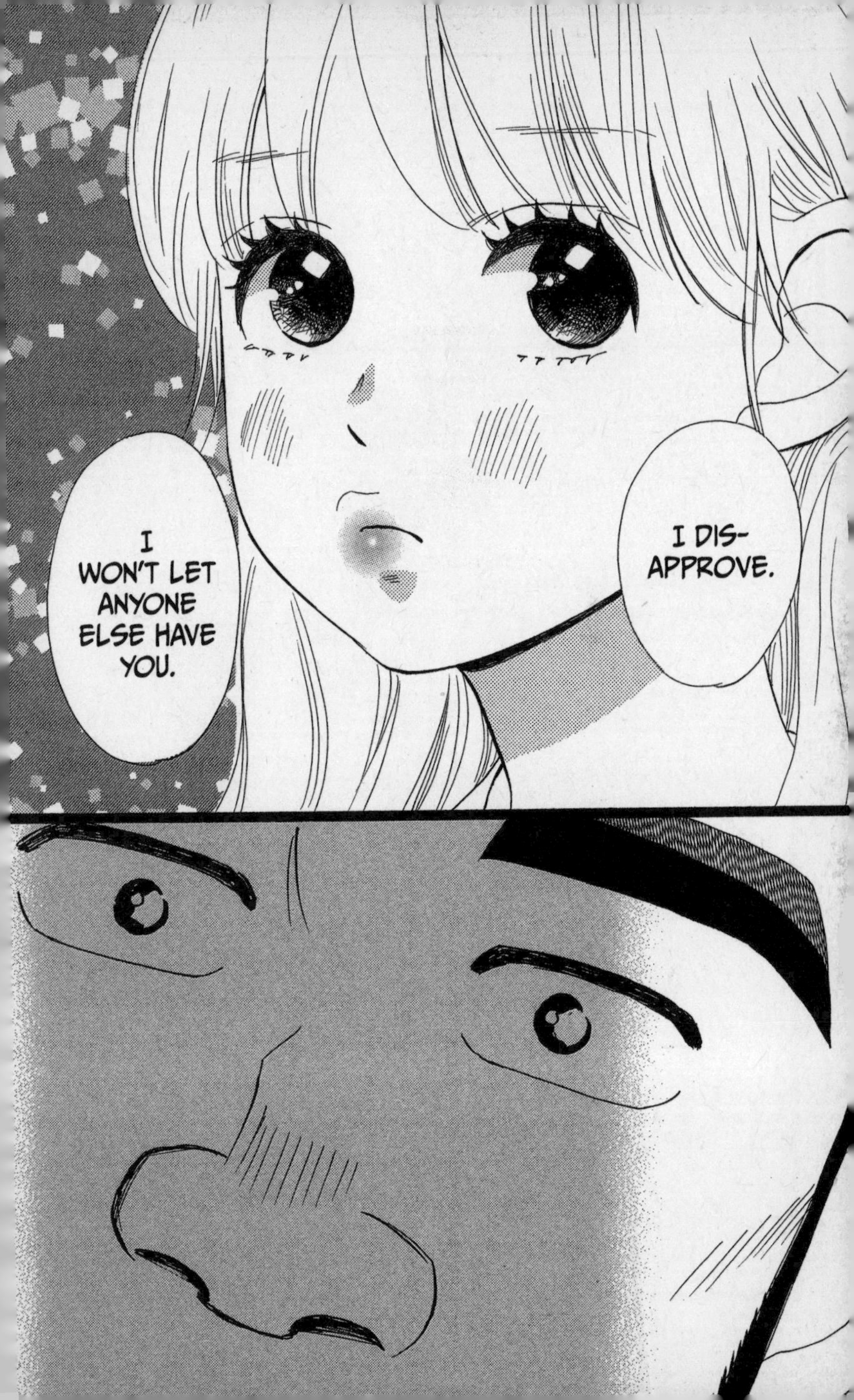
I DIS-APPROVE.
I WON'T LET ANYONE ELSE HAVE YOU.

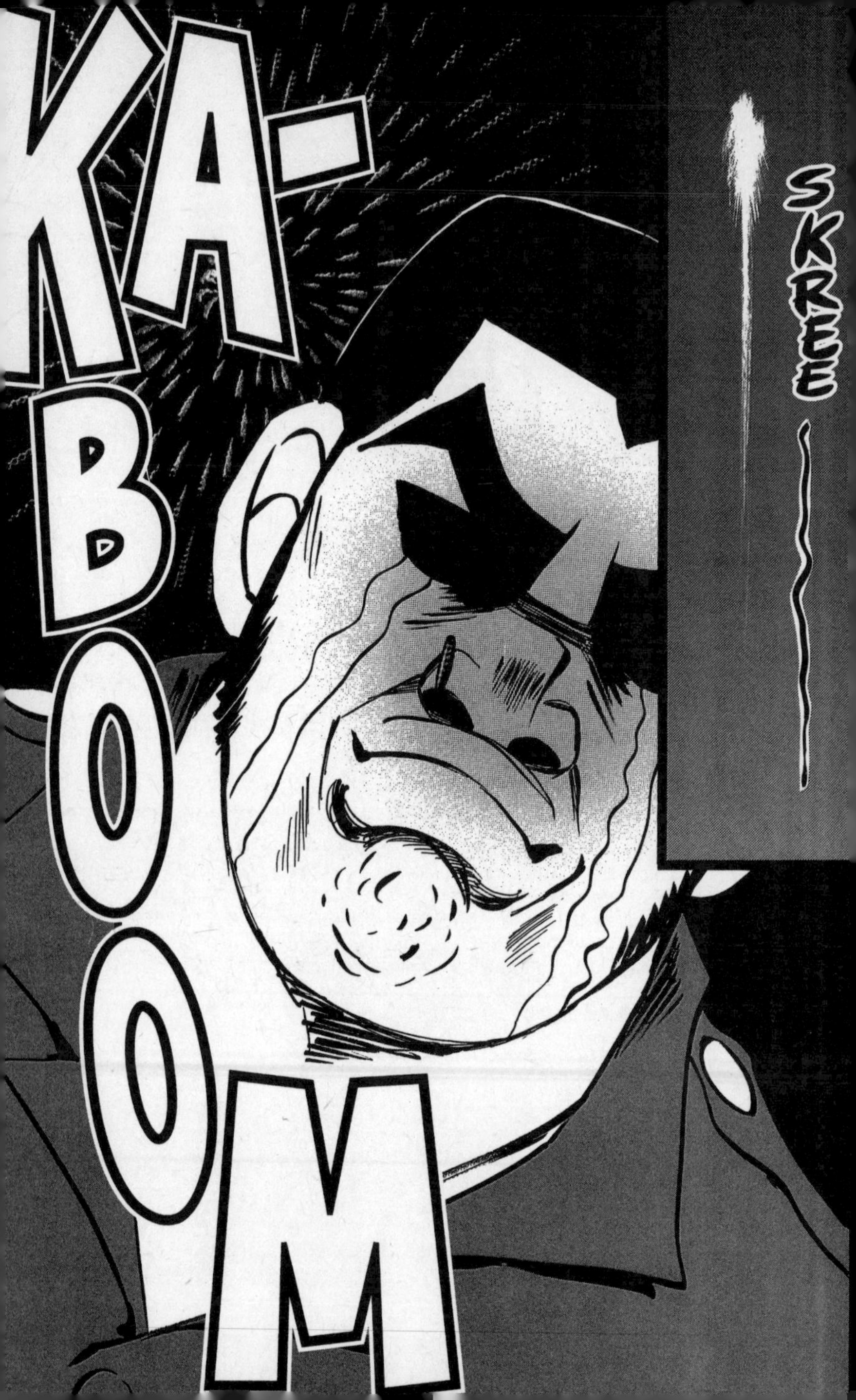

SKREE———
KA-BOOOM

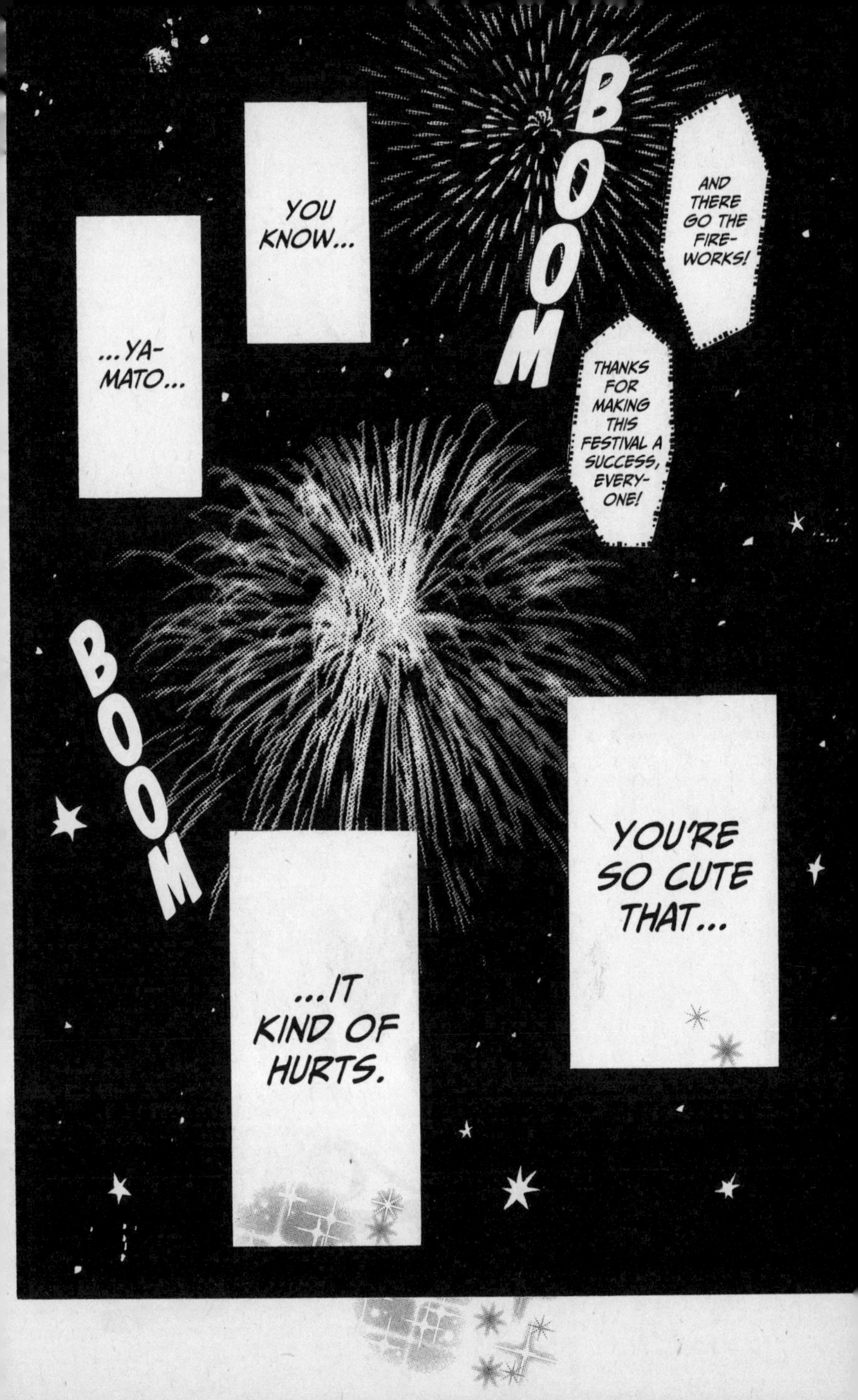
BOOM
AND THERE GO THE FIRE-WORKS!
THANKS FOR MAKING THIS FESTIVAL A SUCCESS, EVERY-ONE!
YOU KNOW...
...YA-MATO...
BOOM
YOU'RE SO CUTE THAT...
...IT KIND OF HURTS.

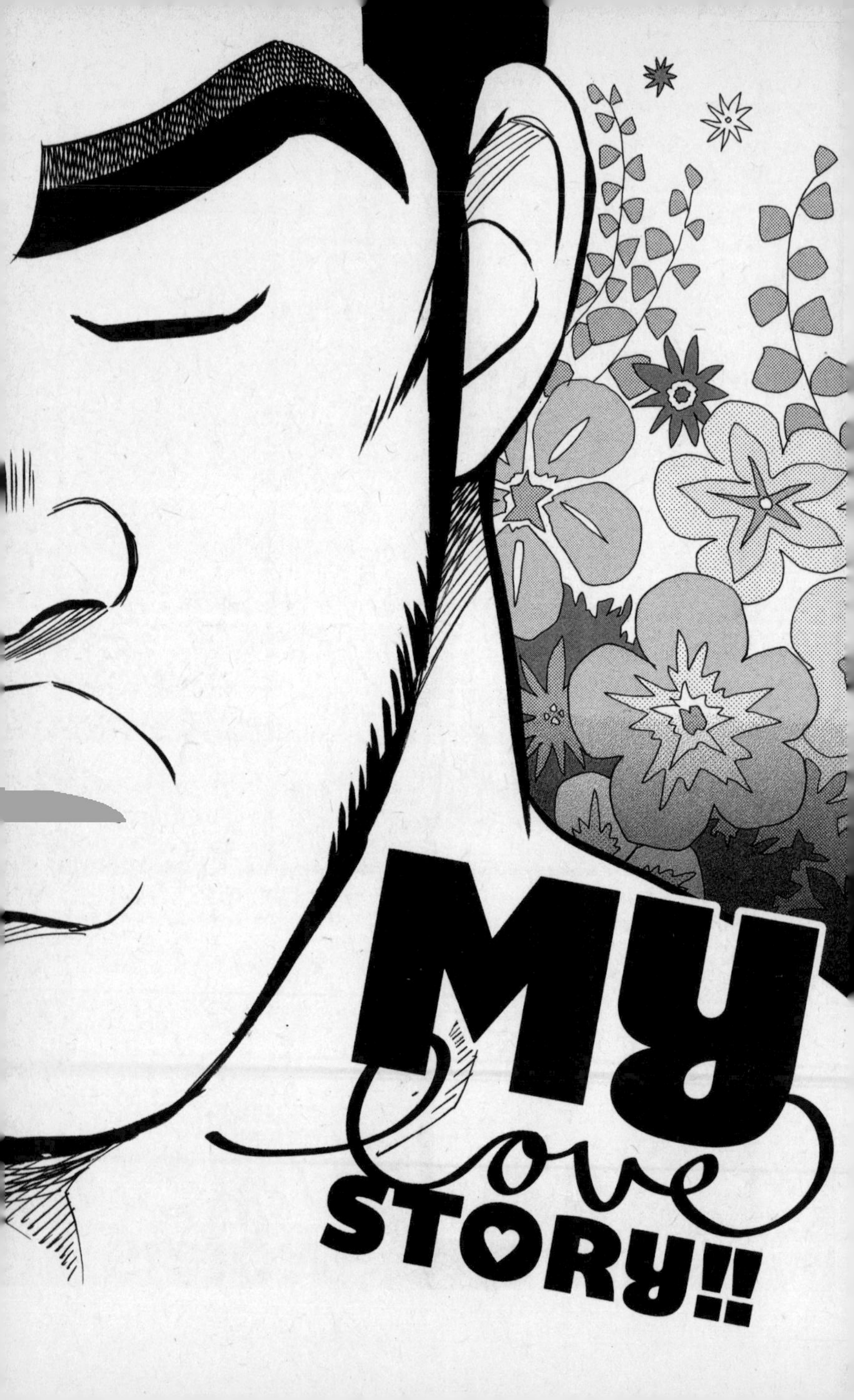
MY
love
STORY!!

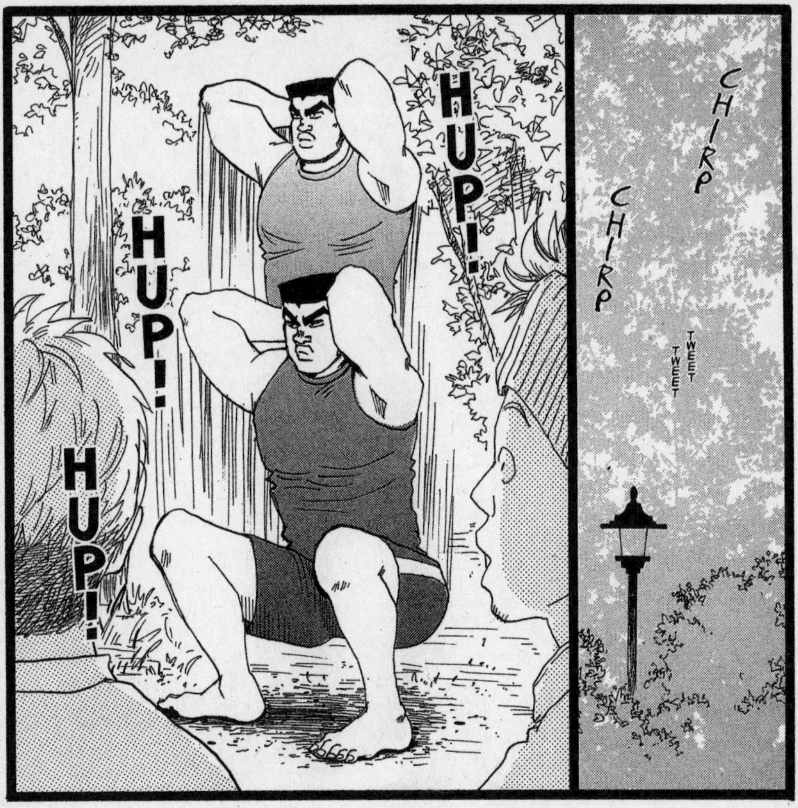
CHIRP
CHIRP
TWEET
TWEET
HUP!!
HUP!!
HUP!!

MY love STORY!!

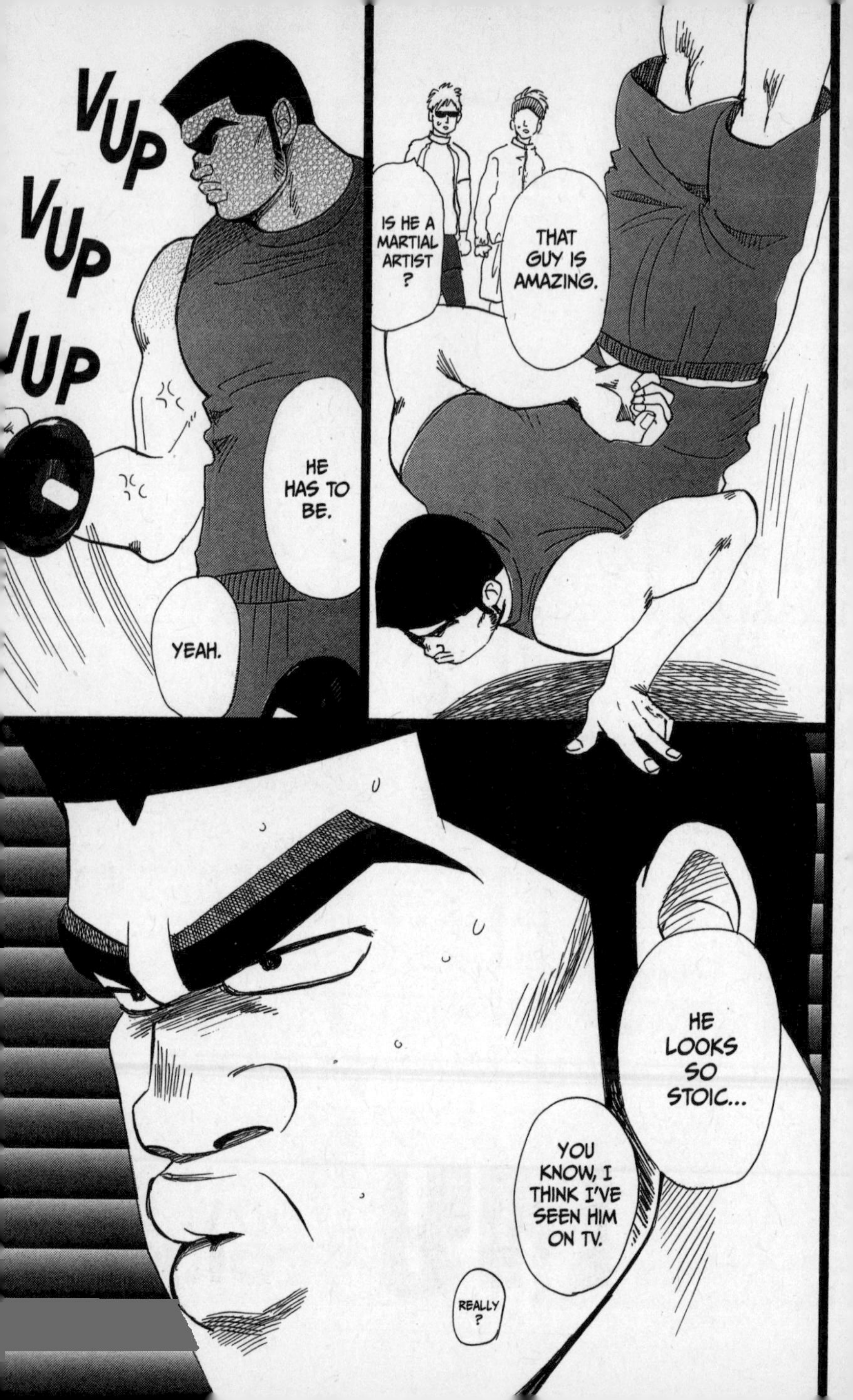

THAT GUY IS AMAZING.
IS HE A MARTIAL ARTIST?
VUP VUP VUP
HE HAS TO BE.
YEAH.
HE LOOKS SO STOIC...
YOU KNOW, I THINK I'VE SEEN HIM ON TV.
REALLY?

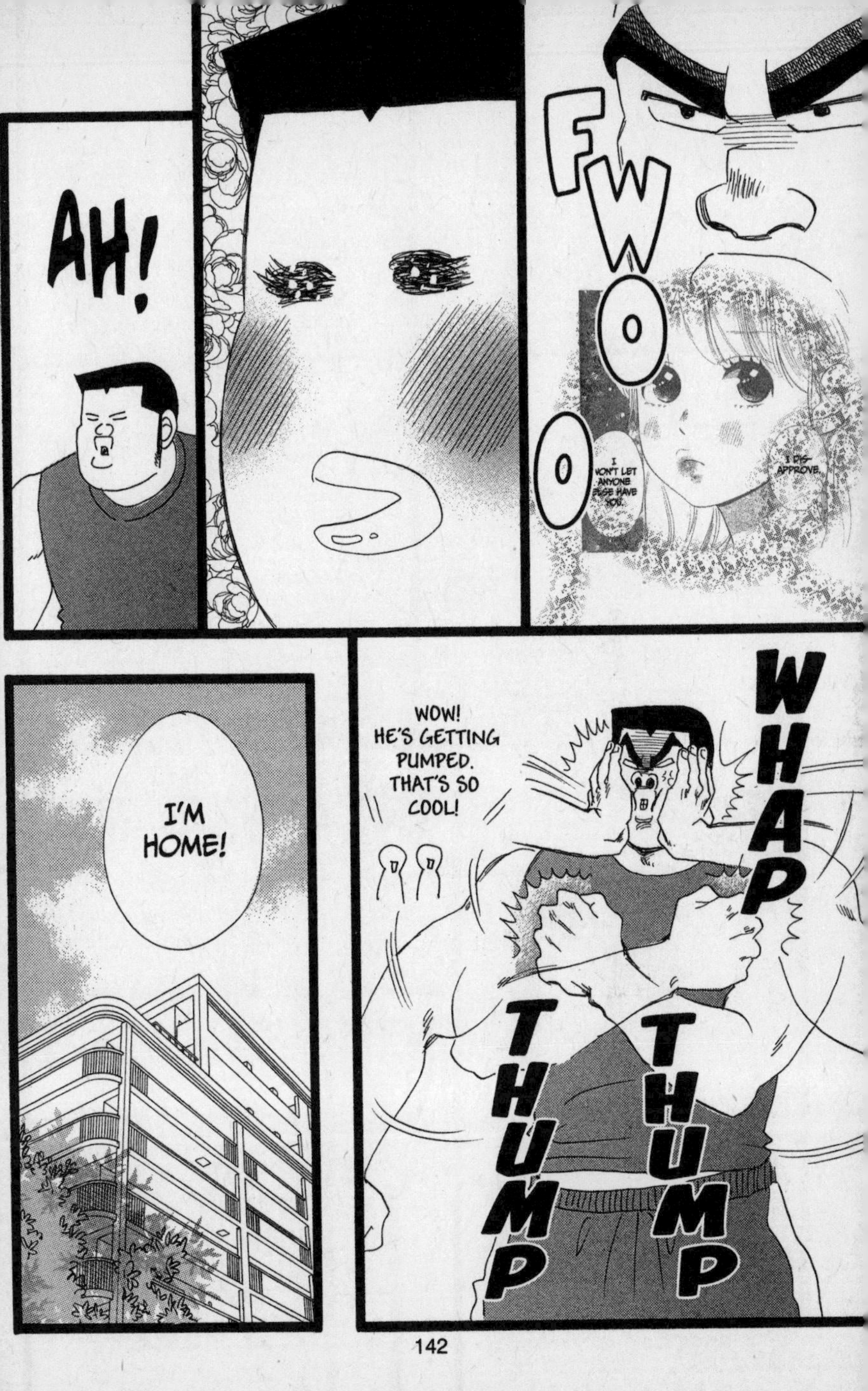
FWOOO
I DIS-APPROVE.
I WON'T LET ANYONE ELSE HAVE YOU.
AH!
WHAP
WOW! HE'S GETTING PUMPED. THAT'S SO COOL!
THUMP THUMP
I'M HOME!

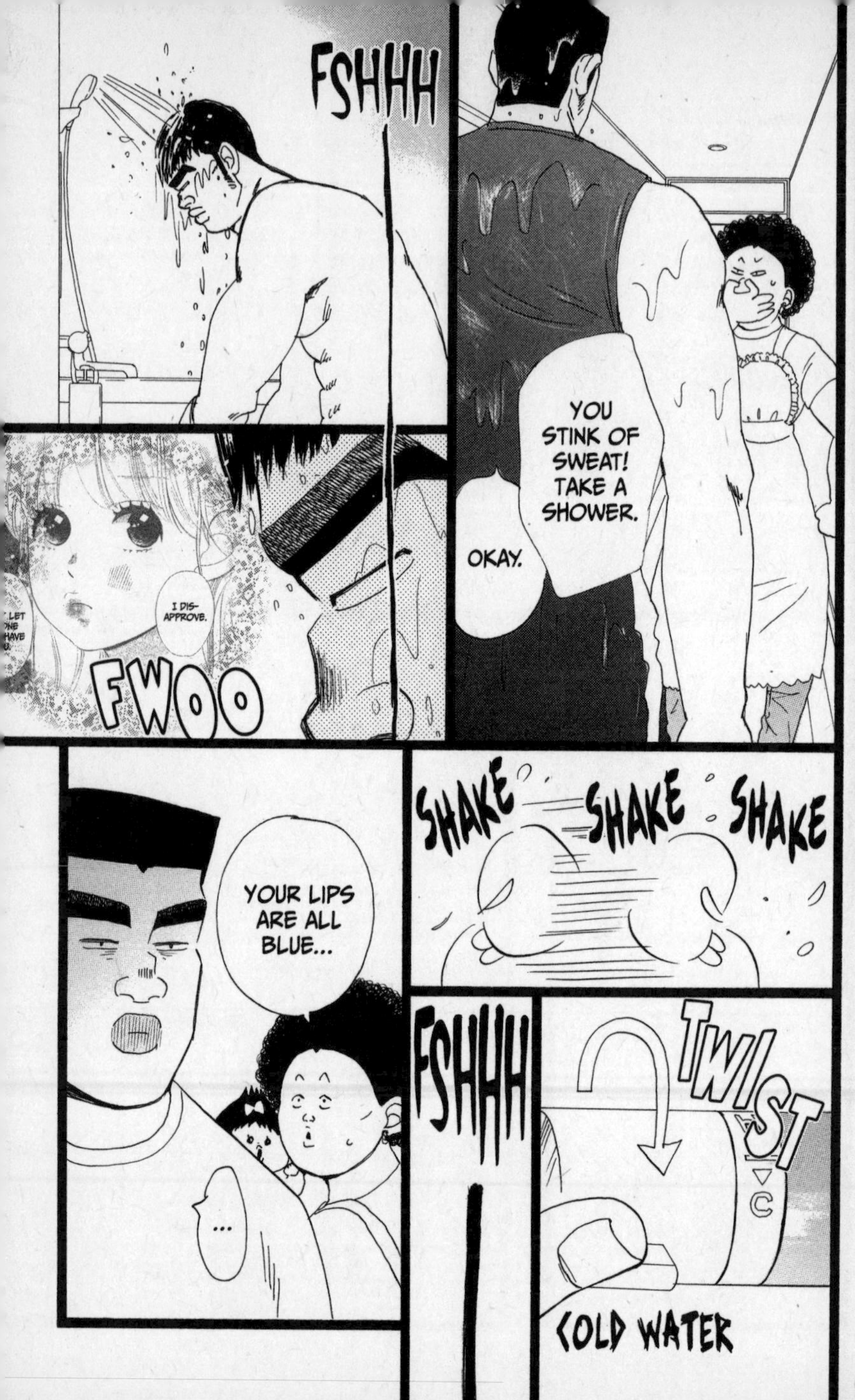
YOU STINK OF SWEAT! TAKE A SHOWER.
OKAY.
FSHHH
I DIS-APPROVE.
FWOO
SHAKE SHAKE SHAKE
TWIST
COLD WATER
FSHHH
YOUR LIPS ARE ALL BLUE...
...

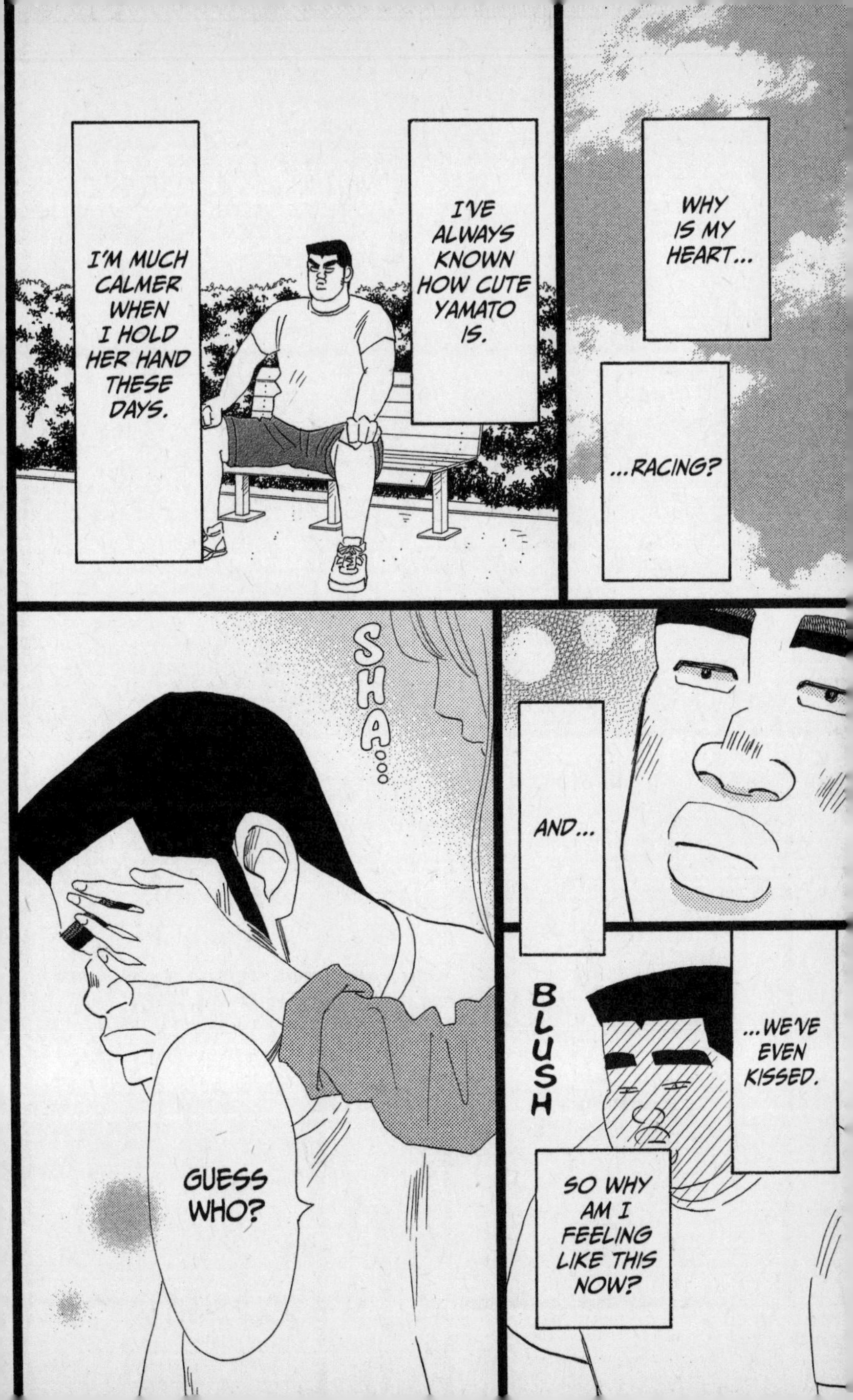
WHY IS MY HEART...
...RACING?
I'VE ALWAYS KNOWN HOW CUTE YAMATO IS.
I'M MUCH CALMER WHEN I HOLD HER HAND THESE DAYS.
AND...
...WE'VE EVEN KISSED.
BLUSH
SO WHY AM I FEELING LIKE THIS NOW?
SHA...
GUESS WHO?

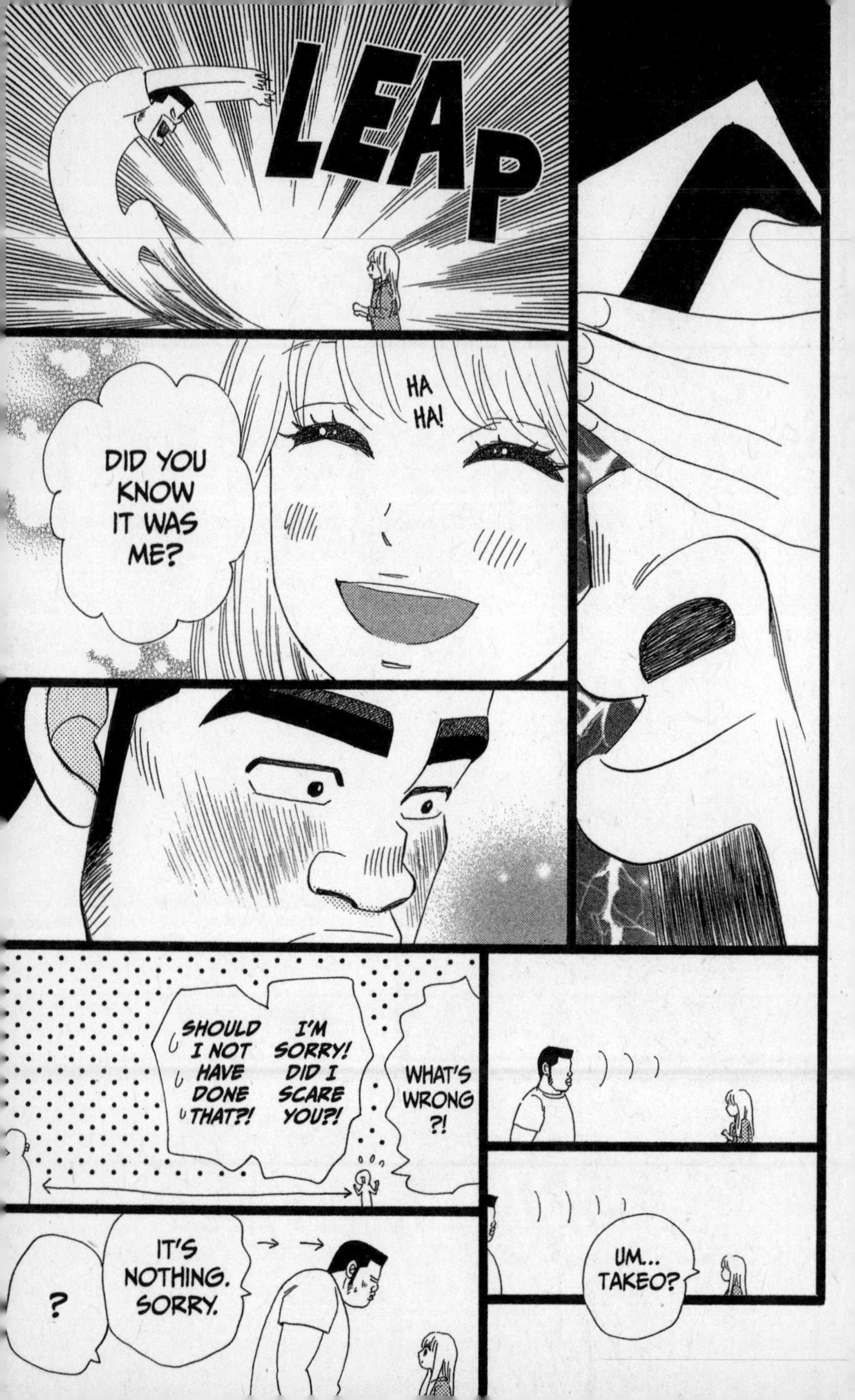
LEAP
HA HA!
DID YOU KNOW IT WAS ME?
UM... TAKEO?
WHAT'S WRONG?!
I'M SORRY! DID I SCARE YOU?!
SHOULD I NOT HAVE DONE THAT?!
IT'S NOTHING. SORRY.
?

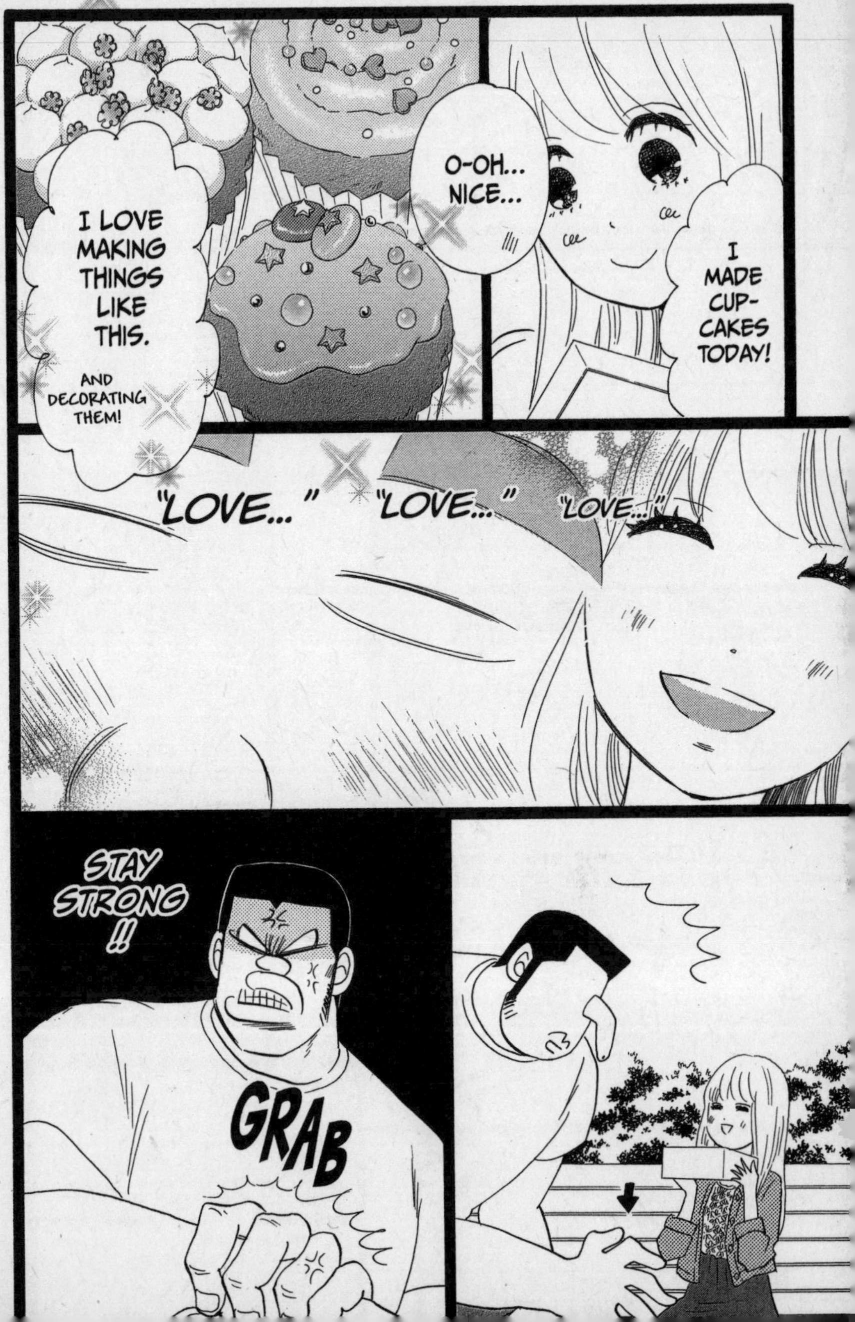

I MADE CUP-CAKES TODAY!
O-OH... NICE...
I LOVE MAKING THINGS LIKE THIS.
AND DECORATING THEM!
"LOVE..." "LOVE..." "LOVE..."
STAY STRONG !!
GRAB

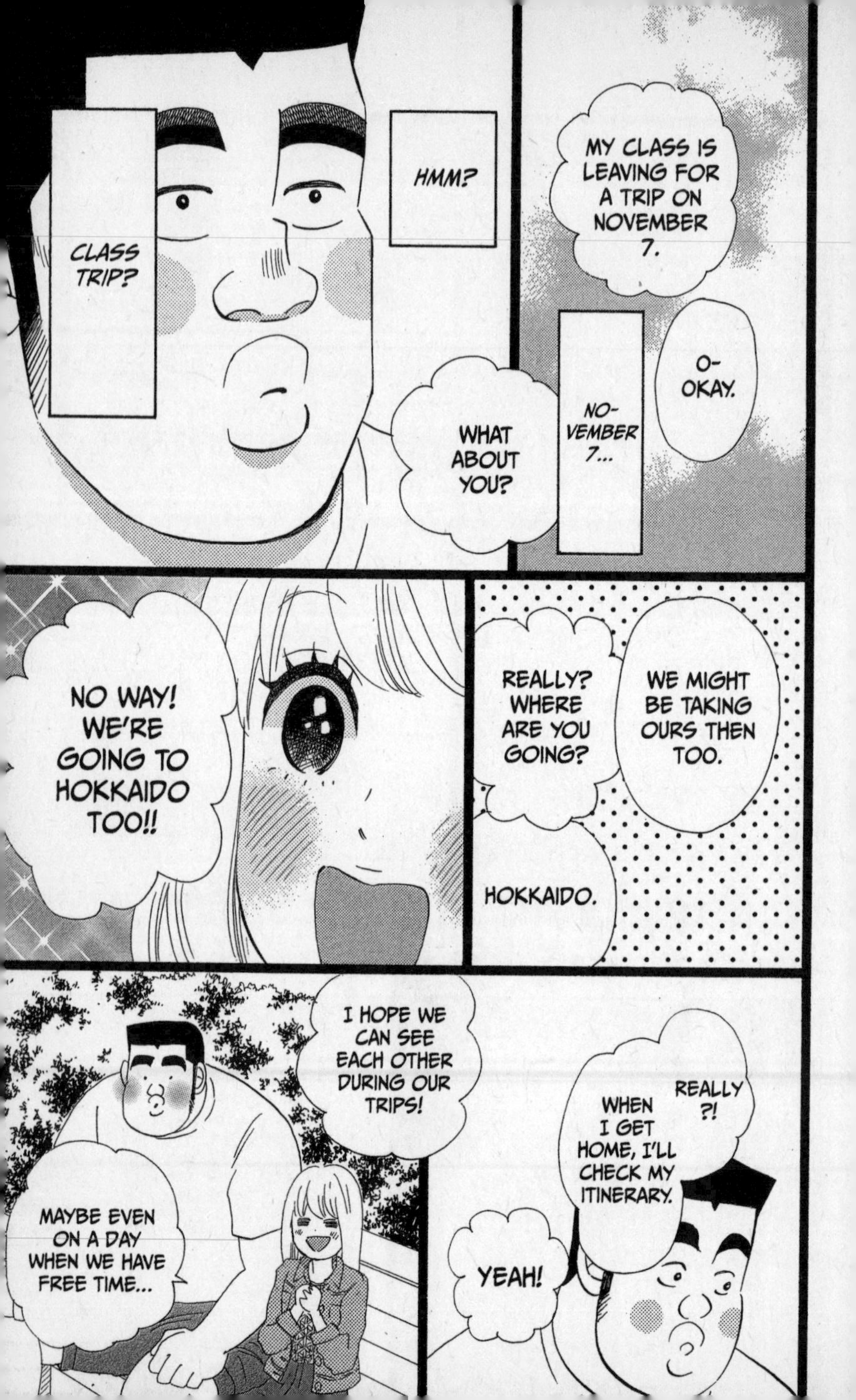

MY CLASS IS LEAVING FOR A TRIP ON NOVEMBER 7.
O-OKAY.
NO-VEMBER 7...
WHAT ABOUT YOU?
HMM?
CLASS TRIP?
WE MIGHT BE TAKING OURS THEN TOO.
REALLY? WHERE ARE YOU GOING?
HOKKAIDO.
NO WAY! WE'RE GOING TO HOKKAIDO TOO!!
REALLY ?!
WHEN I GET HOME, I'LL CHECK MY ITINERARY.
YEAH!
I HOPE WE CAN SEE EACH OTHER DURING OUR TRIPS!
MAYBE EVEN ON A DAY WHEN WE HAVE FREE TIME...

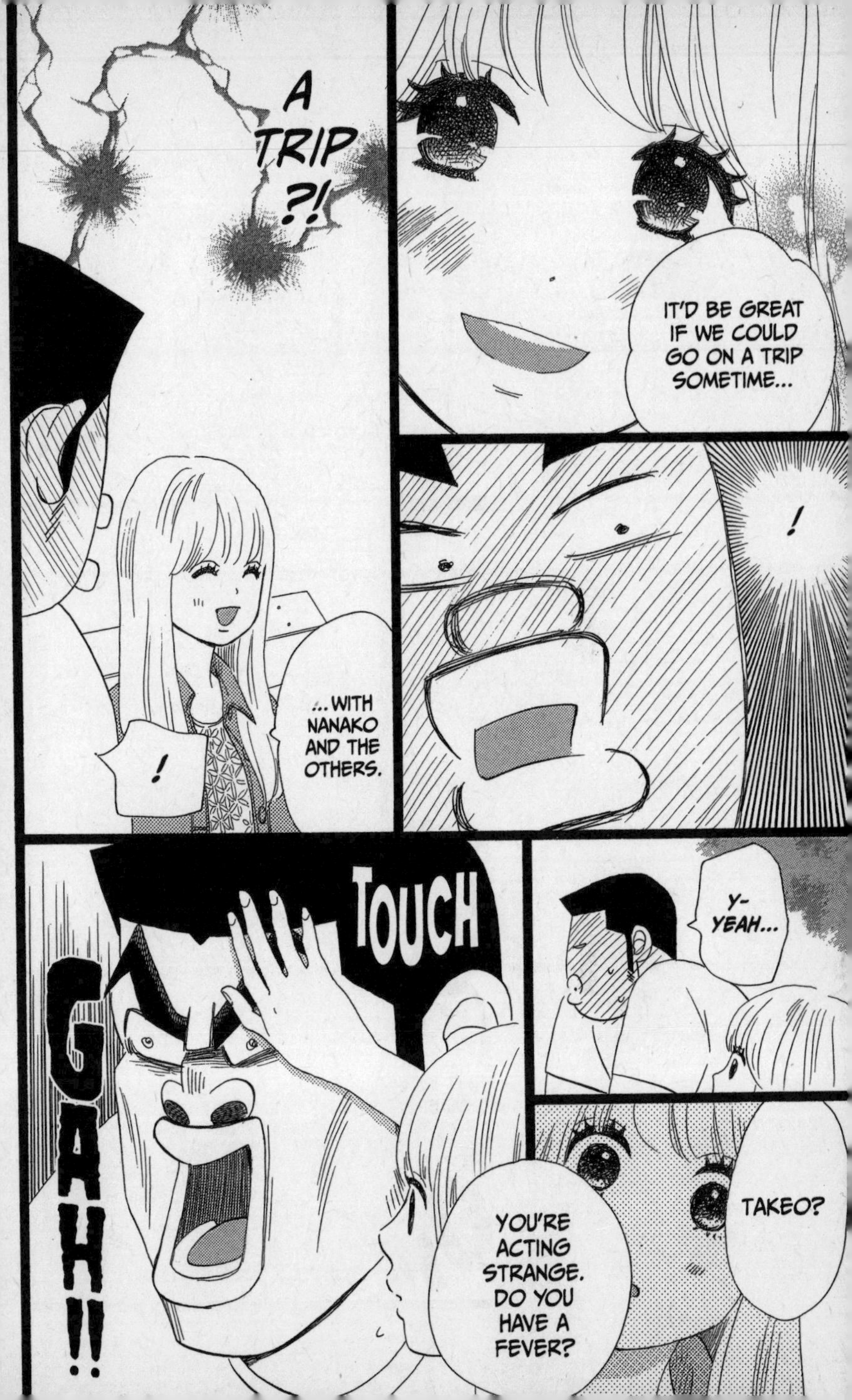
IT'D BE GREAT IF WE COULD GO ON A TRIP SOMETIME...
!
A TRIP ?!
...WITH NANAKO AND THE OTHERS.
!
Y-YEAH...
TAKEO?
TOUCH
GAH!!
YOU'RE ACTING STRANGE. DO YOU HAVE A FEVER?

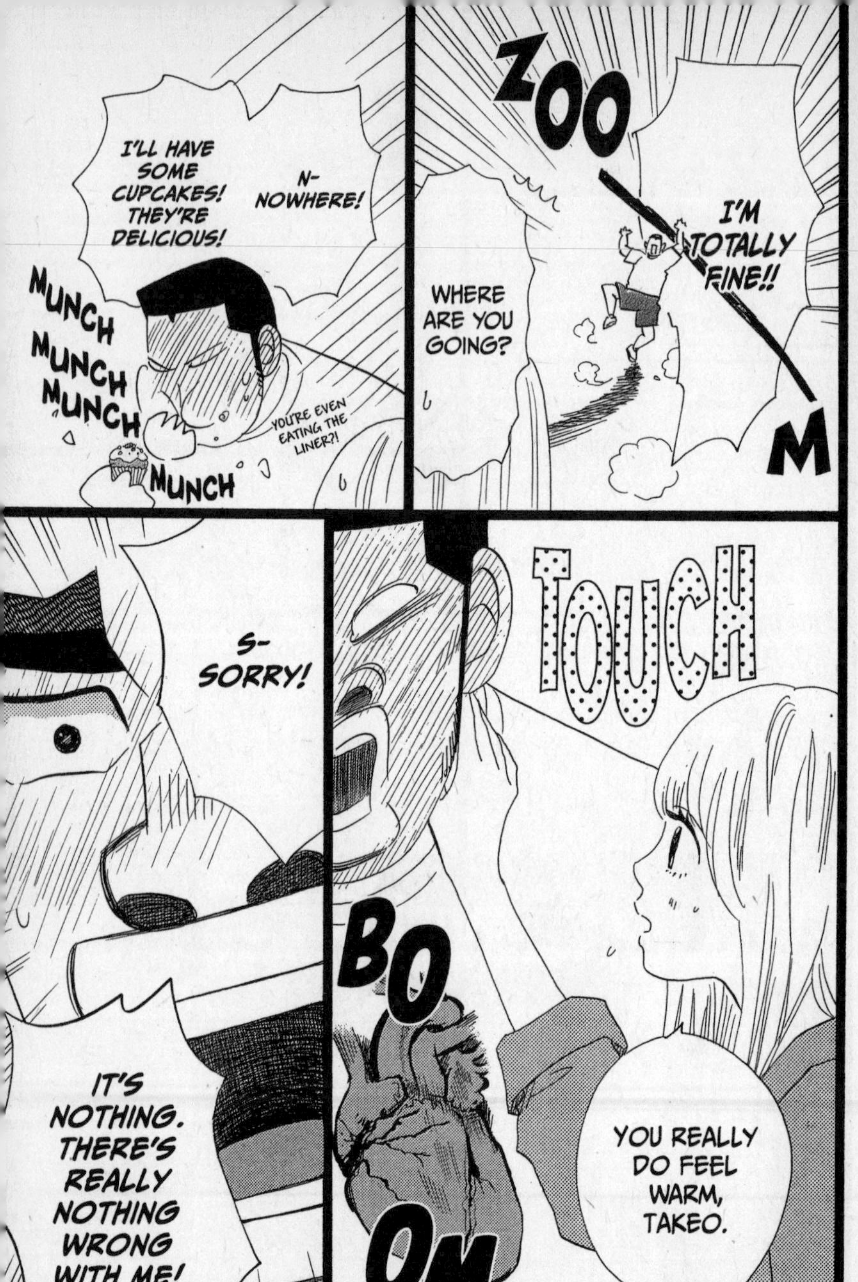
ZOOOM
I'M TOTALLY FINE!!
WHERE ARE YOU GOING?
N- NOWHERE!
I'LL HAVE SOME CUPCAKES! THEY'RE DELICIOUS!
MUNCH MUNCH MUNCH
YOU'RE EVEN EATING THE LINER?!
MUNCH
TOUCH
YOU REALLY DO FEEL WARM, TAKEO.
BOOM
S- SORRY!
IT'S NOTHING. THERE'S REALLY NOTHING WRONG WITH ME!

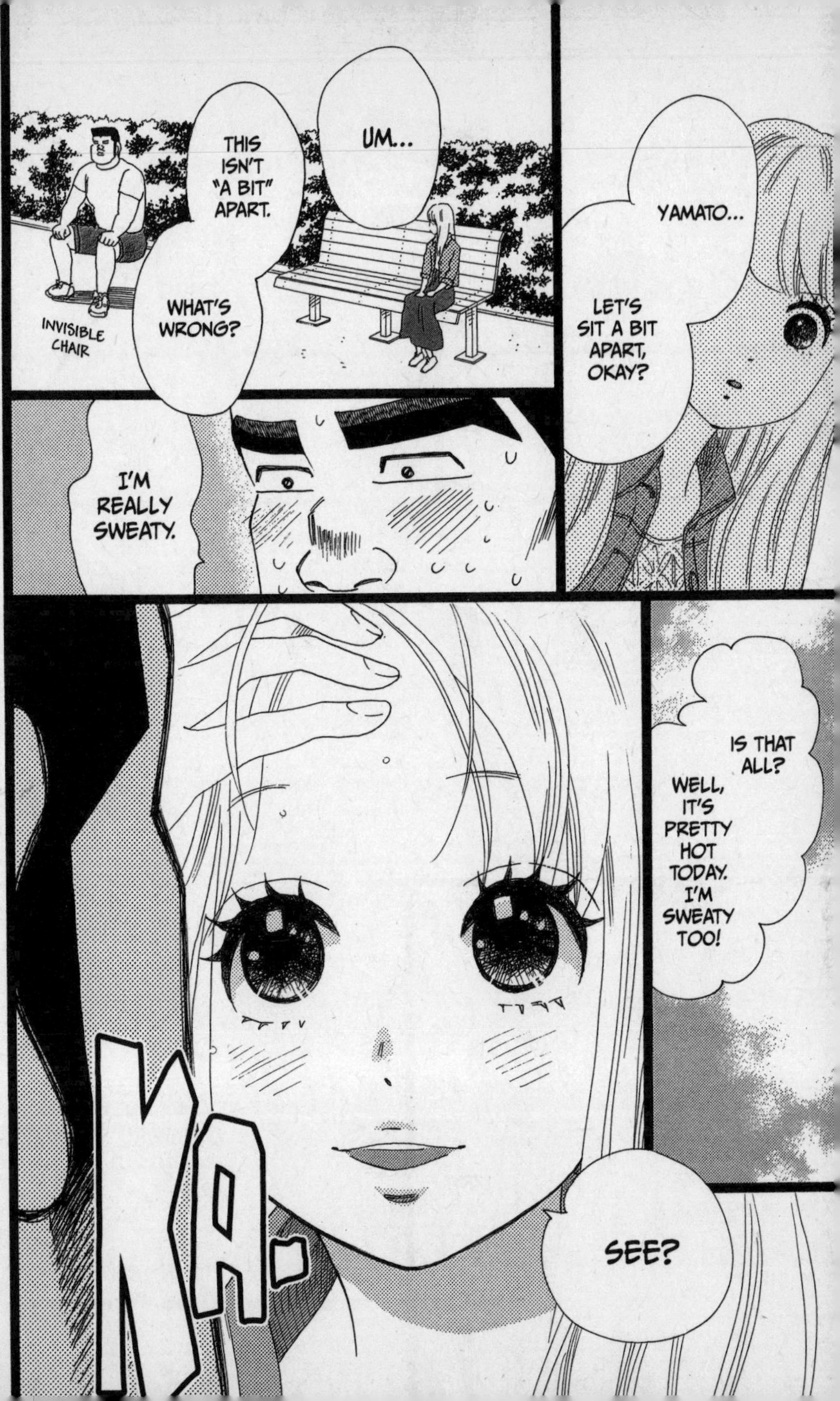

YAMATO...
LET'S SIT A BIT APART, OKAY?
UM...
THIS ISN'T "A BIT" APART.
WHAT'S WRONG?
INVISIBLE CHAIR
I'M REALLY SWEATY.
IS THAT ALL?
WELL, IT'S PRETTY HOT TODAY. I'M SWEATY TOO!
SEE?
MA.

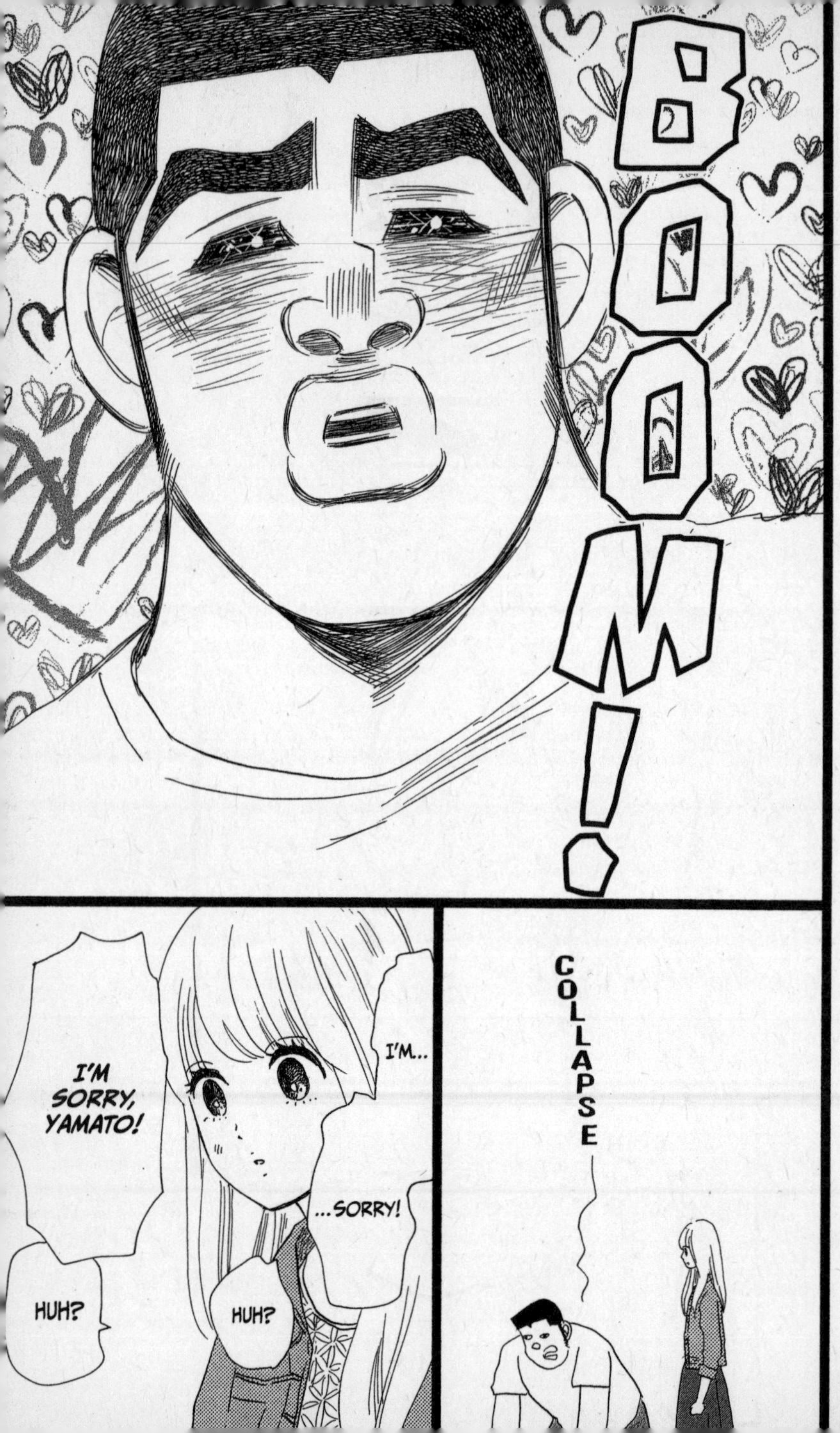
BOOM!
COLLAPSE
I'M...
...SORRY!
I'M SORRY, YAMATO!
HUH?
HUH?

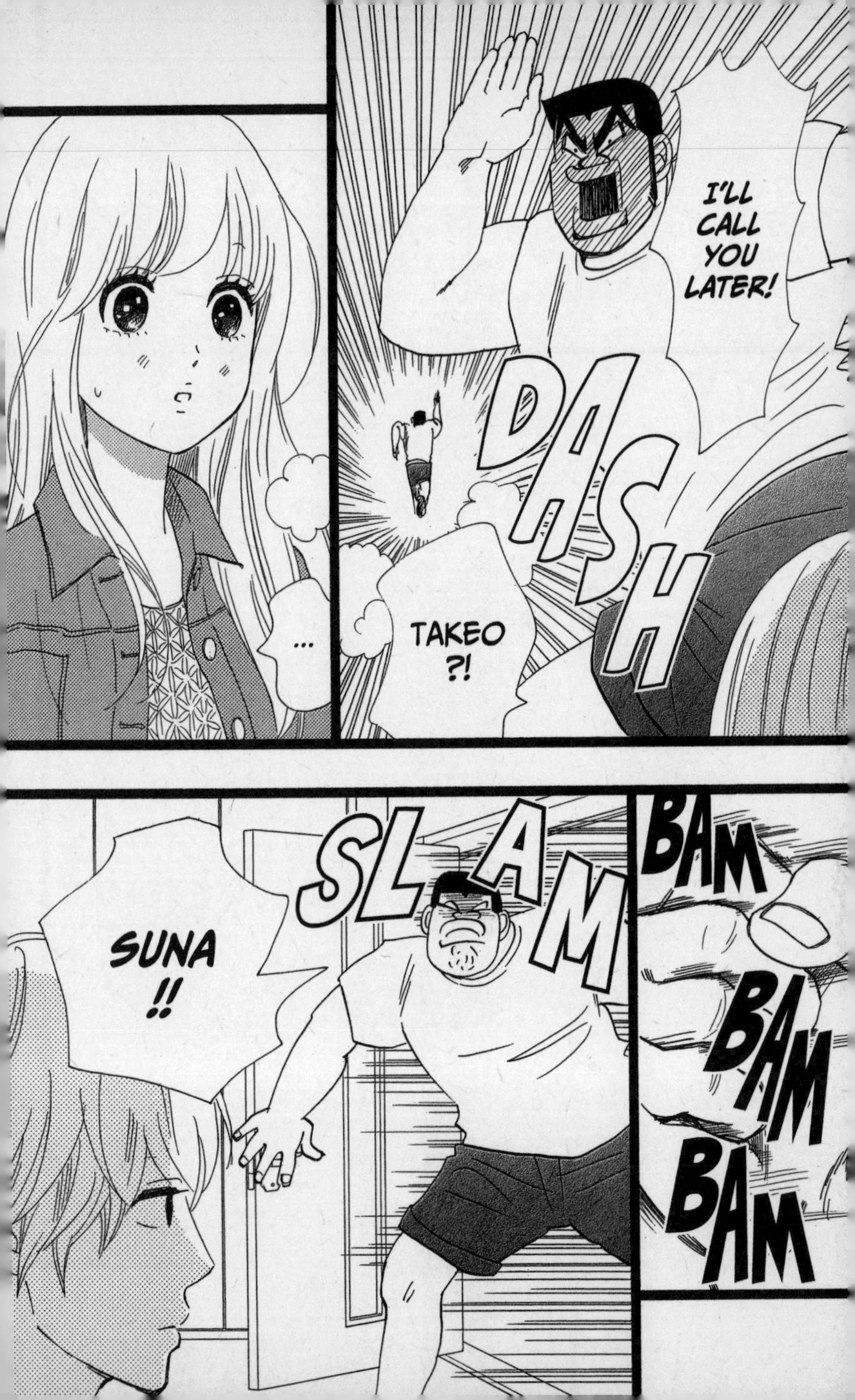
I'LL CALL YOU LATER!
DASH
TAKEO ?!
...
BAM BAM BAM BAM
SLAM
SUNA !!

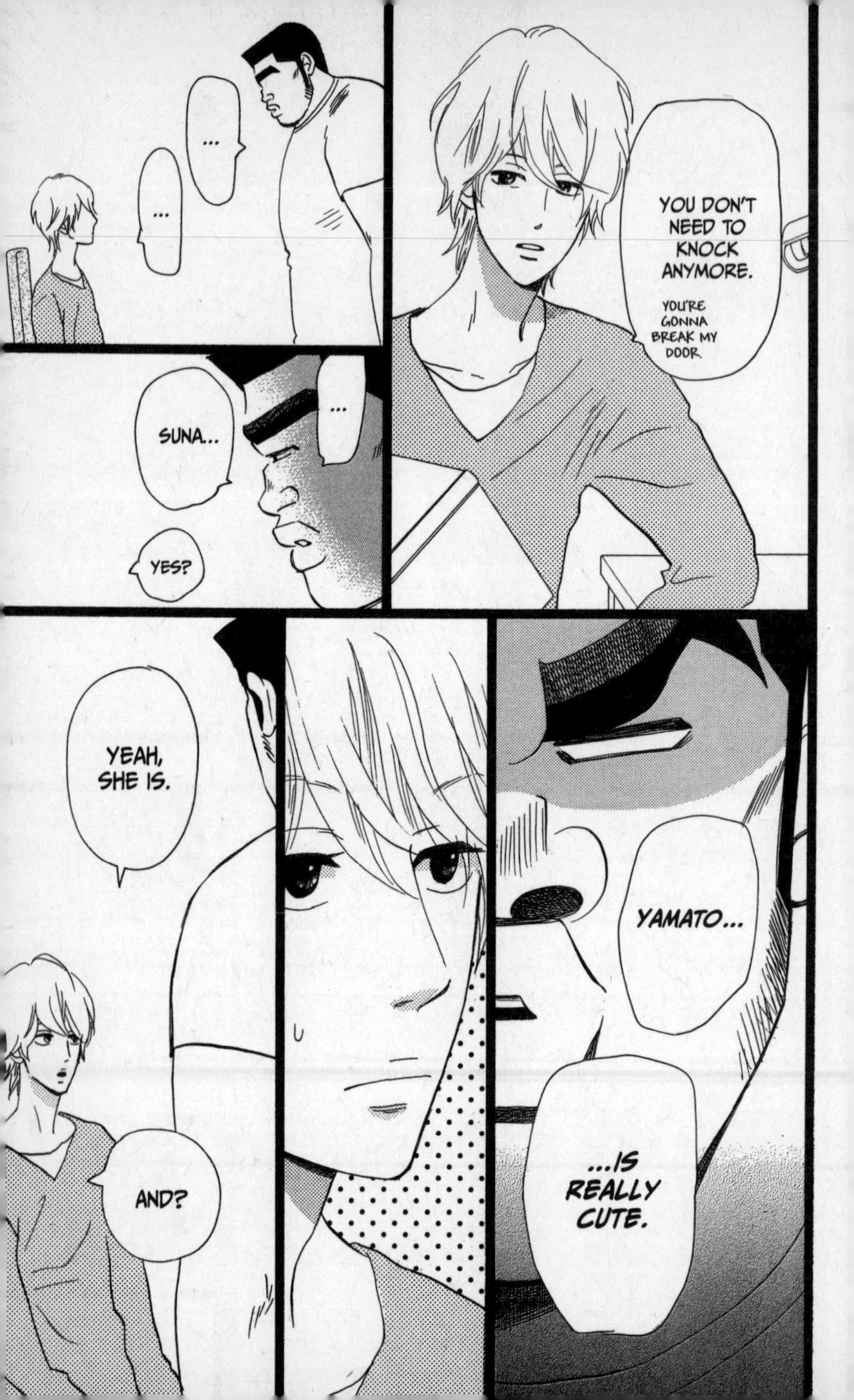
YOU DON'T NEED TO KNOCK ANYMORE.
YOU'RE GONNA BREAK MY DOOR.
...
...
...
SUNA...
YES?
YAMATO...
...IS REALLY CUTE.
YEAH, SHE IS.
AND?

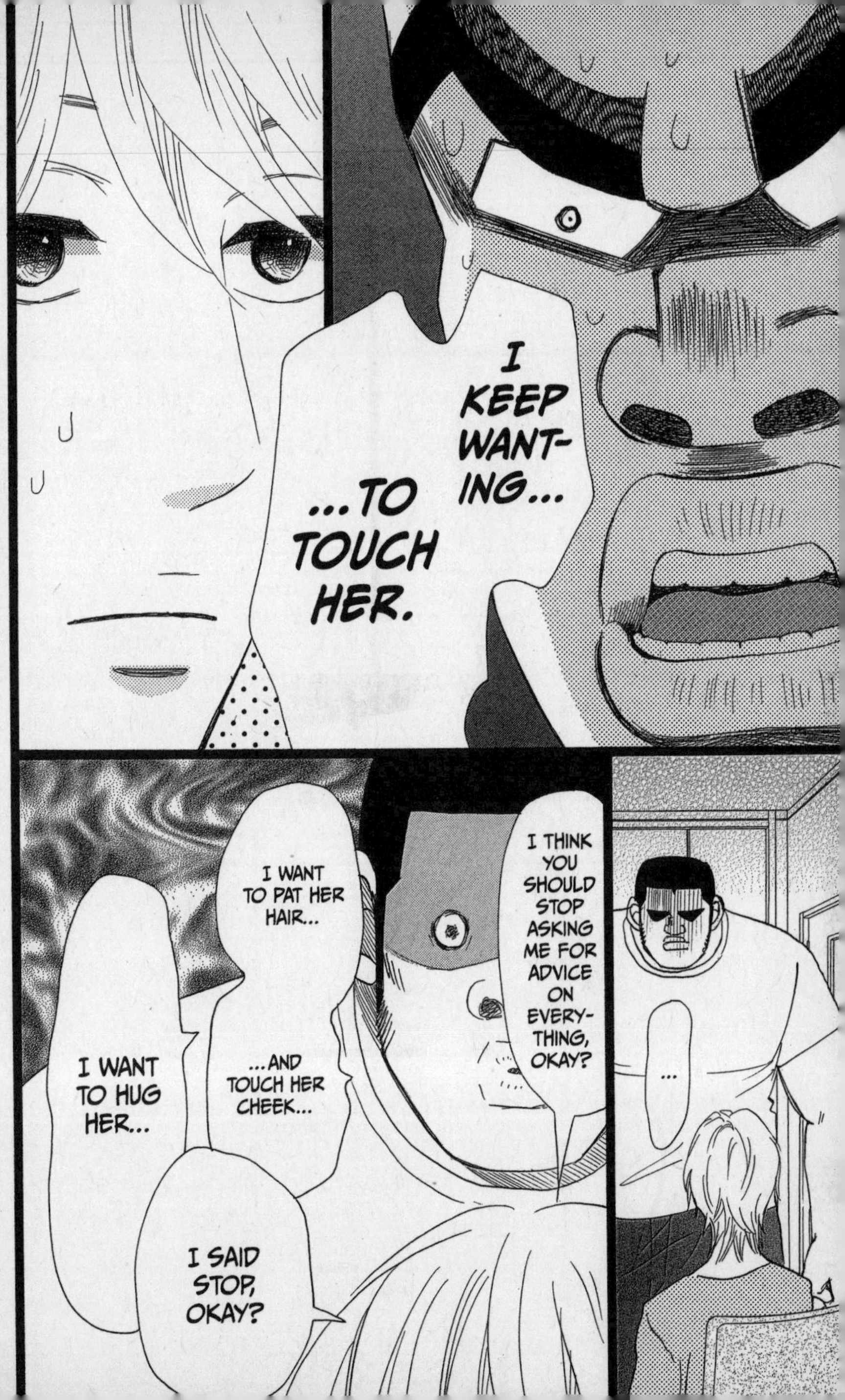
I KEEP WANTING...
...TO TOUCH HER.
...
I THINK YOU SHOULD STOP ASKING ME FOR ADVICE ON EVERYTHING, OKAY?
I WANT TO PAT HER HAIR...
...AND TOUCH HER CHEEK...
I WANT TO HUG HER...
I SAID STOP, OKAY?

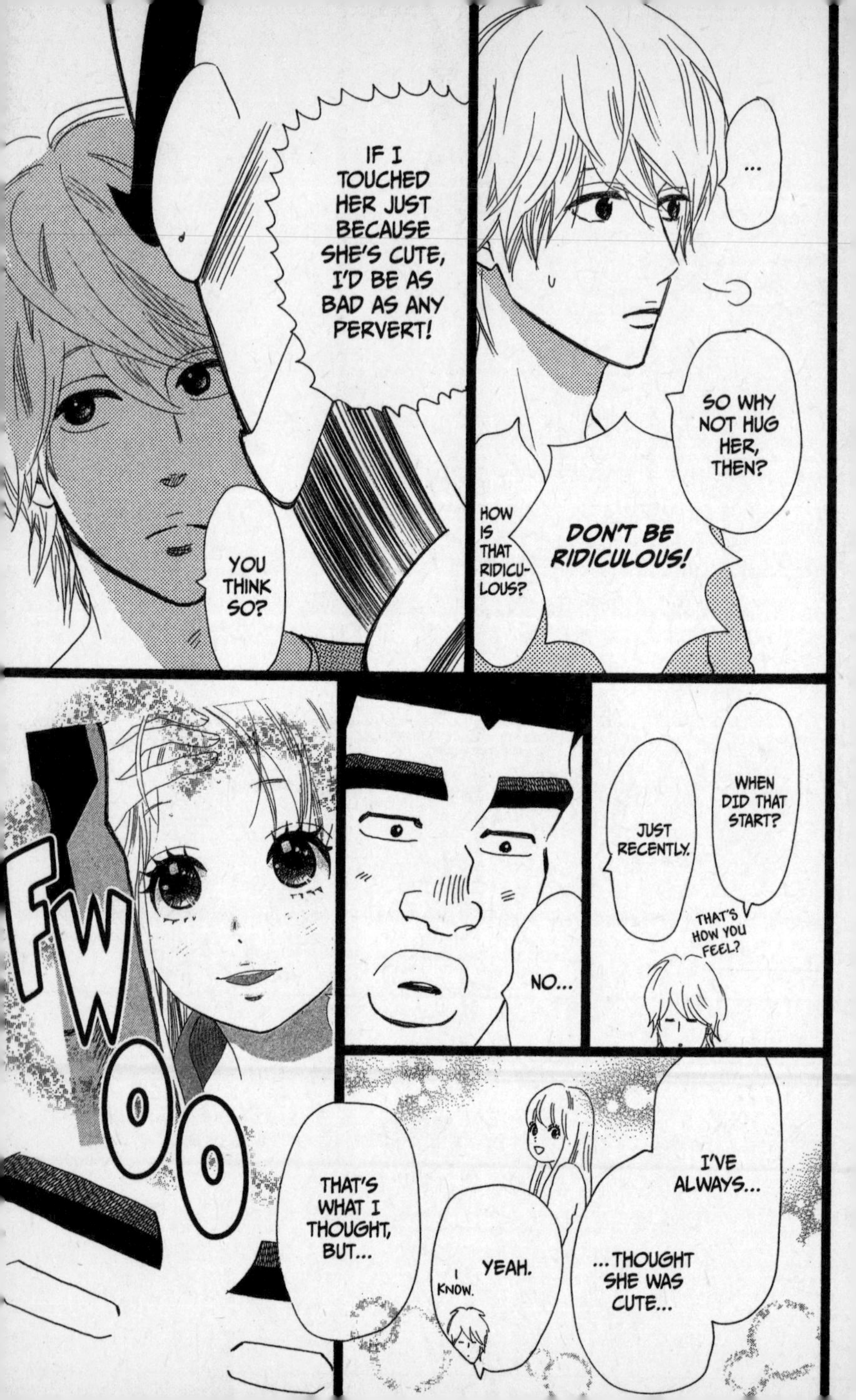
...
SO WHY NOT HUG HER, THEN?
DON'T BE RIDICULOUS!
HOW IS THAT RIDICULOUS?
IF I TOUCHED HER JUST BECAUSE SHE'S CUTE, I'D BE AS BAD AS ANY PERVERT!
YOU THINK SO?
WHEN DID THAT START?
JUST RECENTLY.
THAT'S HOW YOU FEEL?
NO...
I'VE ALWAYS...
...THOUGHT SHE WAS CUTE...
YEAH.
I KNOW.
THAT'S WHAT I THOUGHT, BUT...
FWOOO

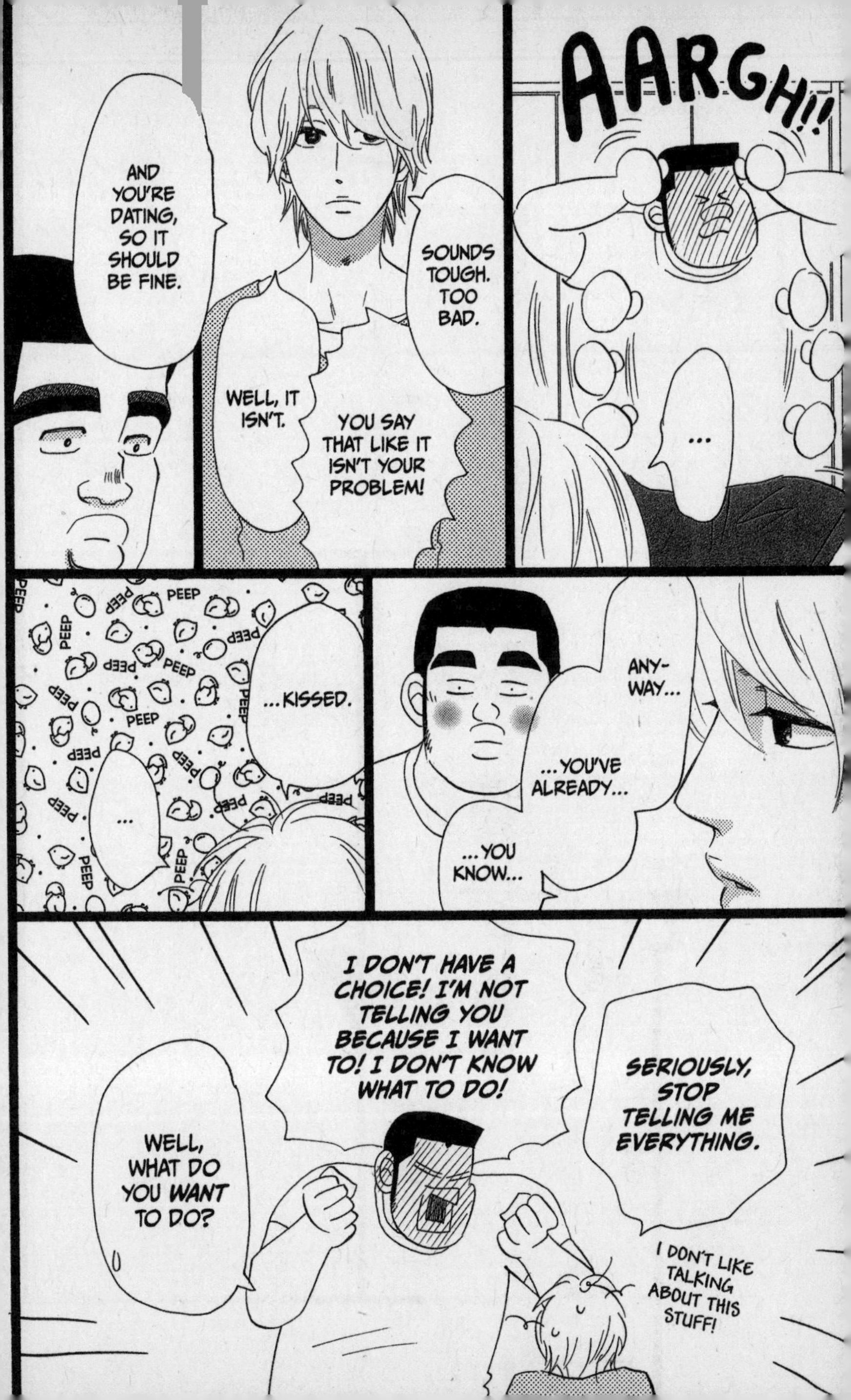
AARGH!!
...
SOUNDS TOUGH. TOO BAD.
YOU SAY THAT LIKE IT ISN'T YOUR PROBLEM!
WELL, IT ISN'T.
AND YOU'RE DATING, SO IT SHOULD BE FINE.
ANY-WAY...
...YOU'VE ALREADY...
...YOU KNOW...
...KISSED.
...
PEEP PEEP PEEP PEEP
SERIOUSLY, STOP TELLING ME EVERYTHING.
I DON'T HAVE A CHOICE! I'M NOT TELLING YOU BECAUSE I WANT TO! I DON'T KNOW WHAT TO DO!
WELL, WHAT DO YOU WANT TO DO?
I DON'T LIKE TALKING ABOUT THIS STUFF!

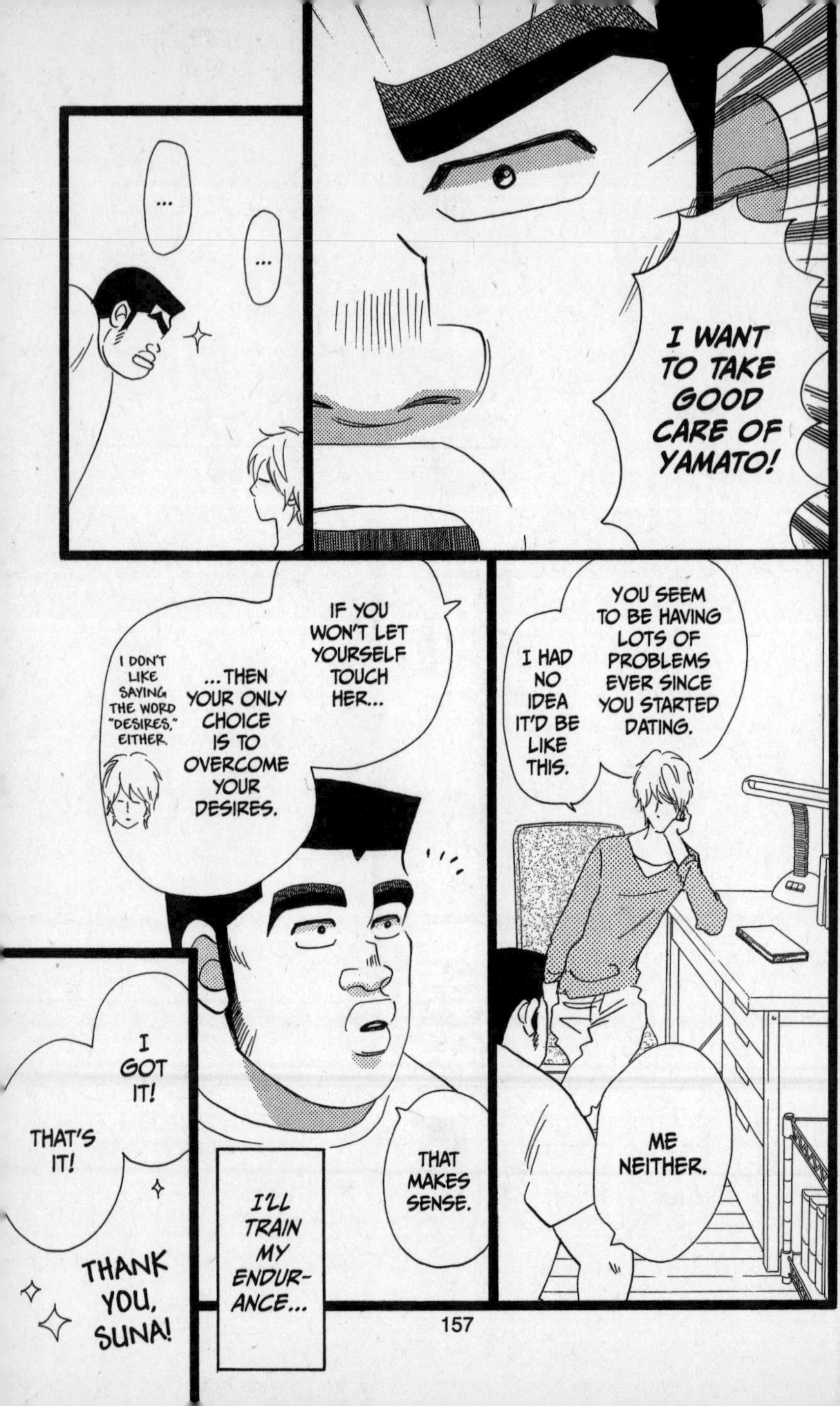
I WANT TO TAKE GOOD CARE OF YAMATO!
...
...
YOU SEEM TO BE HAVING LOTS OF PROBLEMS EVER SINCE YOU STARTED DATING.
I HAD NO IDEA IT'D BE LIKE THIS.
ME NEITHER.
IF YOU WON'T LET YOURSELF TOUCH HER...
...THEN YOUR ONLY CHOICE IS TO OVERCOME YOUR DESIRES.
I DON'T LIKE SAYING THE WORD "DESIRES," EITHER.
THAT MAKES SENSE.
I'LL TRAIN MY ENDURANCE...
I GOT IT!
THAT'S IT!
THANK YOU, SUNA!

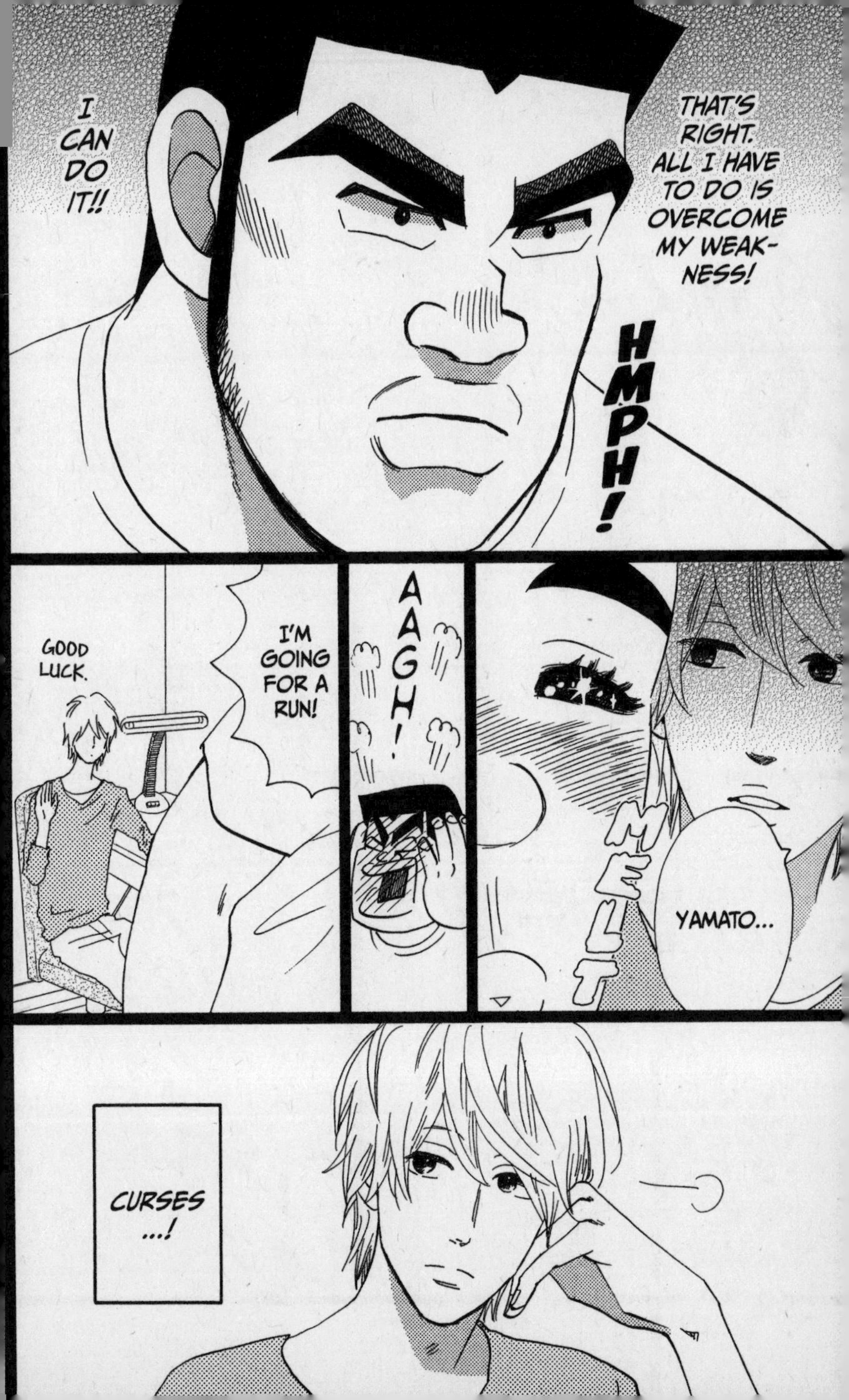
THAT'S RIGHT. ALL I HAVE TO DO IS OVERCOME MY WEAK-NESS!
HMPH!
I CAN DO IT!!
YAMATO...
MELT
AAGH!
I'M GOING FOR A RUN!
GOOD LUCK.
CURSES ...!

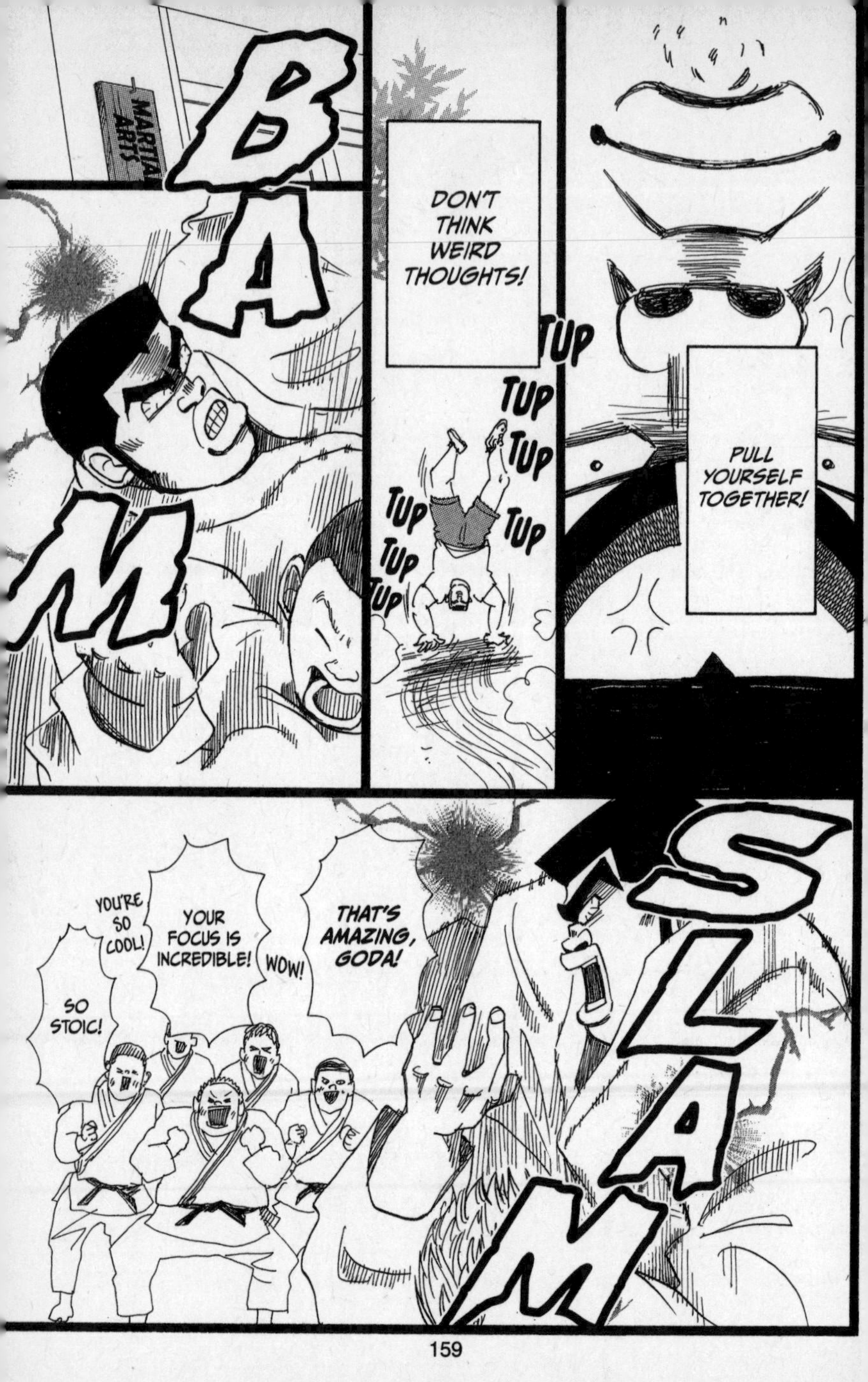
PULL YOURSELF TOGETHER!
DON'T THINK WEIRD THOUGHTS!
TUP TUP TUP TUP TUP TUP TUP
MARTIAL ARTS
BAM
SLAM
THAT'S AMAZING, GODA!
WOW!
YOUR FOCUS IS INCREDIBLE!
YOU'RE SO COOL!
SO STOIC!

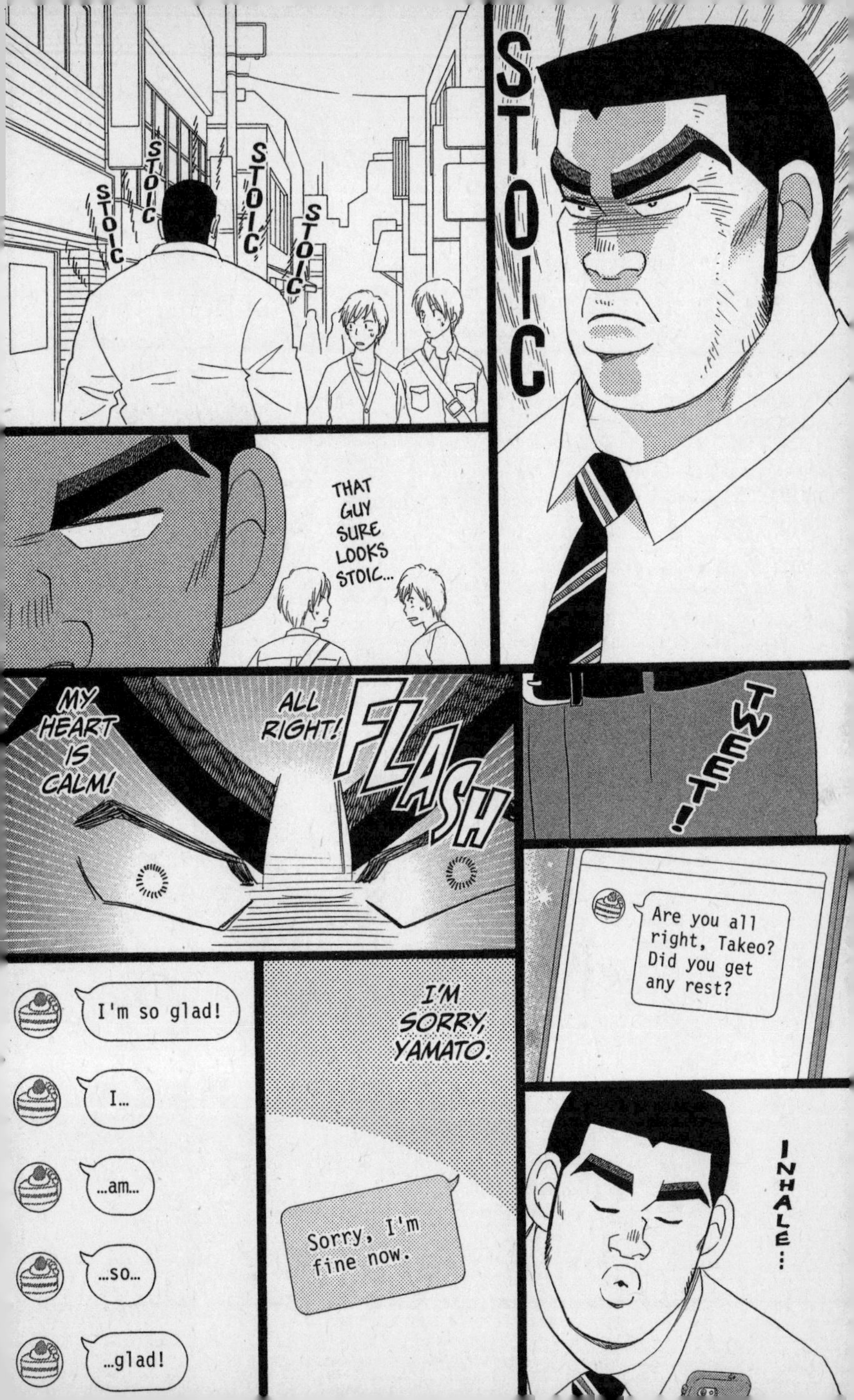
STOIC
STOIC
STOIC
STOIC
STOIC
THAT GUY SURE LOOKS STOIC...
TWEET!
FLASH
ALL RIGHT!
MY HEART IS CALM!
Are you all right, Takeo? Did you get any rest?
INHALE...
I'M SORRY, YAMATO.
Sorry, I'm fine now.
I'm so glad!
I...
...am...
...so...
...glad!

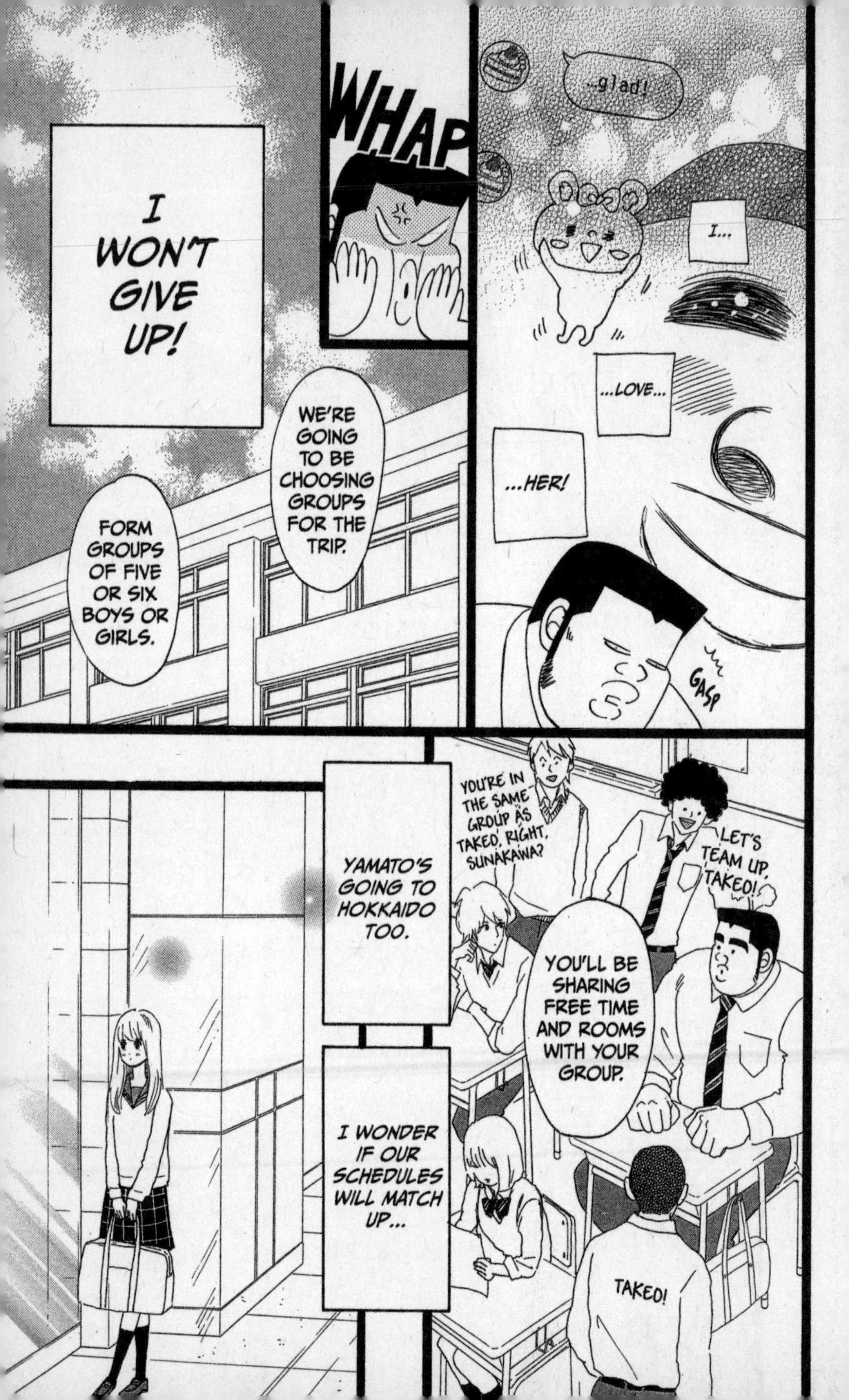
...glad!
I...
...LOVE...
...HER!
GASP
WHAP
I WON'T GIVE UP!
WE'RE GOING TO BE CHOOSING GROUPS FOR THE TRIP.
FORM GROUPS OF FIVE OR SIX BOYS OR GIRLS.
LET'S TEAM UP, TAKEO!
YOU'RE IN THE SAME GROUP AS TAKEO, RIGHT, SUNAKAWA?
YOU'LL BE SHARING FREE TIME AND ROOMS WITH YOUR GROUP.
TAKEO!
YAMATO'S GOING TO HOKKAIDO TOO.
I WONDER IF OUR SCHEDULES WILL MATCH UP...

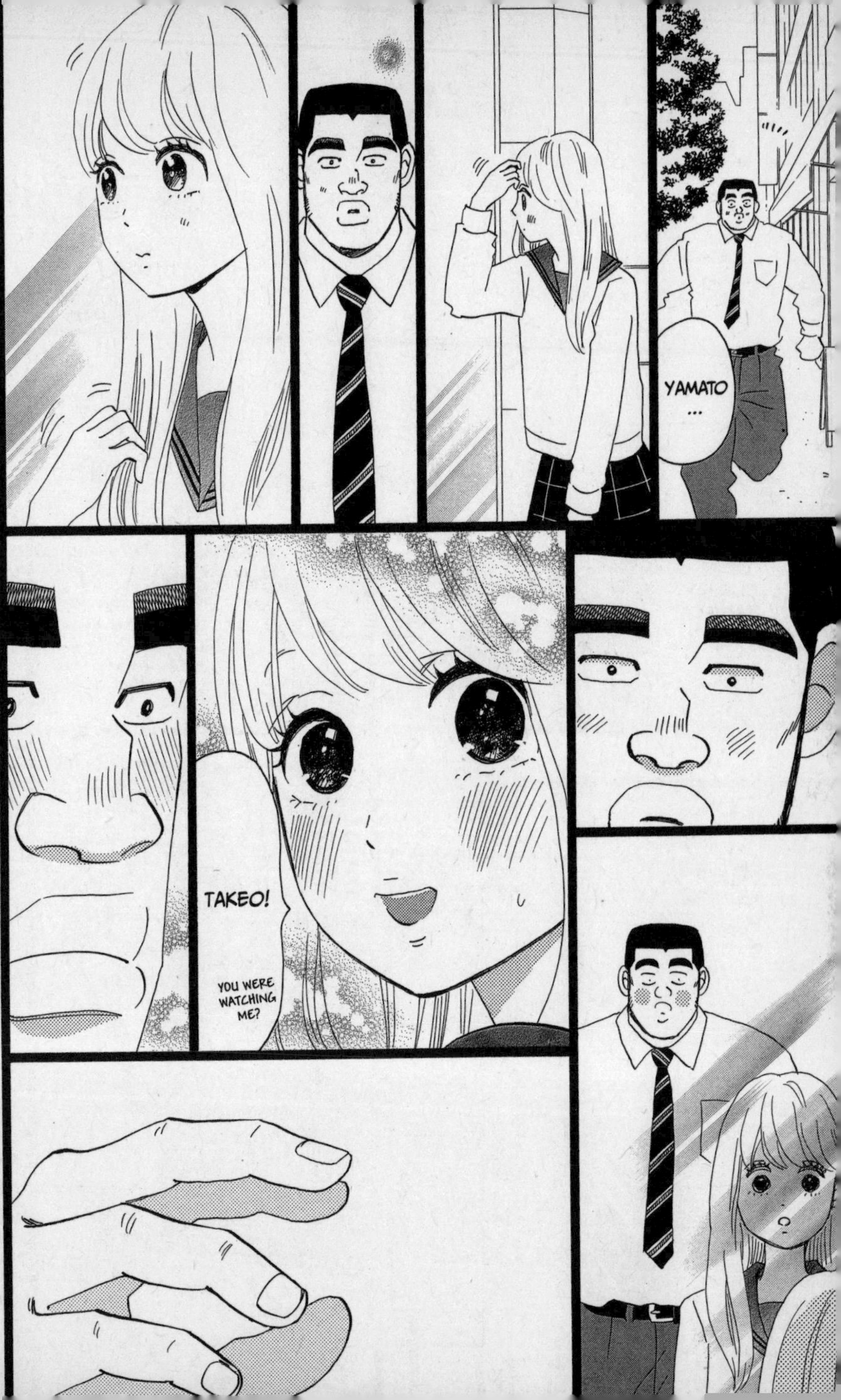
YAMATO ...
TAKEO!
YOU WERE WATCHING ME?

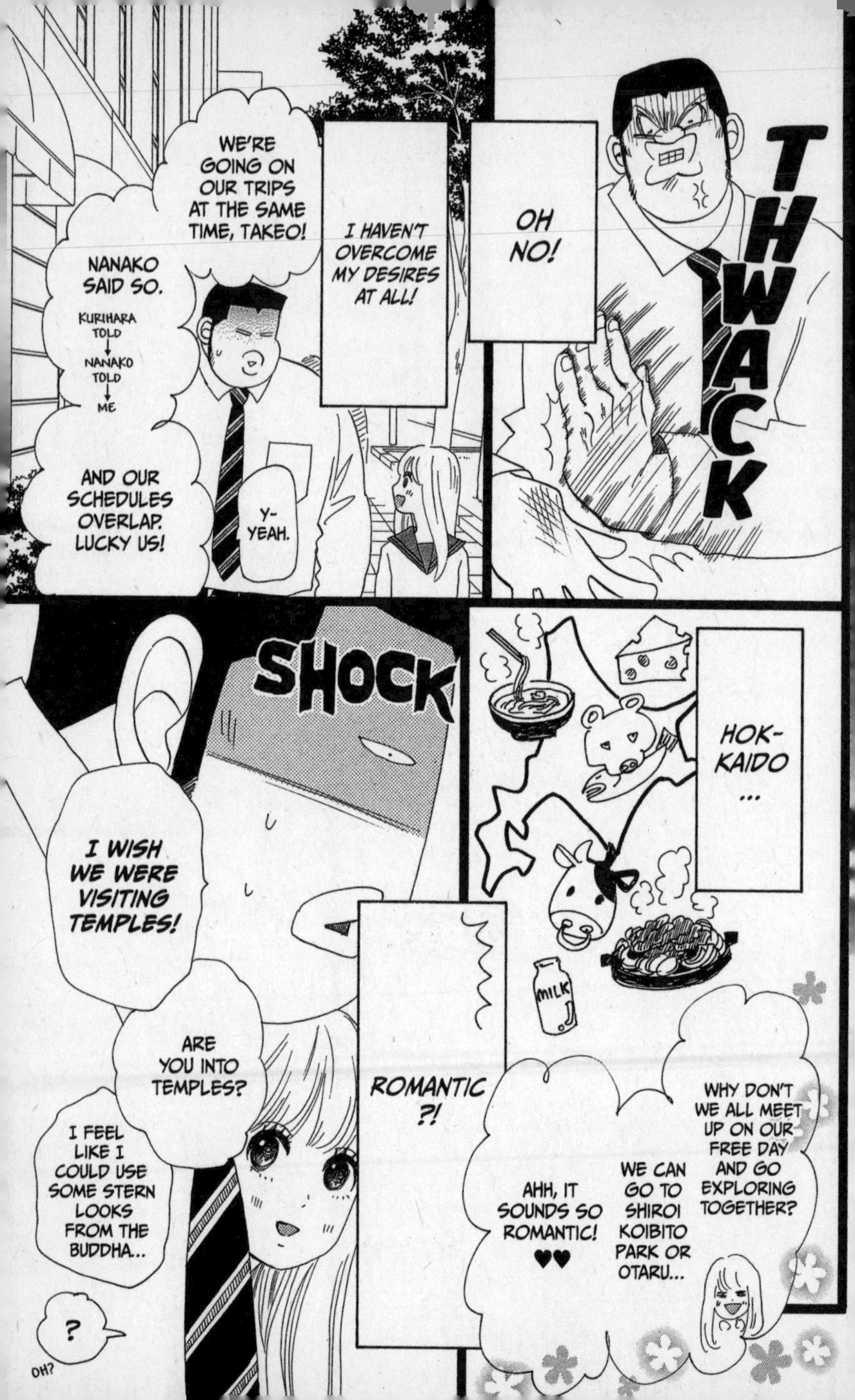
OH NO!
THWACK
I HAVEN'T OVERCOME MY DESIRES AT ALL!
WE'RE GOING ON OUR TRIPS AT THE SAME TIME, TAKEO!
NANAKO SAID SO.
KURIHARA TOLD → NANAKO TOLD → ME
AND OUR SCHEDULES OVERLAP. LUCKY US!
Y-YEAH.
HOK-KAIDO...
MILK
WHY DON'T WE ALL MEET UP ON OUR FREE DAY AND GO EXPLORING TOGETHER?
WE CAN GO TO SHIROI KOIBITO PARK OR OTARU...
AHH, IT SOUNDS SO ROMANTIC! ♥♥
ROMANTIC?!
SHOCK
I WISH WE WERE VISITING TEMPLES!
ARE YOU INTO TEMPLES?
I FEEL LIKE I COULD USE SOME STERN LOOKS FROM THE BUDDHA...
?
OH?

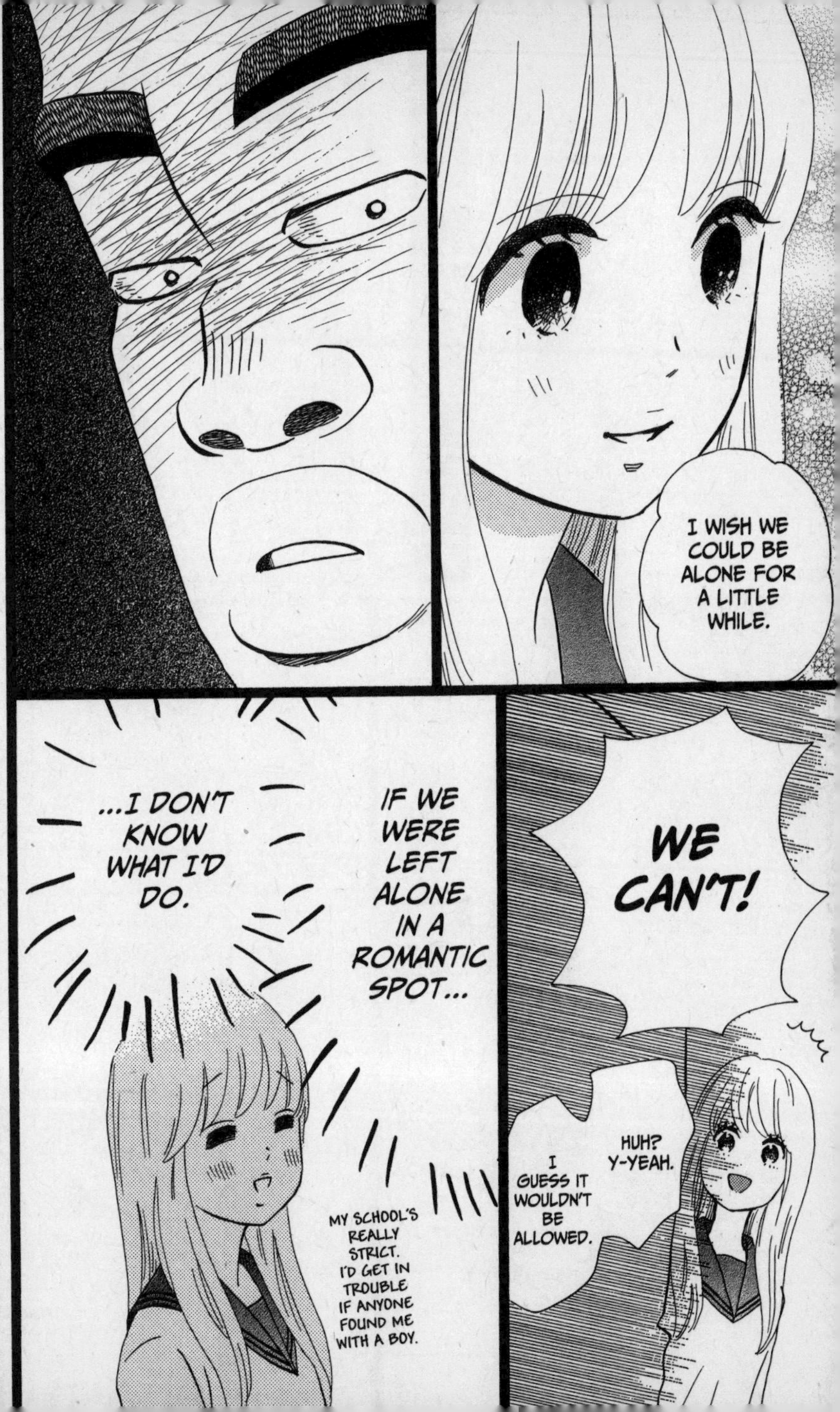
I WISH WE COULD BE ALONE FOR A LITTLE WHILE.
WE CAN'T!
HUH? Y-YEAH.
I GUESS IT WOULDN'T BE ALLOWED.
IF WE WERE LEFT ALONE IN A ROMANTIC SPOT...
...I DON'T KNOW WHAT I'D DO.
MY SCHOOL'S REALLY STRICT. I'D GET IN TROUBLE IF ANYONE FOUND ME WITH A BOY.

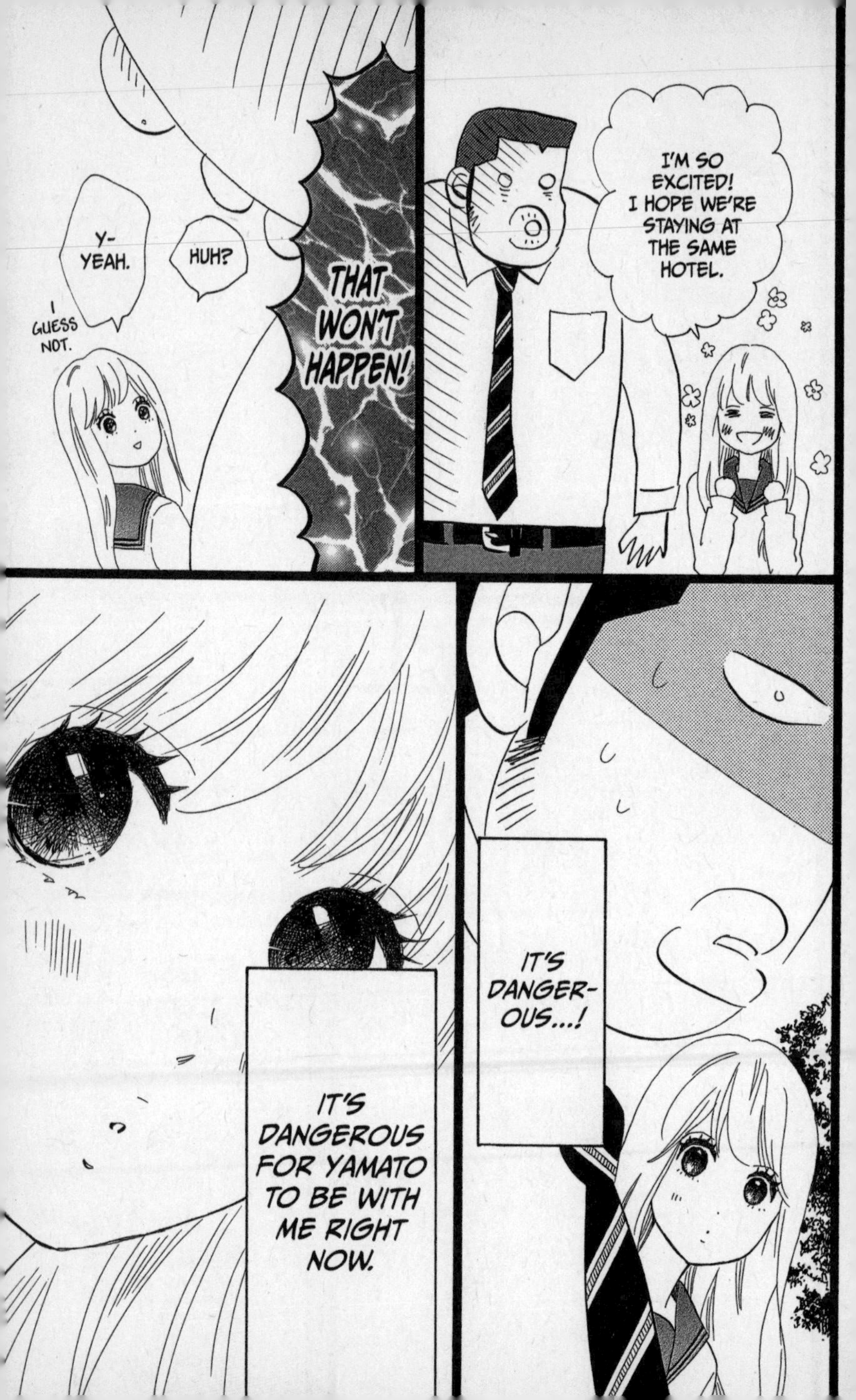
I'M SO EXCITED! I HOPE WE'RE STAYING AT THE SAME HOTEL.
THAT WON'T HAPPEN!
HUH?
Y-YEAH.
I GUESS NOT.
IT'S DANGER-OUS...!
IT'S DANGEROUS FOR YAMATO TO BE WITH ME RIGHT NOW.

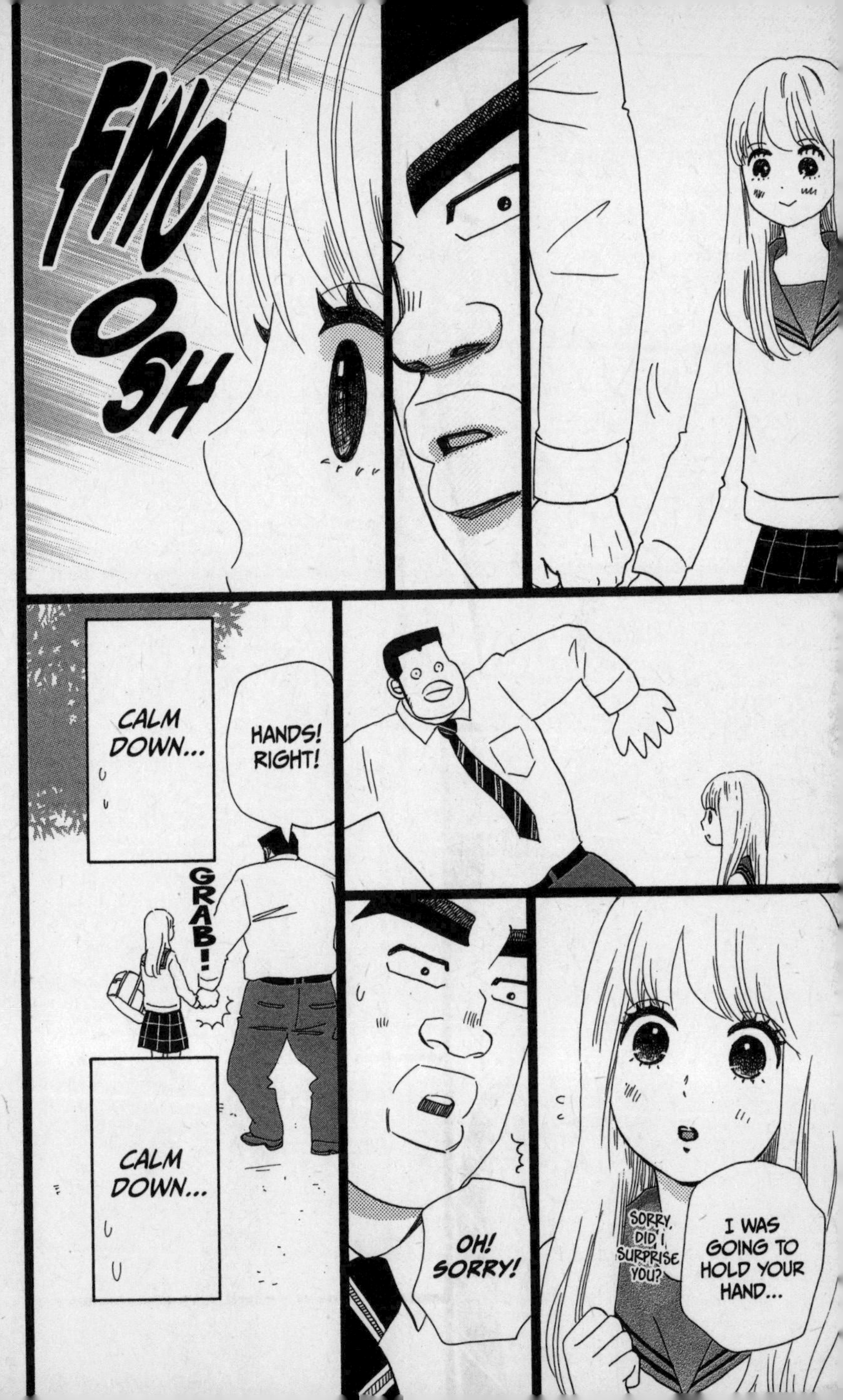
FWOOSH
I WAS GOING TO HOLD YOUR HAND...
SORRY, DID I SURPRISE YOU?
OH! SORRY!
CALM DOWN...
HANDS! RIGHT!
GRAB!
CALM DOWN...

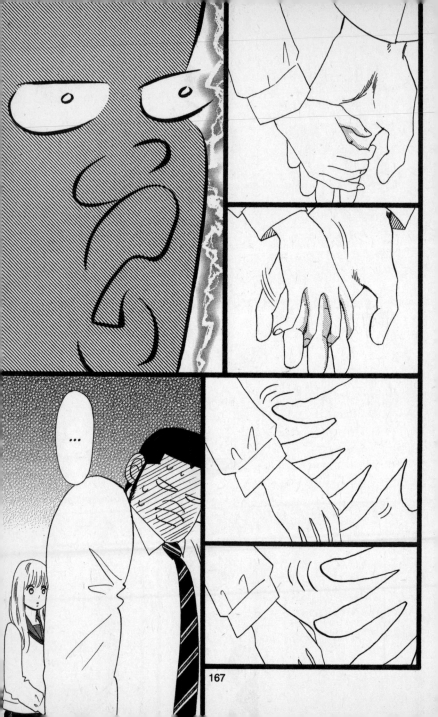

167

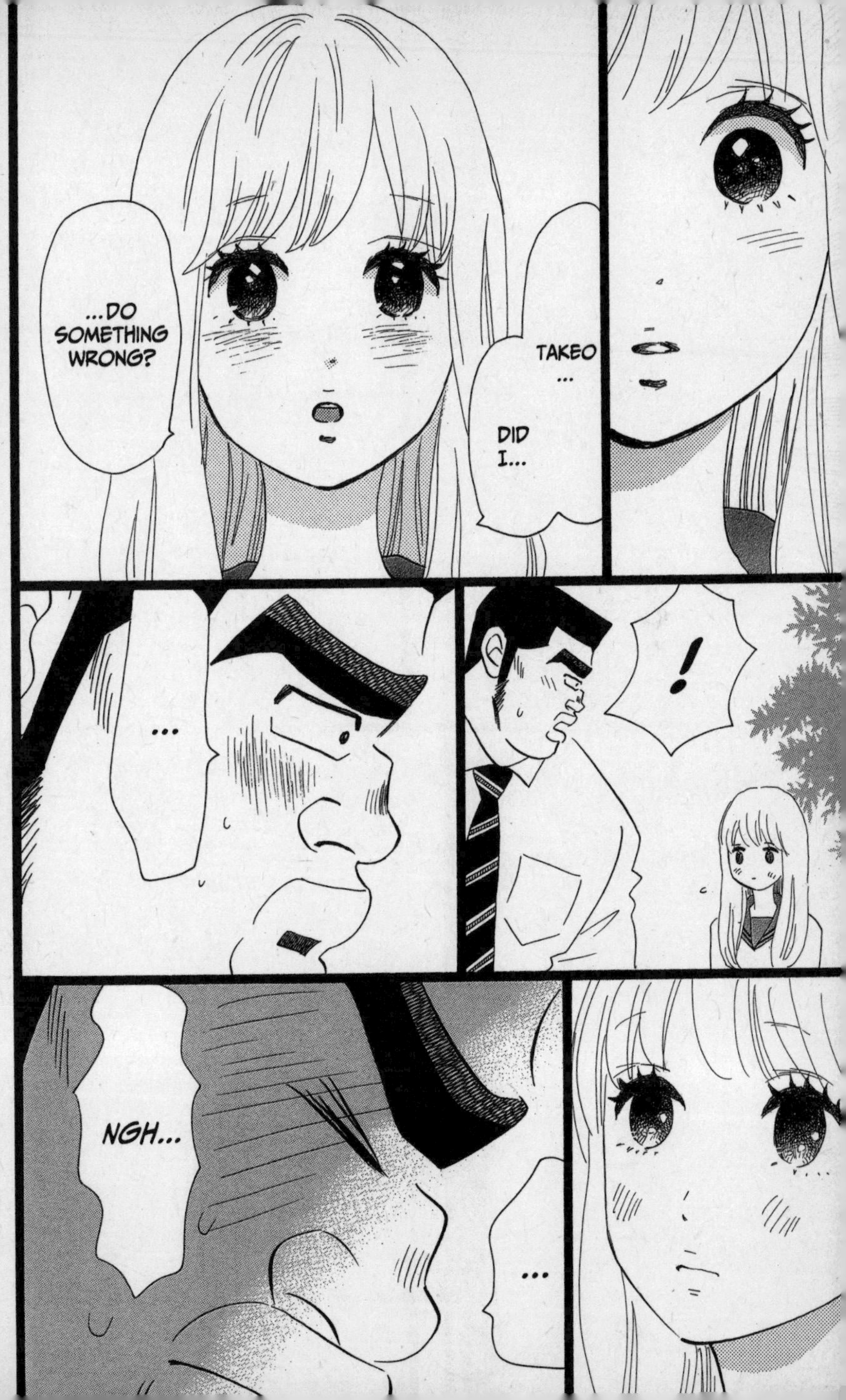
TAKEO ...
DID I...
...DO SOMETHING WRONG?
!
...
...
NGH...

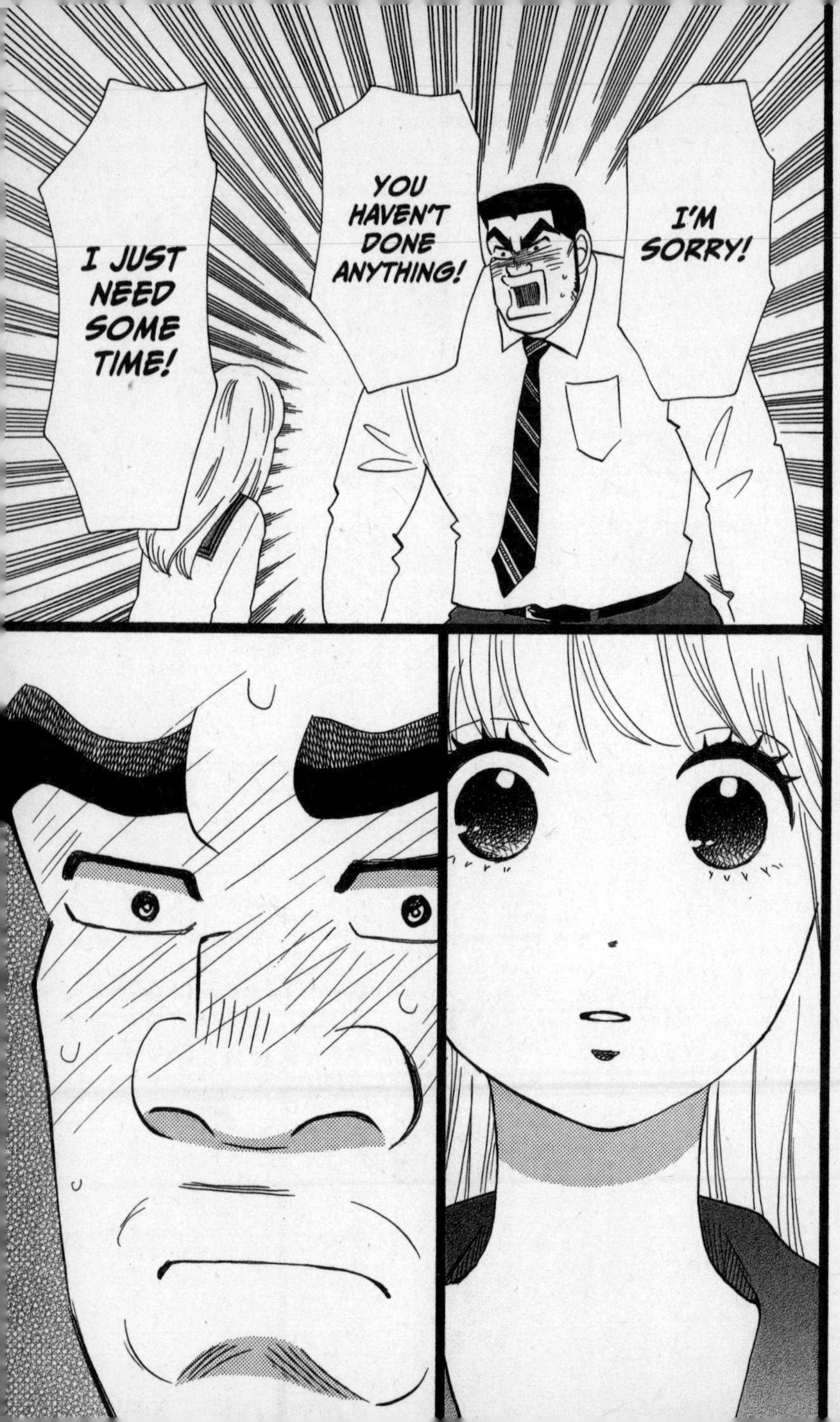
I'M SORRY!
YOU HAVEN'T DONE ANYTHING!
I JUST NEED SOME TIME!

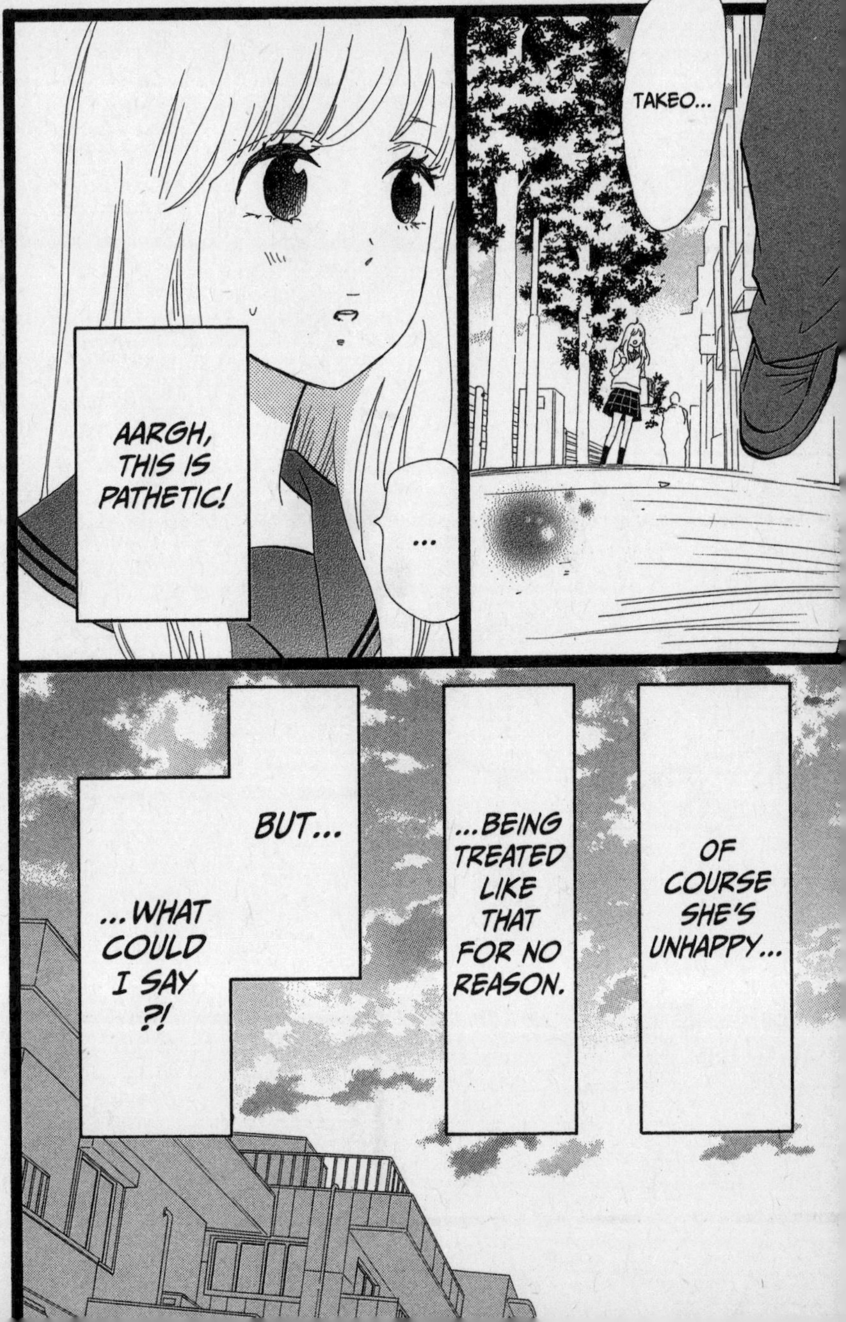
TAKEO...
...
AARGH, THIS IS PATHETIC!
OF COURSE SHE'S UNHAPPY...
...BEING TREATED LIKE THAT FOR NO REASON.
BUT...
...WHAT COULD I SAY ?!

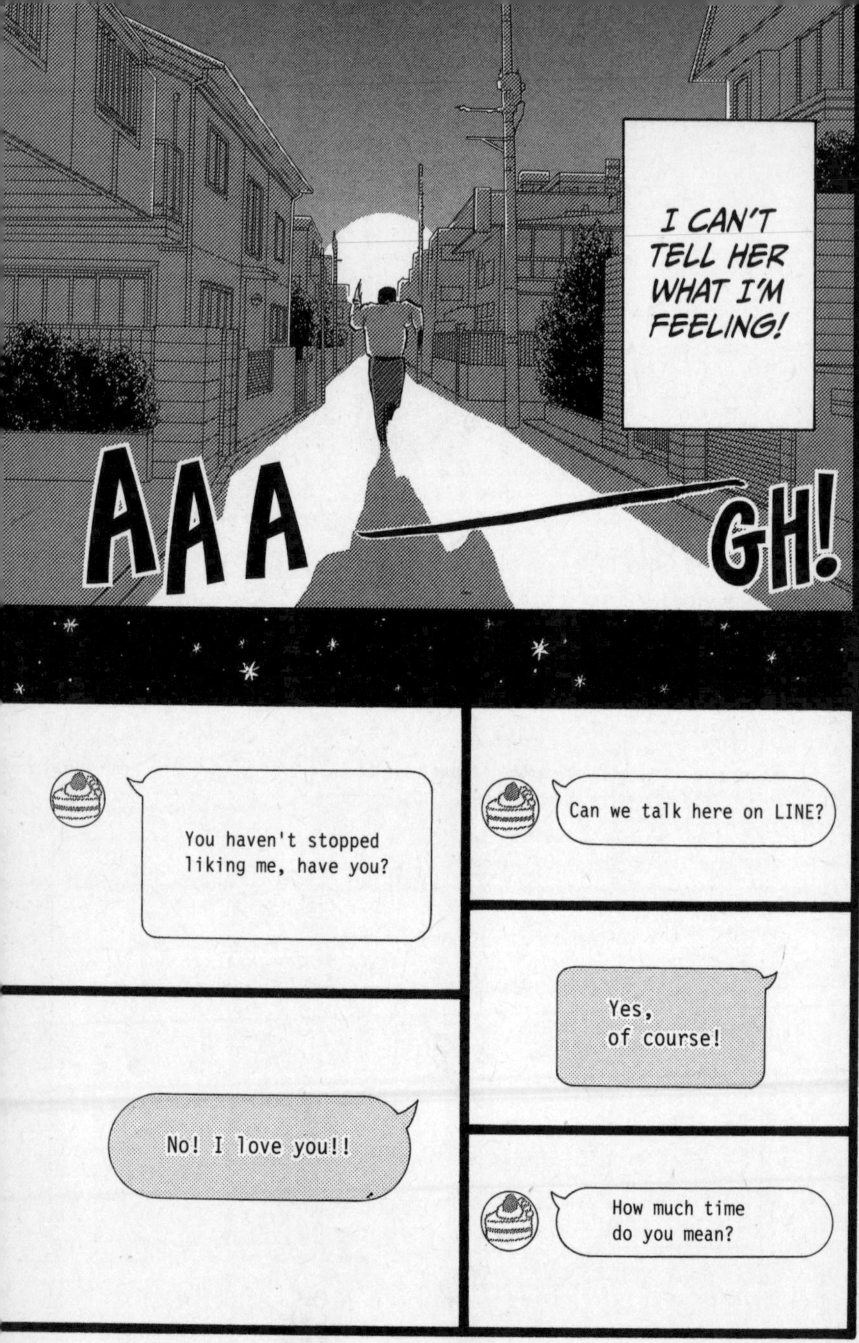
I CAN'T TELL HER WHAT I'M FEELING!
AAA—GH!
Can we talk here on LINE?
Yes, of course!
How much time do you mean?
You haven't stopped liking me, have you?
No! I love you!!

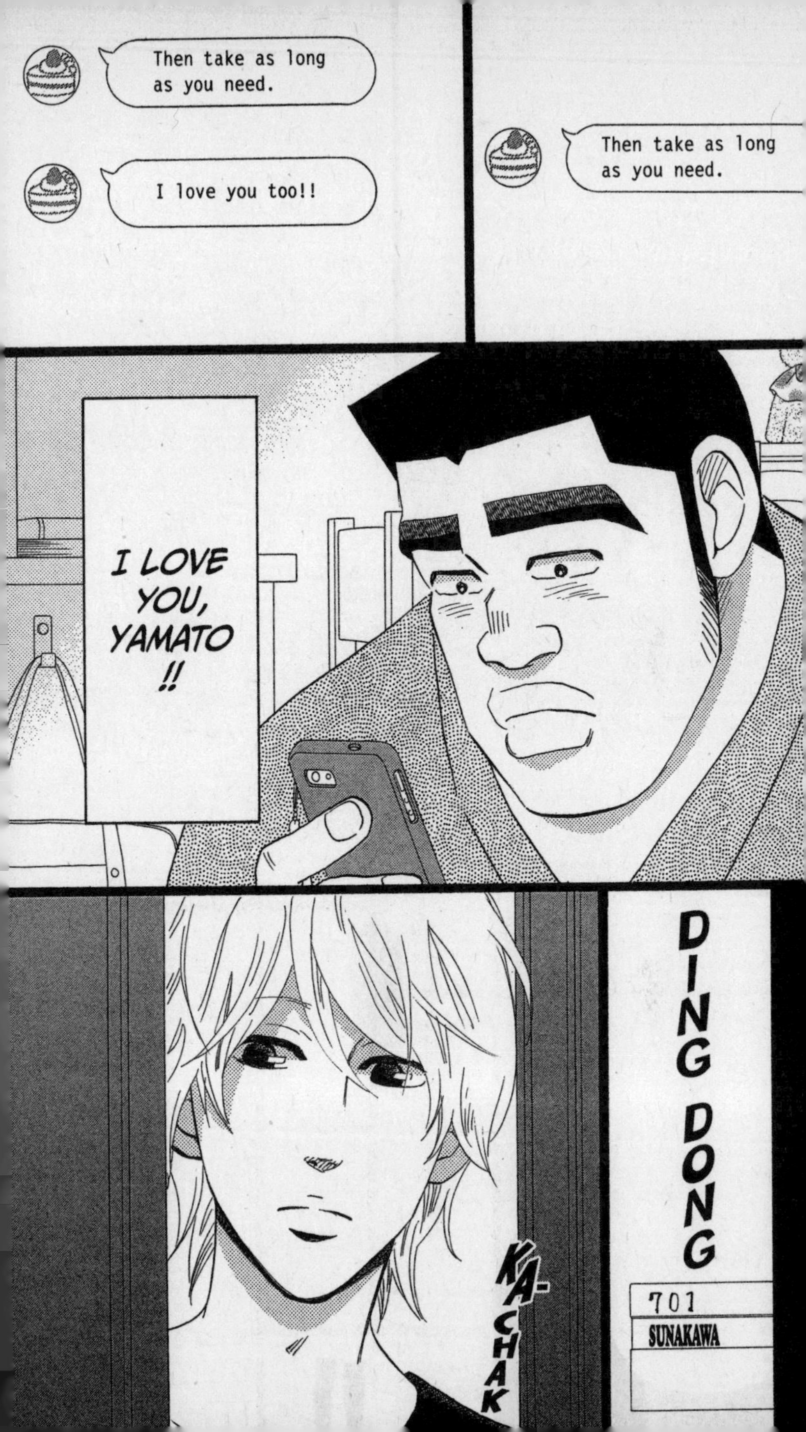
Then take as long as you need.
Then take as long as you need.
I love you too!!
I LOVE YOU, YAMATO !!
DING DONG
701
SUNAKAWA
KA-CHAK

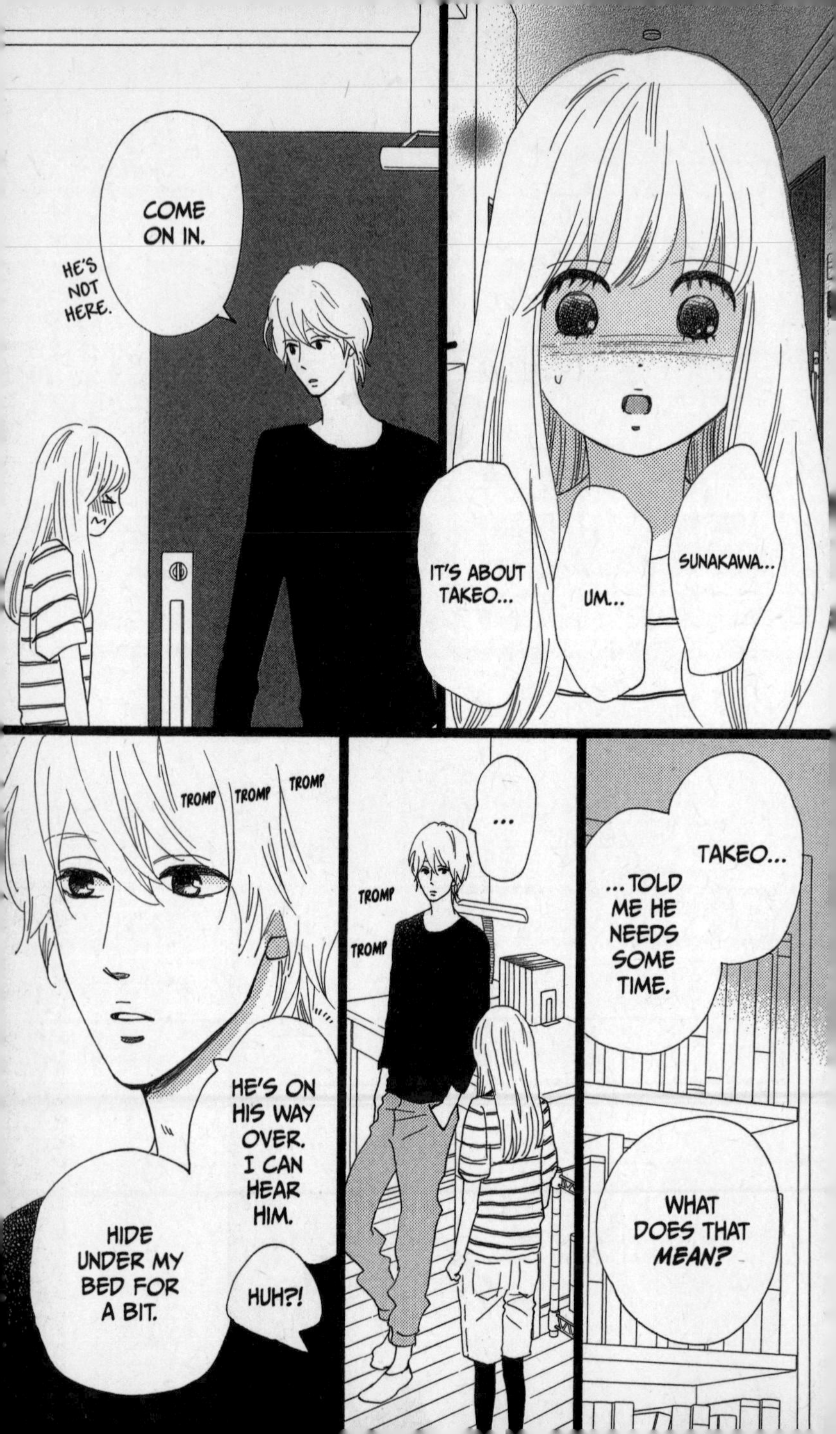
SUNAKAWA...
UM...
IT'S ABOUT TAKEO...
COME ON IN.
HE'S NOT HERE.
TAKEO...
...TOLD ME HE NEEDS SOME TIME.
WHAT DOES THAT *MEAN?*
...
TROMP
TROMP
TROMP
TROMP
TROMP
HE'S ON HIS WAY OVER. I CAN HEAR HIM.
HUH?!
HIDE UNDER MY BED FOR A BIT.

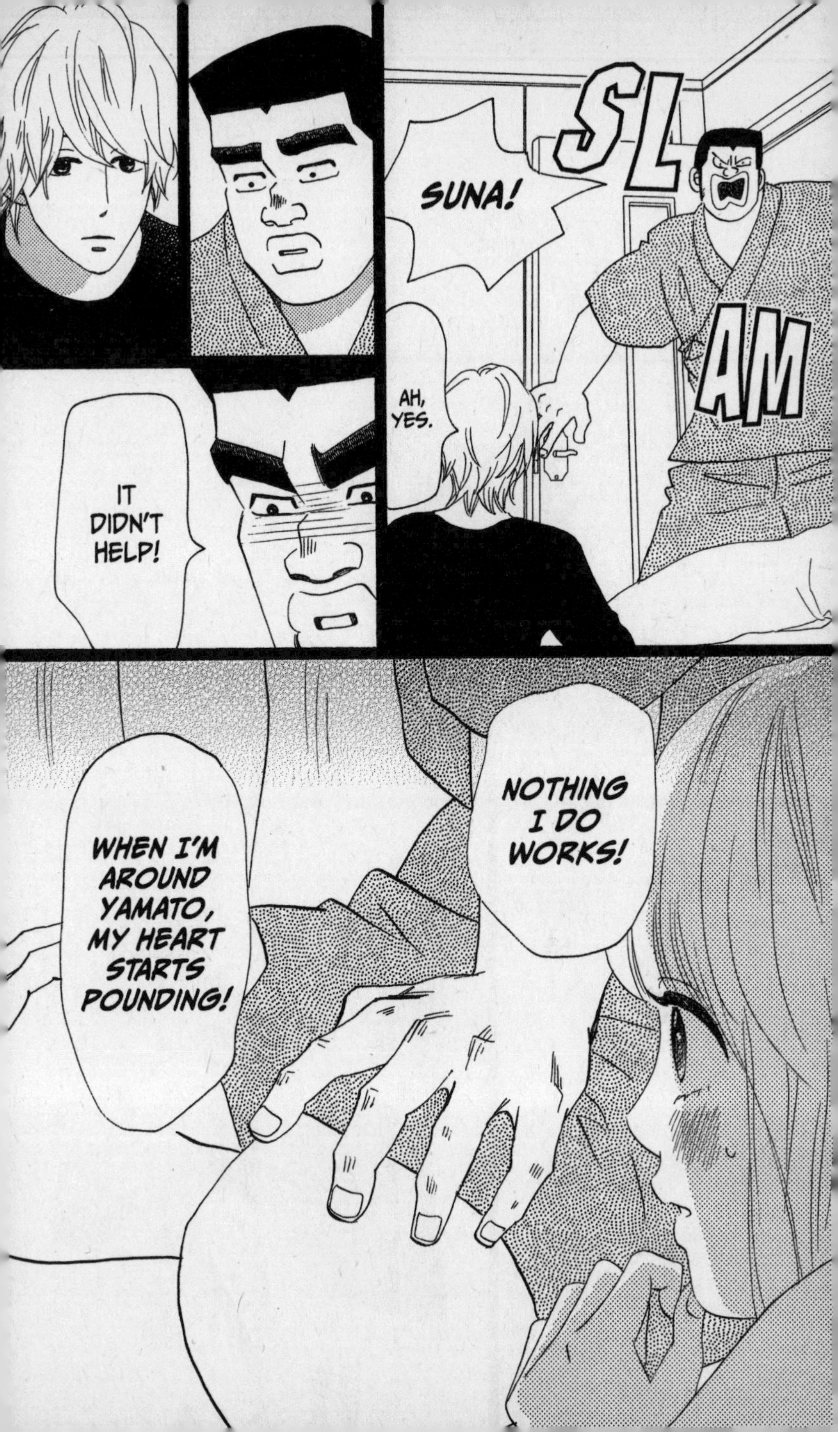
SLAM
SUNA!
AH, YES.
IT DIDN'T HELP!
NOTHING I DO WORKS!
WHEN I'M AROUND YAMATO, MY HEART STARTS POUNDING!

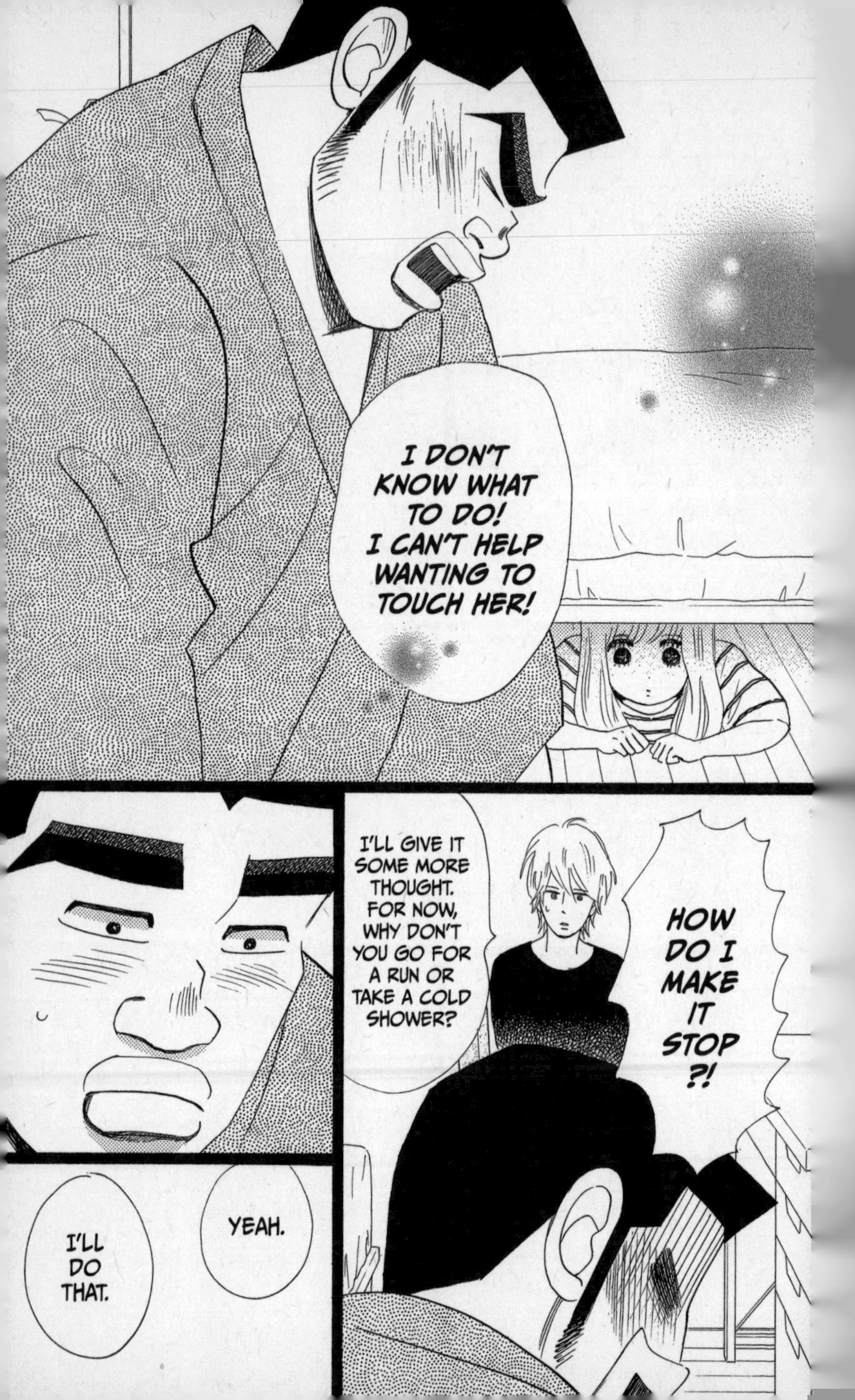
I DON'T KNOW WHAT TO DO! I CAN'T HELP WANTING TO TOUCH HER!
HOW DO I MAKE IT STOP?!
I'LL GIVE IT SOME MORE THOUGHT. FOR NOW, WHY DON'T YOU GO FOR A RUN OR TAKE A COLD SHOWER?
YEAH.
I'LL DO THAT.

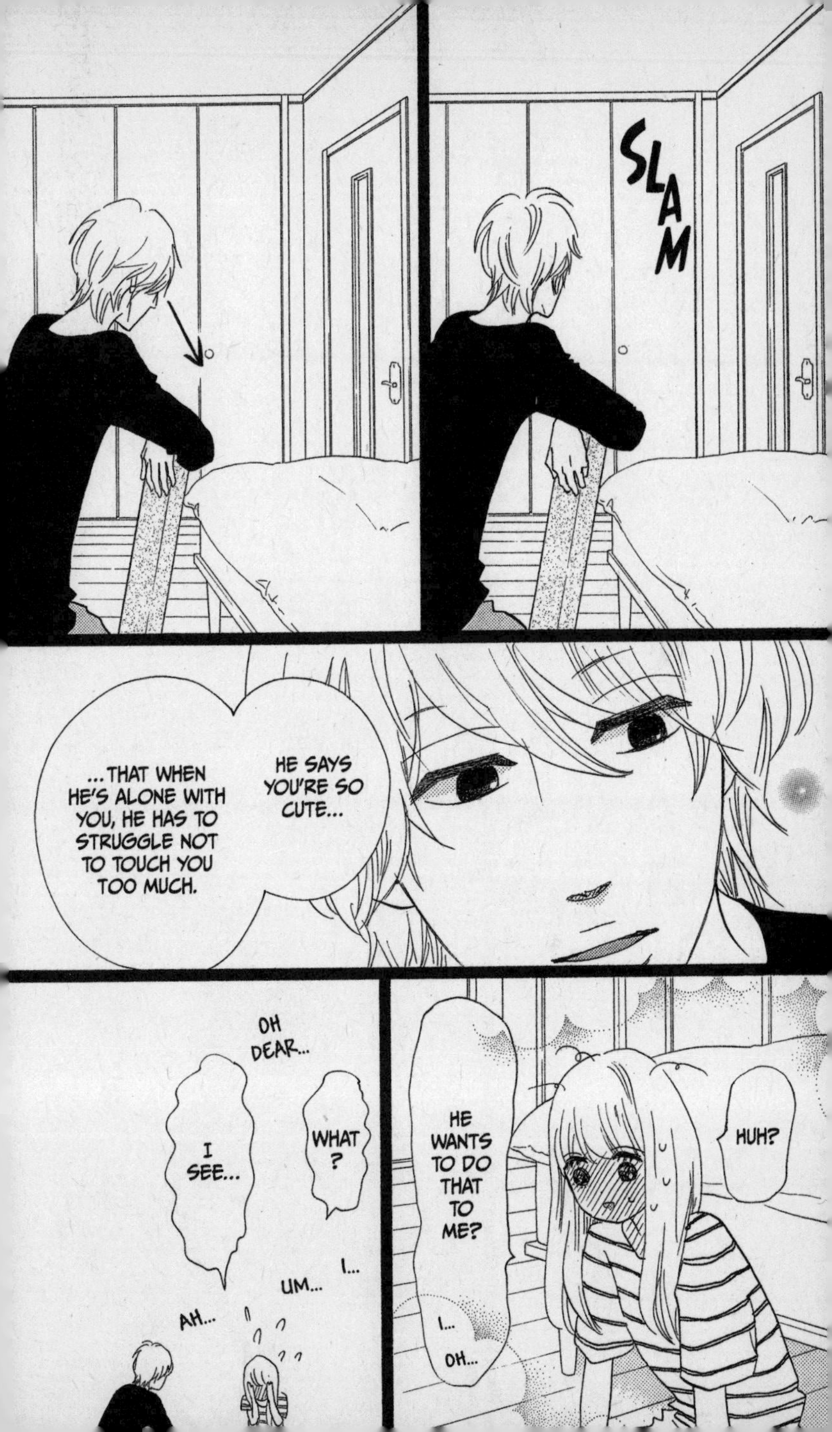
SLAM
HE SAYS YOU'RE SO CUTE...
...THAT WHEN HE'S ALONE WITH YOU, HE HAS TO STRUGGLE NOT TO TOUCH YOU TOO MUCH.
HUH?
HE WANTS TO DO THAT TO ME?
I... OH...
OH DEAR...
WHAT?
I SEE...
I...
UM...
AH...

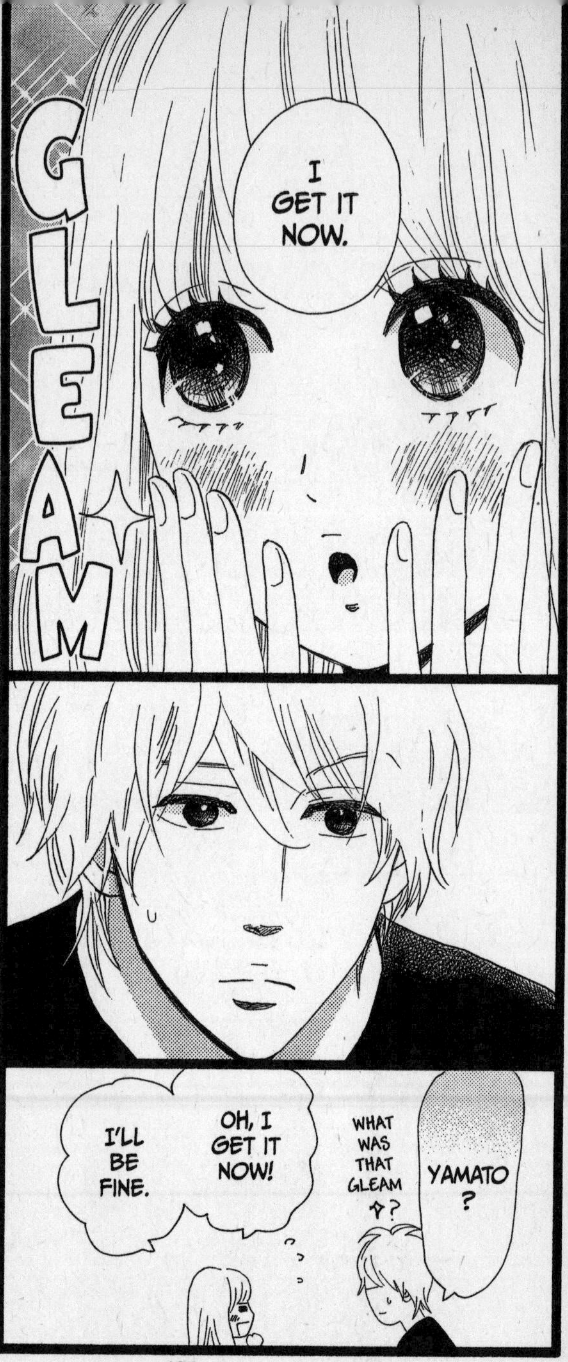
I GET IT NOW.
GLEAM
YAMATO?
WHAT WAS THAT GLEAM ✧?
OH, I GET IT NOW!
I'LL BE FINE.

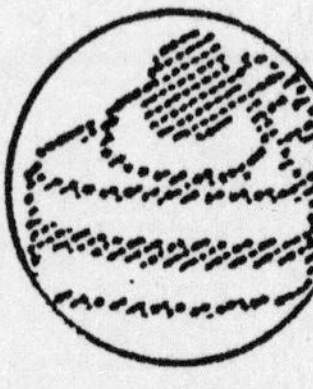

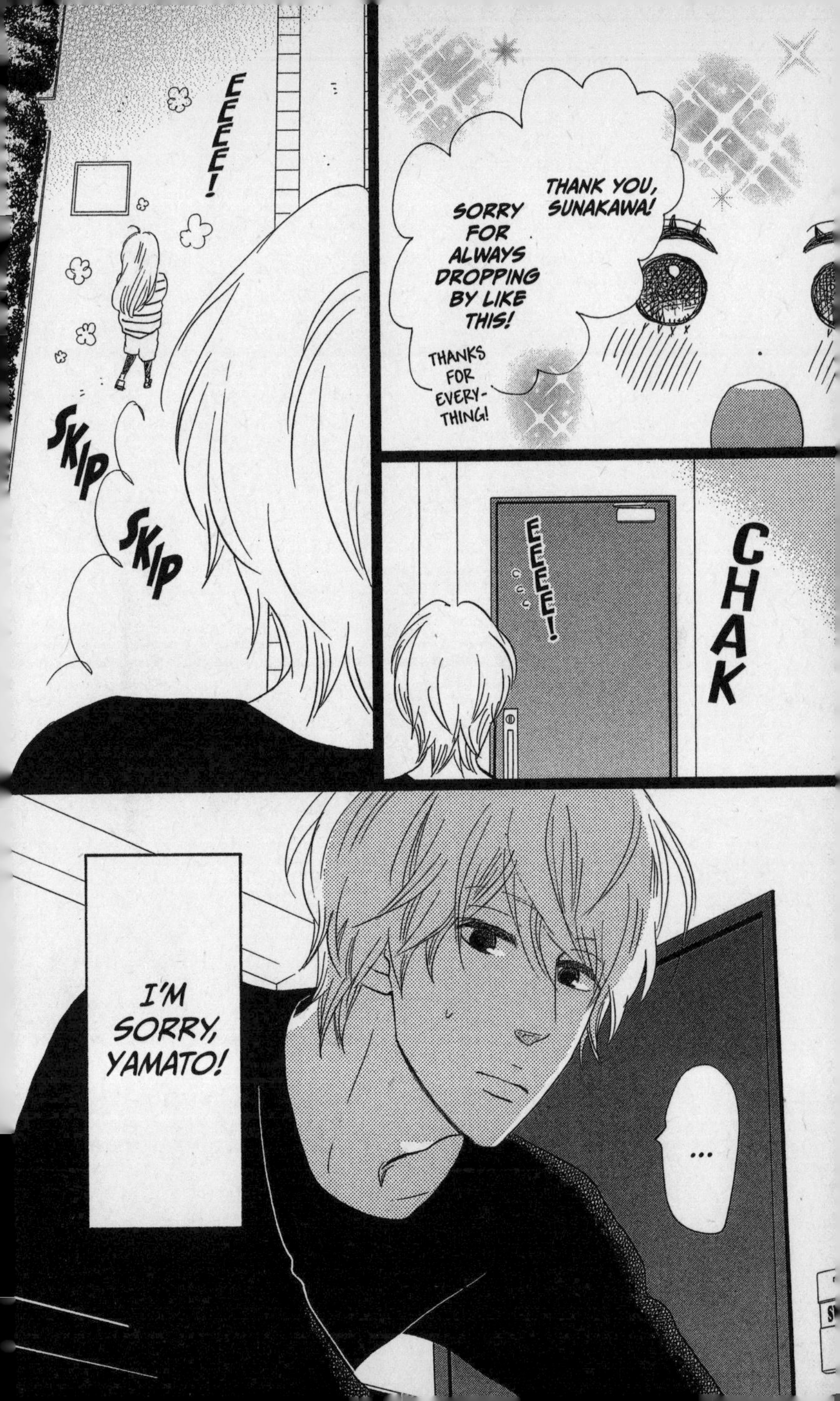
THANK YOU, SUNAKAWA!
SORRY FOR ALWAYS DROPPING BY LIKE THIS!
THANKS FOR EVERY-THING!
CHAK
EEEE!
EEEE!
SKIP
SKIP
...
I'M SORRY, YAMATO!

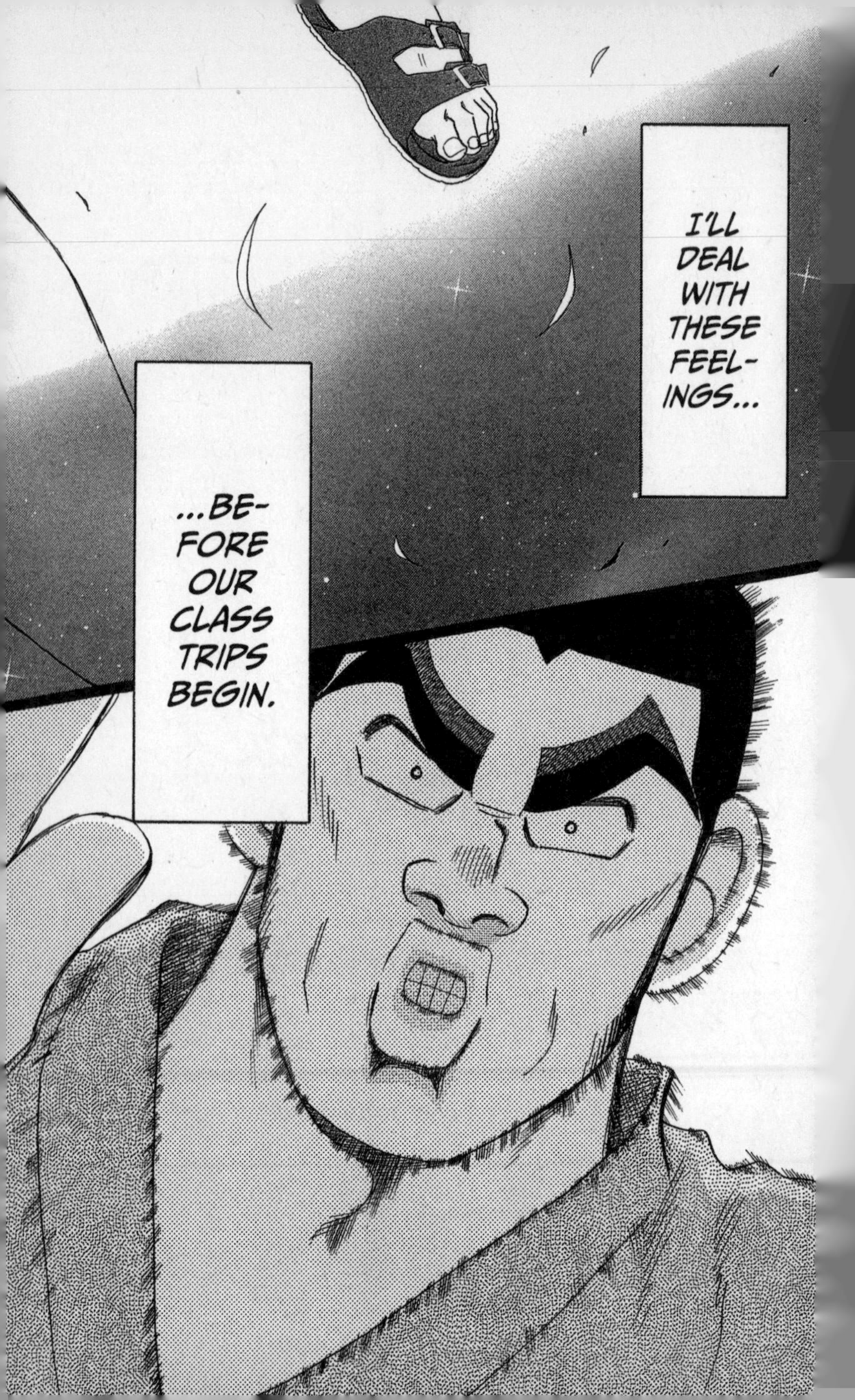
I'LL DEAL WITH THESE FEEL-INGS...
...BE-FORE OUR CLASS TRIPS BEGIN.

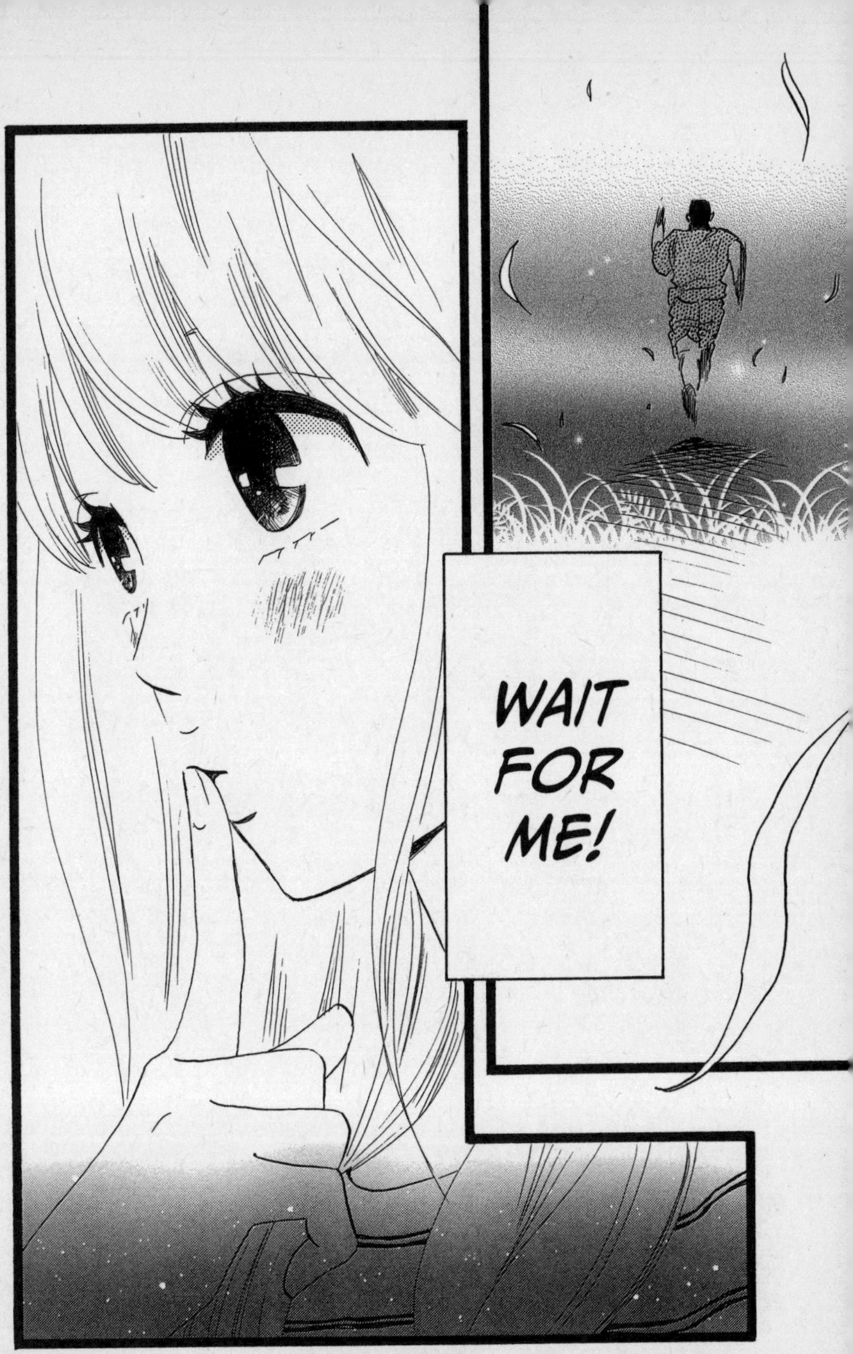
WAIT FOR ME!

TO BE CONTINUED...

MY love STORY!!

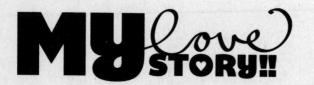

MY LOVE STORY!! 10

We hit the double digits!

Thank you so much! That was fast.

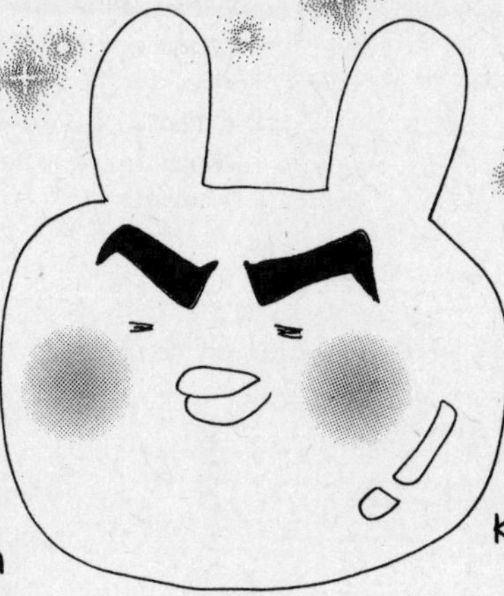

I feel so lucky to have met so many wonderful people through *My Love Story!!* I'm happy to be involved with such a wonderful series.

Thank you very much, Kawahara Sensei!

I'm talking like this is the final volume, but there is another one after this! I hope we'll meet again in volume 11. Thank you for your support!

I want to do weight training and get toned. I want to get so muscular that anyone who hasn't seen me in a while won't recognize me anymore!

But I'll wind up only thinking about it.

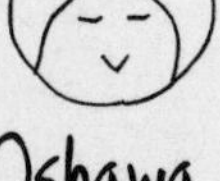

Oshawa

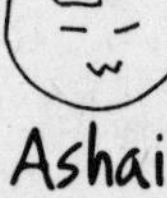

Ashai

I'd like to thank my assistants.

August 2015, Aruko

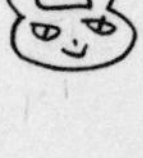

Hello! Thank you very much for picking up the graphic novel version of *My Love Story!!* I'm always grateful for your letters and comments. I'm going to try my best!

I feel so happy! Amazingly, *My Love Story!!* has been made into a movie. I've only seen the previews, but Suzuki, the actor who plays Takeo, is pretty great, isn't he? I had no idea he was so good at acting with his expressions and his poses (?). Seeing Suzuki's Takeo made me want to pay more attention to the expressions and poses in the manga. I want you to see Suzuki's take on Takeo, so I hope you can watch the movie.

(But you might not have enough spare cash...)

And it's not just Suzuki! There's Nagano, a model I adore. I think it's great how normal she looks. (She's really pretty, though.) I got teary eyed when she said her line in the trailer. Sakaguchi is really handsome, but I had no idea he would do such things... He was really physical... I thought it was wonderful.
In the movie, Takeo's parents are really splendid. My sister messaged me that the father was played by the guy from *Aibo*. Such amazing people play the parents in both the movie and the anime...
How lucky!
Of course, the main cast is amazing too!!

I'm really excited by all this! Anyway, I'm going to work hard on the manga. Oh, I mean the story! I'll try my best. But sometimes I feel tired.

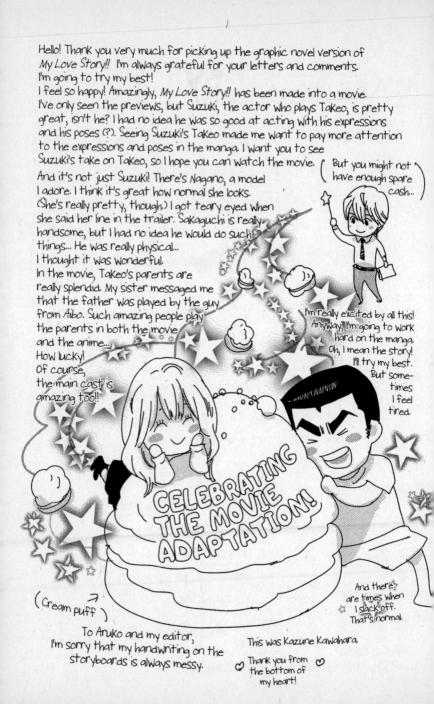

CELEBRATING THE MOVIE ADAPTATION!

(Cream puff)

And there are times when I slack off. That's normal.

To Aruko and my editor, I'm sorry that my handwriting on the storyboards is always messy.

This was Kazune Kawahara.

♡ Thank you from the bottom of my heart! ♡

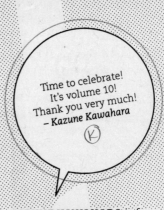

Time to celebrate!
It's volume 10!
Thank you very much!
– Kazune Kawahara

ARUKO is from Ishikawa Prefecture in Japan and was born on July 26 (a Leo!). She made her manga debut with *Ame Nochi Hare* (Clear After the Rain). Her other works include *Yasuko to Kenji*, and her hobbies include laughing and getting lost.

KAZUNE KAWAHARA is from Hokkaido Prefecture in Japan and was born on March 11 (a Pisces!). She made her manga debut at age 18 with *Kare no Ichiban Sukina Hito* (His Most Favorite Person). Her best-selling shojo manga series *High School Debut* is available in North America from VIZ Media. Her hobby is interior redecorating.

I have Post-MLS Anime Depression Syndrome. (Translation: I'm sad that the anime of *My Love Story!!* has ended.) For the cover illustration of volume 10, I used the same design as the poster for the *My Love Story!!* movie!
– Aruko

MY LOVE STORY!!

Volume 10
Shojo Beat Edition

Story by **KAZUNE KAWAHARA**
Art by **ARUKO**

---//---

English Adaptation ♡ **Ysabet Reinhardt MacFarlane**
Translation ♡ **JN Productions**
Touch-up Art & Lettering ♡ **Mark McMurray**
Design ♡ **Fawn Lau**
Editor ♡ **Amy Yu**

---//---

ORE MONOGATARI!!
© 2011 by Kazune Kawahara, Aruko
All rights reserved.
First published in Japan in 2011 by SHUEISHA Inc., Tokyo
English translation rights arranged by SHUEISHA Inc.

The stories, characters and incidents mentioned in
this publication are entirely fictional.

Printed in the U.S.A.

Published by VIZ Media, LLC
P.O. Box 77010
San Francisco, CA 94107

10 9 8 7 6 5 4 3 2 1
First printing, October 2016

www.viz.com

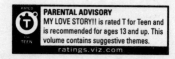

PARENTAL ADVISORY
MY LOVE STORY!! is rated T for Teen and
is recommended for ages 13 and up. This
volume contains suggestive themes.
ratings.viz.com

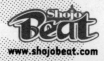
www.shojobeat.com

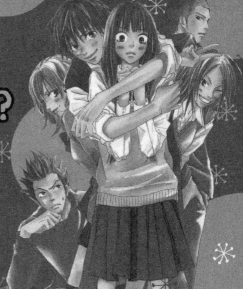
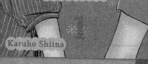
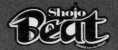

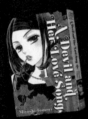
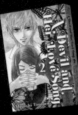
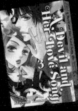
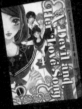

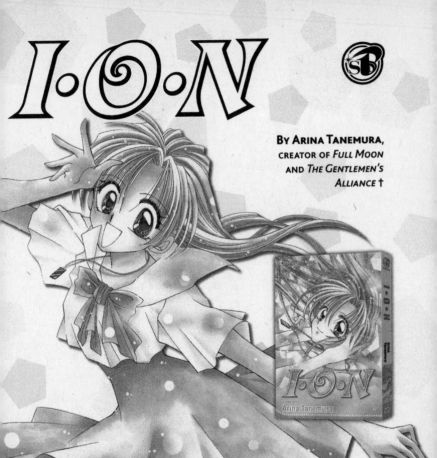

I·O·N

BY ARINA TANEMURA, CREATOR OF *FULL MOON* AND *THE GENTLEMEN'S ALLIANCE †*

Ion Tsuburagi is a normal junior high girl with normal junior high problems. But when a mysterious substance grants her telekinetic powers, she finds herself struggling to keep everything together! Are her new abilities a blessing...or a curse?

Find out in *I·O·N*—manga on sale now!

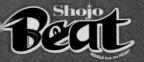

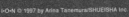

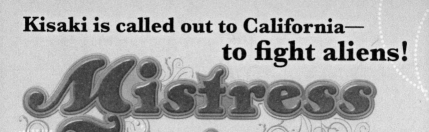

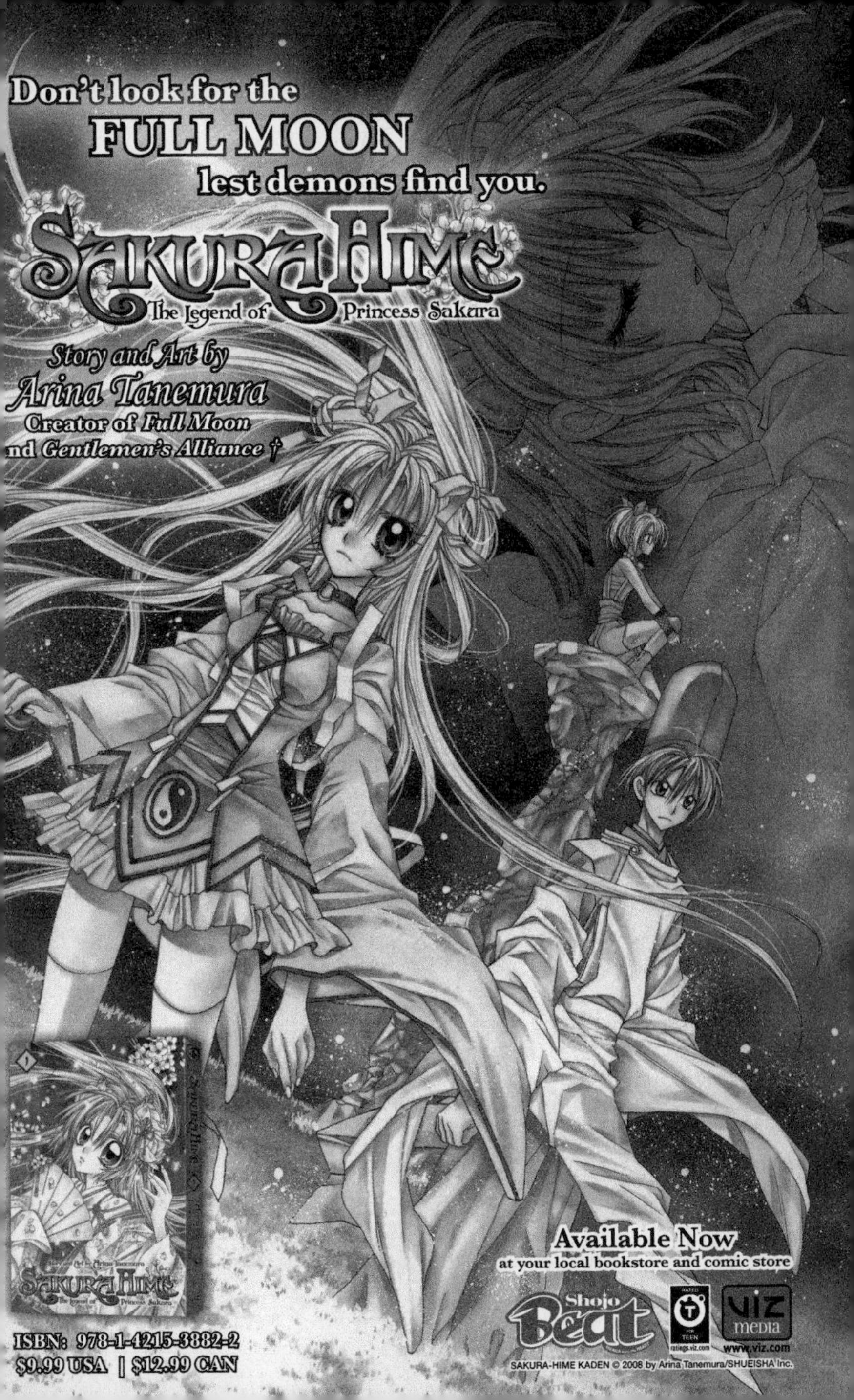

Don't look for the
FULL MOON
lest demons find you.
SAKURA HIME
The Legend of Princess Sakura
Story and Art by
Arina Tanemura
Creator of Full Moon
and Gentlemen's Alliance †
ISBN: 978-1-4215-3882-2
$9.99 USA | $12.99 CAN
Available Now
at your local bookstore and comic store
Shojo Beat
RATED T FOR TEEN ratings.viz.com
VIZ media
www.viz.com
SAKURA-HIME KADEN © 2008 by Arina Tanemura/SHUEISHA Inc.

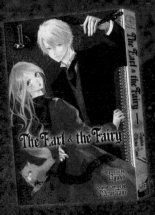

You may be r

wrong

IT'S TRUE: In keeping with the original Japanese comic format, this book reads from right to left—so action, sound effects, and word balloons are completely reversed. This preserves the orientation of the original artwork—plus, it's fun! Check out the diagram shown here to get the hang of things, and then turn to the other side of the book to get started!

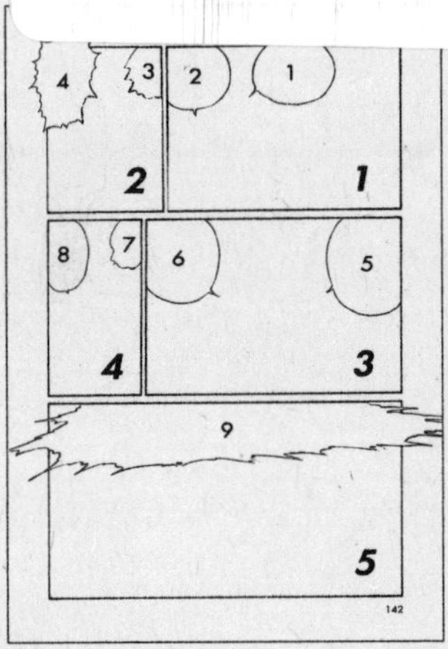
1
2
1
3
4
2
5
6
3
7
8
4
9
5
142

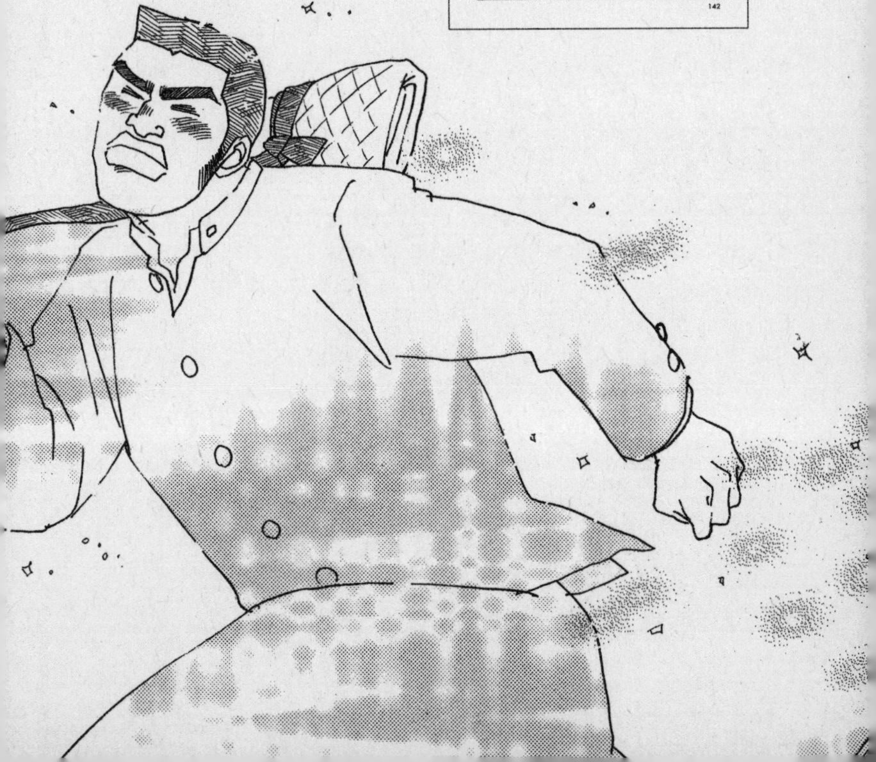